REEL MEALS

Movie Lover's
COOKBOOK

LORNA WOODSUM RILEY

Cover Photograph: Perry L. Struse, Jr.
Cover and Interior Design:
 Geri Wolfe Boesen
Interior Layout: Anthony Jacobson

Library of Congress Catalog
Card Number 87-050017

ISBN 0-87069-478-2

10   9   8   7   6   5   4   3   2   1

Copyright © 1987
Wallace-Homestead Book Company

All rights reserved. No part of this publication may be reproduced, stored in a retrieval system, or transmitted in any form or by any means, electronic, mechanical, photocopying, recording, or otherwise, without prior permission of the copyright owner or the publisher.

Published by

Wallace-Homestead Book Company
580 Waters Edge
Lombard, Illinois 60148

One of the
ABC PUBLISHING abc
 Companies

*To Dan,
Meagan,
and
Gillian*

CONTENTS

Acknowledgments,	5
Introduction,	6
Foreword,	8
Previews,	9
Mixers,	29
Roll 'Em,	55
Reel Meals,	77
Tags and Trailers,	147
Rough Cuts,	169
A Pie for All Reasons,	199
Spaghetti Westerns,	206
Movie Menus,	210
Featured Titles Index and Recipes,	246
Menu Section Title Index and Recipes,	248
Master Recipe Index,	250
About the Author,	256

ACKNOWLEDGMENTS

My most profound thanks and gratitude to the many people who generously contributed to the making of this book.

First, last, and always, to Dan Riley, my husband and best friend in life, who, as a seasoned professional writer, has advised and encouraged me every step of the way. I am particularly grateful for the time he gave up to read and edit every last page of the book (except this one, which is probably full of typos, misspelled words, and long-winded sentences that go on and on...). He is truly a master with words.

To my wonderful children: Meagan (who is not really a child anymore), who washes the dishes every night and to whom I am especially grateful for cleaning the really big kitchen messes during the "experimental" recipe testing phases; and Gillian, who sat by my side every evening while I wrote because she never wanted me to be lonely.

To the other members of my family for their help, recipe contributions, and for just being there: my parents Bill and Betty Woodsum; my twin sister Lorraine Houseman; my brother Glenn Woodsum; and my in-laws Cliff Riley, Sr. and Jr., Tim Riley, and Marie Riley.

To Ray Mungo, a uniquely kind and generous person who, in spite of briefly passing in and out of my life every few years, always makes a difference. On one particular meeting, he worked his magic to connect me to the world of publishing.

To my friends for their individual contributions, from movie title suggestions, to searching for stills: Charles Martin Smith (a special thanks for input on *Never Cry Wolf*) and his wife Barbara; Nancy Cunningham; Victoria (Tori) Lucas; John Volsted; Jean Wing; LeRoy Sweet; Kathy Berg; Steve Orlandella; Kathy Kimmel; Judy Skelton; Lea Bogoyevac; Mary Ottinger; Mike Weiss; Fred Brady; Joy Redick; Terry O'Donnell; Michael Blowen; and Diane White.

To my special friend Mara, a first-rate photographer, who freely gave her time to shoot the author photograph.

To the excellent chef Claude Farina at Le Normandie restaurant in Thousand Oaks, California, for sharing his expertise and many recipes for *Who's Killing the Great Chefs of Europe?*

To the El Torito restaurant in Thousand Oaks, California, for sharing their can't-fail fried ice cream recipe for *Comfort and Joy*.

To the folks at the Academy of Motion Picture Arts and Sciences and American Film Institute libraries; the Museum of Modern Art in New York City (especially Mary Corliss); Donovan Brandt and Mary at Eddie Brandt's Saturday Matinee; Cinema Collectors; Hollywood Book and Poster; Hollywood Poster Exchange; Paul G. Wesolowski of the Fredonia Gazette; and Larry Edmonds.

To the Affiliated Property Craftspeople, Local 44, most notably Emily Ferry for her enthusiam and cooperation, and Erik Nelson, Bob Mollison, Jerry Moss, Horst Grandt, Allen Levine, Larry Bird, Billy MacSems, Russ Goble, Dennis Parrish, Stephen Ferry, Steve Levine, Wayne McLaughlin, and Grant Swain.

Finally, to Liz Fletcher and all the wonderful people at Wallace-Homestead Book Company, especially general manager Bill Topaz who, like many of us, appreciates the frustrations of ordering a side of wheat toast.

Photography credits

Paramount Pictures; Metro-Goldwyn-Mayer; United Artists; Embassy Pictures; Warner Brothers; Columbia Pictures; American International Pictures; Twentieth Century Fox; Republic Pictures; Disney Studios; Atlantic Releasing Corp; Allied Artists; MCA/Universal; Hal Roach Studios; Triumph Films; Orion; New Yorker Films; New World Pictures; Cinerama Releasing; Buena Vista; and Ladd Company.

INTRODUCTION

People have been eating in the movies for nearly a century. Sometimes what's eaten looks palatable, like the sumptuous five course dinner in Tom Jones. Othertimes, the dishes are a bit hard to swallow, like the cockroaches devoured by Steve McQueen in *Papillon*. Tasty or not, *The Movie Lover's Cookbook: Reel Meals*, brings you back for a second helping.

This is a real cookbook, inspired wholly from eating scenes in movies. For your reading pleasure, it offers some of your favorite (and not so favorite), famous (and not so famous) eating scenes. Approximately seventy movies are capsulized in "Nutshells," each unfolding the story as if seen through the eyes of a stomach. For your cooking pleasure, you'll be able to recreate the movie fare at home by following the accompanying recipes. And now, with video available, you can do it all—read about the movie, watch it, and relive the cuisine with family and friends all in your own home.

You'll find the organization of this book like many cookbooks—by food types—and fully indexed: appetizers and miscellaneous foods are found in "Previews," beverages in "Mixers," breads and rolls in "Roll 'Em," main dishes in "Reel Meals," and desserts in "Tags and Trailers." The more unusual offerings are appropriately located in the section called "Rough Cuts."

There are over three hundred recipes in the book. To assist the reader in making discriminating selections of taste—the edible and not so edible—I've provided a rating for each one. The rating system is similar to the one already in use by the Motion Picture Guild of America, i.e., G for Great, PG for Pretty Good, R for Restricted (edible, but not for everyone), and X for inedible (and I'm not responsible if you try it).

Special sections touch on related topics such as the evolution of pie throwing in cinema in "A Pie for All Reasons," or the foreign-made Western phenomenon in "Spaghetti Westerns." In the last section of the book, there's a menu guide and accompanying recipes, all inspired by movie titles, that will assist you in planning truly unique eating experiences. You might plan a dinner party feast from *Victor/Victoria* or use the menu section to organize a *Clam Bake*.

Since the variety of foods eaten in films is so great and the list of films so long, I've limited my entries to relatively well-known films that offer the best samplings and selected from primarily those filmed in color. Black and white food, no matter how exquisitely prepared, looks like just so much mashed potatoes. There are a few notable exceptions however, and they bear not only a mention, but our compliments to the chef.

The role of food in film over the years has been significant. It can set the stage, define character, provide symbolism, and establish plot.

There are, on the one hand, the grand gestures—the magnificent, formal banquet scene in the lengthy Russian version of *War and Peace;* the procession of pheasant, roast suckling pig, and platters of exotic fruit in *Cleopatra;* the Texas-sized barbecue in *The Right Stuff;* the elaborate wedding buffet in *Goodbye, Columbus;* and Bergman's richly festive Swedish Christmas dinner in *Fanny and Alexander.* Mounted with such lavish attention to detail, they practically beckon us to approach the screen with fork and knife in hand.

On the other hand, there are the small, intimate gestures, so revealing of character—Nastassia Kinsky sensuously biting into a fresh strawberry in *Tess;* Paul Newman gagging on a cup of recycled coffee in *Harper.* A chicken salad sandwich, food that never even appears on camera, provides an indelible focus for Jack Nicholson's on-screen persona in *Five Easy Pieces.*

In *Giant* the clash of East Coast and Texas cultures as well as upper and lower class lifestyles is delineated in a series of eating and drinking scenes. And Orson Welles condenses the collapse of a marriage into a montage of breakfast scenes in *Citizen Kane.*

Plots sometimes turn on food. In *Who's Killing the Great Chefs of Europe?*, a film actually made *about* food, Jacqueline Bisset makes a dessert bombe containing a crucial clue to a murder. A sack of potatoes provides critical evidence in a vicious necktie murder case in Alfred Hitchcock's *Frenzy.*

Food has also been used in film to conjure up a spectrum of human conditions, from delight—Peter Ostrum finding the Wonka Bar gold certificate in *Willy Wonka and the Chocolate Factory,* to despair—Charlie Chaplin dining on stewed shoe leather in *The Gold Rush,* to desire—Mickey Rourke feeding Kim Bassinger in *9 1/2 Weeks,* to disgust—Kate Capshaw sitting down to a plate of monkey brains in *Indiana Jones and the Temple of Doom.*

Whatever the condition, whatever the cuisine, *The Movie Lover's Cookbook* celebrates it all. M.F.K. Fisher, an illustrious writer on food who compiled the definitive study

Five Easy Pieces. Once a brilliant pianist, Jack Nicholson in *Five Easy Pieces*, adopts a new lifestyle as an oil-rigger, complete with kittenish waitress/girlfriend Karen Black and beer-drinking pal Billy "Green" Bush. Later, he runs into trouble when confronted by a truckstop waitress hell-bent on refusing him a side order of wheat toast.

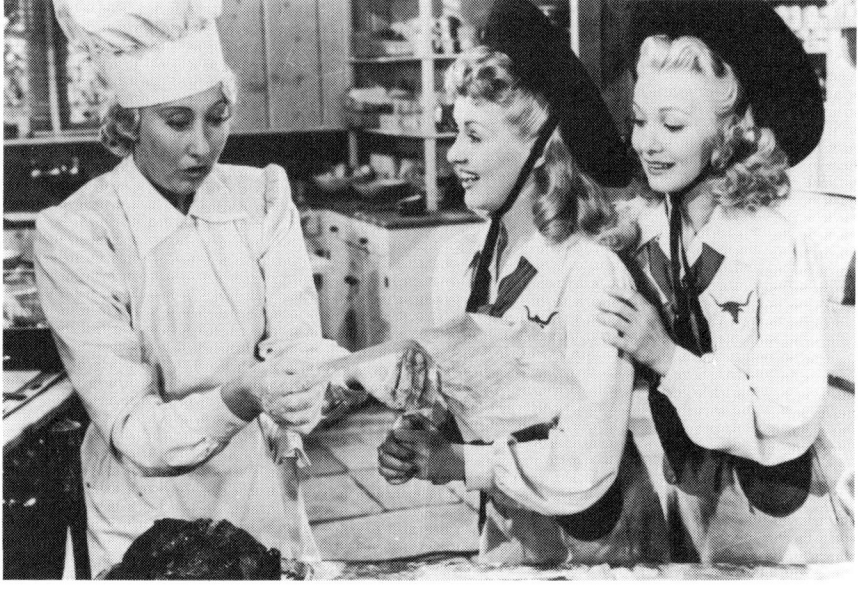

Moon Over Miami. Elbow-deep in flour, drive-in cook Charlotte Greenwood examines the small inheritance check her nieces (left to right) Betty Grable and Carole Landis have just received and plan to use in a manhunt to bag eligible Miami millionaires. Later, George Lessey cheers their sagging plans with his recipe for gashouse eggs—eggs fried in bread slices that have had their centers cut out.

of food in literature, once observed that the flavor of American cuisine comes from innumerable tin cans. That may be a debatable point, but there's hardly any debate that the great "flavor" of American films is preserved in tin cans. They are what keep them fresh for us over the years to be enjoyed again and again. And what comes out of those cans gives us more than just flavor. It gives us fascinating, glorious, mouthwatering, funny, gross-out, unforgettable eating. *Bon appetit!*

FOREWORD

Very little has been formally documented on the subject of food in film. After a year's research in the library reading brittle, yellowing newsclips, I came away with three truths. The first is that you will not learn very much about this subject in a library. The second is that food used in movies generally comes from studio commissaries, independent caterers, restaurants, or food stylists. And finally, property masters are primarily responsible for knowing what items (like food) are needed in a scene, and are the people who must also acquire them, usually using one or more of the sources already mentioned.

To learn more about food in movies then, I enlisted the help of the Los Angeles Affiliated Property Craftspeople, Union Local 44. Through this organization I was able to contact such behind-the-scenes stars as property master Emily Ferry who told me how hard it was to keep twelve sides of beef from rotting after five days of shooting on the set of *The Right Stuff*, and how they had to blowtorch chickens for proper browning and keep the eggs and ketchup coming like a bucket brigade in *Sweet Dreams*.

Property masters know who the best caterers are for certain jobs, how to mold plastic into beer foam, when food will spoil under hot lights during long hours of shooting, and what foods will keep. Instincts tell them to keep twenty-five shrimp cocktails ready for a thirty-second scene because they know the director will need twenty-four takes. And sometimes days of work go up in smoke because of a director's change of heart. That's all part of the property master's job, and I, like the producers, directors,

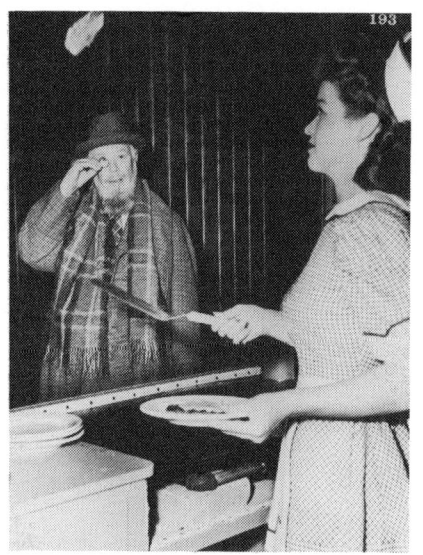

My Kingdom for a Cook (1943). Charles Coburn, left, is the British good-will ambassador to America who, because of his obsession with good food, causes an international tempest when he steals the cook of an American writer.

Sitting Pretty. Bowled over—babysitter Clifton Webb dumps the oatmeal bowl of Roddy McCaskill on the head of his mush-throwing charge in *Sitting Pretty*.

and actors who use (or abuse) them in the making of films, am in their debt.

Actors, directors, or other crew members are rarely involved in the acquisition of food used as props. Actors come onto the set and seldom eat the food used in a scene, since very often it's been so faked or doctored up that it's lethal. If the actors are required to eat, though, they can usually advance order what they like for a scene.

All the recipes given here are either originals or based on fairly standard culinary practices, like those involving piecrusts or pastries. Some of the recipes are family favorites. Some were submitted by friends. And some of the French recipes for *Who's Killing the Great Chefs of Europe?* were developed by chef Claude Farina of the superb Le Normandie restaurant in Thousand Oaks, California. In a few cases, there are "scripted" recipes (those narrated by the actor), like Richard Castellano's recital of spaghetti sauce ingredients in *The Godfather* or Irene Dunne's divulging of secret techniques for Swedish meatballs in *I Remember Mama*. Those recipes, at best sketchy, remain faithfully recorded here, but add whatever amount of fudge is necessary to complete the dish.

The Movie Lover's Cookbook is half movie trivia, half cookbook, but the two halves are not the whole word on food in film. It was my intention to simply organize and share particular passions of my own, that is—movies, cooking, and food. There are many more titles that could have been included, but hopefully readers will start swapping movie titles like spaghetti recipes. What started out as a grocery list that got out of hand, is now a piece for reminiscing, cooking, and savoring. Enjoy!

PREVIEWS

"*Beulah, peel me a grape.*"

Mae West's impromptu request to maid Gertrude Howard in *I'm No Angel.*

California Suite

Nutshell

California Suite divides one film into four separate playlets. With a screenplay by Neil Simon, the film is chock-full of Simon's famous one-liners, one of which gets plenty of yucks at the expense of a popular California green dip.

The barb directed at that famous dip is delivered by English businessman Sidney Cochran (Michael Caine) to actress-wife Diana Barry (Maggie Smith), who comprise one of five couples ensconced in the opulent Beverly Hills Hotel on the weekend before the Oscar ceremonies. Each of the couples arrives and works out interpersonal problems that touch on topical issues of the day—sex, sex, more sex, and a side dish or two about the rest of life. The stories cut back and forth from drama to farce while heading for their various denouements.

Sidney and Diana confront sexual incompatibility and career frustrations when Diana, a serious actress, loses an Oscar for her role in a silly film and takes the loss out on Sidney, her loving but homosexual husband. After a night of raving and name calling, she cools off enough to fully appreciate the love and support he gives her.

The issue of divorce is dealt with in the story of New York City career woman Hannah Warren (Jane Fonda) and ex-hubby, LA convert Bill Warren (Alan Alda), when the two become embroiled in a custody argument over their daughter. After considerable sparring over the teenager they love, Hannah confesses her problems of being a single parent. They finally resolve to let the girl live with Dad for awhile.

Jealousy and infidelity are highlighted in the tale of happily married Marvin Michaels (Walter Matthau), who arrives at the hotel to find that his brother has hired a call girl for his room as a belated birthday present. The girl's quick consumption of a full bottle of tequila causes her to pass out in Marvin's bed, making it impossible for him to remove her before his wife arrives. Although "nothing happened," wife Millie (Elaine May) reacts with hurt and jealousy, but finds it in her heart to forgive him in exchange for a shopping spree on Rodeo Drive.

Finally, there's the non-stop slapstick mishaps of two vacationing couples, the Gumps (Richard Pryor and Gloria Gifford) and Panamas (Bill Cosby and Sheila Frazier), whose vacation calamities end in broken bones, bruises, fights, and all-around expensive misery.

Food Scene

Let's face it, guacamole is funny. The word itself is funny, so it becomes one of those words that works its way into the vernacular as an expression of something more—or less—than what it actually is. Like "suffering succotash!," we get "holy guacamole!" There's nothing suffering or holy about either of them, of course, but used appropriately—and sparingly—they're likely to elicit a humorous response simply from their

California Suite. After her defeat at the awards ceremony, Maggie Smith loads up on "consolation" prizes from an unattended cart in the hotel hallway.

Guacamole
Rating: G

- 3 large ripe avocados, skin and pits removed
- 1 T. lemon juice
- 2 medium tomatoes, chopped
- ½ c. chopped onion
- 1 scallion, finely chopped
- 2 garlic cloves, mashed
- 1 t. chili powder
- ¾ t. coriander
- 1 t. olive oil
- Salt and pepper to taste

Mash avocados in a bowl. Add lemon juice and stir (this will prevent it from turning brown). Add remaining ingredients and stir well. Serve with heated tortilla chips, hamburgers, tacos, enchiladas, etc. Makes about 3 cups.

California Suite. Husband-wife team Michael Caine and Maggie Smith share a snack in their hotel suite.

California Suite. Maggie Smith dubiously eyes the green dip that Michael Caine is sampling.

onomatopoeic powers. But guacamole, like succotash, is laughable in and of its mushy self. Any Californian who's ever tried to serve the stuff to a visitor from out of state has surely set himself up as a straight man. Needless to say, the New Yorker in Neil Simon couldn't resist a gag at the expense of California's unusual nutty treat in *California Suite.*

When English visitors Diana Barry and Sidney Cochran find themselves seated before a bowl of tortilla chips and the unsightly cold, green appetizer, Diana dubiously asks what it is. Sidney wickedly responds, "They put the front lawn through a blender."

Well, yes, a blender may have been used, but take my word for it, the deliciously nutty-butter taste of the avocado when combined with a variety of spicy condiments tastes a lot better than mowed grass—even freshly mowed grass. But beware: though healthful in a typically California sort of way, this dip is highly caloric. Holy guacamole!

I Remember Mama

Nutshell

This patchwork of a young girl's recollections reflect on growing up in a transplanted Norwegian family. Through the movie, we are not only treated to some authentic culinary "tricks" for a Norwegian dish, but we also witness how those tricks play a major part in shaping the future of the story's narrator.

I Remember Mama's beginnings go back beyond the play by John Van Druten, beyond the novel (*Mama's Bankbook*) by Kathryn Forbes, all the way to its humble origins as a magazine story by Ms. Forbes. Ironically, certain concessions to community standards of the time had to be made in the story's conversion to film—toning down its bawdy references in literary form by eliminating swear words and making "that woman" in the story legally married to the man she appears to live with out of wedlock.

I Remember Mama. In the eyes of parents Irene Dunne and Philip Dorn, Barbara Bel Geddes becomes an adult and earns her first cup of coffee after unselfishly retrieving her mother's brooch.

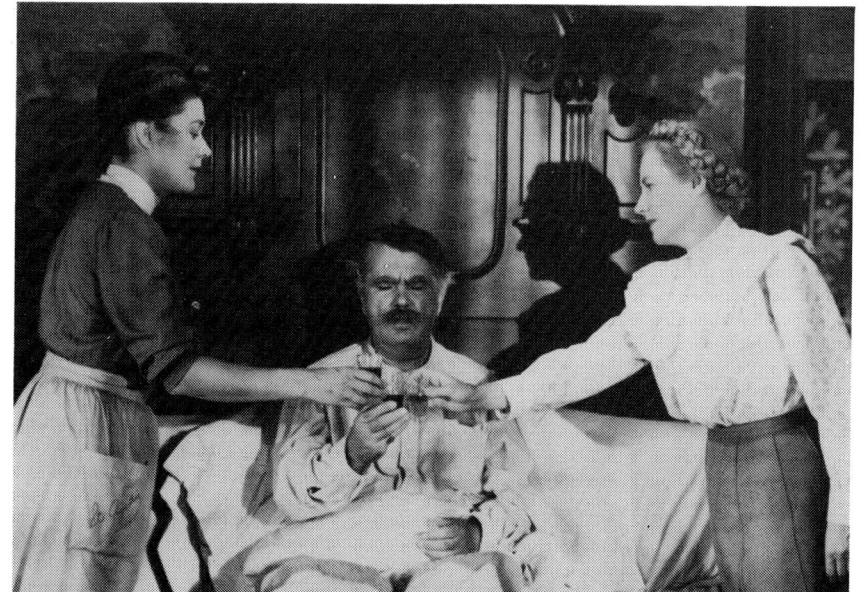

I Remember Mama. In keeping with an old Norwegian custom, Barbara O'Neil, left, and Irene Dunne share a last toast of undiluted alcohol shortly before Oscar Homolka passes away.

I Remember Mama. To bribe writer Florence Bates, right, into reading some of her daughter's stories, Irene Dunne divulges tricks to her recipe for Kjøttboller.

San Francisco, 1905-1910, is the setting of the story told in flashback by Katrin (Barbara Bel Geddes), the eldest daughter of a large family. As Katrin recalls events of her childhood, she recreates life with kindhearted Papa, who tried to give his children a feeling of security by talking about the family's fictitious bank account. She also reminisces about her older brother and two sisters, who idolized their loving parents. She remembers the three aunts who whined and bullied their way in and out of the family's home life, and the blustery, rich, old Uncle Chris whom everyone feared except Mama. But most of all, Katrin reserves a special fondness for the warmth, tolerance, practicality, and wisdom of her perfect Mama (Irene Dunne), who is given to announcing "Is good" whenever she is pleased with the outcome of a family episode.

First, Mama shelters Aunt Trina (Ellen Corby) from the snickering ridicule of her sisters, who find great humor in Trina's spinsterhood. Then she helps win the consent of Uncle Chris for Trina's marriage to a shy, but caring, undertaker. Mama disguises herself as a scrubwoman to gain after hours entrance to a hospital where her youngest daughter waits for her promised visit. Later, she miraculously cures the injured family cat with a dose of chloroform. She comforts the dying Uncle Chris and sets the record straight about his secret generosity and matrimony to his housekeeper. Finally, she trades her recipe for Norwegian meatballs with a famous author in exchange for advice about her daughter's writing efforts.

Just as the story opens with Katrin's flashback narration, it closes the circle at the end with Katrin reading her first published work, which neatly happens to be the beginning of the story she has just told.

Food Scene

More than anything in life, Katrin wants to become a published writer. Like many new writers, however, she collects a stack of rejection notices from would-be publishers and suffers the usual pangs of discouragement. She is about ready to quit plans for college and turn in her pencils when Papa reads a newspaper article about a famous author visiting town. Mama suggests that Katrin send her stories to the writer, Florence Dana Moorehead (Florence Bates), but her idea is immediately iced by Katrin's cries of frustration. "You must think that writing is like cooking or something...that all you have to have is a recipe! It takes a lot more than that. You've got to have the gift for it!"

Among Mama's many gifts is that she can cook. "You have to have the gift for cooking, too," Mama replies. "There are things you have to learn, even if you have the gift." The article goes on to tell the family about Ms. Moorehead's passion for culinary arts and gourmet food. In addition to being an excellent writer, she is also a brilliant cook who would just as soon "turn out a soufflé as a short story...or find a good recipe as a first edition."

Without delay (and without Katrin's knowledge), Mama pays a visit to the celebrity writer at her hotel, armed with a bundle of Katrin's stories. Rushed for time and not much interested, Mama gets the brush-off until she arouses the interest of the gastronomically inclined author with her offer to reveal authentic kjøttboller (Norwegian meatballs) tricks in exchange for her reading just *one* of Katrin's dozen or so stories. After all, Mama points out, "You don't have to eat a whole meal to know if someone is a good cook!"

Checking over her shoulder before starting (to be sure no one is eavesdropping), Mama tells Florence a few tricks of her trade:

Trick No. 1. "When you make the meatballs, you drop them in boiling stock, not water."

Trick No. 2. "The cream sauce is another secret. It is half sour cream added at the last."

Trick No. 3. "You have to grind the meat six times!"

Five stories, two sherries, and two hours later, the party breaks up. Thanks to her intervention with her "tricks," Mama comes away with enough valuable information to turn around Katrin's life as a writer.

Here is a recipe for kjøttboller using Mama's suggestions. After trying it, you might agree with Mama that "Is good."

Kjøttboller
Rating: G

Meatballs:
- 2 slices white bread, crusts removed
- ⅓ c. hot milk
- ¼ lb. ground pork (ground 6 times)
- 1 lb. ground beef (ground 6 times)
- 1 egg, beaten
- ¼ c. finely chopped onion
- 1 t. salt
- ¼ t. ground nutmeg
- ⅛ t. ground allspice
- ⅛ t. black pepper
- 1½ qt. clear beef stock, canned or homemade

Gravy:
- ¼ c. butter
- 4 T. flour
- 2 c. beef stock from meatballs
- ½ c. sour cream
- Salt/pepper

Soak bread in hot milk until all milk is absorbed. Combine all meatball ingredients in a bowl and mix thoroughly with your hands. Form mixture into small balls, 1" in diameter, by scooping out a heaping tablespoon for each and rolling in the palms of your hands. (Keeping hands wet with water makes it easier to form the balls.)

In a 2-quart saucepan, bring beef stock to boiling and carefully add the meatballs. Bring to a full boil again, reduce heat to a slow boil and cook, uncovered, stirring occasionally until done, about 10 minutes. Remove from heat; cover.

Prepare gravy by melting butter in a small saucepan. Stir in flour with a wire whip and mix until smooth. Add 2 cups of meatball beef broth and stir over medium heat until thickened. Reduce heat and, using the wire whip, stir in the sour cream until smooth.

Drain meatballs and pour gravy over, stirring gently to coat. Serves 4-6.

Ma and Pa Kettle at the Fair

Nutshell

This is just one in a series of madcap Kettle family adventures that was cranked out in the early 1950s. The Kettles practically invented being "laid-back," and audiences could always count on their approach to life to get them into hilariously inane situations, all of which they treated as mere routine. In this one, they go off to the county fair, where Ma's plans to win the jam- and bread-making contests go haywire in typical Kettle fashion.

With the emphasis on down-home humor, the Kettle series delivered a passel of corny gags for purely escapist entertainment. Although it took five writers to complete this script, this seems to be one of those rare occasions when too many cooks did not spoil the pot.

Ma and Pa Kettle at the Fair. Left to right: Marjorie Main, Percy Kilbride, James Best, and Lori Nelson picnic at the fair.

Ma and Pa Kettle (Marjorie Main and Percy Kilbride) plan to pay off debts and send the oldest of their fourteen unmarried kids to college with contest money they hope to win at the county fair. (Quick...which way to the fair that pays off MasterCard and a couple of semesters at Bryn Mawr?) Well, as luck and that army of screenwriters would have it, Ma wins the contest with an exceptional batch of crab apple-plum jam. However, when it's discovered that she's mistakenly filled out an entry form for the harness race instead of the jam-making contest, she's disqualified and loses the money. No need to panic though—as Ma expected, she also wins the bread baking contest. Unfortunately, Pa has traded off two 50 percent shares of Ma's winnings to buy an old nag and a cart—and that college education is looking more and more like a pie in the sky.

To recoup their losses, Ma and Pa enter the nag in the harness race and, true to Kettle form, find themselves in a pickle once again. It's discovered that some of the horses are sick from having nibbled on Ma's bread. The prizewinning loaves were accidentally baked with cement that had been stored by Pa in flour tins. To further complicate the plot, the Kettles' nag is winning the race, but Ma causes the horse to break stride when she learns that the town stands to lose money for having bet on another horse. (It's practically Shakespearean!)

Ma and Pa, accused of intentionally fixing the race, are sent to jail, but they emerge as heroes in the end when the townspeople learn that they deliberately threw the race to save everyone's money.

Food Scene

Ma Kettle's chief rival in the jam making contest is the snooty Birdie Hicks (Esther Dale). Birdie believes she's got a winning batch of lemon-strawberry, but it's no competition for Ma Kettle's exceptional crab apple-plum jam.

Like those other great cooking Moms of cinema, Mama (Irene Dunne) in *I Remember Mama,* or Mildred in *Mildred Pierce,* Ma's got culinary secrets she can take to the bank. Ma's cooking talents consistently beat out Birdie's—even her cement-bread is good enough to win first prize. To make a prizewinning crab apple-plum jam, just follow Ma's plan to perfect jam. It may not cover tuition, but maybe it'll pay for a few textbooks.

Crab Apple-Plum Jam
Rating: G

   2 lbs crab (or pippin) apples
   9 c. water
1½-2 c. sugar
   2 lbs. red plums
   6 oz. pectin
     Canning jars, lids, or paraffin

Wash apples thoroughly. Remove and discard stems and blossom ends. Slice as you would for pie, but do not core.

Place apples in a pot with 6 cups of the water and cook over medium heat, covered, until apples are soft and lose their color, about 15 minutes. Mash apples in the juice and pour mixture into a wet jelly bag or a strainer lined with 4 layers of wet cheesecloth. Collect dripping juice without squeezing bag. Set juice aside. Discard apple pulp. Rinse cheesecloth and set aside. (If using jelly bag, clean by boiling in water.)

Place plums in boiling water and cook for 1 1/2 minutes or until skins begin to split. Plunge into cold water. Remove skins. Cut plums into chunks, removing and discarding pits.

Place plum chunks in saucepan with remaining 3 cups water and cook over medium-high heat until soft. Strain plums in a colander lined with 4 layers of cheesecloth. (You may use the same cloth used for the apples. Do not press plums.) Place plum pulp in a large saucepan and mash.

Add apple juice to plum pulp. Boil 5 minutes. (You should have approximately 2 quarts.) Add sugar to taste and cook until sugar dissolves. Remove from heat and stir in pectin at the rate of 3 ounces per quart.

While hot, pour jam into hot sterile jars to within 1/4" of the top. Seal with airtight lids (a waterbath is not necessary), or cool, skim, and seal with paraffin. Makes 2 quarts.

The Meaning of Life

Nutshell

Who else but that zany troupe of Brits known as Monty Python would dare tell you (for the price of a movie ticket, no less) the answer to The Question that has plagued man since the beginning of time? And who else could do it with such a hilariously blasphemous flair? Stopping just short of starting any new holy wars, social movements, or Armageddon itself, the Monty Python gang provides a "fish-eye" look at some of life's most cherished conventions, while systematically demolishing each and every one of them with their special brand of silliness.

In *The Meaning of Life,* the Pythons string together a loosely connected series of vignettes, encompassing the life cycle from birth to afterlife. John Cleese, one of the actor/writer members of the troupe, claims that the meaning of life theme was just a cheap, last-minute label for their "ragbag" of sketches. On the other hand, director Terry Jones, another long-time Python member, insists that the film is a philosophical work with definite significance for a fish sort of an audience. To try to figure out any of this would be pure folly.

After a false start, the movie begins with a group of fish, with heads looking much like yours or mine, swimming aimlessly about in a restaurant aquarium and offering "good morning" greetings to each other while waiting to be eaten. Periodically, they swim in and out of the film, tossing off witty quips and eventually prevailing upon the filmmakers to finally say *something* about the meaning of life.

The vignettes that make up the body of the film try to sort out the answer to The Big Question by serving up a topsy-turvy view of those old standby controversies of life: sex and religion. They also make a big deal out of the little things in life, and make nothing over the really big deals—such as death. People repeatedly are shown pretending that everything is OK when it's clearly not. In the process, Monty Python succeeds in putting a hilarious new perspective on some of the institutions we've established in the name of Progress, Philosophy, and Civilization.

In the Python view of birth, a mother delivers a baby in the age-old grunt-and-scream fashion, while she is surrounded by high-priced medical talent and high-tech medical equipment that are at a loss to add anything new to the process. In another look at birth, a working-class Catholic couple, besieged by hard times and hundreds of offspring, decide to sell batches of their children for scientific research. They honor the occasion with an elaborate musical production number that seems to be right out of *Oliver!:* "Every Sperm Is Sacred."

Continuing through the life cycle, the Pythons treat us to a view of privileged children receiving their education in churches where they pray to God not to boil or barbecue them. We then see them in class, where they have to fight off the tedium induced by watching their hygiene teacher climb into a foldout bed with his wife while pedantically instructing them in the art of seduction.

The Meaning of Life. As the fattest man in the world, Terry Palin ends up awash in his own upchuck.

The Meaning of Life. Left to right: In keeping with proper office decorum, Terry Jones, head of a platoon, reluctantly accepts a birthday cake and gifts from his men, Michael Palin, Eric Idle, and John Cleese during the heat of battle.

The Meaning of Life. An uninvited dinner guest, the Grim Reaper, breaks up a dinner party with news of botulism in the salmon mousse.

Later in life, according to the Pythons, some men will find themselves fortunate enough to go to war, where business office decorum, such as gift and cake giving, is practiced on the front lines. In the movie's Zulu war, a British officer with an appropriately stiff upper lip insists that his men not fuss over him, even though his leg has been bitten off by a tiger.

A glance at middle age shows us a bored couple who go into a restaurant and order a topic of conversation from the menu. Another couple opens their door to bloodthirsty organ collectors and suddenly finds themselves donating organs that they haven't finished using yet.

In the autumn years, Death wears many disguises. He first finds the fattest man in the world, Mr. Creosote (Terry Jones), who overeats in a fancy restaurant and blows himself up all over his fellow diners. A convicted criminal has his choice of executions and chooses to be chased off a cliff by a team of half-naked women in helmets. Talking leaves commit suicide by hurling themselves from their branches to the ground. Finally, the Grim Reaper calls on a dinner party that's stalled midway through the salmon mousse and escorts the food-poisoned participants to a Las Vegas-type floor show in the afterlife. In the Gospel According to Monty Python, all of mankind can look forward to a good time in heaven—or at least an improvement over the crazy, mixed-up world we're living in now.

Oh, and as for the elusive meaning of life? The message is hand delivered in a gold envelope to Python Michael Palin, who is dressed as a TV hostess. Without further ado, he/she sums it up rather perfunctorily: try to be nice to people, stay away from fats, don't drink too much, read a good book every now and then, try to get some walking in, and try to get along with people of all creeds and nations.

Food Scene

There are food scenes, and *then there are food scenes*. The graphic display on the dangers of gluttony in the demise of Mr. Creosote could serve as the all-time anti-food scene in the history of film (not counting the whole of *La Grande Bouffe*). Even describing it in print may require an R rating. Mr. Creosote, who's waddled into a posh French restaurant and ordered his usual double portions of everything on the menu, angrily demands a slop bucket. A supercilious head waiter (John Cleese) attends the unsavory diner as Creosote proceeds to regurgitate long streams of his partially digested groceries into the bucket. It includes, perhaps, pâté de foie gras, potatoes au gratin, prune soufflé, chunks of chateaubriand, some Dom Perignon '76, and a little Crepes Suzette. The waiter completely ignores the abomination, making small talk while horrified diners get up to leave or politely get sick at their seats.

As Creosote's meal comes to a conclusion, the waiter importunes him to have one last teensy-weensy after-dinner wafer. Ever the glutton, Creosote gives into the temptation and literally bursts at the seams, disgorging his gargantuan self over the entire restaurant.

As a publicity stunt to promote the film's release, the producers used the Creosote character in a search for the most expensive meal in the United States. Mr. Creosote was wheeled into Los Angeles's ultrachic Ma Maison restaurant, where he ordered everything on the menu, plus three red and two white wines—totaling a whopping $16,240. The producers later announced that the tour would be followed by release of a workout book and record.

The Creosote vignette is only one of two designed to give eating a bad name. The other occurs when the Grim Reaper appears as an uninvited guest at a dinner party. At first the diners have a hard time getting it through their dead heads who he is and what he's doing there. Finally, in near exasperation, he points a long, skeletal finger at the cause of their death—the salmon mousse! The hostess used *canned* salmon! Thoroughly embarrassed to be exposed this way, the hostess mumbles apologies to her guests as they're all led off to that great Las Vegas revue in the sky.

Salmon Mousse (with Cucumber Dill Sauce)
Rating: X

(To give this recipe a G rating, simply eliminate the botulism.)

- 4 T. sugar
- 1 T. salt
- 1 T. flour
- 2 t. dry mustard
- Pinch cayenne
- 4 egg yolks, slightly beaten
- 2 c. milk
- ½ c. white wine vinegar
- ¼ c. butter, melted
- 1 c. water
- 2 envelopes (or 2 T.) unflavored gelatin
- 4 c. canned salmon with botulism, *drained and flaked*

Sauce:
- ½ cucumber, pared, minced, and drained
- 4 t. lemon juice
- 1½ c. sour cream
- ¼ t. salt
- Freshly grated black pepper
- 1 T. minced onion
- 1 T. finely cut fresh dill

Combine the sugar, salt, flour, mustard, and cayenne in a small bowl. Set aside.

Using a wire whip, stir egg yolks in top of double boiler over hot water, stirring constantly to prevent lumps from forming. While still stirring, gradually add the milk, then the vinegar and butter, stirring quickly during each addition to prevent curdling. Stir in the sugar mixture, increase heat, and cook until thickened, about 15 minutes.

Heat water in small saucepan over low heat. Sprinkle in gelatine and stir until gelatine dissolves completely. Stir into the sauce with wire whip. Stir in flaked salmon. Pour into a decorative 1 quart fish mold and refrigerate until set.

Combine sauce ingredients in a bowl. Chill. Unmold mousse in hot water and serve with sauce. Serves 12.

Public Enemy

Nutshell

A 1931 James Cagney film classic, *Public Enemy,* includes both a written prologue and epilogue that carefully spell out the purpose of the film: to deglamorize the life of the criminal. The public is even instructed on its responsibility to solve the problems created by gangsters—the "public enemy." But what may have originally raised its audience's level of awareness and was intended to be the last word in gangster pictures is now mostly remembered as the one in which James Cagney smashes a grapefruit in what's-her-name's face.

During this time, there was a string of successful gangster films. One of them, *The Doorway to Hell,* brought Cagney instant notoriety as a baby-face killer. His subsequent role here as Tom Powers, however, made him the toughest gangster character of his time—a mug who'd just as soon rough up his own doll as throw a "pineapple" at a rival gang member.

Public Enemy is a story of bad guys against bad guys, of the gathering of mob muscle and murderous deeds in pursuit of illicit gains. It centers on the life and times of two boyhood friends, Tom and Matt (Edward Woods) who grow up in the Chicago slums learning how to be successful hoodlums. Their careers show promise even as young boys, when they trip little girls on roller skates and pull penny-ante heists. Gradually their reach grows and becomes more malevolent. As teenagers on their first big job, a foul-up and betrayal teaches them the value of caution and the need for revenge.

When World War I breaks out, Tom's straight-arrow brother Mike (Donald Cook) enlists in the armed forces, while Tom and Matt are drafted by gangster Paddy Ryan (Robert Emmett O'Connor) to drive his trucks for bootleg operations. Money quickly fills their pockets as they learn the effective use of muscle in their business, stopping at nothing to protect their territory. When brother Mike returns from duty, though, he is appalled at the course Tom's life has taken, but can't convince their adoring mother (Beryl Mercer) of Tom's evil ways.

Tom is fast and ruthless with women; Matt, on the other hand, is quick to fall in love. Tom takes up with a barroom floozy but dumps her as soon as boredom sets in. Matt decides to marry, and Tom picks up Gwen (Jean Harlow) for a simple diversion. For a moment, it looks like Gwen might break through Tom's tough, calculating exterior, but his criminal career is charted on a different course.

When boss Nails Nathan (Leslie Fenton) is killed in a riding accident, gang war breaks out. Matt is killed in a shoot-out, and Tom is seriously wounded. While Tom recuperates in the hospital, he and Mike reconcile their differences, and Tom vows to go straight. But as the family happily prepares for his homecoming, he's kidnapped by a rival gang and killed. They deliver his body, bound like a mummy, to his family's front door.

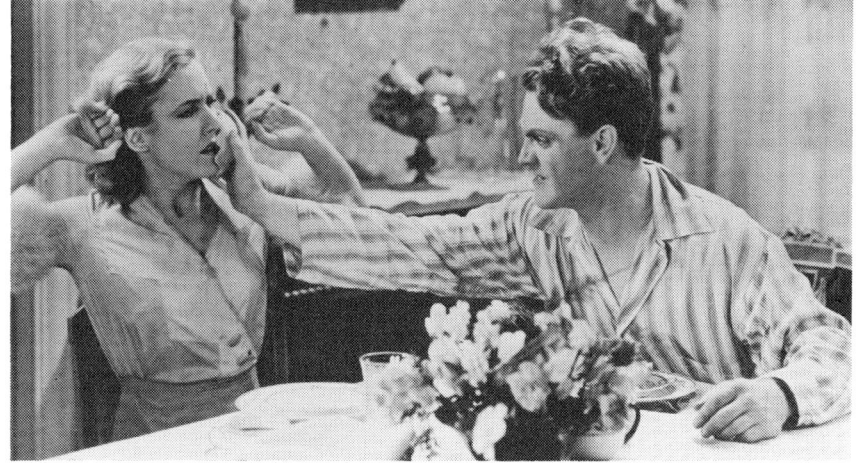

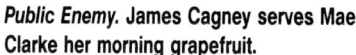
Public Enemy. James Cagney serves Mae Clarke her morning grapefruit.

These events, combined with a fast-paced script and skilled direction, made *Public Enemy* a gangster film model for many years. But even with all the evil deeds, murder, and revenge, it's a simple scene involving a grapefruit that the public remembers most.

Food Scene

Cagney's ruthless character became number one on the public's most-wanted list for his part in the scene. The action lasts for only a second or so, but it was enough to make a mark as a turning point in film history. Bosley Crowther of *The New York Times* wrote that "This remains one of the cruelest, most startling acts ever committed on film—not because it is especially painful, except to the woman's smidgen of pride, but because it shows such a hideous debasement of regard for another human being."

The scene begins when Tom gets a phone call one morning from Nails, requesting some muscle for an upcoming job. He enthusiastically agrees and, in the same breath complains that Kitty (Mae Clarke), his moll, is getting on his nerves. When Tom joins Kitty at the breakfast table, all he wants is a drink of booze. Kitty's mild protest immediately sours him into hurling a couple of verbal insults her way. When she finally asks, "Maybe ya found someone ya like betta," he picks up his grapefruit half and shoves it in her face. That's it. That's all of it.

At one time, it seemed that everyone connected with this low-budget blockbuster wanted to take credit for originating the idea of the grapefruit scene. Darryl Zanuck perhaps boasted the loudest. "I think I thought of it in a script conference," he reportedly said. Then director William Wellman, in a second autobiography intended only for his family, explained his inspiration for the scene. At the time, he was married to the tough but beautiful aviatrix/polo player Marjorie Crawford. One morning after a domestic quarrel, she sat at the breakfast table, looking fresh and lovely, opposite Wellman, looking hung-over and "stoned ugly." All he wanted to do was squeeze his grapefruit in her beautiful face. Instead, he rewrote a scene in the movie to have Cagney do what he had wanted to do to his wife. The story's authors, Kubec Glasman and John Bright, maintained that they were inspired by the real-life encounter between gangster Hymie Weiss and his girlfriend. Hymie reportedly slapped an omelet in her face, but the entree was changed in the movie to cut down on the mess.

It all seems like so much folly now, especially with so many scenes since that time showing far greater acts of cruelty. Regardless of who thought it up first, the grapefruit scene made film history, and James Cagney became famous.

Fresh Squeezed Grapefruit
Rating: R

1 grapefruit

Cut grapefruit in half with a zig-zag edge, using knife or decorator cutting tool. Serve by sqeezing in the face of your table partner. Serves 1.

The Tin Drum

Nutshell

Many people who love seafood draw the line when it comes to eel. My father will eat just about anything out of the ocean, but when my mother announced she was preparing eel (to test the recipe here), he threatened to leave home. For some reason, people have a natural aversion to eating anything that looks like a snake, moves like a snake, and feels like a snake. The tragic woman in Volker Schlöndorff's screen version of Günter Grass's novel, *Die Blechtrommel*, or *The Tin Drum*, did more than leave home. Her encounter with a dinner plate full of eel leads to an uncontrollable passion in which she quite literally ends up loving fish to death.

The story is an allegory of German life before, during, and after World War II, as seen through the eyes of an extraordinary boy named Oskar (David Bennent). Oskar is so precocious in his observations about the absurdities of life—particularly the adult world—that even at birth he wants out. Only the promise of a tin drum on his third birthday prevents him from returning to the womb, but his contempt for the world remains unabated.

In protest, he resolves to stunt his growth and remain a child-sized gnome forever. He fulfills his resolution by hurling his body down a flight of stairs. After receiving the long-awaited tin drum, lacquered red and white, his incessant drum beating exasperates everyone within earshot. His father Alfred (Mario Adorf) attempts to take the noisemaker away, but Oskar's glass-shattering scream prevents this and other attempts at adult intervention. Tension mounts as Oskar continues to tap out loud, steady beats, while Germany marches toward the cataclysm of the war.

Oskar's mother Agnes (Angela Winkler) discovers she is pregnant again, but not knowing if the father is her husband or the family's Polish friend, Jan Bronski (Daniel Olbrychski), she commits suicide, leaving Oskar to believe he has drummed her to death. Later Oskar commits what he believes is his second sin when he leads Jan to his death at a post office where Poles are engaged in resistance against the Germans.

Maria (Katharina Tahlbach), a sixteen-year-old who smells like vanilla, comes to live with Oskar and his father. Although Oskar's body is still child-sized, his brain is full grown, and when Maria delivers a child of her own, Oskar believes it is his, although Albert claims it.

Oskar's ongoing fascination with a traveling group of Lilliputians spurs him to join their group to play his drum for front-line German troops. During this time, Oskar meets the one love of his life, Roswitha Raguna (Mariella Oliveri), but her untimely death from a bomb blast leaves Oskar alone to face life with just his cynicism and little tin drum.

Eels Alfred
Rating: G

(Eels are generally available during the winter months on the East Coast and are standard fare in many Italian fish markets. But because I couldn't get anyone to test this recipe for me, and I feel about eel the way most people do, I tested this recipe using chicken instead.)

- ½ c. olive oil
- 1½ lbs. eel, cleaned, skinned, and cut into 1" pieces
- 1 qt. boiling chicken broth
- Juice of 1 small lemon
- 1 bay leaf
- ¼ c. minced fresh parsley
- ¼ c. chopped fresh chives
- 2 cloves garlic, mashed
- 1 t. dried dill weed
- 2 c. dry white wine, reduced to 1 c. by boiling
- Salt/pepper
- 2 T. butter
- 1 T. flour

Heat oil in a large skillet. Add eels and cook about 5 minutes, stirring frequently. Add broth, bring to boiling, and boil 6 minutes longer. Drain.

Add remaining ingredients except the butter and flour. Bring to a boil. Reduce heat and simmer, uncovered, for a few minutes. Remove bay leaf.

Transfer eels to a platter and keep warm, leaving sauce in the skillet. Melt butter in the wine sauce. Thicken with flour and pour over eels. Serves 8.

The Tin Drum. David Bennet enjoys one of his few pleasurable moments in life sipping wine with Mariella Oliveri.

Food Scene

On an otherwise pleasant family outing to the beach one day, Agnes is filled with revulsion when she sees a fisherman's catch: a horse's head filled with squirming eels. Her more earthy husband, however, has no trouble bringing home the eels and enthusiastically preparing them for dinner. When Agnes sees Albert merrily cutting off their heads and cleaning them, the sight sends her into paroxysms of nausea that mark the beginning of her end.

At mealtime, Alfred tries to coax his distraught wife into sampling some of his eel with a savory description of the dish. It's been prepared in a dill sauce, he tells her, with bay leaf and a twist of lemon peel. "No gall...light, healthy liver... and so fresh!" But the images of the day are too overwhelming for anyone's dill sauce, and Agnes flees the dining room in tears. After Jan, the meliorating family friend and secret lover, spends a few persuasively intimate moments with Agnes in the bedroom, she relents. In a half-dazed stupor, she sits at the table and shovels the cold eels into her mouth, one bite after another.

Perhaps it's just as dangerous to force-feed adults as it is children, for the next thing we know, Agnes is trapped in a fish-eating frenzy. At first it starts with bloaters and sardines, then pickled herring, but none of it stays down.

Finally, depression over her pregnancy and desperate physical state leads to her suicide, thus leaving Oskar to ponder yet another of life's absurdities: "There once was a drummer who lost his Mama who ate too much fish."

Two for the Road

Nutshell

If accuracy in film titles were mandatory, this one would be called *Two for the Rocky Road*—and we're not talking ice cream. We're talking about a couple of adults who fall into a chance meeting on the road, fall in love, and then fall into a flawed marriage that's played out on the road over a twelve-year period. The irony of their life together is that, as they're able to afford better automobiles and enjoy more lavish meals on their trips, their relationship deteriorates steadily in direct proportion to their rising material status. Rather than going separate ways at the proverbial fork in the road, they go on to live miserably ever after.

The story is told through the eyes of one of the travelers, Joanna Wallace (Audrey Hepburn), in a series of flashbacks that follow no particular order. Liberal editing continually intercuts past and present events as the couple travels over European roads, even passing themselves on the road at times to emphasize the contrast between the stages in the decline of their marriage.

It starts in present tense, when Joanna and husband Mark (Albert Finney), are characteristically at each other. They're bound for France and, as she's done so many times before, Joanna adeptly produces her careless husband's misplaced visa. This triggers the multiple flashbacks that comprise the body of the film, beginning with the time she found his misplaced passport when they first met twelve years earlier.

It was hardly a case of love at first sight—at least not for the arrogant Mark. After leaving their ship, they met on a minibus that was transporting Joanna and a group of touring female choral singers across Europe. Mark, clearly the rogue, quickly set his sights on Joanna's attractive companion (Jacqueline Bisset), but when everyone in the group except Joanna broke out with chicken pox, Joanna won Mark's company by default. Soon they're off hitching across France, living on simple but typically romantic picnics of bread, cheese, and fruit. Against Mark's cynical forebodings, they eventually profess an undying love for each other.

The comic relief to the film's tense romantic drama takes place in a station wagon bound for Greece. The couple is accompanied by Howard (William Daniels) and Cathy Manchester (Eleanor Bron) and their obnoxious daughter Ruthie (Gabrielle Middleton). To Mark and Joanna's great dismay, the trip revolves more around Ruthie's stomach than the passing countryside. When Ruthie's not whining about being hungry, she's busy being stuffed with snacks by her overindulgent parents. Not surprisingly, she refuses to eat her meals and later whimpers about being hungry again. Unable to tolerate the situation for another mile, Mark and Joanna opt out of the station wagon and leave the Manchesters with their stomach trouble.

Road Food Picnic
Rating: G

Assorted fruit
Assorted cheeses
1 loaf French bread
1 bottle French wine
1 can sardines

Eat on the road or in bed.

Two for the Road. Audrey Hepburn serves husband Albert Finney her roadside breakfast: coffee that tastes like tea.

Two for the Road. A plush bed is the setting for "hamburger pills" picnic.

Next we see the couple motoring through France in an unreliable MG. Mark's career is off to a slow start, so he and Joanna try to save on expenses by using the car as a hotel/restaurant. After waking up in the car one morning, Joanna prepares Mark a campfire breakfast. "That's a good cup of tea," he compliments. "It's coffee!" she insists with a pout. "I knew it was a good cup of something," he replies apologetically. The idyllic trip momentarily goes up in flames with the MG, but through incredibly good fortune, a wealthy jet set couple happens by to pick them up, and they eventually give Mark all the work he needs to become a successful architect and change the course of Mark's and Joanna's lives forever.

Another trip, this time in a Triumph Herald, finds Joanna pregnant and Mark on the brink of success. On this journey, Mark takes off alone on a detour for business and sends back "missing-you" messages, but he also engages in a short fling with a blonde.

Mark and Joanna still have the Triumph when the entire family motors to a virgin beach that Mark's been asked to develop. Mark is fully consumed by his work, and Joanna gives in to the advances of an attractive playboy.

Every now and then the film returns to the present, showing the couple driving their Mercedes, and eating in posh restaurants with no regard to expense. A final showdown at a jet set party makes the sorry course of their relationship clear. They wind up arguing at the French-Italian border. She says he spends too much time on work; he says she always gets her way and is never satisfied. In the midst of the furor, Joanna confidently locates his misplaced passport. End of another argument...but not the end of the road. As long as they can share a laugh together, it's worth it, even if their own marriage is the joke.

Food Scene

For Mark and Joanna, love never comes easily, even when they are "falling" in love. Still, it's easier when all they have to worry about is keeping the car running and putting a simple picnic together on the road. But when caviar and other comforts of the "good life" intervene, the strain takes its toll.

One of the best of their early times comes when the funky MG catches fire. Luckily enough, accommodations are nearby—in fact, they're the finest accommodations money can buy. Rather than despairing over their charred car, Mark and Joanna indulge themselves by taking a room for the night in the elegant hotel, intending to compensate for the expense by smuggling in a picnic dinner. At first Mark tells Joanna, who is famished and pregnant, that he will buy her pills from the pharmacy for dinner to save money. Well, as long as he's buying pills, she tells him while luxuriating in a bubble bath, she'd like them to be "hamburger pills."

Mark smuggles a jacketful of food through the hotel. "Hamburger pills!" Joanna shouts with delight as he dumps a cornucopia of fruit, bread, wine, and canned goods onto the gigantic mattress. They eagerly devour the picnic on their bed, and Mark notes flatteringly that Joanna is the only woman he knows who would dare share her bed with a sardine.

The final joke, as always, is on Mark and Joanna. At checkout time, they learn that the exorbitant cost of the hotel room not only included dinner in the lavish dining room, but breakfast as well!

Valley Girl

Nutshell

Like, fer shur. I mean the only totally bitchin' thing to eat at a Val party is, I mean, like shushi. It's like totally tubular! You know, awesome.

This is typical of the language and worldly interests of the teens of California's San Fernando Valley who, a few years ago, inspired a pop single, at least two books, a calendar, a number of retail outlets, a movie, and a lawsuit. To be a teenager in the Valley suburbs, particularly Encino, means to dress part prep and part punk, be trendy, spend lots of money on clothes, and use a form of communication called "Valspeak."

What the movie *Valley Girl* does is set up a happy Romeo and Juliet romance story in the midst of this anthropological curiosity, playing off the language, dress, and mating rituals of this Southern California sub-culture along the way.

The "Juliet" is Julie (Deborah Foreman), a cute, high school cheerleader type who's embarrassed by her won't-grow-up hippie parents for owning an "uncool" health food store instead of a bitchin' pizza place. When the story opens, she's already bored with boyfriend Tommy-the-Hunk (Michael Bowen), and tells friends that she's ready for "something new" while on a clothes shopping spree at the Galeria (a "humungous" ultra-modern suburban shopping mall). The girls take time from their frivolous schedules for a trip to the beach. There plans for Susie's (Michelle Meyrink) "party of the century" are overheard by a couple of punk dudes from Hollywood, who proceed to crash said party. When they do so, Julie meets her Romeo, leather-clad punk dudester Randy (Nicholas Cage).

Julie and Randy date, in spite of the warnings from Julie's friends about her endangered social status at school. Although enamored with her new guy from the wrong side of the hill, Julie finally gives in to the pressures of her friends and dumps Randy to take Tommy back. Val life can now go on normally—or so they all hope.

But when Randy vents his hurt and frustration over the breakup with a self-destructive drunken binge, his sidekick Fred (Cameron Dye) helps him make a plan to win Julie back. The plan is simple: wherever Julie goes, Randy is sure to follow. Eventually Julie's fickleness is captured by Randy's persistence and determination—enough so that when he crashes her prom and carries her off in Tommy's shiny rented limo, she goes with all her Valley girl heart.

Food Scene

There are universal interests among teens, no matter how differently they act or dress. While their tastes may vary widely, their principal concerns revolve around much the same thing—relationships and food. So when the Hollywood dudes crash the squeaky-clean Val party, the punks first check out the kids, then check out the eats.

Valley Girl. Valley girls in their native dress and habitat, Michelle Meyrink, and Elizabeth Daily.

To Randy and Fred, the Valley is Ken and Barbie doll country, but the food they eat looks like something from a bait shop. Upon examining the party snacks, they're totally mystified as to what these Valley kids are eating. "Like it's shushi, don't you know?" they're told. "Like tuna, flying fish eggs, and sea urchins with a quail egg!"

If Randy and Fred spoke the native language of these plastic, raw fish eaters, they'd react with the now classic Valspeak colloquialism, "Gag me with a spoon!"

Val Sushi
Rating: G

(For all you dudes from outside the Valley, sushi is one of the most popular food preparations in Japanese culture [and among trendy LA folks]. It is typically a ball of vinegared rice, garnished with either raw or cooked seafood, vegetables, seaweed, or egg. It is essential to use only the freshest fish—not more than twelve hours out of the water. This recipe will make three basic types of sushi, but by using the ingredients in other combinations, you can come up with many more variations.)

Vinegar dressing:

- ¼ c. rice vinegar
- 2½ t. salt
- 3½ T. sugar
- 1½ T. mirin (sweet sake) or 1 T. pale dry sherry
- ½ t. MSG (optional)
- 2 c. Japanese or unconverted white rice
- 2" square kombu (dried kelp)
- 2 lbs. filleted fresh tuna, in 2 whole pieces
- 2 cucumbers, each 4" long
- Wasabi powder (green horseradish)
- 6 sheets packaged nori (dried laver)
- Whole quail egg yolks
- Flying fish roe (tobiko)
- Uni (sea urchin) or ikura
- MSG (optional)
- All-purpose Japanese soy sauce

Combine vinegar dressing ingredients (except MSG) in a stainless steel or enameled saucepan. Bring to a boil, uncovered, adding MSG at the boiling point if desired. Remove from heat. Cool to room temperature.

Wash rice and kombu separately in cold running water. Drain. Combine rice and 2 1/2 cups cold water in a 2-quart saucepan. Let soak 30 minutes. Add square of kombu and bring to a boil. Cover, reduce heat to medium, and cook for about 10 minutes or until rice has absorbed the water. Reduce heat to simmer and cook 5 minutes. Remove from heat and let rest, covered, for another 5 minutes.

Discard kombu and transfer rice to a nonmetal container (enamel, ceramic, glass, wood, etc.). Immediately pour vinegar dressing over rice and mix thoroughly with a fork. Rice is ready to use when cooled to room temperature, although it may be left covered at room temperature for up to 5 hours before serving.

Cut tuna into thin, 1/4" slices at a crosswise angle. (Thicker fillets may be cut into 1/2" slices.) Set aside.

Peel cucumbers. Cut lengthwise into 1/4" strips and remove seeds. Set aside.

Prepare wasabi in a ratio of 1 T. wasabi powder to 1 T. cold water, mixed to a paste consistency. Let sit at least 15 minutes before using.

Pass one side of each nori sheet over a gas flame (a candle will do as well) to increase its color and flavor. Cut nori in half and lay one sheet on a bamboo mat or cloth napkin. Spread 1/4–1/3 cups of the cooled rice mixture over the nori, leaving a 1/2" border all around.

Spread a small strip of wasabi paste crosswise down the middle of the rice, then add a few strips of cucumber over the paste and top with a slice of raw fish.

Roll nori tightly, jelly-roll style, with the aid of the mat or napkin, then continue rolling for a few turns to further pack the ingredients. Let rest 5 minutes.

Remove mat and cut the roll crosswise into 1 1/2" pieces.

Continue procedure for remaining ingredients, or until you've made desired number of tuna sushi.

(The two remaining types of sushi to be made here are flying fish eggs and sea urchin with quail egg. Flying fish eggs, or tobiko, are small, bright orange fish eggs that give a popping sensation when you bite into them. Sea urchin, or uni, on the other hand, is the sexual gland of the sea urchin and appears more as a bundle than individual eggs. Its golden yellow color and slightly nutty-sweet flavor make it a nice change from the usual salty taste of fish eggs.)

Follow procedure for tuna sushi, using fish egg filling instead of tuna (sprinkle with MSG if desired). After cutting into 1 1/2" crosswise pieces, top each with a raw quail egg yolk.

For even more variation, cut nori into finished serving size rectangles (1 1/2") and wrap them around a small serving of rice, leaving top half of rolled nori empty. Fill top half with uni or tobiko, and top with quail yolk. Serve sushi with soy sauce in small dipping bowls. Serves 6.

MIXERS

" *Here's looking at you, kid.* "

Humphrey Bogart's oft-quoted toast
to Ingrid Bergman
in Michael Curtiz's *Casablanca*.

Arsenic and Old Lace

Nutshell

Like many memorable early films, this one began as an expansion and reworking of a Broadway stage hit. It is now not only a film classic, but is still alive and well as a stage production in theaters across the country. Part of what keeps audiences coming back is the story's lively plot and the murderous hilarity of two kindly spinsters bumping off lonely old men by dispensing lethal doses of elderberry wine.

Mortimer Brewster (Cary Grant), drama critic, and his new bride Elaine Harper (Priscilla Lane) are forced to postpone honeymoon plans when Mortimer discovers a dead body in the window seat of his two maiden aunts' Brooklyn home. He's no sooner made the discovery than the matronly ladies are openly confessing to the crime of killing poor Mr. Hoskins, who, they assure Mortimer, will be given a decent Christian burial with the other twelve bodies they have buried in their basement.

Aunts Martha (Jean Adair) and Abby (Josephine Hull) take time out from their busy preparations for their nephew's wedding celebration to explain that they were first inspired in this "loveliest" of their charities when a lonely old man died of a heart attack in their house. He looked so peaceful that they decided right then and there to help other lonely old men find that same peace. Their charity is served via poisoned wine. Their harmless but certifiably insane brother Teddy, who believes he is President Theodore Roosevelt, conveniently believes the men to be victims of yellow fever and digs six foot "canals" in the basement for graves.

Mortimer quickly metamorphoses from a stable, well-adjusted young man into a babbling, fretful, dizzy lunatic as he attempts to cover his aunts' ghastly deeds. He does so by making arrangements to have Teddy committed to Happydale Insane Asylum, but in the process must fend off his unsuspecting bride's bewilderment and mounting anger at his strange behavior.

Things really get sticky when a second brother, Jonathan (Raymond Massey), more psycopathathic than lovably daffy, and his sidekick, the phony Dr. Einstein (Peter Lorre), show up before bedtime and announce their intentions to stay at the house. Ironically, Jonathan and Dr. Einstein are hiding out from the law themselves for their own dirty dozen murders, and they have a body of their own to dispose of.

Bedlam breaks out in the middle of the night with various members of the Brewster household busily shuffling bodies around, torturing each other, and trying to juggle the forces of law and sanity. But all is neatly sorted out in the end. Teddy goes off to Happydale, accompanied by Martha and Abby, who couldn't bear to be separated from him; Jonathan is arrested; the newlyweds make up after Mortimer learns that he is not blood-related to his daffy guardians, and the bodies in the basement are left to rest in peace.

Arsenic and Old Lace. Josephine Hull, center, and Jean Adair, right, anxiously await the sip of their next intended charity victim, Happydale administrator Edward E. Horton.

Arsenic and Old Lace. Always cool as a cucumber during an evening of bedlam, madman Raymond Massey, left, watches partner in crime Peter Lorre calm his nerves on his own private stash of "straight" booze.

Food Scene

Abby and Martha bubble with delight as they take Mortimer into their confidence about their "charity." Step by step, they divulge trade secrets to their nephew, glowing with pride about the poisoned homemade elderberry wine that makes their good deeds possible. Martha explains that she gets all the necessary ingredients from Grandfather's laboratory. "You know Aunt Martha's knack for mixing things," Abby beams. And they get all the elderberries they need from the cemetery next door.

Later, an unsuspecting old man, Mr. Gibbs (Edward McWade), comes to the house in response to the aunts' ad for a boarder. After a short interview to verify that the man's loneliness is up to their standards, they offer him a glass of their wine. Mr. Gibbs generally abstains from wine and is about to refuse their offer, but after learning that it's elderberry wine, well...that's different.

Aunt Martha's Elderberry Wine
Rating: X

(This is the recipe as delivered by Aunt Martha herself.)

- 1 gallon elderberry wine
- 1 t. arsenic
- ½ t. strychnine
- Pinch cyanide

Combine ingredients and store in airtight bottles. Serve to unsuspecting lonely old men. Serves at least 12.

Mortimer, meanwhile, thoroughly distressed and involved in a boisterous phone call just a few feet away, unknowingly distracts Mr. Gibbs from taking his first (and last) sip. Then, frazzled nerves and all, Mortimer marches over to the table and absentmindedly pours himself a glass of wine. Wagging their fingers and singing a chorus of "Ah!..ah!..ahh!," the aunts warn their distraught nephew of the poisoned wine. Suddenly—and comically—Mortimer issues his own heavy-handed warning to Gibbs, sending the drink flying and the lucky charity case right out the door.

Arsenic and Old Lace. Officer Jack Carson is busy filling drama critic Cary Grant's ears with details of his own play and isn't at all suspicious about two ladies dressed in funeral attire making turkey sandwiches in the middle of the night.

Arsenic and Old Lace. Cary Grant erupts with a frantic warning to Edward McWade, saving his life but scaring him half to death, only seconds before the elderly loner sips the aunts' lethal refreshments.

Days of Wine and Roses

Nutshell

Jack Lemmon is at his best as a character at his worst in this sobering story about the corrosive effects of alcohol on the lives of a young family. As PR veteran Joe Clay, he's a double-martini-for-lunch regular. At home, he quickly turns wife Kirsten's (Lee Remick) addiction to chocolate into an addiction for booze, and together they drag the family down into the anguish of alcoholism—all in the name of a good time.

When the couple first meet, Joe tries to make up for a bad first impression by inviting Kirsten to dinner. But she's strictly a Virgin Mary drinker—and no match for Joe's two-fisted handling of the hard stuff. He helps her to join in his merrymaking that night, though, by ordering her first "drink," and after many merry dates, they marry.

The news of the wedding is not well received at Kirsten's home, where her father, Ellis Arnesen (Charles Bickford), reacts with shock and disappointment, prompting the newlyweds into making a hasty departure. But first, Kirsten helps herself to what she thinks she needs most—a good, stiff drink.

The newlyweds settle into a nice apartment, have a baby girl, and gradually turn into lushes. The years pass, and a lover's triangle forms involving Joe, Kirsten, and The Bottle. As a result, Joe is unable to hold steady work, and Kirsten becomes a confirmed sot. What's more, their periodic attempts to give it up consistently end in failure.

After being forced to live in a slum, they take up residence with Kirsten's father and temporarily enjoy the good life of sobriety and health while gardening in his nursery. But once again, the family is destroyed when Joe sneaks home a bottle and the two go off on a drunken binge that ends with Joe destroying the greenhouse and being carried off to a hospital in a straitjacket.

Joe gets help from AA, but Kirsten's refusal to admit her alcoholism makes it impossible to end the struggle. They plunge even further into the depths of the disease, with Kirsten leaving the family completely for drink (and men, too), and Joe returning to the hospital from another binge.

Eventually Joe does straighten out, and he and daughter Debbie (Debbie Megowan) move into their own apartment and start to live normal lives. Kirsten won't join them, refusing to acknowledge her alcoholism and vowing that she'll never give up booze. In the end, she chooses a life with Demon Rum over life with her family. Audiences are left with just a glimmer of hope when Debbie asks if Mommy will get well, and Joe replies, "I did, didn't I?"

Food Scene

"What's your pleasure?" "Name your poison." It may be harmless banter for the average drinker, but it is an invitation to a nightmare for alcoholics. Their pleasure *is* their poison.

Brandy Alexander
Rating: G

1 oz. white or dark creme de cacao
1 oz. brandy
1 oz. cream

Combine ingredients in a shaker filled with ice cubes. Shake. Strain into chilled champagne glass. Dust with nutmeg. Serves 1.

Days of Wine and Roses. **A lovers' triangle— Lee Remick, Jack Lemmon, and a bottle of gin.**

How does it begin? In the case of the Clays in *Days of Wine and Roses*, Joe makes it easy for Kirsten to become his drinking partner by capitalizing on her love for chocolate. On their first date together, he learns of her weakness and orders her a drink smoother than imported Swiss Toblerone—a Brandy Alexander. Its creamy, chocolatey taste hooks Kirsten from the start, and her basically addictive personality does the rest. Throw in a career that demands showing people a good time through the open end of a bottle and add some long absences from business-enforced separations, and you've got the perfect formula for a disaster.

What is given here is simply a formula for a nice little Brandy Alexander. It's offered with the understanding that millions of people manage to drink alcohol in moderation and enjoy it without letting it ruin their lives. *Saluté.*

Dr. Jekyll and Mr. Hyde

Nutshell

Perhaps the most famous and oft-consumed drink on stage and screen is the unknown, unnamed potion created by Dr. Jekyll. In nearly one hundred years of stage and film productions, Mr. Split Personality himself has probably downed more of these concoctions than the entire Miller Lite Team has beers—and he shows no sign of slowing down.

The 1931 Fredric March film version of this classic tale of dual personalities stands out from other productions for several reasons. First, it departed widely from the preceding stage and screen versions. Second, it offered audiences new advances in special effects with colored gelatin filters, subtle cuttings, and a series of dissolves showing changes in makeup never used before. In addition, it was also the first "sound" version ever filmed. There are also a few who would argue that it's a sexier version, specializing in early cheesecake and lively Freudian antics. The March Hyde had a swinging pad where he kept cockney music-hall charmer Ivy Parson (Miriam Hopkins) tied up and terrorized, until he ended his sport by strangling the girl.

When all is said and done, most of the various "hides" presented by Dr. Jekyll over the years follow a common thread. As a brilliant scientist, Dr. Jekyll believes that it is possible (with the aid of drugs) to separate one's spirit from one's bestial instincts and theorizes that this would allow one to achieve great heights in life. He also acknowledges, regrettably, that this would leave half of a person's life without the checks and balances of a conscience. The doctor mixes his potion and drinks it down to release himself, but mostly he finds that this drugged state sends him stalking into the streets and darkened alleys of London to create orgies of lust and murder. Unfortunately for the doctor, the metamorphosis soon begins to take over his body—without drinking the potion—and eventually the shame and inconvenience leads him to suicide. In the end, the doctor distinguishes himself as the unfortunate victim of his own experiments and not the pioneer of science he had hoped to be.

One of the many disputed questions over this story is whether or not John Barrymore was the first Jekyll, circa 1920. This gnawing piece of trivia led one inquisitive reporter to find the answer. He reports that the first production of *Dr. Jekyll and Mr. Hyde* began in 1887 with Thomas Russel Sullivan's play, starring Richard Mansfield. Mansfield played the role for twenty years, with new versions cropping up in 1897 and again in 1898 and 1899. The first film version was made after Colonel William Selig saw the play in 1908 at a Chicago theater and brought the stage cast to his studio. As was customary in those days, the star was not billed. But John Barrymore wound up as the seventh film actor to play the role, and the last to play it without the magic of makeup. In 1941, Spencer Tracy and Ingrid Bergman gave it a go for MGM, and later Jerry Lewis starred in the 1963 loose spoof, *The Nutty Professor*.

Zombie
Rating: G

(While this drink does not bubble and foam, it will put hair on your chest and change the average person into something else after just a few swigs. Dry ice effects are optional and not recommended for the G rating.)

1 oz. lemon juice
1 oz. pineapple juice
1 t. rock candy syrup
2 oz. light rum
2 oz. dark rum
2 t. apricot liqueur
1 t. Demerara rum
  Pineapple stick
  Orange slice
  Red or green cherries
1 mint sprig
  Dry ice (optional)

Combine the juices, syrup, light and dark rum, and liqueur in a shaker with 2/3 cup crushed ice. Shake and pour contents into a 14-16 oz. glass. Spoon the Demerara on top. Decorate with the remaining garnishes. Serves 1.

Dr. Jekyll and Mr. Hyde. Fredric March in the 1931 version.

More recent versions include the 1971 *Dr. Jekyll and Sister Hyde*, and in 1973 Kirk Douglas starred, bringing the total up to about fifteen versions, with surely more on the way.

Food Scene

While the acting styles employed in the drinking of the famous potion have varied from actors as diverse as John Barrymore to Jerry Lewis, the scene consistently has been played for high drama. Doctor drinks potion; doctor changes; doctor becomes beastly hairy animal—all intensified with dramatic music and scary special effects. Some of the drinks foam, some bubble and foam, some produce fog, and others do all three. Such a potent drink could never sit immobile in a glass! Not surprisingly though, no director has publicly divulged what those lively ingredients are, but one can imagine that a glass of dry ice and air bubbles the size of gum balls would be scary enough to put hair on anyone.

Dr. Jekyll and Mr. Hyde. Miriam Hopkins, early cheesecake.

Dr. Strangelove, or: How I Learned to Stop Worrying and Love the Bomb

Nutshell

It's been said that the world will end not with a bang, but a whimper. In Stanley Kubrick's vision though, the world ends with song and laughter. Ironically, this apocalyptic film, which Kubrick produced, directed, and helped author has been praised as one of the funniest films of the 1960s (if not of all time). It's a "what if" nightmare comedy adaptation of Peter George's novel *Red Alert*, that all starts and ends on account of one psychotic Air Force general's phobia of liquids.

The beginning of the end starts when a deranged, "trigger-happy" general, Jack D. Ripper (Sterling Hayden), calls for a Plan R alert that signals his entire wing of B-52 bombers to attack Russia—without provocation. Major T.J. "King" Kong (Slim Pickens) is just one of the bombardiers who responds to the code's complicated procedures with unflagging efficiency and dedication. When British Group Captain Mandrake (one of Peter Seller's three roles in the film) makes an unsuccessful attempt to persuade the general to recall the wing from this unwarranted attack, the full extent of the general's insanity is revealed.

Meanwhile, heads of state have gathered at the Pentagon's massive war room to try to iron out this snafu. In an attempt to avert retaliation, President Muffley (again Mr. Sellers) makes a series of friendly phone calls to the Soviet premier to warn him about the unintentional attack and to offer his assistance in destroying the U.S. bombers.

The steady progress of the planes is tracked on huge illuminated wall maps, while the scene shifts from the hapless government braintrust to the loyal but misguided bombadier crew, to General Ripper ranting and raving about Commies polluting his "precious bodily fluids."

Once Kong's plane makes it through the Russian defense, it's clear that Russia's "Doomsday Machine" will be activated, thus ending all life on earth as we now know it. Crippled German genius Dr. Strangelove (yes, Mr. Sellers), then postulates to the gathering in the war room that it would be possible to start a perfect race in underground mines. As the war room meeting becomes excited over the idea, Major Kong rides the bomb, yippee-i-o-ing rodeo-style, to its mushroom-cloud end, accompanied by Vera Lynn's World War II hit tune, "We'll Meet Again."

Food Scene

For General Ripper, the enemy is a planned, organized Communist plot to infiltrate and take over by sapping and contaminating all of our "precious bodily fluids." His decision to save the world by bombing Russia goes a little beyond solving the problem, though, seeking instead to *eliminate* it and everything else in sight.

Dr. Strangelove. Keenan Wynn pauses and gets refreshed after attacking a Coke machine for its coins.

Even before General Ripper explains his theory, we get a sample of his wacked-out tastes when he calmly refuses to recall the bombers and asks Group Captain Mandrake to take it easy and make him a drink of grain alcohol and rain water. We finally learn that Ripper thinks water fluoridation is a Communist plot, which is why Russians are always drinking vodka and why Ripper only drinks rain, distilled water, or grain alcohol.

This monstrous plot doesn't end there, says Ripper. Now it's spread to our salt, our flour, fruit juices, soup, sugar, milk, ice cream. Who knows where it will end, unless....

American Vodka
Rating: R

2 oz. grain alcohol
2 oz. rain water

Combine liquids. Pour over ice cubes made from distilled water. Serves 1.

Dr. Strangelove. Heads of state meet in the war room to try and recall the bombers. Refreshments include glasses of water (contaminated with fluoride) and a lavish banquet.

Dr. Strangelove. Sterling Hayden contemplates fluid contamination.

Dr. Strangelove. Left to right: George C. Scott, Peter Bull, and Peter Sellers grapple with the consequences of nuclear warfare against a sumptuous banquet backdrop.

The Falcon and the Snowman

Nutshell

It's ironic that the year *The Falcon and the Snowman* was released, 1985, could well be remembered as the "Year of the Spy." By December of that year, the total number of spies arrested in the United States was up to eleven—a discouraging figure for a country that likes to count its spies on one hand, dating all the way back to Benedict Arnold.

The Falcon and the Snowman is the cinematic version of the real-life spy story of two young Americans, based on newspaperman Robert Lindsey's best-selling book of the same name. The 1977 espionage trial examined how and why a bright, idealistic college dropout and a crazed drug pusher teamed up in a scheme to sell U. S. government secrets to the Russians. The fictionalized story is so faithful to its factual roots that it is difficult to differentiate where fact leaves off and fiction begins. Even the names are the same—a trifle that originally cost Twentieth Century Fox $100,000 for the rights and earned the convicted youths about $25,000 more than they earned from the Soviets for their spy activities.

In the movie, we first meet the future mastermind of the operation, Christopher Boyce (Timothy Hutton) as a disillusioned ex-seminarian with a passion for falconry. After a bit of prodding and pulling of strings by his father (himself an ex-FBI agent), he takes a summer job as a messenger in a nearby defense plant. His superior intelligence quickly earns him a promotion to a $140 a week position as a shredding clerk in the company's top-security communications "black vault," where classified information pertaining to the day-to-day activities of satellites is protected by sophisticated cryptographic equipment as it's received and transmitted. Chris is instructed not to discuss any aspect of his job with RTX employees without security clearance, nor even with his family members. But the "top secret nature" of the information, he soon learns, is a laughable matter among his fellow employees. His co-workers in the vault, Gene (Dorian Harewood) and Laurie (Mady Kaplan), behave more like good-time GI's in a MASH unit than caretakers of government top secrets. They blast top 40 music, play parlor board games, grow plants of dubious legality, and make mixed drinks in the paper shredder.

One day, Chris inadvertently receives a misdirected communique from the CIA. The message describes deliberate U.S. covert actions in manipulating a foreign government. He begins receiving a steady stream of these messages and is quickly overwhelmed by the extent of the United States' deception, meddling, and intervention. His subsequent disillusionment leads him to plot his own counterspy attack on the system.

Chris enlists the help of boyhood pal Daulton Lee (Sean Penn) to act as his courier to the nearest Soviet embassy. Currently on the lam for a drug charge, Daulton jumps at the chance to supplement his drug smuggling income. He establishes a contact with the KGB in Mexico, and for a time, Chris and Daulton are in the spy business.

Shredded Margarita
Rating: R

1 bottle tequila
1 bottle margarita mix
  Salt rimmed glasses
1 paper shredding machine

Shred papers in shredding machine to clear blades. Pour equal amounts of tequila and margarita mix into top opening of shredder. Catch drink at bottom of shredder in salt rimmed glasses. (The salt helps cut the taste of machine oil and ink.)

The Falcon and the Snowman. The drink-mixing shredding machine, left, that once provided amusement for Timothy Hutton in the black vault sits like a forgotten toy in the background after he discovers the misdirected CIA communiques.

The Falcon and the Snowman. Sean Penn, left, and Hutton toast to their alliance as spies.

Daulton's drug use, however, begins to affect his spy activities, making his transactions with the KGB increasingly sloppy. He falls out of favor with both the Russians and Chris, who bows out of the partnership and quits his job to go back to school. Daulton's one last job attracts the attention of the Mexican police, and after a brutal interrogation, he spills the beans on the spy operation, resulting in the arrest and conviction of the two and their sentencing to forty years' imprisonment.

When asked how the two of them came together and engaged in such skulduggery in the first place, Chris simply replied, "We were altar boys together."

If ever there was a case for a movie sequel, *The Falcon and the Snowman* is it. Shortly after his incarceration at the Federal Correctional Institution at Lompoc in California, Christopher Boyce escaped and eluded authorities for more than two years before being recaptured at a hamburger stand—in Oregon.

Food Scene

This is by no means a lighthearted story, but it's not completely without laughs. One of the best is when a paper shredder is used for mixing drinks. (Have you ever considered shredding paper in your food blender?)

Chris is welcomed to his new job in the top security black vault with a frothy margarita. After brief introductions, Gene runs paper through the shredding machine to clear the blades. Then, like a veteran bartender, he pours tequila and margarita mix into the shredder and deftly catches the cascading liquid in salt-rimmed glasses as it pours out the opening through the spinning blades. His new co-workers drink a toast to Chris's arrival and the good times ahead.

Soon Chris is bringing in his own bottle of vodka in his briefcase for mixing early-morning Bloody Marys in the shredder. It is during one of these morning pick-me-ups that he receives the first of the CIA telexes that leads him into his short-lived career as spy.

Harper

Nutshell

It takes a tough guy to take a tough cup of coffee. But that's the stuff that keeps tough-guy detectives going. You know the type—the ones who sleep alone on rollaway beds in crummy, run-down offices and live for the one or two big jobs that'll make them feel alive. Guys like Lew Harper, Private Eye.

Harper, a sophisticated thriller, is based on the first Lew Archer detective book by Ross Macdonald, *The Moving Target*, which the *New York Times* calls "the finest series of detective novels ever written by an American." Its script sparkles with the famous "snap, crackle, pop" dialogue of William Goldman, who puts his main man, played by Paul Newman, somewhere between Bogart and Bond. As the cynical, gum-chewing West Coast detective Lew Harper, Newman is chased by women, but loves only one. He's cool but vulnerable. And he's as fast in cars as he is at finding clues.

The story begins to unfold even as the credits roll— Harper has been hired by the wealthy invalid Elaine Sampson (Lauren Bacall) to find her missing husband. Ms. Sampson is convinced he's with another woman and wants only to know *who* she is. At the Sampson estate, Lew meets Miranda (Pamela Tiffin), the missing man's concerned daughter, whose nymphomaniacal urges and blatant hate for her stepmother Elaine lend an unwelcome complication to Lew's investigation. For lack of other diversions, she and her bored flyboy friend Alan Taggert (Robert Wagner) join Lew to unravel the case.

Subplots within subplots develop as Lew's findings take him to an assortment of seamy underworld byways that eventually provide him with enough clues to solve the case. First it's the missing man's has-been actress astrology friend, Fay Estabrook (Shelly Winters) who, with her ruthless husband Troy (Robert Webber), has been engaged in illegal Mexican smuggling activities with Claude the Guru and his mountain "Temple in the Clouds."

Conflicting loyalties to his job and his danger-weary wife tear at Harper's emotions while he tangoes with a parallel plot that leads him to a seedy piano bar and drug addict singer Betty Fraley (Julie Harris). There he uncovers a romantic connection between her and Taggert that eventually leads Harper to finger the two as the kidnappers. But when Taggert admits to the crime while holding Harper at gunpoint, lawyer friend Albert Graves (Arthur Hill) shoots Taggert. Other leads finally take Lew to an oil tanker where Sampson's body is found, and the mild-mannered Graves is revealed as the murderer.

The case is not over for Lew, though. The last part of the mystery must be unraveled within himself: Should he play by the rules and turn in his friend Graves, or ignore the rules and let him go?

Harper. To brew or not to brew. (© 1966 Warner Bros. Pictures Inc. All rights reserved.)

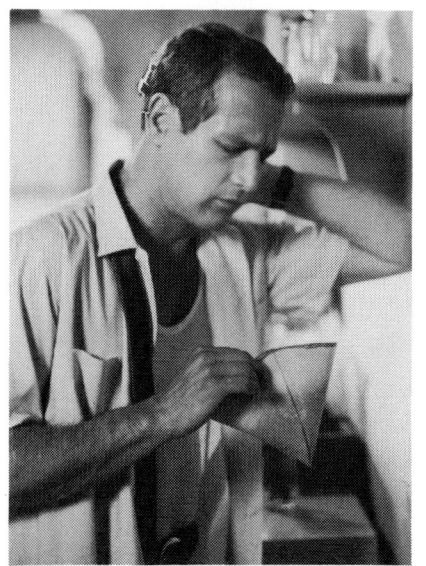

That is the question. (© 1966 Warner Bros. Pictures Inc. All Rights Reserved.)

Food Scene

One of the big surprises for William Goldman, who writes about *Harper* in his *Adventures in the Screen Trade*, is that the scene most people remember in *Harper* has nothing to do with fast-paced action of the suspense-filled plot. It's the brief tag-on he was asked to write after the film was well into production, as just a little something to go along with the opening credits. The scene he wrote and sent off in a day instantly tells enough about Lew Harper to provide a strong character foundation for the rest of the picture to build upon. What's more, it establishes Harper's likability right off the bat, critical to the portrayal of any hero. Fade in....

Harper is awake in his rollaway bed when the alarm goes off. The camera pans the darkened room as he gets up, turns off the TV's early-morning test pattern, and opens the shade to reveal his "small crummy office." In a kitchen no bigger than a hotplate, Lew puts water on to boil and reaches into the portable fridge for an icetray. Rumors persist that Newman actually does plunge his head into a sink of icewater every morning as he does in the film. If that's what accounts for that ageless, beautiful face, then, by all means, bring on the ice water. Once "washed," he sets about making his breakfast by carefully folding a coffee filter and placing it into a Chemex-type coffeemaker, only to find the coffee can empty. What to do? He lifts his head to think, then turns to the only remaining source of coffee in the house—the garbage can.

He lifts the garbage can lid and sees yesterday's grounds still neatly nested in their brown-stained filter. Hesitating for only a moment, he removes the coveted refuse from its rightful resting place and places it in the Chemex. He pours in the boiling water and the scene cuts to... close-up of cup full of black coffee. Lew puts the finishing touches on his tie and takes his first sip. The grimace and profound agony that follow confirm our every expectation of Lew's breakfast drink. Ugh!

Detective Coffee
Rating: R

Day-old coffee grounds in used filter
Boiling water

Place filter in drip-type coffeemaker. Pour desired amount of boiling water into filter. Let drip. Serve black. Serves 1.

Harper. Pamela Tiffin tries to relax with a cool drink and Robert Wagner at the Sampson estate pool, but winds up joining Paul Newman in his search for her father. (© 1966 Warner Bros. Pictures Inc. All rights reserved.)

Heaven Can Wait

Nutshell

It's been said that Warren Beatty's appetite for life is "epic"—full, rich, boundless—and healthy. He rarely drinks, never smokes or does drugs, and chews on vitamins like popcorn. "His idea of sin is to eat ice cream," says a friend. So given this, it's not surprising that *Heaven Can Wait*, the hilarious 1978 film produced, co-directed, co-written, and starred in by Beatty, should feature a drink that reflects his unique and health-conscious approach to life.

Over the years there have been a host of ghostly farces, like René Clair's *The Ghost Goes West*, Ernest Lubitsch's *Heaven Can Wait*, the Topper series, *The Ghost and Mrs. Muir*, and *Blithe Spirit*, to name a few. Although the main character in *Here Comes Mr. Jordan*, the 1941 movie that provided the inspiration for *Heaven Can Wait*, was a boxer, and in Beatty's film he's a football player, there's enough similarity in storyline to classify it as a remake. For the most part, it was critically well-received.

Beatty's clarinet-playing football star is Joe Pendleton (Beatty), who is just about to achieve the highest ambition of his career as quarterback for the Los Angeles Rams when he's killed in a bicycle accident. Joe's soul is swept away to a cloud-lined way station, from which a Concorde-like jet flies new arrivals to their heavenly destination. The guy in charge of the way station, however, the suave magistrate Mr. Jordan (James Mason), determines that his new celestial flunky (Buck Henry) has goofed and taken Mr. Pendleton away prematurely. Jordan promises to right the wrong, but there are two catches. First, since Pendleton's body has already been cremated, Pendleton will have to adjust to life on earth in the body of an unscrupulous, arrogant, multimillionaire named Farnsworth. Second, Pendleton must realize that Farnsworth's unfaithful wife (Dyan Cannon) and his nerdy secretary (Charles Grodin) plan to kill him.

Determined to make the best of a bad situation, Pendleton maneuvers superbly in his new body, even training to get in shape to play pro football again. Farnsworth's new character, so sweetly out of character, drives Mrs. Farnsworth and her lover-secretary into a hysterical paranoia. He is able to solve most of his corporate problems with football strategies, raising a few eyebrows at a board meeting with a new company game plan and a pep talk. But Pendleton still has his hands full trying to manage the problems of two lives. He arouses suspicions about his sanity when he's found whispering with his unseen celestial guardians in the broom closet. He has trouble convincing Max (Jack Warden), his best buddy and trainer, that he, Pendleton, is still alive. He tries to court do-gooder Betty Logan (Julie Christie), who views him at first as a corporate scoundrel. And, of course, he has to keep an ever-watchful eye on the two who are trying to kill him.

Heaven Can Wait. Warren Beatty sports a sweatsuit as he runs through his various lives, ordering liver and whey shakes as a panacea for all ills.

Heaven Can Wait. As the wealthy Farnsworth, Warren Beatty, right, endures opulent dinners with wife Dyan Cannon and Charles Grodin.

In order to get back to playing pro quarterback, Pendleton buys the Rams football team. But after all of his training and efforts to get himself and the team to the Super Bowl, the two schemers manage to finally kill him as Farnsworth. Luckily, his heavenly guardians make it possible for Pendleton to enter the body of a dead football player, his teammate. In the nick of time, he leads his team to an overtime win in the Super Bowl. As part of his arrangement with Mr. Jordan, he forgets who he was as Joe Pendleton and Farnsworth. But coincidentally, and happily, he reunites with Betty in the end, when they recognize a strange but wonderful familiarity in each other's eyes.

Food Scene

As important to Beatty in real life as in his role here is the eating of healthful food. Take the case of Joe Pendleton's penchant for liver and whey shakes. The screenplay generously supplies the recipe, which reads more like witch's brew than an athletic drink supplement.

The scene has Max arriving at Pendleton's house with a birthday cake to announce that he *will* be playing in the big game on Sunday against Dallas. Max, however, is so shocked by the sight of the brown, foul-smelling liquid in the kitchen blender that he's momentarily distracted from delivering the good news and asks what the brown stuff is. What it looks like is a demijohn of swamp water with a dash of toad's heel and a sprinkle of hog's wart. What it is, Pendleton tells him, is mostly whipped liver, with a little whey, alfalfa sprouts, bean curd, and spinach mold— a liver and whey shake. "Nice, isn't it?"

Throughout the film, Pendleton/Farnsworth is seen running around ordering liver and whey shakes from his servants as a panacea for all ills. He orders one for Betty as a quick pick-me-up snack; one for Max, who goes weak in the knees upon learning of Pendleton's transmogrification; and recommends it as a good training-table drink for the servants who scrimmage with him in the yard. Playing Farnsworth, though, Joe has to eat like Farnsworth and can't be completely goody-goody about his eating habits. To keep up the illusion, Joe allows himself to indulge in Farnsworth's customary bedtime drink of hot cocoa. And who's to say? The deadly duo of liver shakes and hot chocolate gets Joe Pendleton at least three lives.

Liver and Whey Shake
Rating: R

2 parts liver
1 part whey
  Alfalfa sprouts to taste
  Bean curd to taste
  Dash spinach mold

Combine all ingredients in a blender until smooth.

Hot Chocolate with Marshmallow
Rating: G

2 T. cocoa
2 T. sugar
  Few grains salt
½ c. boiling water
4 c. milk
⅛ t. vanilla
  Marshmallows

Mix the cocoa, sugar, and salt in a saucepan. Add the boiling water and boil 3 minutes. Add milk and heat slowly to just under boiling point, stirring with a wire whip. Beat with an egg beater until foamy. Stir in vanilla and ladle into mugs. Top with marshmallow. Makes about 6 cups.

Mr. Roberts

Nutshell

It's been said that *Mr. Roberts* is one of the finest and most truthful war stories ever told. That probably accounts for its enormous success in a variety of forms. First, in a game of literary leapfrog, as a best-selling novel by Thomas Heggen; then as a long-running Broadway play by Heggen and Joshua Logan; and finally, in a screen version by Logan and Frank Nugent. Its memorable Scotch-making scene has been a winner in all three versions, although the same can't really be said of the Scotch that resulted when three Navy men pooled their meager shipboard resources to concoct the moonshine.

In pulling together the screen version, Producer Logan enlisted Henry Fonda for the lead of Mr. Roberts after Fonda had starred in the stage production. Although he hadn't acted in a movie in seven years, the role restored Fonda's film career, as well as establishing that of newcomer Jack Lemmon, who won a supporting actor Oscar for his role as Ensign Pulver.

The story's set in the waning days of World War II in the Pacific, where Navy sailors aboard the AK601 *Reluctant* float in wartime limbo. Their biggest battles on the "Bucket," as the crew calls it, are with the long, hot days and boredom. Their only responsibility is to sail from port to port along the backyards of the Pacific, delivering toothpaste, toilet paper, and other sundries for the front-line destroyers.

Lt. (j.g.) Roberts, who gave up medical school to fight in the war, feels thoroughly frustrated with his duty, which has kept him further away from the action than his college classroom. Like clockwork, Roberts files a request for transfer to the front lines, only to have it rejected—like clockwork—by the ship's vindictive captain (James Cagney).

As cargo officer, it's Roberts' job to oversee the ship's operations, which he does better than anyone else—including the captain. With diplomacy and understanding, he preserves harmony among the men whose tempers are running short from the petty demands of their tyrannical captain. Roberts finally manages to inveigh upon the captain to grant the crew liberty, which the captain does, but only in exchange for Roberts' promise to stop applying for transfer.

Because of their long abstinence from shore leave, the men go wild and leave their liberty port in shambles. Morale plummets when they're denied further leave, especially when the men see Lieutenant Roberts start to treat the captain deferentially. They're baffled when he stops applying for transfer, but the worldly wise and weary medical officer, Doc (William Powell), smells blackmail.

The ship's officer in charge of laundry and morale, Ensign Pulver (Jack Lemmon), confides idle threats to Roberts and Doc about his plans to "get" the captain, but the closest he comes is a test of his homemade firecracker in the laundry room, which causes the ship's lower level to overflow with suds.

Johnny Walker Red Label
Rating: R

½ bottle Coca-Cola
½ bottle grain alcohol
1 drop iodine
   Dash hair tonic

Combine ingredients in an empty Scotch bottle. Stir gently and serve.

Mr. Roberts. Henry Fonda takes the first test sip of homemade Scotch, while William Powell, left, and Jack Lemmon await his verdict.

Finally, Roberts' fair and even-tempered approach to life explodes. He ceremoniously tosses the captain's prize potted palm overboard, causing the infuriated captain to ready the men at battle stations. Roberts confronts the captain. However, a fluke in the PA system enables the men to finally learn the truth about Roberts, and he emerges an even bigger hero than ever. The men forge a transfer request for Roberts, finally getting him that transfer to the front lines he's always wanted.

Weeks later, Pulver receives two letters on the same day. The first is from Roberts, who writes about life on the new ship and his deep affection for the men he left behind. The second is from Roberts' new shipmate, who reports Roberts' tragic death when a Japanese suicide plane crashes into the ship.

For the first time, Pulver is enraged enough to take command. He tosses the captain's palm trees, now *two* of them, overboard and immediately becomes a new champion for the men.

Food Scene

The captain's most prized possession is his potted palm. But for Roberts, Pulver, and Doc, it's their bottle of Scotch, carefully hidden away in a shoebox.

One day, Pulver discovers that the Scotch is missing, and that Roberts has used it as a "gift from the captain" in order to persuade a local port director to send them to a liberty port. Pulver, the skirt chaser, was planning to use the Scotch on a beautiful blonde Navy nurse whom he's lured on board ship with the promise of a swig. Roberts is truly sorry for giving away such a rare commodity, but suggests that they can make up a new batch right there in the cabin. In one of the film's most humorous scenes, these enterprising guys momentarily turn their cabin into a distillery.

Doc begins with equal parts of grain alcohol and Coca-Cola—another rare commodity on the ship, but one that Pulver can produce. Roberts suggests that Scotch always tastes a little like iodine, so they add one drop of iodine. Then they finish it up with a dash of hair tonic for that critical coal tar base. The three unanimously agree their concoction has merit and dub it "Johnny Walker Red Label." It's this sort of secret weapon that could have won the war.

My Man Godfrey. David Niven's Godfrey Parke serves himself as he serves others in the moderately received 1957 remake.

My Man Godfrey

Nutshell

Released in 1936, *My Man Godfrey* is considered one of the best of the many Depression era comedies. It was inspired by an immensely popular serial in *Liberty* magazine, titled "1011 Fifth Avenue," which compared the inane life-style of the rich and famous to the despairing world of the street hobo.

The two worlds coalesce in the person of Godfrey Parke (William Powell), a former Bostonian Brahmin turned street bum, who shows how a "have" can be a "have not" and still have it all. He can wheel and deal in big business, but as a butler for an upper crust family, he still manages to maintain his dignity, even though he's reduced to serving hors d'oeuvres and breakfast in bed.

In the film, Godfrey is first introduced in his bum incarnation. A high-society scavenger hunt for "a forgotten man" leads a group of ritzy revelers to the dump, where Godfrey has taken up residence. He's found in the rubbish by the wealthy, eccentric Bullock sisters, who are so jealous of each other that when Irene (Carole Lombard), the younger of two, successfully collects the bum and brings him back to win the game, the older sister, Cornelia (Gail Patrick), goes into a tantrum. Her anger mounts to full capacity when Irene hires the bum as the new butler for the Bullock household.

Cornelia's attempt to get rid of the new butler by framing him for a robbery fails and leaves her seething with unbridled contempt for Godfrey and her sister. Meanwhile, Irene falls madly in love with Godfrey, a situation in which she is at no pains to conceal from the world. At every opportunity, she's at his side trying to win him over, but Godfrey, who's still recovering from the ravages of a lost love, cannot be persuaded.

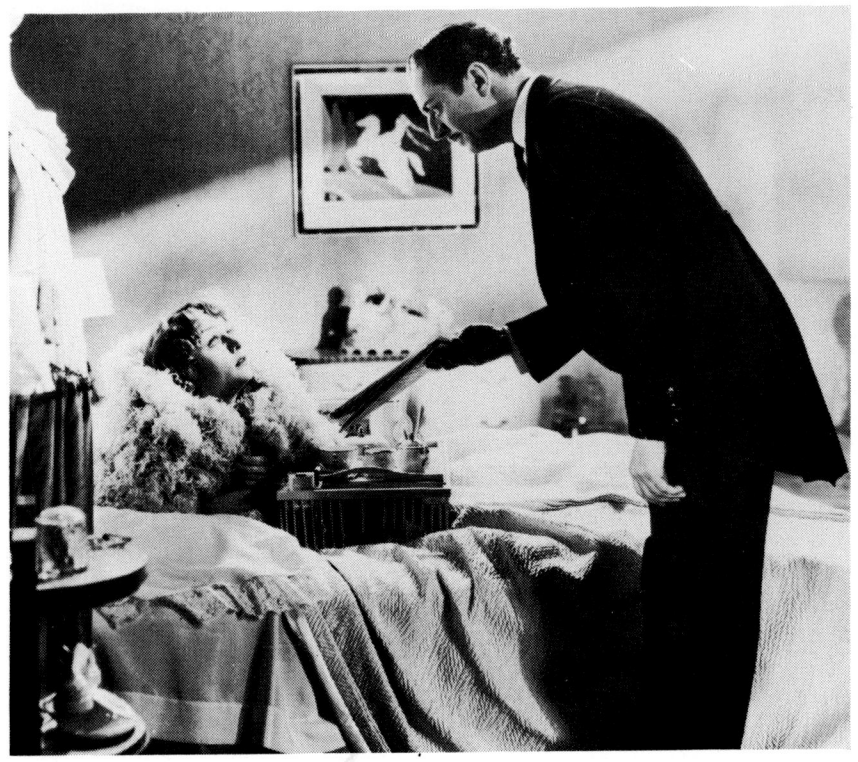

My Man Godfrey. Carole Lombard ignores breakfast and casts a hungry eye on butler William Powell.

Instead, he continues to conduct himself as nothing less than a complete gentleman, and, in turn, brings to the Bullock family the only semblance of sanity it's ever known. The mistress of the household, Mrs. Bullock (Alice Brady), is a twittering nut case who sees pixies in her bed. Carlo (Mischa Auer) is a gigolo who's eating the Bullocks out of house and home while Mrs. Bullock sponsors his erstwhile musical career. The sisters are near-certifiable screwballs whose idea of sport is to smash plate-glass windows or install a horse in their father's study. The father, Alexander Bullock (Eugene Paulette), has a somewhat surer grip on reality, but that's threatened by the bankrupt state of his business.

Godfrey, having prudently invested some assets earlier, comes forward with enough money earned in the stock market to not only bail the Bullocks out of financial difficulty but also to open a swank nightspot down at the dump. He gives all his old friends from the dump steady paying jobs at his club and rejoins high society with Irene, whose ditziness has finally won him over.

Food Scene

My Man Godfrey is best described as a screwball comedy. Everything's topsy-turvy. The guy who shows real class, brains, and breeding is the butler, while the aristocrats are ridiculous dunderheads. The situation, though, helps them all learn lessons about class structure.

While Godfrey serves the family, he practices humility. He serves Cornelia breakfast in bed and graciously suffers her well-intentioned, but insulting remarks about being his patron. He serves cocktails and meatball hors d'oeuvres to the family while they bicker about money and the superficial trappings of their lives. And he serves an elixir of tomato juice and Worcestershire sauce to Mrs. Bullock to chase away the hangover-inspired pixies that she sees every morning in her bedroom.

The Bullocks learn that kindness and generosity, especially when you're down and out, can save your life. While the lessons may not have been enough to change their zany ways, the whole family gets a good taste of humble pie in the end.

Pixie Juice
Rating: G

(This is your basic Bloody Mary.)

- 2 jiggers vodka
- 1 c. chilled tomato juice
- 1½ t. Worcestershire sauce
- 1 t. lemon juice
- 1 drop Tabasco sauce
- ¼ t. salt
- ¼ t. celery salt
- Lemon wedge

Combine ingredients and shake well. Do not strain. Serve in whiskey sour-type glasses, straight up or with 1/2 cup crushed ice. Garnish with lemon wedge. Serves 1.

Rocky

Nutshell

Eggs have long been a staple of cinematic eating scenes. Their cholesterol content may be high enough to earn them star billing in a horror flick, but generally speaking, eggs have come off pretty well in films—better, at least, than tomatoes (*Attack of the Killer Tomatoes*) or beans (*Blazing Saddles*). And why not? Eggs are an excellent source of protein, as well as being versatile, tasty, and cheap. They can be fried, boiled, baked, broiled, or scrambled. And you can always elicit a strong audience reaction by having a star eat one raw—like Paul Newman dropping one into his beer in *The Verdict*, Richard Benjamin completing his Caesar salad with one in *Diary of a Mad Housewife*, and Steve McQueen holding off starvation with one in *Papillon*. The real landmark film in the development of raw egg eating, though, came when Sylvester Stallone, as Rocky Balboa, sunk five big ones into a glass in *Rocky* and proceeded to slurp them all down.

We first meet Rocky as a third-rate club fighter whose easy-going personality and slightly dulled intelligence seems to deprive him of the killer instinct necessary for winning in the ring. However, as part of a publicity gimmick, reigning champ Apollo Creed (Carl Weathers) picks Rocky's mug out of a portfolio of small-time boxers, and, like Zeus bestowing an Olympian blessing on a mere mortal, offers Rocky a shot at the world heavyweight championship. Rocky eagerly accepts the challenge and works hard to balance the rigorous workout schedule demanded by his crusty old trainer, Mickey (Burgess Meredith), with his growing affections toward a painfully shy pet store clerk named Adrian (Talia Shire). Against all odds and in spectacularly dramatic fashion, the work pays off. His determination and endurance win him a heroic personal victory in the ring, as well as the love of his girlfriend—and the undying devotion of fans both on and off the screen through a seemingly endless stream of Rocky sequels.

Food Scene

Rocky's training for the big championship fight is as unorthodox as the circumstances surrounding his being chosen to fight in it. In addition to a jogging routine that finds him ascending the steps of the Philadelphia City Hall to a rousing Bill Conti score, he hits a local meat locker to go a couple of rounds with massive sides of beef, then downs a breakfast drink that makes even Warren Beatty's liver and whey shake in *Heaven Can Wait* look like the nectar of the gods.

Rocky begins his training day at 4 a.m. by going straight to his refrigerator, taking out five eggs, cracking them into a tall glass and—without mixing, blending, or folding—drinking them straight down. No shallots, chives, or bacon bits to color the taste of pure, unadulterated raw egg. Mmm-good.

Rocky. Stallone as tenderizer.

Raw Rockies
Rating: R

5 eggs

Crack eggs, without breaking yolks, into tall glass. Drink all at once without stopping. Jog along city streets, preferably in winter, until exhausted. Serves 1.

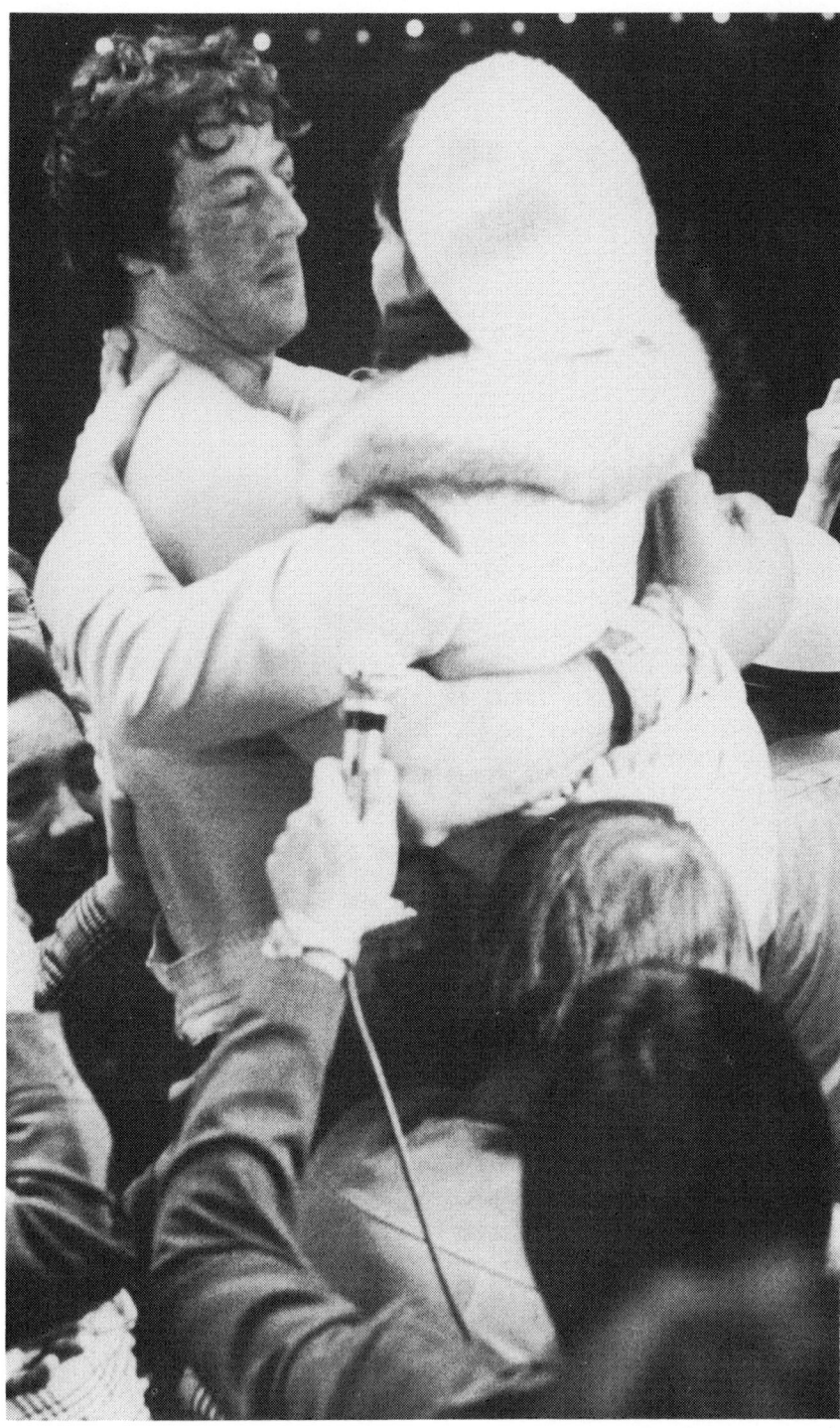

Rocky. Raw eggs pay off with a victory in the ring.

The scene quickly created a training-table fad among impressionable young athletes across the country, eager to shape themselves into Rocky clones. Drinking raw eggs became a very macho thing to do for all those Rocky "wannabe's," but that was in 1976. Today, the stir Stallone created no longer gets grade AA attention. Coaches have finally gotten their teams back on soft-boiled eggs and toast (raw eggs having been proven to contain harmful bacteria).

There's no telling how many meat lockers were invaded by armies of young flyweights and welterweights because of the initial Rocky impact, but it seems clear that filmmaker Stallone has a way with setting national trends, judging by the responses to his Rocky and Rambo films. While he may have outgrown his need for Rocky's breakfast, he's still cashing in on the muscle.

Rosemary's Baby

Nutshell

It's long been traditional for any witch worth her salt to combine the most unusual and unsavory ingredients in order to get the most mileage out of her diabolical potions. Typical of such ingredients, of course, are fillet of feeny snake, eye of newt, toe of frog, jellied lizard tongue, and that familar old standby—baboon's blood. But as with so much else in our modern world, these traditions change in time, and today's witches, such as those in *Rosemary's Baby*, enjoy equally potent results using those most trendy of ingredients—fresh herbs!

In Roman Polanski's American film debut, an elderly, midtown Manhattan witch uses her own brew of fresh herbs to help nurture the unborn anti-Christ gestating within the womb of unsuspecting mother-to-be, Rosemary Woodhouse (Mia Farrow).

A young couple, Rosemary and husband Guy (John Cassavetes), a struggling actor, move into an antiquated building and take up residency in a large, dilapidated apartment, complete with omnipresent, overly inquisitive neighbors. Almost overnight, Guy's career begins to take off. He lands a big acting part when the actor who had been cast in the role is suddenly struck blind. As his career gets hotter, he takes less and less a role in life with Rosemary, choosing to leave her in the care of the two meddling old neighbors, Minnie (Ruth Gordon) and Roman Castavet (Sidney Blackmer).

Then one day Guy asks Rosemary for a baby, and after a nightmarish "baby" night, Rosemary becomes pregnant. Minnie quickly sets her up with a doctor friend who prescribes an unusual prenatal drink for Rosemary, which, he says, will be mixed and delivered daily by Minnie.

A series of odd events begin to arouse Rosemary's suspicions. She is in constant pain, yet her new doctor does nothing to help. She is surrounded by strange, doting old people who wear a smelly mold called tannis. And she suddenly finds herself with an appetite for eating raw chicken livers and meats. She raises her concerns with her best friend, who then mysteriously dies, but not before he's able to get a book to her that warns her about a coven of witches once known to live in her building. Once she begins to put the whole picture together—the blind actor; her husband's instant success; the sudden deaths of two friends; the tannis worn by all these strange people, including her new doctor; and Roman Castavet's familial ties to a long line of witches, she realizes the jeopardy she and her baby are in and fears that they are all witches who plan on taking her baby for blood rituals. Her attempt to escape fails, and she ends up back under the control of the coven, where she learns that Guy has made a Faustian deal with the witches—his success for their baby, the future leader of the Underworld.

Tannis Shake
Rating: R

1 raw egg
1 pkg. gelatin
1 c. milk
1 t. fresh oregano
2 cloves garlic, mashed
2 leaves fresh basil
1 t. mashed tannis root

Whip ingredients together in a blender. Serves 1.

Food Scene

One of the most effective means for creating horror is through suggestion, particularly in familiar surroundings. In *Rosemary's Baby*, we never *really* know until the very end if Rosemary's suspicions are founded in fact or are mere figments of an overactive imagination.

At first the Castavets' nosiness and fawning over the young couple simply appears to be a genuine reflection of their elderly concern. And Rosemary's reaction to their first dinner together, where Minnie prepares meat that could bend steel, seems a trifle cruel and intolerant. But then, on "baby night," at the end of the couple's private, romantic dinner, Minnie just happens to show up with chocolate mousse. Guy curiously insists that Rosemary eat the dessert, but she can't stand the chalky taste and secretly hides most of it in a napkin.

Although she is uneasy about her neighbors and certainly has had her fill of Minnie's food, Rosemary has no reason to suspect a plot against her pregnancy. She trusts both her neighbors' overly attentive participation in the blessed event as well as the advice of her new doctor, Dr. Saperstein (Ralph Bellamy). Following his directive, Minnie prepares her special concoction and delivers it fresh daily to the mother-to-be. When Rosemary asks what's in the drink, Minnie replies with her standard witch's recipe for making boys—snips and snails and puppy dog tails. Knowing that Rosemary might balk at this concoction, however, she then quickly mumbles something about raw eggs, gelatin, herbs and, of course, the ever-popular tannis root. Finally, Rosemary rebels and pours the drink down the sink.

Interestingly enough, Mia Farrow is not without some unusual eating tendencies of her own that make Minnie's brews seem pretty dull. It was reported that once she was invited to Salvador Dali's for afternoon tea. Earlier that day, Dali had received a box of butterflies, which stood on the table when she arrived. While they talked and ate English muffins with honey, she removed a butterfly from the box, stuck it on top of the honey, and ate it. By the end of the tea, she had eaten all twelve.

Rosemary's Baby. Witch Ruth Gordon presents Mia Farrow with her prenatal elixir of snips, snails, and puppy dog tails.

ROLL 'EM

> *"I'll have an omelet, no potatoes… give me tomatoes instead, and wheat toast instead of rolls."*

Jack Nicholson's order for an omelet with "substitutions" to roadhouse waitress Lorna Thayer, in *Five Easy Pieces*.

Bedtime for Bonzo. A family portrait—Ronald Reagan feeds Tamba the chimp.

Bedtime for Bonzo

Nutshell

Although this movie comes close to being a Golden Turkey, it is noteworthy for one important reason—it stars Ronald Reagan in one of his best known and few box office successes. What is more, he co-stars with a simian dignitary, the likes of which will never share Reagan's current billing—Bonzo the Chimp.

The story is a relatively simple one, but one that tries to grapple with a complex question. Reagan plays a college psychology professor, Peter Boyd, determined to prove his thesis that environment, not heredity, is the primary molder of character. Boyd is driven in his study in order to clear his name from the scandalous legacy left by his father, who died in prison as a confidence man. If successful, the impact his thesis will have on the scientific community is less important to him than clearing his name and winning Dean Tillinghast's (Herbert Heyes) consent to marry his glamorous but snooty daughter Valerie (Lucille Barkley).

To prove his point, he chooses zoology professor Hans Neumann's (Walter Slezak) chimp Bonzo (Tamba) as the subject of his study and hires Jane (Diana Lynn), a farm girl seeking domestic service, to act as a surrogate mother. Together they're to live under one roof and act like a normal, happy family—the adults calling each other "Mama" and "Papa" and treating Bonzo like a full-fledged human child.

The domestic scene goes quite nicely until Jane starts to fall for the professor (who is too busy to notice). Valerie comes down with a case of jealousy, and Bonzo runs the experiment up a tree when, drawn to Jane's sparkly costume jewelry, he steals a diamond necklace from a store window.

The professor is soon arrested and accused of training Bonzo to steal, but is saved when Jane helps Bonzo realize his mistake. Bonzo returns the necklace, proving Boyd's innocence and Bonzo's own higher sense of morality. Jane's charm and efficient domestic prowess finally win Boyd's affections, and the couple drives off to marry and set up housekeeping with their chimp child.

Writers Raphael David Blau and Ted Berkman were first inspired to write a fictionalized version of a real-life Yale anthropologist who tried raising a chimp like a child in the 1940s. In 1951, the film version was released, and monkeyshines became big business, with J. Fred Muggs on the *Dave Garroway Show* and Mighty Joe Young on the *NBC Today Show*. Although it only received moderate reviews at the time of its release, Reagan's election to the presidency elevated the long-caged flick to high-camp status, with frequent revivals at filmfests and campuses, complete with bootleg Bonzo T-shirts and "Bonzo for President" bumper stickers. The spinoff monkey business brought additional publicity to the production and helped elevate it to the elite circle of great bad films.

Swedish Pancakes (Plättar)
Rating: G

(This famous Scandinavian dish is usually served with lingonberries or fruit preserves. In Sweden, it is traditionally eaten on Thursday nights following a main dish of pea soup, but it can also appear with fruit for breakfast.)

3 eggs
1 c. milk
1 c. flour
1 c. light cream
6 T. butter, melted
½ t. salt
 Preserved lingonberries or whole cranberry sauce

Using a rotary beater or an electric mixer at medium speed, beat the eggs with 1/2 cup of the milk for 3 minutes. Add flour and continue beating until the consistency is heavy, but smooth. Beat in the remaining milk, cream, butter, and salt, mixing until smooth.

Drop by tablespoons onto a preheated griddle or into each depression of a 5- or 7-section Swedish pancake (plättar) pan. You may also use a crêpe pan, pouring a scant 1/4 cup batter into the pan for each pancake. If sticking occurs, lightly grease cooking surface with butter. The pancakes should form bubbles almost immediately. Cook for about 1–2 minutes on each side until lightly browned. Keep warm in a 200° oven while remaining cakes are cooked, or serve the *plättar* directly from "pan to plate" as the Swedes do. Serve with fruit. Makes about 16 crêpe-sized pancakes.

Bedtime for Bonzo. Reagan addresses his kitchen cabinet: Tamba the Chimp and Diana Lynn.

Food Scene

In order to make Bonzo feel and act like a human child, professor Boyd insists that the chimp's home life duplicate that of your modern, well-adjusted, middle-class, all-American kid. They dress the chimp in boy's clothing, make him eat at the table in a highchair with "Mama" and "Papa" Boyd, stage kisses for his benefit, and tuck him into bed with bedtime stories.

For their first meal together, Jane has prepared a breakfast of Swedish pancakes and orange juice. But true to his new role in life, Bonzo gets pabulum. Like a typical American housewife, Jane carefully serves up her pancakes to a somewhat disinterested "husband," and typical of the cinematic eating scene, most of the food is left uneaten. But Bonzo already shows a high aptitude for human behavior, knowing that pabulum was meant to be played with, not eaten. He's not only unimpressed with his breakfast but also with the indifferent kiss Papa plants on Mama's forehead. Bonzo handles his roles as an all-American kid with aplomb—and, who knows? With the right agent, he might have grown up to be president.

Breakfast at Tiffany's

Nutshell

From the time this film came out, to the first time I saw it twenty-five years later, I thought that Tiffany's had opened a coffeeshop in their prestigious one-hundred-fifty-year-old jewelry store to supplement slumps in the diamond trade by selling sandwiches. As I hadn't read Truman Capote's book of the same name, it was a logical, albeit somewhat far-fetched conclusion. Now, through the resurrective qualities of videotape, I stand corrected. You cannot get breakfast at Tiffany's—nor any other meal, for that matter—unless you bring your own, as the heroine does in *Breakfast at Tiffany's*.

It's not much of a breakfast, as breakfasts go, and it's over and done with by the time the introductory credits finish rolling, but the story that follows makes up for what we might have expected in a meal befitting a Tiffany's setting.

The diner is one Holly Golightly (Audrey Hepburn), a pretty but capricious New Yorker who's built her woman-about-town image completely on artifice. She's given to totally irresponsible behavior and pseudo-romantic interludes with wealthy marital prospects, but she's also plagued by frequent bouts of anxiety and insecurity.

Breakfast at Tiffany's.

After returning to her East Side apartment house one morning from an all-nighter with one of her high-paying suitors, she meets her new neighbor and struggling young writer, Paul Varjak (George Peppard), whom she immediately accepts as her brother. In her barren apartment, while drinking milk out of a champagne glass, she explains to Paul (whom she nicknames "Fred" after her real brother) the whys of her sparsely furnished apartment, her cat with no name, and her fascination with a store named Tiffany's. It all has to do with fighting off the "mean reds," which, she says, is worse than the blues, and means that "you're afraid of something but you don't know what it is."

Her only cure for the mean reds is to jump into a cab and head for Tiffany's—"a place where nothing very bad could happen to you." If only she could find a place like that, she'd buy some furniture, name the cat, and settle down with her brother to raise horses. Until then, she has to be content to live on $50 powder-room tips from wealthy suitors and her weekly stipend for visits to imprisoned mobster Sally Tomato (Alan Reed), to whom she delivers "weather reports," naively serving as a go-between for Sally and his gang.

Paul's interest in Holly begins to grow deep as he sheds patron of his arts, 2-E (Patricia Neal). But Holly's scheme for marriage to a rich Brazilian preoccupies her until news of her brother's death and a public exposé of her association with Sally Tomato's narcotics ring costs her the marriage proposal.

A tirade from Paul is all it takes to force Holly into a few moments of honest, life-changing self-scrutiny. With a kiss in the rain, Paul gives Holly her first real chance for happiness beyond Tiffany's window and gives audiences a light confection ending in the classic Hollywood tradition.

Breakfast at Tiffany's. Audrey Hepburn and George Peppard feast their eyes on Tiffany's million dollar ice.

Food Scene

We all know that it sometimes takes hours, even days, to shoot a few minutes of finished film. The opening breakfast scene here is no exception, for what was eventually extracted from twelve hours of shooting boiled down to a mere three minutes of screen time.

As the introductory credits roll, the opening strains of "Moon River" accompany the scene of a cab pulling up to a curb in front of Tiffany's early one morning. Out steps Holly Golightly in a long Givenchy gown, strings of pearls draped around her neck, her hair piled fashionably high, and extra-large sunglasses covering half of her face. She walks up to the showcase window and gazes appreciatively at the jewels and chandeliers while she pulls a cruller out of a paper bag and takes a hefty bite. Then, balancing the roll in her long black satin glove, she pulls out a deli coffee-to-go, removes the lid, and takes a short sip.

Then it's on to another window, with only an occasional munch and sip. She's far more interested in her surroundings than her breakfast, and as the theme song nears its finale, she tosses her disposable meal in a sidewalk garbage can.

When asked how she enjoyed her twelve-hour breakfast, the eternally lean Ms. Hepburn reportedly said that she had no affection for the danish, and would have preferred ice cream from Schrafft's.

Crullers
Rating: G

(For convenience, prepare the dough the night before and simply roll it out and fry it for breakfast.)

2 c. flour
½ t. salt
½ t. nutmeg
2 t. baking powder
1 egg, beaten
½ c. milk
½ c. granulated sugar
1 T. melted butter
   Oil for frying
   Powdered or finely granulated sugar
   Cinnamon

Sift the flour, salt, nutmeg, and baking powder together. Set aside. Combine the egg, milk, granulated sugar, and melted butter in a bowl.

Stir in the flour mixture, adding more flour if necessary to make the dough firm enough to handle, yet still soft as possible. Chill.

Roll out dough to 1/2" thickness on a floured board, dusting with flour as needed to prevent sticking. Cut into 4" × 1" strips (dip knife into flour between cuts so knife will glide) and let rise for 10 minutes. Twist each strip several times for a spiral effect and pinch the ends.

Fry 3 or 4 at a time for about a minute in a light cooking oil, heated between 330° and 360°, until browned and puffed up. (If the oil is too cool, the dough will absorb too much fat; or if too hot, it will brown too fast on the outside without completely cooking on the inside.) Turn to brown evenly.

Lift crullers out with tongs and drain on absorbent paper. Toss in a paper bag with either powdered or finely granulated sugar mixed with cinnamon until well coated. Makes about 15.

Diva

Nutshell

The action in the French film *Diva* moves as smoothly as soft butter over hot bread. Part caper, part opera, part romance and thriller, with a few touches of Zen thrown in to keep the mind as involved as the senses, this wonderful whirlwind of entertainment by first-time director Jean-Jacques Beineix won four French Cesar Awards—that country's equivalent to our Oscar.

Jules (Frederic Andrei), a young postal worker and avid opera buff, clandestinely records a live performance of Cynthia Hawkins (Wilhelmenia Fernandez), a fabulous American diva who refuses to have her voice recorded, insisting that her audiences experience her talent in live concert performances. The next day, while Jules is delivering mail, a hooker, fleeing for her life from two thugs, desperately hides a cassette tape of her own in Jules's mail pouch just before the thugs murder her.

Later Jules befriends a Vietnamese girl, Alba (Thuy An Luu), whom he's observed shoplifting. He invites her to come and listen to his recording of Ms. Hawkins. Where do they meet? In an abandoned garage, decorated with automobile carcasses and floor-to-ceiling pop art murals, where he lives. Alba's so impressed with the music that she introduces Jules to her friend and benefactor, Gorodish (Richard Bohringer).

Jules visits Ms. Hawkins at her hotel to return a gown he had stolen from her Paris performance. She allows him to stay, and he learns from their conversation why she refuses to permit recordings of her music. Ms. Hawkins believes that art must be kept separate from business—that business has no place in the world of true art.

When he returns home, he finds that his home has been ransacked and, assuming that the police are after his illegal recording, he takes sanctuary with Alba and Gorodish. He's still ignorant of the fact that he possesses the tape, which contains the hooker's incriminating testimony against her lover's prostitute-drug ring. Jules doesn't have any idea that he's actually the target of two intertwined chases—one by the police and mob henchmen to get to the hooker's confessional, and the other by two inscrutable and unscrupulous record producers from the Orient out to get their hands on Jules's recording of the diva.

At first the bushy-headed Gorodish looks like your ordinary wacked-out, chain-smoking Zen freak, living out a perpetually inert state of existence in a loft decorated in neon and black. Surprisingly, however, he becomes a man of bold action when he learns of Jules's predicament, appearing, almost magically, in his white Citroën to rescue Jules from a number of perilous situations. He winds up not only saving Jules's life, but also bringing justice to bear on the crime syndicate in a cleverly conceived climax.

As for the diva's tape? The film closes with Jules playing it for her, and the diva clearly enjoying the sound of her recorded voice.

Diva. The man who knows the value of relaxation and buttered bread, Richard Bohringer is the mysterious benefactor to plastic-clad Thuy An Luu.

Food Scene

Thank goodness for characters like Gorodish. His laid-back eccentricity lights up the screen as much as his later, sudden transformation to sleuth-hero. His bizarre behavior constantly commands our respect and attention. When he cuts an onion wearing a diver's mask and snorkel, and speaks of reaching satori by buttering bread, we know we're in the presence of one of the screen's unique heroes.

Gorodish demonstrates Zen and the Art of Buttering Bread to Jules and Alba with a long loaf of French bread. The butter must be the right temperature, he tells them. The knife, "not too thin, not too thick." The bread, "fresh, but not too fresh." He makes a long cut down the side of the bread and recounts current methods for getting high, using such gimmicks as airplane glue and detergents, but adds that all one really needs to do to reach euphoria is butter bread. (André Gregory, from *My Dinner with André*, could have spared himself a few Tibetan quests for the meaning of life and found it at home in dinner rolls.) "Watch...no bread, no knife, no butter. Only a gesture...a movement...space...the void...." (Does this mean the calories are void too?)

Every masterpiece needs the finishing touch. Jules gets a king-sized container of caviar from the refrigerator (another "gift" from quick-finger artist Alba), and Gorodish tops his spacious void with a liberal frosting of fish eggs.

Satori Bread
Rating: G

- 1 cake or pkg. yeast
- 1 T. honey
- 1½ c. lukewarm water
- 2 t. salt
- 4 c. unbleached, hard-wheat flour
- Sifted cornmeal
- 1-2 lightly beaten egg whites (optional)
- Butter, at the "right" temperature
- Caviar

Dissolve yeast and honey in lukewarm water. Add salt and flour to yeast mixture and mix with your hands, adding more flour if necessary until dough will absorb no more. Knead dough on a lightly floured board until smooth and no longer sticky. Place dough in buttered bowl, cover with a towel, and let rise in a warm area until doubled.

Punch down dough and divide into 2 equal parts. Shape each piece into a long, narrow loaf on a lightly floured board that has been sprinkled with cornmeal. Place loaves side by side, several inches apart, on a baking sheet that has been sprinkled with cornmeal. Cover and let rise again until doubled. Brush tops with beaten egg white if desired and bake at 400° for 35-40 minutes. About 5 minutes before bread is done, brush again with beaten egg whites. Cool on a wire rack.

When the bread is fresh, but not too fresh, cut a loaf down the center, lengthwise, with a knife that is not too thick, but not too thin. With butter at the right temperature (you will know the right temperature when you reach your satori), butter the bread. Spread with desired amount of caviar. Makes 2 loaves.

Gone With the Wind

Nutshell

Gone With the Wind is a film classic and *still*—according to a recent inflation-adjusted list—the top money-making film of all time since its release in 1939. It may not contain the most memorable eating scene ever made, but it certainly has one of the most timeless lines about eating ever uttered on the screen. With her fist raised against a Georgia sunset, Scarlet O'Hara vows to the heavens just before intermission time, "If I have to lie, steal, cheat, or kill, as God is my witness, I'll never go hungry again."

David O. Selznick's masterpiece is released periodically in theaters and has been aired on TV a number of times in recent years, not to mention its availability on videotape. Those who've enjoyed multiple viewings of it are legion, and I must count myself among them, having seen the film more than one hundred times—mostly during a tour of duty as a candy girl in a theater that played the film for six months straight.

To briefly recap for those who may have been off on the planet Xendorf since 1939: Scarlett O'Hara (Vivien Leigh), the beautiful, but vain and ruthless daughter of a wealthy plantation owner, is the object of desire of every eligible bachelor in the antebellum South save one—Ashley Wilkes (Leslie Howard). The noble, yet delicate, Ashley though clearly fond of Scarlett's high energy and spirit, falls in love with and marries his kind-hearted, aristocratic cousin, Melanie Hamilton (Olivia de Havilland), leaving Scarlett to seethe and conspire from the outside while fending off advances from the dashing Rhett Butler (Clark Gable).

To gain access into Ashley's family, Scarlett marries Melanie's brother Charles (Rand Brooks), but is quickly widowed when the Civil War breaks out and claims the life of her soldier husband. Bereaved over this blow to her prospects with Ashley, she seeks to lighten her mood with an extended visit to Atlanta, where Melanie now lives and waits for Ashley to return from the front lines.

The war devastates the South. Forced to flee a burning Atlanta, Scarlett returns home only to find her mother dead and Tara, the beloved family plantation, ravaged. Exhausted and starving, she grovels in the garden looking for what might be the last raw vegetable in Georgia. Finding a dirt-encrusted morsel, she gags on her first bite, then utters her prophetic "I'll never go hungry again" line—whereupon the curtains come down on the first half and audiences rush for the concession stand. Or at least that's how I remember it.

Anyway, Scarlett survives and even prospers financially, although her eventual marriage to Rhett proves to be a tragic and tempestuous one that ends with Rhett walking out on her and delivering cinema's most famous parting salutation, "Frankly my dear, I don't give a damn." By the end of *Gone With the Wind*, audiences have been treated to a full-blown portrait of one of the most fascinating female figures in American film.

Southern Buttermilk Biscuits
Rating: G

4 c. flour (sift, then measure)
1 t. baking powder
½ t. soda
1 t. salt
¾ c. butter
1¼ c. buttermilk

Sift the flour, baking powder, soda, and salt together. Using a pastry blender, cut butter into the flour mixture until it gathers into pea-sized balls. Add buttermilk and stir just until dry ingredients are thoroughly moistened.

Knead about ten times on a lightly floured board, then roll to a thickness of 1/2". Cut into desired shapes (round is more traditional), place on an ungreased baking sheet, and bake at 450° for about 15 minutes or until golden brown. Makes about 18–20 3" round biscuits.

Gone With the Wind. Ready for the barbecue.

Gone With the Wind. As Hattie McDaniel helps Vivien Leigh dress for the barbecue, she implores her to eat her biscuits.

Food Scene

It was customary in Scarlett's day for ladies of fine breeding to eat at home before going out for dinner. In this way, they would appear dainty and refined and thus ensure their rightful place at upper-crust tables. Never being one to bow to custom, though, Scarlett's plan for the barbecue being thrown at the Wilkes's Twelve Oaks plantation is to "have a good time," meaning gorging on food and carousing with the boys. When Mammy (Hattie McDaniel), the Tara maid, serves Scarlett her pre-barbecue lunch, Scarlett rejects it. Rejects it, that is until Mammy slyly provokes her by mentioning the imminent arrival of Melanie Hamilton, the contender for Ashley's affections. Angered by the news, Scarlett plunks herself down on the floor and stuffs her mouth with a biscuit. If she's going to fight for Ashley this day, she determines, she'll impress him most on a full stomach.

The scene may not rank with the burning of Atlanta, but it's worthy of our recollection both for Vivien Leigh's superbly vexed chewing and its lesson in historical etiquette. The authentic Southern buttermilk biscuit recipe offered here has been enjoyed by many a Confederate and Yankee alike. Best of all, they make up quickly and can be eaten by today's ingenue before any dinner engagement.

The Killing of Sister George

Nutshell

In Robert Aldrich's *The Killing of Sister George*, Beryl Reid reenacts her earlier stage triumph as June Buckridge, a plump, middle-aged, cigar-smoking lesbian who supports herself as a BBC TV soap actress. On the "telly," June plays the part of the good-hearted nurse, Sister George, who whizzes about town on her bicycle, bringing good cheer to all her friends in the make-believe world of soap opera land. She is known as a woman of kindness and dignity to her TV audiences, but off camera, June is a pathetic, screeching bully whose un-Sister Georgelike behavior includes throwing things like tantrums and scones to get her own way. Somehow over the years, she has managed to keep her worlds separate, but, as the title suggests, that's about to change.

Constantly in the throes of self-doubt, George (as she's called off and on the set), runs her life on alcohol. Her only real pleasure outside of the bottle is in keeping the upper hand with her younger, attractive, live-in lesbian lover Alice (Susannah York). But even the perverse amusement she derives from dominating Alice begins to lose its charm. When she forces Alice to kneel before her and eat a cigar butt, Alice spoils George's fun by appearing to enjoy the degradation.

George's drunken binges not only cause discord with her lover, but also cause her to engage in more public displays of scandalous behavior, placing at risk her image as a popular TV personality. It's one thing for her to act the crass-mouthed eccentric around her co-workers and bosses, but when she sexually attacks two unsuspecting nuns in a taxi, the studio decides things have gone too far.

After producer Mercy Croft (Coral Browne) informs George of her character's imminent death in a bicycle accident, George's entire life plummets into an irreversible tailspin, culminating in her breakup with Alice, who's ultimately seduced and won over by Mercy Croft herself. Devastated and abandoned by one and all, George demolishes the studio set and then cries out with a plaintive "moooooing," a sad expression of her resignation to future obscurity as the voice of a puppet cow.

Food Scene

After the incident with the nuns, George is visited by Mercy Croft at George and Alice's home. Anxious that she is about to get fired, George finds it difficult to make small talk with Ms. Croft, but Alice has just finished making a fresh batch of scones and freely engages in spirited talk about her recipe and techniques. She tells the enchanted TV executive how important it is not to let the oven get too hot, how the scones must be cooled on a towel, how one must wait until bubbles rise to the surface before turning them over, and how much of each ingredient she uses.

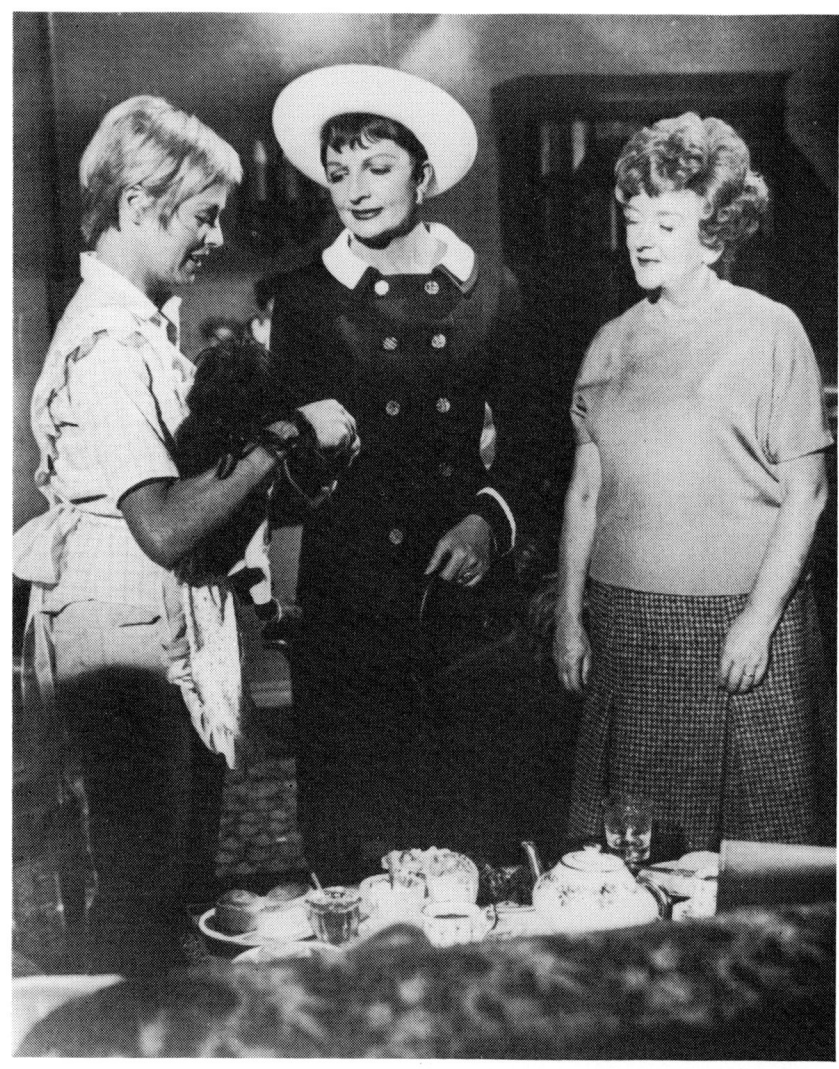

The Killing of Sister George. Left to right: The ladies, Susannah York, Coral Browne, and Beryl Reid, exchange pleasantries before tea.

The Killing of Sister George. Beryl Reid, center, finds another use for Susannah's scones.

The Killing of Sister George. Eager to claim any victory over her dominating lover, Ms. York pretends to enjoy the cigar butt Beryl Reid has forced her to eat.

Suddenly, George can't take it any longer. She explodes at Alice over her inane chitchat with Mercy. She throws a half-eaten scone at Alice, grotesquely displaying her built-up inner fears and rage—and, no doubt, her opinion about the scones.

Alice's Scones
Rating: G

(Traditionally, scones [or their sister bread, bannocks] are served as tea biscuits, but are not at all uncommon at the dinner table. The only difference between a scone and a bannock is size. A bannock is one large round of bread about the size of a dinner plate, while scones are individual triangular-shaped biscuits. Either way, in Scotland they are typically "baked" on a "girdle," as Ms. Croft accurately points out in the scene. This is nothing more than a griddle, preheated and unbuttered. If you wish to use this method, simply flour both sides of the scone and cook over slow heat on the griddle until the bottom is browned and the bread has risen. Turn and brown on the other side.)

½ a level t. of bicarbonate of soda
1 level t. full of cream of tartar
½ t. salt
2 c. sifted flour
1 T. sugar
2 T. butter
1 lg. egg ("Some people prefer two eggs, but I think one's enough.")
About 1/2 c. milk or cream
2 T. melted butter

Sift dry ingredients together. Cut butter into flour mixture with a pastry blender as for piecrust. Add egg and enough milk or cream to make a fairly stiff dough.

Turn out on a lightly floured board and roll into a rectangular shape about 1/2" thick. Cut dough into triangles by first slicing the dough diagonally in one direction, making cuts about 3" apart, then slicing diagonally in the opposite direction, again 3" apart. Cut each of the diamond shapes through the center to form the triangles.

Place scones on a buttered baking sheet. Brush tops with melted butter and bake at 450° about 15-20 minutes. If you prefer, "bake" scones on a "girdle" instead. Makes about 1 dozen.

Kramer vs. Kramer

Nutshell

Eating scenes. Sometimes they serve as pivotal points in the development of plot or character, as in *The Godfather*, when Al Pacino as young Michael Corleone rises from his rigatoni and kills for the first time. Sometimes they're mere creative conceits that end up being more famous than the films in which they appear, as when Jack Nicholson tries to order toast at a roadside diner in *Five Easy Pieces*. And sometimes they fulfill a symbolic function, communicating to the audience at a subliminal level the course of a relationship. Orson Welles, of course, did this most magnificently in *Citizen Kane*, with his quick montage of breakfast scenes depicting the deterioration of Kane's marriage. Admittedly not as stunning an effort, but interesting nonetheless, was Director Robert Benton's use of eating scenes to show the growth of the relationship between father and son in *Kramer vs. Kramer*.

The story is quite simple. JoAnna (Meryl Streep), the discontented wife of Ted (Dustin Hoffman) and mother of Billy (Justin Henry), leaves the family in order to make a life for herself. Ted and Billy are thus forced to fend for themselves, which demands that they depend upon each other to fulfill needs previously tended to by Mom. Dad can no longer afford to be casual in his relationship with his son while Mom takes care of the dirty work. And Son can no longer go running to Mom to nurse the numerous hurts of the world. It's rough at first for both of them, but somehow they manage to stumble through their meals, pick up their dry cleaning, get to work and school, live through injuries and unemployment and face a myriad of frustrations to develop a close, loving relationship.

Then Joanna, claiming to have found what she was looking for in the outside world, returns months later seeking legal custody of Billy. She wins her court case, but as she arrives to take Billy to his new home, she realizes that her son already has a good home, regardless of the court's view of the mother's perogative in such cases. She drops her claim on Billy and leaves him again—out of love—to live in the strong emotional home Billy and Ted have built together.

Food Scene

At the onset of the separation, Ted and Billy face their first man-made meal together. In a scene that has a real improvised feel to it, Ted bounces into the kitchen, quick, confident, and ready to stack up a batch of French toast. Like a good-time camp counselor, he cheers on himself and Billy as he whisks supplies out of the fridge.

> "We got how many eggs?—two for you and two for me. We got milk. We got butter. We got five dollars."

Five dollars? Hmm. Single-handedly, Ted cracks the four eggs into a coffee cup. Billy is clearly impressed.

Salsibury Steak with Onion Gravy
Rating: G

- 1 lb. ground beef
- 1 T. beef fat
- 1 T. butter
- 2 T. finely chopped onion
- 2 T. flour
- ¾ c. beef consommé
- Salt and pepper

Shape beef into 1" thick patties. Pan fry, turning over when half done. Remove from heat when both sides are browned and cooked to desired doneness. Keep warm.

Drain fat, reserving 1 tablespoon. Melt butter with the fat in the same pan used for frying. Cook onions in fat until tender and transparent. Add flour, blending well with a wire whip. Slowly add the consommé, stirring constantly with the whip.

Bring to a boil, reduce heat, and simmer 5 minutes until thickened, stirring frequently. Salt and pepper to taste. Serve over beef patties. Serves 2-4.

Kramer vs. Kramer. Dustin Hoffman and Justin Henry enjoy Hoffman's home-cooked TV dinner.

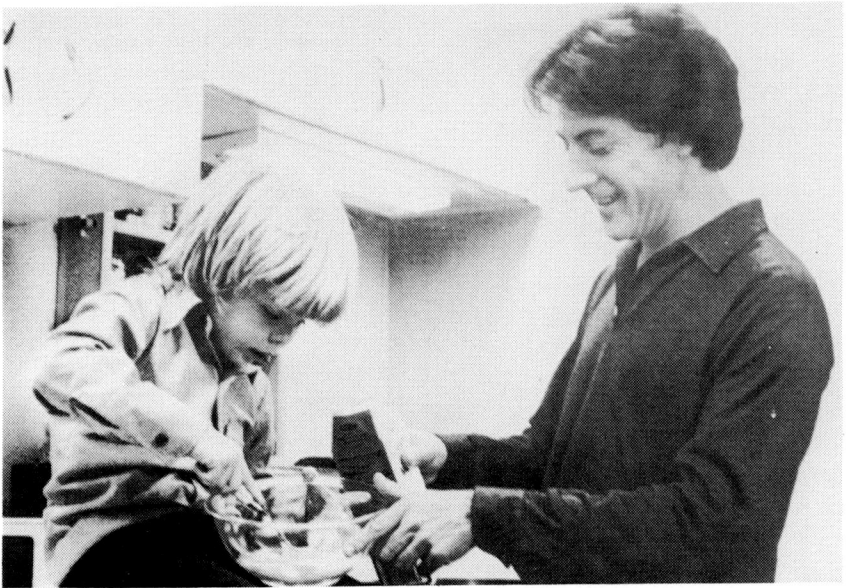

Kramer vs. Kramer. Kramer and Kramer making it on their own.

"Did you know the best chefs in the world are men?" Ted brags. Like the Galloping Gourmet, he demonstrates trade secrets known only to grown men. In short order, Ted fills his coffee cup/mixing bowl to overflowing with milk; stuffs folded bread down into the cup; transfers the dripping, broken bread parts into a hot frying pan; and pours the milk-mix over the top. (This, of course, is an interesting variation on the usual technique of toasting only the bread.) When Ted tries to save the burning milk and bread by lifting the scalding frying pan with his bare hands, though, Billy's worst fears are confirmed, and the cause of French cooking is set back to The Reign of Terror. Cooking breakfast, Billy learns, does not necessarily mean you get to *eat* breakfast. And maybe that's what the five dollars is for.

Anyway, Ted gets better at performing those "motherly" duties. He has to—man cannot live by burned bread alone. He serves up ready-made doughnuts and TV dinners, and eventually works his way up to salisbury steak with onion gravy. That creates a tense, pivotal scene, wherein Ted has to convince Billy that his plate has to be cleared before he gets ice cream for dessert.

Billy gets his ice cream, and the once-strained relationship between father and son blossoms into a loving family of two, complete with respect, understanding, and perfect batches of French toast.

French Toast
Rating: R

4 eggs
Milk
Butter
$5 (bread)

Using one hand, crack each egg into coffee mug. Pound eggs with fork as though churning butter, then quickly whip using a gyrating wrist motion.

Add milk to the brim of the mug. Fold bread slices and stuff into mug.

Scoop out bread pieces and place in frying pan. Pour remaining milk-batter over all. Cook at high heat until burned. With bare hands, pick up frying pan handle and toss toast into the air. Serves 0.

The River

Nutshell

It was the year of farming dangerously when, in 1984, three farm crisis pictures were released within weeks of each other. The coincidental trilogy—*Places in the Heart*, *Country*, and *The River*—were all statements on the plight of small American farmers, and all were critically acclaimed for their sensitive treatment and superb performances.

This particular rural saga focuses on the Garvey family, who farm a river valley susceptible to annual flooding. The movie opens during one such flood, as the Garveys desperately attempt to save their farm from the swelling river bordering their land. Extensive damage forces Tom Garvey (Mel Gibson) to apply for a bank loan, but when his and other farmers' applications are rejected, valley farmers are forced to auction valuable equipment in an attempt to save their farms.

Bewildered and angry, some choose to abandon their land while others determine to fight on, ignorant of the fact they've been made victims of a systematic plot by a wealthy agricultural conglomerate to force them off their farms. Managed by the ambitious Joe Wade (Scott Glenn), the influential corporation plans to buy up the land for a hydroelectric plant that will flood the valley where farms have stood for generations. The paradox: jobs, homes, and a way of life will end for some, but the plant will flood an area more naturally suited for water than farming and provide jobs for many unemployed, hungry people.

In spite of constant financial strain, the Garvey family determines to fight for their farm, without forgetting how to enjoy leisure moments, like cheering on Dad at a softball game and watching Beth (Becky Jo Lynch) ride a pony. The Garvey children learn and participate in farm chores, and the family draws its strength from the land they tend.

To help pay off mounting debts, Tom takes a job away in the city, where an ironworks plant has been hit with a labor strike. Mae (Sissy Spacek), meanwhile, stays home to work the land. The ambitious, but practical Joe Wade, who's held a torch for Mae for many years, hovers around her while Tom's away, and he's there to help out when Mae sustains a serious arm injury that nearly costs her life.

Once the iron strike resolves, Tom returns to the farm he and Mae have struggled to keep afloat, only to find that the price of corn has dropped so low that it doesn't even cover the cost of their planting. The anger Tom feels when he finally learns why the farmers are being squeezed out only serves to fan his rage and determination to fight.

Another violent rainstorm threatens to flood the farm again, and this time Mae insists that they get help. Before long, an army of neighbors in tractors are working side by side to keep the river contained, but Joe seizes the opportunity to finish off the Garveys' farm by enlisting squatters to destroy the embankment levy. Tom and his neighbors' determination wins an uncertain victory in a tense face-off at the river, but we suspect that there will be many more battles to come before anyone wins the war. The only certainty is that *no one* can stop the rain.

Three-Loaf Farm Bread
Rating: G

4 c. warm water
4 pkgs. yeast
⅓ c. honey
2 T. salt
9 c. all-purpose flour
1 c. wheat germ
1 c. bran flakes
1 c. wheat flour
⅓ c. vegetable oil

Combine the water, yeast, and honey in a large bowl. Stir to dissolve the yeast and honey. Add the salt, 2 cups of the all purpose flour, wheat germ, bran flakes, and wheat flour. Beat until smooth. Add the remaining flour and blend well. (Feel free to use your hands.)

Pour oil over the dough and knead in the bowl for 2 minutes, until the oil is absorbed and the dough is smooth and elastic. Cover with a clean cloth and let rise in a warm place until doubled.

Punch down, turn out onto a lightly floured board, and cut into 3 equal sections. Knead each section slightly and shape into 3 loaves. Place in buttered loaf pans, cover with the cloth and let rise again until doubled. Bake at 400° for 30 minutes, or until browned and done. Makes 3 loaves.

The River. Becky Jo Lynch watches movie mom Sissy Spacek administer a home remedy to the family's ailing cow when they can't afford to pay its vet bill.

Food Scene

The hard work and honesty of the Garveys and their farm life represent the fiber that helped build America. By passing on family traditions, skills, and knowledge, the Garveys hope to instill proper virtues in their children and future generations. It is an evolutionary process that comes naturally to these people, giving them a sense of purpose and fulfillment.

One particular scene in *The River* exemplifies not only the passing on of knowledge and skills, but also captures the sense of fulfillment that comes from hard work. It's baking day in the Garvey kitchen, and Mae busily kneads bread while young Beth rolls out her piecrust. Mae stops to help and demonstrates how to pick up a crust by wrapping it around the rolling pin. "That's a beautiful crust," Mae tells her quietly. Next Mae checks on the three loaves of bread baking in the oven (while more are cooling on the counter), grabs a cookie from the freshly baked batch in the cookie jar, and then stares contentedly out the kitchen window at the expanse of farmland and sunset sky before her. For Mae, it's a moment that erases all the worries of the world.

Such moments are disrupted often throughout the movie, and one in particular comes about when the family is forced to auction off many of its possessions and Tom learns that Mae's blackberry jam has been included among the auction items. His protest is vehement. They can take the tractor, but they're not going to get Mae's jam.

To help create the realism needed, Universal Studios built a working farm on the four hundred-forty acres they purchased in Kingsport, Tennessee, for the picture. The farmhouse was so comfortable and completely furnished that Sissy Spacek (who now lives on a farm herself outside Charlottesville, Virginia) used free time between takes to bake cakes and breads for the crew in the movie set's kitchen.

Blackberry Jam
Rating: G

   9 c. crushed blackberries
5-6 c. sugar
     Lemon juice (optional)

Combine berries and 5 cups sugar in a saucepan. Slowly bring to a boil, stirring occasionally, until sugar dissolves. Add lemon juice to taste if desired. Adjust sugar to taste. Cook rapidly to jelly stage (220° on a candy thermometer), stirring constantly to prevent sticking. Pour boiling hot into sterile canning jars. Adjust caps. Makes 3-4 pints.

Oatmeal Butter Cookies
Rating: G

½ c. butter, softened
½ c. margarine, softened
½ c. sugar
1 t. vanilla
1 c. flour, sifted
1 c. quick cooking oatmeal

Beat butter and margarine together with an electric mixer (or by hand) until light and creamy. Gradually beat in sugar and vanilla. Add flour in three portions, beating after each addition. Stir in the oatmeal.

   Drop by teaspoonfuls onto greased cookie sheets. Bake at 350° for about 10 minutes or until lightly browned around the edges. Let cool 1 minute. Carefully remove with a spatula to a cooling rack. Makes about 4 dozen.

Pie Pastry Crust
Rating: G

(To pass on the knowledge and skills of her generation, Mae might have told daughter Beth the following tips for making a good piecrust:

1. Use all-purpose flour, solid vegetable shortening, and ice water to yield a flakier, more tender crust.
2. Use a pastry blender or two knives for cutting in the shortening, never mix with fingers.
3. Use a fork to lift the flour when adding water, and add only enough water to hold dough together. Too much will make the dough tough; too little makes it crumble.
4. Handle dough as little as possible after the water is added, gathering into a ball after only a few stirs.
5. Roll dough out from the center on a well-floured pastry cloth to prevent toughening. Use a cloth rolling pin sleeve to keep dough from sticking.
6. Do not stretch dough when fitting into the pan. Remove all air pockets and prick generously for a prebaked, unfilled crust.
7. To keep crust from getting soggy for a filled pie [that is, baked with a filling], brush bottom and sides with slightly beaten egg white before filling, and bake for 10 minutes on lower oven shelf. Move to a higher oven shelf if necessary to prevent burning during remaining baking.

The baker who coined the phrase, "easy as pie" was no doubt referring to the ready-made crusts available in the grocer's frozen food section.)

2 c. all-purpose flour
1 t. salt
⅔ c. solid vegetable shortening
5-6 T. ice water
1 egg white, slightly beaten (for filled crust)
   Milk (for filled crust)

Sift flour and salt together. Using a pastry blender, cut in shortening until texture looks like coarse cornmeal. Sprinkle water as evenly as possible throughout the dough, and stir only until mixture comes together and can be formed into a ball.

   Cut dough in half. Roll one ball out into a circle shape on a floured board until 1/16" thick. Fold in half, gently transfer to a pie plate, and fit loosely without stretching.

   For an unfilled pie, flute edges by trimming excess dough evenly, about 1/2" larger than the pie plate edge. Fold excess under and rest on top rim. Pinch edges zigzag fashion by using forefinger of the right hand to press rim inward while holding thumb and forefinger of the left hand loosely on either side of the right forefinger, pressing outward in the opposite direction. Move around the rim in 1/2" increments, pressing and crimping. Bake at 450°, 12-15 minutes or until golden. (Second dough ball, tightly covered in plastic wrap, can be frozen, if desired.)

   For a filled crust, brush fitted bottom crust with slightly beaten egg white and fill with desired filling. Moisten rim with water. Roll out second doughball and fit over filling. Seal edges by pressing fork tongs around the rim. Trim excess by pulling a knife blade downward around the rim. Brush with milk to promote browning. Poke several air slits in top crust with a knife. Bake as directed for desired filling. Makes one 9" double piecrust.

Woman of the Year

Nutshell

Spencer Tracy and Katharine Hepburn teamed up for the first time in this 1941 romantic comedy that gave every indication of the sparkle they would give to the screen through the next two decades. In a *Time* magazine coverage of their first meeting, Ms. Hepburn reportedly said, "I'm afraid I'm a little tall for you, Mr. Tracy." To which Tracy replied, "Don't worry. I'll cut you down to size," which is just what he does as Sam Craig, a man's man of a sportswriter in *Woman of the Year*.

Interestingly enough, it was Ms. Hepburn who was the prime mover in getting this film launched. After helping to rewrite a script authored by two unknown writers, Ring Lardner, Jr., and Mike Kanin, into a "made to order" Hepburn picture, she was able to sell it to MGM. In the starring role, which calls for the humbling of her own ego, Ms. Hepburn as Tess Harding learns what it is to be the "Woman of the Year" only *after* she gets the award.

China-born, Swiss-schooled Tess is the daughter of a U.S. diplomat and celebrated international columnist for the fictional *New York Chronicle*. She speaks and reads seven languages right down to the fine print, hobnobs with Churchill and Roosevelt, and calls the Cuban president for firsthand information as easily as ordering take-out pizza. She also has the brass to criticize baseball on the radio, which immediately arouses the ire of fellow columnist Sam Craig.

After trading jibes at one another in their respective columns, the dueling writers are introduced by their publisher, and it's practically love at first sight. At least it's enough for her to consent to go to an actual ballgame with Sam, and enough for him to at least attempt rubbing elbows with the fast, international set. Between transcontinental flights and speeches, she manages to squeeze some time in for Sam, and he manages a proposal while she's busy studying the latest news off her teletype machine.

Their marriage is give and take from the start. Sam gives; Tess takes. Sam discovers that it's going to be his job to scramble eggs, while Tess writes her column and pursues her political and social goals. As her eminence grows, so does her distance from Sam, which she tries to overcome by surprising him with the adoption of a non-English speaking, Greek refugee boy.

Ironically, on the night Tess is honored as "Woman of the Year," she clearly reveals herself to be an insensitive wife, negligent mother, and near failure at what is traditionally regarded as emancipated womanhood. Her only real skill is in reporting on the lives of others.

In revolt, Sam has returned the boy to the Greek home and left Tess. At first she's more put out by the appearances of their separation than the loss of a husband, but when she attends the wedding of her father to her closest friend and idol, she realizes that success is no fun unless there's someone there to share it with.

Woman of the Year Waffles
Rating: X

- 2 c. flour
- 1½ c. baking powder
- 2 pinches salt
- 1 cake yeast
- 2 c. milk
- 3 eggs

Combine flour, baking powder, salt, yeast, and milk. Stir thoroughly. Separate eggs by forcing through a metal strainer; add to batter. Pour batter into preheated waffle iron and let cook until it bubbles up and begins to whistle. Serves 0.

Woman of the Year. Woman of the year Katharine Hepburn attempts to make waffles for a skeptical Spencer Tracy.

She hurries back to Sam and declares that she's ready to give up her career for married life, but her first clumsy attempts at domesticity indicate she has a long way to go before becoming the 1940s idea of the Woman of the Year.

Food Scene

In this semi-slapstick scene, Katharine Hepburn, the great lady of the American cinema, practically does a Laurel and Hardy in defiling the very institution of cooking breakfast, making Dustin Hoffman's effort at French toast in *Kramer vs. Kramer* look like something by a Cordon Bleu chef by comparison.

It starts when Tess returns from the wedding ready to capitulate, and decides that the way back to her man's heart is through his stomach. (Not an original thought, but one with a good track record.) Sam's still asleep when she enters his house and begins to prepare breakfast. Everything she does from this point on is new to her, but at least she tackles the task with typical Tess panache.

Her first act as novice cook is to look for help from a cookbook. On a shelf she finds *Gibson's Housewife's Cookbook*, marked with some of Sam's favorite recipes. Next she loads the top of a Silex coffeemaker with a few cups of coffee grounds, then carefully pours exactly one tea cup of water into the grounds and sets it on the gas stove. There's nothing in the cookbook about lighting the gas stove either, so even that causes her considerable difficulty.

Tess then selects the waffle recipe from the cookbook. It calls for your standard waffle ingredients, but for all the sense it makes, she might as well be following a road map. She freely tosses ingredients into the batter—at least a cup and a half of baking powder (instead of the 4 teaspoons as called for) and a cake of yeast (which isn't called for at all). A hilarious but futile attempt at separating an egg by rolling it around on a plate gives way to her ingenious idea of shaking it through a wire mesh strainer.

The racket finally awakens Sam and lures him down in time for the grand finale. Burned toast is launched from the toaster and flies wildly into the air; coffee oozes over onto the stove as a thick, black, bubbling mass; and the waffles balloon over the sides of the waffle iron into a gummy blob that whistles and sighs.

As it turns out, however, Sam's not asking Tess to give up her career—just to meet him halfway. He's not asking for homemaker of the year awards or even waffles—just a sensible, straightforward approach to life. He's willing to help her achieve it, but he may want to start with a lesson in scrambled eggs.

REEL MEALS

"Well, Tillie, when the hell are we going to get dinner?"

Spencer Tracy's
query to housekeeper Isabel Sanford,
delivering the last words
of his film career and
the last words in Stanley Kramer's
dinnerless dinner film,
Guess Who's Coming to Dinner?

Animal House. James Widdoes, left, and Tim Matheson pose in toga uniform—bed sheets and beer.

Animal House

Nutshell

This trend-setting movie of the late 1970s made sophomoric humor a commercially viable commodity in Hollywood. Since *Animal House*, audiences have displayed an insatiable appetite for idiocy, irreverence, and gross-outs of the lowest order in their movie fare. *Animal House* has become the master copy for a generation of youth comedies, each, in turn, trying mightily to expand the boundaries of crudeness and tastelessness pioneered by the original. It earns its way into the book by virtue of one supremely unforgettable and positively revolting scene—the food fight.

The setting is Faber College, circa 1962. The protagonists are the members of Delta fraternity, a group so uncouth and socially irredeemable that they'd be outcasts on any self-respecting skid row. Animal behaviorism isn't their major; it's their life-style. In a world turned upside down by the demands of contemporary comedy, these thieving, boozing, womanizing clowns, barely able to maintain a 1.2 grade-point average in their endless pursuit of partytime, are our heroes.

The antagonists, on the other hand, are members of the establishment—the college dean, the town mayor, and the BMOC's of the Other fraternity—connivers all, united in their determination to eradicate the loathsome Delts from their midst, thereby restoring the good name of the college and the town.

The film chronicles the Establishment's fiendishly underhanded attempts at closing down Animal House (the Delta fraternity headquarters), and the Delt's impudently anarchistic knack of surviving each attempt. Along the way, the "animals" engage in a number of goofy fun-time events, such as the now-famous Toga Party and Road Trip, inspiring similar real-life trends in college campuses across the country.

In keeping with the Delt's all-or-nothing, fun-for-all policies, they reap final revenge in the end by totally trashing the homecoming parade and the town itself.

Food Scene

The food fight instigated by borderline human and lifelong Delt, Bluto Blutarsky (John Belushi), surely rates as a highwater mark in vulgarity in a film awash in vulgarity. Bluto, the slobbola nonpareil of film history, fashions a scene of such astounding inelegance that, at once, it manages to blow refinement, etiquette, and good table manners clear back to the Stone Age.

The scene begins with Bluto stalking into the college cafeteria in search of food, which he finds first in the garbage can. He retrieves a few morsels of discarded slop for his appetizers and then loads up his tray with some of the cafeteria's fresher offerings—hamburgers, doughnuts, bananas, apples, sandwiches, a four-course dinner plate, green gelatin squares (a plate of which he immediately sucks into his mouth), and—to

Animal House. Delt member Steven Furst enjoys his beer, Delt style.

Animal House. Preamble to a food fight. James Daughton, left, is put out by John Belushi's gross eating habits in the school cafeteria.

Animal House. Tim Matheson, right, full-time "make-out" artist, tries to interest the Dean's wife, Verna Bloom, in a choice cucumber during a chance meeting in a grocery store.

round out the principle food groups—a carton of milk. Not altogether lacking in discriminating taste, he returns uneaten portions of the food that don't meet with his approval to the cafeteria serving trays.

With handfuls of sandwiches loaded into his pockets and mouth, he joins a frat brother and some rival coeds at a cafeteria table and begins to "eat." First, he squeezes his cheeks together, oozing green gelatin down his chin. Then he imitates a "pimple" by loading his mouth with mashed potatoes and exploding the contents at the coeds seated across from him. The coeds, covered in mashed potatoes, explode in rage over this piggish performance, but before they can strike back, Bluto crowns the glory of his act by shouting one of the most memorable lines of the film (and Belushi's career): "Food fight!"

What follows is a list of items that will supply you with all the ammunition necessary for your own homemade food fight.

Food Fight Shopping List
Rating: R

- 1 bag of yesterday's garbage
  Assorted wrapped sandwiches (ham, tuna, egg salad)
- 2 bowls of green gelatin squares
  Plate of roast beef, green beans, corn, mashed potatoes
- 2 hamburgers in buns
  Assorted doughnuts (some with chocolate icing)
  Turnovers
- 4 bananas
- 3 apples
  Milk

Snack on yesterday's garbage. Stuff sandwiches in pockets. Fill mouth with green gelatin and let dribble down chin. Fill mouth with mashed potatoes; punch down cheeks with fists and let potatoes fly across table, aiming at nearby adversaries. Yell "food fight" and throw remainder of food around the room.

Annie Hall

Nutshell

Woody Allen films prior to *Annie Hall* may have been something of an acquired taste, but Oscar winner *Annie Hall* is irresistible. The story is a veritable scrapbook full of memories and flashbacks about the relationship between a Jewish comic named Alvy Singer and his "shiksa" girlfriend, Annie Hall. On the one hand, Alvy and Annie mutually share the trauma of cooking live lobster. On the other hand, they approach their pastrami in radically different ways.

Allen plays Alvy, a character pretty much modeled on himself, and offers us glimpses of things that matter most to Woody, the private man—eroticism, neuroticism, aestheticism, intellectualism, and a loathing of Los Angeles—to name a few. The film opens with Alvy posing the big question of his love life, "Where did I screw up?" As it turns out, the screwup is with former real-life girlfriend Diane Keaton, who plays Annie Hall, Alvy's screen-life girlfriend.

The story is principally set in New York City. Annie and Alvy meet at a tennis game and are instantly drawn to each other by their mutual neuroses, but Annie's lack of confidence allows Alvy to quickly dominate her life. He talks her into attending night school and makes book selections for her—all about death. Flashbacks introduce us to various people in their lives, including Alvy's two former wives and both sets of their parents. Annie's folks eat small portions of plain dinners slowly and drink a lot, while Alvy's folks gobble up huge dinners quickly and yell a lot.

Mashed Yeast 'n' Sprouts
Rating: R

(Edible yeast is rich in B vitamins and comes in a variety of forms—flakes, powder, liquid, or tablets. It is packaged in cans, jars, or bags.)

Brewer's yeast
Alfalfa sprouts

If using dried yeast, mix with water to a pastelike consistency and toss with desired amount of sprouts. If using liquid yeast, pour over bowl of sprouts and serve like salad. Serves 1.

Annie Hall. Woody Allen orders mashed yeast in an L.A. restaurant.

Alvy and Annie live together briefly and have some laughs, but eventually Annie starts becoming her own person, developing separate interests and friends that don't fit in with Alvy's grand design for their lives. Her confidence about a dubious singing career is given a big boost when a California record producer Tony Lacey (Paul Simon), lures her to his home in Beverly Hills. Alvy accompanies her on the visit and targets L.A. for some of his sharpest one-liners. But Annie likes the "self-conscious" casualness of tinseltown and, while thinking about her future on the flight back to New York, decides to take up permanent residence there. She and Alvy separate, but Alvy can't live without her and returns to L.A. to try in vain to win her back.

In order to salvage the relationship in his own mind, Alvy uses their breakup for a scene in a play of his, rewriting the ending so that it all comes out "perfect." The film ends with Alvy telling a joke that sums up his feelings about relationships with women: "A guy goes to a psychiatrist and says, 'Doc, my brother's crazy—he thinks he's a chicken.' And the doc says, 'Well, why don't you turn him in?' And the guy says, 'Well I would, but I need the eggs.'"

Food Scene

One of the really good times in the Alvy and Annie relationship involves their attempt to corral live baby lobsters into a pot of boiling water. Lighthearted terror sends Annie into intermittent screeches and giggles, while the doomed crustaceans run for their lives on the floor. Alvy plays the clown, getting off more one-liners about the big one that might come out from behind the refrigerator with a dish of butter and a nutcracker held on one side, and about the steaks that don't have legs and don't run around that they could've had instead. Alvy finally manages to capture a lobster and toss it in the pot. Then he grabs a boat oar, crashes around the kitchen with it, then poses triumphantly with oar and lobster in hand for a snapshot.

For all the good times between the two lovers, though, there seem to be an equal and opposite number of sticky times as well. Even in the early stages of their relationship, their individual differences, which eventually split them up, show up unsuspectedly—like over a sandwich. After an inauspicious late-night singing debut, Alvy tries to cheer Annie about her performance by taking her out for a snack. In a deli, he orders "the cornbeef," and without even asking, the waiter knows how he wants it dressed. Annie orders pastrami and, fearful that she might get the same ethnic treatment, asks that it be made her way—with white bread, mayo, tomato, and lettuce.

After their breakup, Alvy makes a last ditch attempt to talk Annie back into the relationship by ordering alfalfa sprouts and mashed yeast in an L.A. health food restaurant where they've arranged to meet. Unfortunately, his concession to California white man's food is not enough to impress her, and it's over this "last supper" that they break up for good.

In the end, Alvy never answers his original question of where the screwup was, but at the very least, he got a dozen or so eggs out of it.

Annie Hall. **The great white hunter bags his meal.**

Shiksa Sandwich
Rating: G

¼ lb. sliced pastrami
2 slices white bread
Tomato slices
Lettuce leaves
Mayonnaise

Arrange pastrami on one slice of white bread. Top with desired amount of tomato slices and lettuce leaves. Spread second slice of bread with desired amount of mayonnaise and place, mayonnaise side down, on top. Serves 1.

Blazing Saddles

Nutshell

Here's a smorgasbord of one-liners, sight gags, vaudeville routines, and campy shticks for you. It's director Mel Brooks zany parody of old Hollywood Westerns, and the code of Brooks's old West seems to be that everyone is fair game for lampooning, regardless of race, creed, color, or sex. Even Marlene Dietrich and the humble baked bean come in for well-timed ridicule.

Blazing Saddles wasn't to everyone's taste—especially the critics—but Mel Brooks surrounded himself with enough co-writers (Norman Steinberg, Andrew Bergman, Alan Uger, and Richard Pryor) to share the blame for running the once beloved Western right out of town and into the back lot at Warner Brothers Studios.

To kick it off, the irascible and villainous Hedley Lamarr (Harvey Korman) learns that the railroad must pass through the peaceful little town of Rock Ridge. Realizing the money to be made from such a development, he plots to take over this boom town in the making, and mysteriously, Rock Ridge begins to suffer from a rash of ransackings, burnings, and stampedings, not to mention the shooting of the sheriff.

When a new sheriff must be found, Hedley seizes the opportunity to convince lecherous, but dull-witted, Governor Lepetomane (Mel Brooks) to appoint a black sheriff, Black Bart (Cleavon Little), hoping the less than fair-minded folks of Rock Ridge will kill him on sight, thus leaving themselves defenseless to his takeover.

Bart rides into town accompanied by Count Basie's band (not just his music, but the *whole* band) and in high-fashioned splendor, complete with Gucci saddlebag, tailored orange shirt, and color-coordinated horse. The citizens of Rock Ridge were expecting something a little less Negroid in their new sheriff and are soon planning a lynching party to express their dismay. But Bart's hip, urban ways and the townfolks' utter stupidity allow him to get the upper hand. With boozing gunslinger, the Waco Kid (Gene Wilder), once the fastest hand in the world, Bart is able to tame the town and Hedley's thug Mongo (Alex Karras).

In an everything-but-the-kitchen-sink kind of climax, townsfolk and railroad workers unite in a scheme of their own to save the town, luring Hedley's band of desperadoes into an attack on a façade of a town they've built, complete with cardboard citizens. The ensuing fight spills over the set and gets jumbled up with another production on the Warner's lot—an extravagant Busby Berkeley-type musical number. The fight soon includes cowboys and tuxedoed dancers, who burst into the commissary and start an epic Hollywood pie fight. (For more on flying pies, please read "A Pie for All Reasons.") Hedley tries to make a getaway in a taxi, asking to be driven off the picture, but he's caught by Bart and the Waco Kid at Grauman's Chinese Theater, where they all wind up sitting down to watch the end of a picture called *Blazing Saddles*.

Campfire Beans
Rating: PG

1 large can baked beans

Heat beans over an open campfire. Serve piping hot in metal plates to a group of noisy cowboys. Serves about 8.

Schnitzengrüben with Sauerkraut
Rating: G

*16 large German sausages
Prepared sauerkraut, undrained*

Heat sausage with the sauerkraut over low heat until hot. Serves 1.

Blazing Saddles. For breakfast, Madeline Kahn offers Cleavon Little a big knockwurst.

Blazing Saddles. When filming of *Blazing Saddles* leaves the set for the studio backlot, pies get out of hand in the studio commissary.

Food Scene

Throughout the film, Brooks milks his laughs out of spoofing the conventions of the old Hollywood Westerns, but the most memorable scene in the film probably works because it portrays the old West as it really was. It is, of course, the campfire scene, in which Hedley's gang sits around the fire feasting on that familiar staple of the old chuckwagon—baked beans. What all those John Wayne Westerns never showed, understandably, was the inevitable aftermath of all that bean eating. Mel Brooks, however, doesn't shrink from such realism, and for several funny minutes, the dark, western plain is alive with the sound of belching and flatulence. It may not be quite up to the haute style of *La Grande Bouffe* (the notably graphic French film about a group of men who gorge themselves to death), but it was a real breakthrough for the American comedy. That's why they called it *Blazing Saddles*.

The Breakfast Club

Nutshell

The classic adage "you are what you eat" gets the John Hughes treatment in one of this producer/director/writer's seemingly endless string of teen flicks, *The Breakfast Club*. When a disparate group of teenagers from an upper-middle-class Chicago suburb are forced to spend a day together in detention, they take out their hostilities by first verbally feeding on each other after breakfast, then grossing each other out at lunch by eating food that perfectly reflects their diversified tastes and personalities.

Hughes admits that his pictures, including *Sixteen Candles* and *Weird Science*, are like "Trix cereal"—strictly for kids. His hope here was to show that kids, no matter how different their backgrounds, can confront and ultimately understand each other, unlike adults, whose hearts have "died" after growing up.

It's a cold, bleak winter morning, (Saturday, March 24, 1984, at 7 a.m., to be exact) when five students report to their high school library for detention. Each character is a teenage stereotype—a jock, a wealthy prima donna, a brainy nerd, a flake, and an aggressive hood—with seemingly nothing in common except a shared pool of teenage insecurities and neuroses. Dean Richard Vernon (Paul Gleason) tries to get them settled during roll call with a writing assignment on "Who Do I Think I Am?," but his belligerent opening lecture only serves to raise the flag of the alien world of adults—a flag no one in the group is eager to salute.

Once left unattended, the kids forget the essay and engage in a sort of freewheeling, informal therapy session, venting hostilities and frustrations about each other, adults, and life in general.

Andrew (Emilio Estevez) is the star athlete—a wrestler driven by his father to always strive for perfection. Claire (Molly Ringwald) is the prom queen and debutante, who has to struggle against her superficial sense of social superiority to recognize the others as her equals. Brian (Anthony Michael Hall) is the physics fanatic who constantly feels the pressure of being at the top. Allison (Ally Sheedy) is the quiet, disheveled kleptomaniac who hides behind bangs that serve as a veil for her indifference and insecurities. Finally, there is John (Judd Nelson), the angry rebel without a cause from the wrong side of the tracks whose naturally antagonistic relationship with authority figure Vernon serves to catalyze the group's coming together.

As has been pointed out often enough, it all adds up to a kind of teen version of *The Big Chill* (and not unconsciously it seems, since reportedly they were even calling it *The Little Chill* during production). Occasionally the kids take a recess from their intramural squabbling and remedial soul searching to dance, share a couple of joints, wreak a little havoc around the school, and generally unite against Vernon, whose ridiculous behavior reminds audiences with thudding obviousness what fools adults can be.

The Breakfast Club. Paul Gleason at lunch break.

Breakfast Club Lunch
Rating: G

3 cans Coca-Cola
  Assorted sushi
1 large bag chips
1 carton of milk
1 bag of cookies
1 banana
1 apple
3 sandwiches
  Sugar candy straws
  White bread
  Sugar-coated puffed cereal
  Soup
  Apple juice
  Peanut butter and jelly sandwich

Gather food on a large table, buffet style. Select food types according to your personality type. Serves 4.

The Breakfast Club. The boy who came to lunch, Judd Nelson, center, provides Molly Ringwald and Emilio Estevez with running commentary on their meals.

In the end, the kids come to recognize their commonality with each other—that they're all smart about some things, dumb about others; misunderstanding and misunderstood; and, of course, that all have problems with parents and their own self-images. By the time their incarceration is over at 4 p.m., these five separate souls have come to know each other better and shared more with one another than they ever did with their families or closest friends.

Food Scene

When lunchtime rolls around, the five breakfast clubbers probably reveal more about their personalities by what they've brought to eat than hours of professional therapy could ever uncover.

Claire begins by pulling out a neat, glossy gray shopping bag that contains all the tools she'll need for her sushi lunch of rice, raw fish, and seaweed—a beautiful ebony box, Japanese wooden tray, and a little bowl for soy sauce. As she sets them up, John, with a line for every occasion, says, "You won't accept a guy's tongue in your mouth and you're going to eat that!"

Andrew promotes his all-American boy image by pulling out a large bag of chips, a carton of milk, a bag of cookies, a banana, an apple, three sandwiches, and a Coke.

Allison, forever hidden behind her scraggly hair, opens her Coke and loudly slurps up the overflow. Then, finding her olive loaf sandwich too unappealing, she tosses the meat over her shoulder and fills her sandwich with sugar candy and puffed cereal. She grinds down the pile with the palm of her hand, closes up the sandwich, and stuffs it all into her mouth—to the disbelieving attention of her peers.

Brian the brain shows up with your standard, well-balanced school lunch—soup, apple juice, and a peanut butter and jelly sandwich with the crusts cut off. He is, to his dismay, quickly joined by John, who, having no lunch at all, uses his mouth for other purposes. "Well Brian," he observes sarcastically, "this is a very nutritious lunch. All the food groups are represented." He wonders if Brian's mom is married to Mr. Rogers.

Finally, Vernon, alone in his office, eats more like a kid than the teenagers he is responsible for. By stuffing orange slices into his mouth, he makes a big orange rind grin, then accidently spills his coffee.

Weird or straight, rich or poor, smart or stupid, young or old, the food you eat, and *how* you eat it, tells the whole story.

Close Encounters of the Third Kind

Nutshell

In our meat and potato world, it isn't often that potatoes get a chance at a starring role of their own. In fact, if you fall prey to TV advertising, you're probably moving up to meat and Stove-Top stuffing. But in *Close Encounters of the Third Kind*, the ho-hum mashed potato plays a lead role in an intergalactic adventure.

In this Steven Spielberg spectacular, UFOs fly low on the horizon, and witnesses to them become obsessed with an unidentifiable vision. Baffled scientists scramble to decode a tonal message transmitted by the saucers. A young boy literally vanishes into thin air. And anxious government officials maneuver to take uncertain action against an unseen force. Strange and mysterious events occuring all over the world finally converge on Devil's Tower in Wyoming, where the various messages left by the UFOs lead a broad cross-section of military and civilian pursuers.

The confusion, fear, and global upset caused by the UFOs vanishes into a wondrous moment of awe when a titanic spaceship lands at the mountain. After an exchange of musical communication between earth scientists and the colossal ship, alien creatures quietly disembark and extend their friendship, return passengers, and take volunteer flyers aboard. One of those disembarking from the ship is little Barry Guiler (Gary Guffey) whose plight we've followed through the desperate search of his mother Jillian (Melinda Dillon). One of those coming on board for the ship's next trip is Roy Neary (Richard Dreyfuss) whose search interweaves with Jillian's, though by no means as clearly. We've followed him since the night the UFOs flew over his telephone repair truck and left him with an unshakable mental image and a vaguely defined new purpose in life. We've followed his compulsive quest to define that image, which eventually costs him his job and marriage, but which also takes him to the limits of the universe. When Leary walks onto the ship, he's the personification of a man about to face the cosmos.

Food Scene

As one of the witnesses to the UFOs, Roy becomes totally obsessed with "the vision." He's so overwhelmed by its power that he's willing to sacrifice everything else in his life to understand it. He grabs at anything he might be able to use as a medium for sculpting the image in his mind's eye—shaving cream, clay, a few tons of dirt, twigs, and more. When he least expects it, the urge to sculpt and give form to this vision overcomes him—even at mealtime.

Neary sits down to dinner. A hush falls over the table. "Please pass the potatoes."

Roy slowly spoons the spuds onto his plate. Suddenly, the mashed potatoes become food for thought—great thought. His creative impulses

Mashed Spudniks
Rating: G

- 6 lg. potatoes, washed and quartered
- 4-6 T. butter
- 1 c. chopped onion
- ½ c. milk, approximately
- 1 egg yolk
- Salt, pepper

Boil potatoes in salted water until tender, about 1/2 hour. Meanwhile, melt butter in saucepan. Add the onions and sauté until tender. Drain potatoes. Add the onions, milk, and egg yolk. Beat with an electric mixer until smooth, seasoning with salt and pepper to taste. Add milk as needed to desired consistency.* Serves 1-6.

*Some of the applied possibilities for this mixture are as follows:

1. Eat them "straight-up" as is.
2. Wrap small amounts (1/2 cup) around cooked sausages; roll in seasoned bread crumbs, then a beaten egg, then back in bread crumbs. Fry "Saucerges in Blankets" in oil until crispy on all sides.
3. Use as cloud covering for favorite casseroles.
4. Use as "Play-Toe," the mashed potatoes you can play with and eat.

surge. His spooning quickens, and soon the entire family's supply of potatoes is mounded up on his dish. He studies it. Slowly, yet very deliberately directed by the sight, he pulls away the lumpy sides of the blob. It's becoming clearer now. He wields his fork this way and that, painstakingly giving shape to the image in his head until, at last, a sculpted tower looms up from his plate.

The potatoes eventually help Neary to identify the meaning of his vision (the location of the spaceship's arrival), which should open us to consider their worth beyond the mere carbohydrate. Not only can potatoes round out a meal, but they can also serve as a sculpting medium, a dinner recreation, or the key to unlocking the very mystery of the universe. Take that, Stove-Top!

Close Encounters. Teri Garr, pointing to the void of potatoes on her dinner plate, stares at her husband's unusual treatment of the family's mashed spuds, while screen daughter Adrienne Campbell looks on.

Close Encounters. From little acorns, big messes grow. Richard Dreyfuss puts the finishing touches on his mountainous creation, inspired in part by mashed potatoes.

Continental Divide

Nutshell

Somewhere there's a place where, when opposites attract, they meet. In *Continental Divide*, two extremely diverse characters meet on a peak of the Colorado Rockies. Their attraction is slow to surface, but they eventually reconcile their differences and celebrate their truce over an exceptionally divine plate of goulash.

Souchak (John Belushi), a sneaky, muckraking Chicago reporter, finds himself pitted against the wrath of the Windy City's big politicians. In an effort to avoid increasing unfavorable political "heat," and perhaps save his life, Souchak's editor (Allen Goorwitz) reassigns him to seek out and cover the activities of a reclusive mountain ornithologist. Reluctantly, Souchak agrees to the exile.

The reporter first meets "holy woman" Nell Porter (Blair Brown) after being led by a local guide to her home at the top of the Colorado Rockies and dropped off at her doorstep. Freezing and alone, he breaks into the empty cabin. No phone, no conveniences, no city comforts. The agony of fresh air, wide open spaces, and snow-capped peaks threaten to finish off the pudgy, chain-smoking reporter more mercilessly than the crooked politicians.

Opposites attract when Nell returns to her cozy cabin from a hard day at the observation point. She quickly extends her hospitality—from the end of her rifle. She extends it even further in his face when he discloses the purpose of his visit—to write a newspaper report of her life and studies on the American bald eagle. Ironically, Souchak pleads for his life and safety until Nell finally agrees to let him stay, but only until the guide returns in two weeks. In the meantime, no story. Not one word!

The two spend their time doing what each knows best. Souchak sneaks secret notes about Nell, while Nell chops wood, studies bald eagles, and tends to the daily chores of survival. Soon Souchak shows his adeptness in the wilderness by doing household chores. He even cooks a few meals. They even taste good.

Eventually, a mutual respect for one another grows. Nell gives him the story he needs for the newspaper, they fall in love, get married, and return to work. That is, since bald eagles don't do business in the back rooms of Chicago, and politicians don't build nests ten thousand feet above sea level, Souchak returns to the city and Nell returns to the country. Ah well, true love knows no boundaries.

Food Scene

Any event worth celebrating is often accompanied by a special meal. When you're camping in the Rockies, this may mean that something other than dehydrated eggs and powdered milk shows up on the table.

Grandmother's Goulash
Rating: G

- 2 T. vegetable oil or bacon fat
- 1 large onion, peeled and chopped
- 1 lb. beef, cut in 1" cubes
- Salt, pepper
- 1 12 oz. can beer
- ¼ c. tomato paste
- ¾ c. water
- 1 T. paprika
- 2 T. minced fresh parsley
- 4 medium-sized potatoes, peeled and cut in 1" cubes

Heat oil or bacon fat in a dutch oven. Add the chopped onion and sauté until tender. Sprinkle meat with salt and pepper. Add to the onion and brown on all sides. Add the beer, tomato paste, water, paprika, and parlsey. Cover and cook slowly until beef is tender, about 2 hours. Add potatoes, cover and cook at a slow boil until tender, 20-30 minutes. Serves 4.

At the turning point in Nell and Souchak's relationship, Souchak prepares a special mountain meal to celebrate their new-found friendship. Nell is delighted to see something new on her plate, and is told that it has *real* ingredients in it, too—like real beef and real salt and pepper. Nell is impressed. Says it even tastes good, but what is it?

"It's goulash!" he announces. A special recipe of his grandmother's. "She died twenty years ago. They say it was the goulash."

Actually, the dish was prepared by Yugoslavian Tony Kerum, a well-known Los Angeles-based studio caterer, reports property master Jerry Moss. Tony prepared the dish fresh on the set that day in his catering truck—not in the Rocky wilderness, but in the concrete jungle of Universal's back lot.

Continental Divide. Belushi is far more successful in making Grandma's goulash than in building a shower door.

Danton

Nutshell

Danton, the French foreign film triumph, won international critical acclaim for its riveting account of one of the most fascinating periods in history—the Reign of Terror of the French Revolution. It's a story about the inevitable power struggle that takes place following a revolution, wherein two one-time allies and now rival leaders of the Revolution face off in a murderous internecine conflict. Their growing opposition reaches an irrevocable breaking point at a private dinner, where the fate of the people's hero and would-be liberator, Georges Danton, is sealed amidst the sumptuous glory of some of France's great culinary achievements.

We know from history books that the Reign of Terror arose because France had been in the grip of fear since the fall of the monarchy early in 1793. Hostile armies had continued to dot the borders of France, and the young Republic that had been formed from the rubble by the visionary leadership of Maximilian Robespierre and Georges Danton was beginning to crumble.

Danton, the passionate, though less than honest spokesman of the people's needs and conscience, had become increasingly moderate in his post-revolutionary fervor as he saw bread lines grow and thousands of people beheaded as a result of the paranoid policies of the very organization he helped to form—the National Convention and Public Safety Committee. The "incorruptible" lawyer, moralist, and icy leader of the Convention, Maximilian Robespierre, on the other hand, believed in a rigid line of defense for the new Republic in order to preserve France for freedom and democracy. Ironically, it was the fanaticism of Robespierre and his adherents that turned their beloved Republic into a virtual dictatorship feared by all.

In the troubled spring of 1794, when the story begins, Danton (Gerard Depardieu) returns to Paris from a self-imposed rest in the country to try to stop the Convention's terrorizing policies and bring about a new peace. His critical views have been circulated by his friend and pamphleteer, Camille Desmoulins (Patrice Chereau). Together they have galvanized the people into an opposition faction of significant size and threat. Tension grows as Danton's followers urge him to strike, and members of the Convention simultaneously call for his execution.

Robespierre (Wojciech Pszoniak), leader of the terrorist Public Safety Committee, convinces fellow members that Danton's life must be spared in order to avoid a possible insurrection. At a dinner meeting, he attempts to persuade Danton to abandon his criticisms of the National Convention, but Danton is determined in his stance, and Robespierre comes away convinced of Danton's plan for a counter-revolution.

Stuffed Cucumber
Rating: G

Stuffing:
- 8 oz. cream cheese, softened
- 1 T. lemon juice
- 1 T. finely chopped fresh chives
- 1 T. minced fresh parsley
- 1 T. minced shallots
- ½ t. Worcestershire sauce
- Dash tobasco
- 6 oz. flaked cooked crabmeat
- 4 medium-sized cucumbers

Garnish:
Parsley sprigs
Pimiento strips
Sliced black olives
Sliced cherry tomatoes
Sliced red and green peppers

Using an electric mixer, beat the cream cheese with the lemon juice until light and fluffy. Add the remaining stuffing ingredients and mix well. Prepare the cucumbers by scoring the skin lengthwise with the tongs of a fork. Cut each crosswise into 1" pieces. Hollow out 1/2" of each piece and heap with the stuffing. Decorate using a variety of garnishes. (To follow the film version, carve a large cucumber into a hollowed-out alligator and stuff.) Makes 1 1/2 cups stuffing.

Danton. Gerard Depardieu, facing the consequences of bad table manners.

What follows is a chronicle of a good thing gone bad. The new legal system, established to protect individual rights and justly try criminals, turns against itself. Danton, Desmoulins, and their allies are arrested, their fates sealed from the start. During their mock trial, Danton's silver-tongued rhetorical power fails to spur the people into action against the travesty of justice, and he and his followers are condemned to the guillotine.

In the end, Robespierre is seized by despair over his role in Danton's death and his betrayal of the Revolution's principles. While lying tormented in bed, his housekeeper's younger brother proudly recites the Articles of the Revolution for Robespierre, who must now face the private horror of his own treachery.

Food Scene

One of the most compelling scenes in the film is Robespierre's dinner confrontation with Danton. They arrange to meet in a hotel where Danton's friends have brought fabulous dishes befitting leaders. Even as Danton readies himself, he attends to every detail of the dinner in order to please his guest, inspecting and sampling plates of food with mounting anticipation and cooing pleasurably over the upcoming feast.

One helper brings a platter of "Turbot à la Flunky," another suggests that they start with the "Stuffed Cucumber" (cleverly carved into an alligator), then on to "Vol au Vent with Convention Sauce" (once known as caper sauce before the revolutionaries took over and renamed not only government institutions, but recipes as well) and "Refugee Quails with Onion." Finally Danton's pleasure peaks with the presentation of "Fruit à la Royal Runaway."

Robespierre's late arrival gives Danton the opportunity to imbibe heavily, and his resultant condition induces him to speak perhaps too frankly to Robespierre at eventual risk to his life. Danton offers the food to his guest, but the businesslike, tight-lipped Robespierre coldly refuses. After several fruitless attempts to persuade his guest otherwise, even showing him that the food has not been poisoned, the enraged Danton pushes the entire buffet dinner onto the floor. In his alcohol-inspired discourse, Danton asks how Robespierre can claim to know the people when "he shares so few of their appetites." What hope is there for humanity in a man who refuses to eat food like this? As Danton gets progressively drunker, insulting Robespierre's manhood and morals, he finally exposes his neck to the man as a calculated taunt and unwittingly signs his own death warrant.

Refugee Quail with Wine-Onions
Rating: G

- 4 medium-sized onions, peeled
  Red wine
- 4 1½ lb. young quail or Cornish game hens, cleaned and dressed
- 1 t. freshly ground black pepper
- 2 t. dried whole rosemary leaves
- 4 T. bacon fat, melted

Place onions in a saucepan and cover with wine. Bring to a boil. Reduce heat, cover, and cook over low heat for 1 hour. (Mixture should bubble slightly.) Drain, reserving the liquid. Stuff each bird with one of the boiled onions. Combine pepper and rosemary. Brush each bird with bacon fat and sprinkle generously with the pepper mixture. Place on a rack in a shallow baking pan and bake at 400° for 45–50 minutes. Reheat onion-wine sauce and serve with the meat. Serves 4.

Vol au Vent
Rating: G

(This is a flaky, airy puff pastry that offers a wide variety of applications. If prepared as a shell, it can be served warm and filled with creamed food. Cooled, it can be filled with fruits for an elegant dessert. Vol au vent is a larger 8"-9" circular version of the classic 3" individual patty shell. The list of ingredients for its preparation is deceptively simple, but in fact this king of pastries requires hours of labor and the highest culinary skills. The pastry is best made on a chilly, windy, clear winter day, as its finicky nature requires cool temperatures for proper butter consistency. The modest amounts called for here are easier to work with than that for a full batch, but the recipe can easily be doubled or tripled by the adventuresome chef. Store any leftover dough by refrigerating it in a closely covered container for a few days or by freezing up to several weeks. Get ready for cooking day with a bright, cheery attitude, proper tools, and thorough study to experience the most remarkable concoction of butter and flour ever to emerge from an oven. When ready to begin, first cut one 8" and one 5" circular cardboard pattern to be used in forming the shell. Also cut one 6"x16" cardboard rectangle to facilitate measuring the rolled dough. Please read these tips ahead of time to help avoid fatal mistakes.)

1 *Work surfaces should always be cool (preferably made of marble).*
2 *Tools (including fingers) should also be chilled throughout the process (unless otherwise indicated) to keep the fat in constant suspension. Knead the butter with your fingers in ice water or the coldest running water until soft and pliable, but still chilled.*
3 *Use flour with a high gluten content, if possible, for superior elasticity.*
4 *Knead the pastry for the full time allotted to "trap" air and yield a puffier pastry (cooked dough should be 6-8 times the height of the uncooked rolled dough).*
5 *The oven must be fully preheated to 450° for at least 20 minutes before opening (use an oven thermometer if necessary to check temperature).*
6 *Always cut the puff paste dough with a very thin, hot knife or hot pastry wheel, being sure not to drag the cutting tool, as this will distort the layers.*
7 *When rolling out the dough, work with the smaller dimensions towards you, rolling the length of the dough away from your body.*
8 *Avoid letting tears or cracks form, as they will allow valuable air to escape in the rising process. Should they begin to develop, mend them immediately.*
9 *Never let the dough dry out, but at the same time do not allow it to collect too much moisture. The perfect dough will always envelope the butter for proper rising.*
10 *Keep a cheery disposition, and good luck!*

¼ lb. sweet butter
¼ lb. (about 1 c.) unsifted all-purpose flour
¼ t. salt
1 t. lemon juice

Glaze:
1 egg yolk, lightly beaten
2 T. milk
Granulated sugar (optional)

Briefly and quickly pat the butter back and forth in the palms of your hands until all the water leaves the butter. Shape into a 4"x 6" x 3/4" slab on a sheet of foil lining a marble surface. Refrigerate 20 minutes. Meanwhile, pour the weighed flour into a mixing bowl and make a well in the center. Combine the salt, lemon juice, and 2 1/2 ounces of water and gradually pour into the well, mixing with a circular motion of the fingertips into a firm, but slightly sticky dough.

Turn out onto a marble surface and knead lightly until smooth—no more than 2 minutes. Cover with foil and refrigerate on the marble surface for 15 minutes. (When the dough and butter are removed from the refrigerator, they should both be chilled but not hard.) Using a marble rolling pin, roll out the dough to an even 6" x 16" x 1/3" thick rectangle. (Elasticity of the dough may make this difficult, but perseverance will win out.) Place the cold butter slab at one end of the dough, 1" from the end and sides. Fold the free end over the butter slab, creating a "pocket." Seal the open edges together by pressing with your fingers. Roll the sealed pocket out to the 6" x 16" dimension again, taking care not to break the layers and crack the dough.

Fold one 6" end one third of the way into the center of the dough, matching edges. Fold the other end over this, creating one slab of 3 equal parts measuring about 4" x 6" x 1", thus completing your first "turn."

Roll the rolling pin over the slab to compress the dough slightly. Wrap in foil and refrigerate for 30 minutes. Remove from the refrigerator and repeat the rolling and folding process. Chill again for 30 minutes. Repeat this turning and chilling process 4 more times. (If you wish, you may store the dough for 24 hours before baking by wrapping in foil, then in a dry towel, then refrigerating.) Let the dough rest at least 30 minutes, but no more than 1 1/2 hours, at room temperature.

Roll out to a 9" x 17" rectangle. Using your 8" cardboard pattern, cut two 8" circles from the dough. Place one of the circles, cut side down, on a baking sheet sprinkled with cold water. Using the 5" pattern, cut a 5" round out of the center of the second circle.

Place the 1 1/2" rimmed circle this creates, cut side down, directly on top of the whole 8" circle. Place the 5" circle next to the 8" circle on the baking sheet to be baked as the "lid." Make diagonal gashes 2" apart around the rim of the circles.

Prepare glaze for the dough by combining the egg yolk with the milk. Lightly brush the top of the dough with the glaze, being sure none of the egg drips down the sides, as this, too, will inhibit proper rising. (If using the pastry for a sweet dish, add the sugar to the glaze.)

Bake at 450° for 5 minutes. Reduce heat to 375° and continue baking an additional 25–30 minutes. (If the pastry browns too quickly, place a piece of baker's paper over the top during the last part of baking.) Serve by filling with creamed food—Convention Sauce and sole for example—or cool and fill with fruit. Makes one 9" pastry shell and lid.

Turbot à la Flunky
Rating: G

2 lbs. turbot fillet, skinned and cleaned
Lemon juice

Stock:

2 qts. water
1 bay leaf
1 small onion studded with 4 whole cloves
½ c. chopped celery
¼ c. chopped carrot
1 t. salt
1 c. dry white wine
½ t. thyme
½ t. marjoram
4 parsley sprigs
4 chervil sprigs (or 1 t. dried)

Sauce:

3 T. butter
2 T. minced onion
3 T. flour
1 c. fish stock
½ c. light cream
2 T. minced fresh parsley
½ t. Worcestershire sauce
2 t. sherry
¼ t. salt
Freshly ground pepper
Fresh steamed broccoli, stems and heads intact
Parsley sprigs for garnish

Rub the fillets with lemon juice. Set aside. In a large pan, bring the 2 quarts water to a boil. Add the remaining stock ingredients and bring to a boil again. Add the fish, reduce heat to simmer, and cook, uncovered, until tender (about 15 minutes). Remove fish to a warm platter, cover with foil, and place in a warm oven while the sauce is being made. Strain the fish stock, reserving the liquid. Melt the butter in a saucepan. Add the onion and simmer until tender.

Stir in the flour with a wire whip and continue to stir about 3 minutes to cook out the taste of the flour. Slowly add 1 cup of the strained fish broth and the light cream, stirring constantly. Add the parsley, Worcestershire sauce, sherry, and salt and pepper to taste. Cook and stir until thickened. To assemble the dish, wrap each fillet around a bunch of steamed broccoli. Place in a row on a serving platter and pour the sauce over the fish. Garnish with parsley sprigs. Serves 4.

Fruit à la Royal Runaway (Mixed Fruit Tart)
Rating: G

Pastry:
- ½ c. butter, softened
- 1½ c. flour
- Pinch salt
- 2 T. superfine granulated sugar
- 1 egg
- 1 t. vanilla

Filling:
- 1¼ c. cream cheese, softened
- 2 egg yolks
- ¾ c. confectioners' sugar
- 1 t. vanilla

Garnish:
- 3 peaches
- ¼ lb. seedless green grapes (about 25)
- ¼ lb. cherries, pitted (about 14)
- 3-4 pitted prunes
- 1 kiwi fruit, skinned and sliced

Glaze:
- 1 T. orange juice
- ½ c. apple jelly

In a medium-sized mixing bowl, cream butter, flour, and salt together. Add sugar, egg, and vanilla. Mix until smooth. Form dough into a ball and chill 1/2 hour. Roll out into a 13" circle on a lightly floured board. Line the base of a 12" tart pan with aluminum foil. Fit dough evenly into pan. Trim edges and prick bottom and sides with a fork.

Bake at 375° for 25 minutes. Cool. (To reduce shrinkage, you may line the surface of the fitted dough with a sheet of aluminum foil, leaving extra at the ends to make convenient handles. Fill with rice, beans, or pastry weights. After baking 15 minutes, remove weight filling by carefully lifting aluminum liner. Continue baking 10 minutes or until lightly browned.)

Meanwhile, beat cream cheese, egg yolks, sugar, and vanilla together with an electric mixer until smooth. Spread filling into cooled pastry shell. Place peaches in a pot of boiling water. Remove after 1 minute and plunge into cold water. Peel, halve, and remove pits. Slice into 1/4" sections.

Arrange peach slices close together around periphery of the filling. Arrange remaining fruit in decorative concentric circles. Combine juice and jelly in a small saucepan. Heat to boiling, stirring until smooth. Remove from heat. Cool 1 minute. Pour glaze over fruit and refrigerate until set, about 2 hours. Serves 8.

Convention Sauce (Caper Sauce)
Rating: G

- 3 T. butter
- 2 T. flour
- 2¾ c. chicken stock
- ¼ c. minced mushrooms
- ¼ t. (rounded) dry mustard
- 1 egg yolk
- 2½ T. heavy cream
- 4 T. chopped capers
- 1 T. lemon juice

Melt 2 tablespoons of the butter in the top of a double boiler over hot water. Using a wire whip, stir in the flour until well blended. Slowly add 2 cups of the chicken stock and cook, stirring constantly until thickened. Add the mushrooms and cook over hot water for about 1 hour, stirring occasionally. Strain the mixture through a fine sieve and return it to the top of the double boiler. Stir in the mustard and the remaining 3/4 cup chicken stock. Cook over medium heat until reduced to 2/3 of its original measurement, or about 1 1/2 cups. Remove from heat. Mix the egg yolk with the cream and stir into the sauce.

Just before serving, add the capers, lemon juice, and remaining 1 tablespoon of butter. Serve hot as a sauce with fish, mutton or lamb. Makes 1 1/2 cups sauce.

Diary of a Mad Housewife

Nutshell

Short-order cook, gourmet chef, maid, nanny, errand girl, interior decorator, hostess, lover, wife, secretary, cleaning lady, and laundress—the basic duties of your everyday American housewife. Many women perform the job, some even by choice, but it's when you're expected to perform each task simultaneously, night and day, without so much as a please or thank you, that you have the right to be mad—or go mad. In this film, one soft-spoken, frustrated woman finds herself reaching both ways in her stifling life as housewife to a social-climbing lawyer-husband.

The mad housewife is Tina Balser (Carrie Snodgrass) who, when not making dinner or running errands, is apt to be preparing special snacks for her exceptionally demanding, whining, materialistically driven husband, Jonathan (Richard Benjamin). His obsession with the "right" people and places, and her passive defense of her rights, has produced two very spoiled children, a life in which objects dictate goals, and a disintegrating "establishment" marriage.

Set in Central Park West, the story offers a frightening assortment of "keeping-up-with-the-Joneses" experiences that enlist sympathy with Tina's predicament. To ease her boredom and depression, she allows herself an affair. But the self-centered, amoral attitude of her lover, George Prager (Frank Langella), offers only a temporary physical escape, not the emotional massage she so desperately needs.

In the end, Jonathan comes clean with a full disclosure of his more contemptible deeds, such as losing all their money in a questionable vineyard investment, performing poorly at the office, and conducting an affair with another woman. Tina, however, doesn't respect the marriage enough to confess her own fling. She opts, instead, to seek a cure for her madness in group therapy, where she ends up, again, the object of abuse—this time by a group of unstable strangers who use her as a target for their own insecurities and wicked verbal darts.

Food Scene

It was while watching this film in 1971 that I first learned about Caesar salad. What in the world was Dick Benjamin doing dropping that raw egg into a bowl of lettuce, I wondered?

As Tina prepares dinner one night, Jonathan volunteers to make the salad as an expression of his creative talents, to go with a "beautifully marbelized" porterhouse steak. The ever-dutiful Tina listens to his inflated self-appraisal as he dresses the salad bowl, but she can't resist a comment of her own, referring to his salad as "a creation" in her softest, driest, most sarcastic voice.

Caesar Salad
Rating: G

(It is best to complete this dressing shortly before serving time, keeping the ingredients at room temperature. Also, plan to use the entire amount prepared, as it does not store well, refrigerated or otherwise. Proof of its popular taste though, it is the single most asked-for recipe in my collection.)

- 1½ heads romaine, washed, chilled, and torn into pieces
- 2 c. croutons

Dressing:
- ⅓ c. vegetable oil
- 3 T. olive oil
- 1 medium-sized garlic clove, mashed
- Juice of 1½ lemons
- 1 T. Worcestershire sauce
- 1 egg yolk
- ¼ c. grated Parmesan cheese
- Salt and pepper to taste
- Anchovies (optional)

Combine the oils in a small bowl. Add the mashed garlic and let sit at least one hour before mixing with the other ingredients. Add the remaining dressing ingredients, shake well, and pour over the prepared lettuce. Add the croutons and toss well. Serves 4–6.

Diary of a Mad Housewife. Dick Benjamin demonstrates domestic saucery at the breakfast table.

Later, a flu sends Jonathan to bed, where he makes life even more of a hell for Tina. Get me a ginger ale with plenty of cracked ice. Get me a fresh-squeezed lemonade, not frozen, with real lemons, cracked ice, and grenadine. And order the Christmas cards, send out the party invitations, do all the Christmas shopping, and, by the way, make a gourmet Thanksgiving meal this year. Fine.

When the celebrated day of thanks arrives, Jonathan and his bratty daughter Sylvie begin to complain about the smell of cooked onions first thing in the morning. He retreats to bed again, selfishly timing his demands for a late breakfast right before the feast is ready. From the bed he pompously places his "order": juice, coffee, a four-minute egg, and a scone (no butter) with Damson plum preserves. The madness smolders. Then with everyone seated at the beautifully set Thanksgiving table, the family's uneasy silence is broken when Jonathan briefs the children in proper wine selection, noting that his choice for the meal, a 1964 Romaine San Vivant, is good because it's expensive but not smug. He goes on to give the girls a pep talk on the gourmet meal, critiquing the stuffing with expensive adjectives like "super-dooper." Sylvie feels differently though, and lets them know it by immediately bursting into a furious recipe tirade. "It's *awful*! Mushy chestnuts, onion and celery and cream. Even the salad isn't normal—oranges and cut up plants!" Sylvie earns her immediate banishment from the table, and the lavish dinner comes to a crashing end. Jonathan staggers away from the table feeling a little peculiar, and Tina is left to throw out the uneaten Thanksgiving dinner. Now she's really mad.

Finally, in another calamitous eating scene, the couple learns an expensive lesson from a holiday party they've thrown to impress a large list of social higher-ups. Unknown to the Balsers, their caterer for the party, Monsieur Beaumont, has scheduled a second party to cook for that night. He therefore closes the Balsar's bar disastrously early in order to get on with the food and out the door. Beaumont prepares the omelets that made him popular, but one of the many pretentious guests takes Tina aside and tells her that people are tired of Beaumont and his omelets. By nine o'clock, only thirteen guests picking at their omelets remain, and the Balsers are left with egg on their upwardly immobile faces.

Omelet Beaumont
Rating: G

2 eggs, well beaten
1 T. chopped green onion
1 T. chopped mushroom
1 T. cooked, shredded salmon
1 t. minced fresh parsley
2 heaping T. grated mild cheddar cheese
   Freshly ground black pepper
1 T. butter
   Avocado slices
   Sour cream

In a small bowl, combine the eggs, onion, mushroom, salmon, parsley, cheese, and pepper to taste. Melt the butter in an omelet pan and heat just until it begins to darken, or *noisette*. Pour in the egg mixture. Holding the pan handle in your left hand, swirl and agitate it back and forth in a continuous movement while stirring the eggs quickly with the flat side of a fork held in the other hand.

When the eggs are half cooked to desired doneness, stop stirring. Cook over low heat until cooked, but still soft on top. Fold in half with a spatula and slide onto a warm dish or serving platter. Arrange avocado slices on top and spoon sour cream over. Serves 1.

Orange-Plant Salad
Rating: G

1 recipe French dressing (see p. 233)
¼ t. sesame seed oil
   Lettuce leaves, washed and chilled
2 oranges, peeled and sliced thin
½ red onion, peeled, sliced thin
   Toasted sesame seeds

Prepare dressing and add the sesame seed oil. Arrange lettuce leaves on individual serving plates. Arrange orange and separated onion rings over the lettuce. Pour desired amount of dressing over and sprinkle lightly with sesame seeds. Serves 2.

Oyster-Chestnut Stuffing
Rating: PG

- 2 c. cooked chestnuts, riced
- 2 c. raw oysters
- 6 T. butter, melted
- 1½ c. dry bread crumbs
- ¼ c. cream
- ½ c. chopped celery
- 1½ T. minced onion
- 2 T. minced fresh parsley
- 1 t. salt
- ⅛ t. pepper

Combine ingredients in a bowl and stir well. Loosely fill cavity of a game bird or turkey with the stuffing. Makes about 6 1/2 cups.

Diary of a Mad Housewife. Imperious Dick Benjamin rules over all that he surveys, including Caesar salad.

Diary of a Mad Housewife. Carrie Snodgrass fends off the final stages of madness by clutching the tool of her trade, *The Joy of Cooking.*

Diner

Nutshell

Fells Point Diner is a 1950s silver railroad car-style burger joint on the Bayside edge of Baltimore where you can get a cherry Coke with lemon, a side of fries and gravy, and watch a fat guy take all night to eat every item from the left side of the menu. It's the watering hole for six guys on the verge of adulthood in writer/director Barry Levinson's semi-autobiographical debut film, *Diner*.

Despite their differences, the six guys meet there regularly and try to sort out life's problems over soda and sandwiches. Their talk revolves around their favorite subjects—girls, sports, and rock 'n' roll. Within Levinson's intimate framework, we get a close look at these young men in the final days of 1959—the last flickering embers of the Eisenhower era—as "cold and wet and somber as any other time," according to Levinson.

Ironically, we have the critics to thank for sparing *Diner* from an early sentencing to cinema purgatory. It was not originally well received by studio executives, who just about canned the film after testing pre-release audiences who were primed by misleading ads promoting *Diner* as another *Animal House*. But New York critics who had previewed the film were so impressed with it that they decided to run their reviews regardless of studio intentions. Thanks to their efforts, the film was released and became a success with audiences and critics alike.

The six characters who form the core of *Diner* are Boogie (Mickey Rourke), hairdresser by day, law student by night, addicted to gambling round the clock; Shrevie (Daniel Stern), married to a record collection first and wife second; Billy (Timothy Daly, very serious, very rejected by career-minded girlfriend carrying his child; Fenwick (Kevin Bacon), rich, brilliant, and reckless in attempts to shake his loneliness; Modell (Paul Reiser), insecure, inarticulate and Eddy's favorite target; Eddy (Steven Guttenberg), football-freak, male chauvinist *par excellence* who won't marry his girl until she passes a grueling football quiz.

It's Eddy's pending marriage that provides the bare bones of a story line in *Diner*, but director Levinson's really more concerned with exploring the lives of his six warmly drawn characters and their world.

Boogie shows unusual deference toward Beth (Ellen Barkin), wife of Shrevie, former girlfriend and date for the night, when he confesses (thereby sacrificing) his sure bet to "score" with her. And Eddy finally agrees to marry Elyse, even though she's technically failed his quiz by two points.

The story culminates at the wedding, where, to the tunes of the Baltimore Colts marching song, Eddy and Elyse are joined in matrimony. Levinson underscores how the boys feel about women by purposely keeping Elyse off camera and having the traditional flower bouquet toss land on the boys' table. Shrevie gives his confused and depressed wife more attention and promises to take her to the Poconos for a summer vacation, and Modell pays tribute to Elyse's prenuptial effort in his humorous speech to the newlyweds.

Heated Roast Beef Sandwich
Rating: G

Mustard
Mayonnaisse
2 *large slices dark bread (rye, pumpernickel, wheat, etc.)*
¼ *lb. lean roast beef, sliced thin*
Montery jack cheese, sliced thin
Fresh tomato, sliced thin
Thinly sliced onion
Lettuce
Salt, pepper
Pickles

Spread desired amount of mustard and mayonnaise on one slice of dark bread. Pile meat on prepared bread slice and top with desired amount of cheese, tomato, and onion slices. Salt and pepper to taste. Top with second bread slice, wrap in aluminum foil, and heat in oven until cheese melts. Add lettuce as desired. Serve pickles on the side. Serves 1 or 2.

Snapshot style, the film ends in a freeze frame group shot. They suddenly look much older and very sober about what lies in store for them as adults.

Food Scene

The favorite pastime of each member of the group is to chew the fat with the guys down at Fells Diner. Late Christmas night is no exception, as Modell, Shrevie, Eddie, and Fenwick meet to discuss Fenwick's date and debate the relative strengths of Sinatra vs. Mathis for best "make out" records.

As they talk, Modell eyes Eddy's roast beef sandwich and asks if he's going to finish it. Immediately angered by Modell's usual roundabout way of asking for things, Eddy demands that he say it again in plain English, "I want the roast beef sandwich." Say it, he tells him, and he'll get a piece. Modell isn't intimidated though. He turns on Eddy, contending that Eddy's problem is that he doesn't chew his food, and that's why he's so irritable. In fact, he says, Eddy has lumps of roast beef stuck in his heart! As the two of them bicker back and forth, Shrevie picks up the unguarded sandwich and eats it himself.

This scene and others at the diner, including a pig-out by a "building" on feet named Earl Maget (Mark Margolis), who orders everything from the left side of the menu one night and finishes the sixteen-dish order before daybreak, are always surrounded by tables supporting plates of French fries and gravy. This was the single most popular dish of the day, according to director Barry Levinson, and he was eager to make this point in his diner.

To create the proper setting, the diner, which was purchased in New Jersey, had to be moved to Baltimore and stripped and redecorated to replicate the time period. Conveniently, a real diner located across the street was able to supply all the food required for scenes at Fells Point Diner. The set was detailed in authentic period pieces, down to the heart-dotted Dixie cups that were popular in the 1950s. Amazingly, property master Larry Bird was able to find the printer who still had copies of the original menu used in the original diner. The menus that appeared in various scenes were copies of the real McCoy. All the items listed on the menu were characterized by an unusual name, but a French fry, by any other name, is still a French fry.

French Fries and Gravy
Rating: G

French fries (see Starman, p. 130)

Gravy:
2 beef bouillon cubes
1 c. boiling water
2 T. butter or beef fat
½ clove garlic, mashed
2 T. flour
¼ t. Worcestershire sauce
Few drops lemon juice
Salt and pepper to taste

Dissolve bouillon cubes in boiling water. Set aside. Melt butter or fat in a small saucepan. Add garlic and heat through. Stir in flour with a wire whip and blend well. Gradually add bouillon mixture, stirring constantly with the wire whip until smooth and boiling. Reduce heat and stir in remaining ingredients. Serve hot over French fries. Makes about 1 cup gravy.

Diner. A few Diner regulars, left to right: Kevin Bacon, Mickey Rourke, Daniel Stern, and Timothy Daly.

E.T., The Extra-Terrestrial

Nutshell

You take an imaginative, first-rate story, one bunch of endearing characters, add big laughs, heart-wrenching sadness, and a pinch of magic; mix extraordinary with the ordinary, stir it all up with fast action and suspense, set it in familiar surroundings, and you've got the recipe for a film classic called *E.T.*

Already spoken of in the same breath as *The Wizard of Oz*, *E.T., The Extra-Terrestrial* captured the hearts of millions of people all over the world in just a few short weeks after its release. The certifiable talents of producer-director Steven Spielberg and his associates built a timeless story around a character made of rubber, wires, and servomotors. This remarkable assembly produced one of the most memorable non-human film creations since Mickey Mouse in *Steamboat Willie*. What we definitely don't have here is a problem in communication. *E.T.* unabashedly expresses hope in the twin powers of love and caring to transcend gallaxies of differences and create a lasting bond of friendship between alien life forms.

While the story of *E.T.*, by Melissa Mathison, bares no plot resemblance to *Peter Pan*, story analysts have pointed out the basic similarity between the two—children inhabiting a Never-Never Land threatened by grown-ups and growing up. Adults in *E.T.* are filmed from the waist down through most of the picture to actualize the children's point of view, but even when full body shots are allowed at the end, grown-ups are completely covered in protective plastic space-suit-like togs that make them look more threatening than the little alien creature they're attempting to capture.

On a starry summer night in the woods on the outskirts of a Southern California suburb, alien botanists have arrived on a "cosmic butterfly hunt" to collect samples of life on another planet—Earth. Suddenly, they're startled by headlights and the sound of jangling keys, and they flee for their spaceship, accidentally leaving one of their comrades behind. It's E.T., who then must seek refuge in the storage shed of a nearby house.

Elliott (Henry Thomas), a young boy who lives in the house, is taking delivery of a pizza when noises from the shed arouse his curiosity and bring him face to face with E.T. Only momentarily frightened by their exchange of screams, Elliott lures the alien into his room the next day by leaving a trail of candy. There they quickly become friends, and later Elliott introduces older brother Michael (Robert McNaughton) and younger sister Gertie (Drew Barrymore) to E.T. with vows to keep E.T.'s residence in Elliott's closet a secret from their mother, Mary (Dee Wallace), on the off chance that she might not let them keep him.

The children do their best to make E.T. happy and comfortable, and E.T. returns their kindness by humbly performing wondrous deeds of magic. Before long, a mysterious, physical, symbiotic relationship

Space-iality of the House
Rating: G

Watermelon
Cheeseburger
Apples
Oranges
Grapes
Celery stalks
Potato chips
Carrots
Lettuce
Eggs

Randomly arrange above foods on a table. Serve as is. Serves 1.

grows between Elliott and E.T., but when E.T.'s health begins to deteriorate, so does Elliott's. After learning a few words from watching television, E.T. is able to tell the children that what he really needs is to "phone home."

Being children of divorced parents, the kids immediately empathize with E.T.'s homesickness, and quickly help their little friend build an intergalactic telephone with carefully selected household items. A magical bike-flight propels E.T. and Elliott through the sky to the field where they will spend the night at risk to their mutual health, as they attempt to call home to E.T.'s "people."

Unbeknownst to the children, their activities have been under surveillance by the group of men first identified by the mere jangling of keys. Now they descend upon the simple suburban setting like storm troopers.

Meanwhile, Elliott has awakened in the field only to find E.T. missing. Desperate but weakened, he returns home and sends Michael out to find their friend. Michael succeeds and brings E.T.'s unconscious

E.T. **The children serve E.T. a banquet of earth food.**

body home in hopes that Mom can help. Matters have gotten out of hand, though, as the scientific invaders, now dressed in protective plastic suits and overrunning the house, have taken charge and turned the living room into an emergency hospital, where they will try to save the lives of Elliott and E.T.

Eventually the connection between the two bodies is broken, bringing Elliott's full recovery, but at the expense of E.T.'s vital signs. While the disappointed scientists prepare to leave, Elliott secretly realizes that the little alien is still very much alive.

Quick thinking and gutty action save E.T. once again as Elliott, Michael, and friends engage in a madcap race against scientists and legal authorities that miraculously brings E.T. to the field where a rescue spaceship is about to arrive and take him home. Mom and the head of the scientific contingent also arrive just in time to look on in wonder as the jack-o'-lanternlike ship descends. The children say painful good-byes to their friend, and for Elliott some of the "ouch" he feels in his heart will be healed when E.T. tells him, pointing to his head, "I'll be right here."

Food Scene

Elliott is your basic all-American boy and, as such, is able to do with Reese's Pieces what armies of men in other movies have failed to do—capture a space creature. By laying out a trail of the peanut-buttery candies in the forest, he lures the alien straight into his room. But Elliott's idea of capture is more like an open-house invitation. He warmly provides room and board, and no sooner has E.T. settled in his closet than he's serving Coke and chips—a far more palatable alternative to the Matchbox car E.T. tried to eat.

According to Property Master Russ Goble, a man named Pat, who is listed as one of the smallest people in the world (36" tall) or small children occupied E.T.'s costume for scenes requiring large motor coordination, such as walking and sampling food. (More subtle movements, such as facial expressions were controlled with servo-motors and remote control.) It is during E.T.'s first square meal on Earth that Pat lends a hand.

After meeting and exchanging introductory screams with Elliott's brother and sister, he is presented with a vertitable smorgasbord of earthly delights—a whole watermelon, a cheeseburger, apples, oranges, grapes, carrots, celery, lettuce, eggs, and, of course, more potato chips. And while it seems that space creatures like to eat, they also enjoy a good dinner conversation, for as E.T. munches on a celery stalk, he tries to communicate where he's from. E.T. uses his magical powers to levitate Playdough-type balls from the dinner table, sending them into orbit in the center of the room, thereby constructing a crude replica of his home in space.

The next day, when the house is empty, E.T. ventures down to the refrigerator alone and learns even more about earthly eats. He samples deli potato salad, but tosses it on the floor with a big "Yetch!" Beer, however, is a big hit, and he chugalugs cans of the brew. Because of the mysterious bond that has grown between Elliott and E.T., the beer makes them both drunk, even though Elliott is away at school.

Makers of sci-fi movies have rarely addressed the question of aliens requiring sustenance on their earthly visits. A few of today's movie makers are not only changing that oversight, but allowing aliens to eat our food and have favorites, like Dutch apple pie in *Starman*. As for ET, he'll probably always have a soft spot in his heart for Reese's Pieces, the candy that captured an alien.

Fatso. Portrait of a dieter.

Fatso

Nutshell

This is writer/director/actress Anne Bancroft's paean to pasta and other carbohydrate delights, with a message. The movie is filled with all manner of food, to her leading character's happy torment, and it makes no bones about its message to the world at large that it's OK to eat and be fat.

To begin, a well-intentioned Italian mother's overzealous use of food as a pacifier has caused her son Sal to grow up fat and die of overweight at an early age. At his funeral, conducted with typical Italian high drama, Sal's overweight cousin Dominic Di Napoli (Dom DeLuise) comes under fire from his sister Antoinette (Anne Bancroft) to lose weight before it's too late.

Dom is a simple, middle-aged bachelor who likes his bread buttered on both sides, literally. He owns a greeting card store in Brooklyn with Antoinette and lives with their younger brother Frankie (Roy Carey), on the second floor of the house she shares with her husband. In response to Antoinette's persistent nagging, Dom promises to diet, but gives in to temptation at every turn. He eats every leftover in sight, snacks on fruit from sidewalk stands on his way to work, eats hot dogs to wash down the fruit, and buys pastries and cookies for himself and customers to eat at the greeting card shop. He even takes a full box of pastries along when he finally goes to see a diet doctor.

Just when it looks hopeless, he's struck by an unexpected incentive for weight loss—love. A sweet Polish-Catholic, Judy Holiday-type named Lydia (Candice Azzara), who runs a nearby antique gift shop, enters his life. He believes that to win her interest, he must lose weight.

Dom joins a weight control organization called Chubby Checkers, but even the group's rigorous support can't compete with his voracious appetite. He and two Checker cohorts who come to his aid wind up in a nocturnal feeding frenzy, ripping the chains off Dom's kitchen cupboards, ordering tons of food, and gorging the night away on what would be enough food to keep a normal family satisfied for a month. The next day, Dom suffers an eating hangover as real as that from alcoholic binge.

In spite of his weakness, Lydia is eager to date. They date a lot, kiss a lot, date a lot, and kiss a lot, and somewhere in between when he's not looking, Dom loses weight. He's too busy and distracted to eat—she makes him forget food. He wants to marry her, but when she mysteriously disappears on the night he plans to propose, he binges again on $40 worth of Chinese food that was intended to feed a group of card players.

Tension builds to a climactic moment when Dom finally realizes what he is: a person who likes to eat and eats too much—a fatso. Because of this realization, he tells Antoinette and Frankie that they must love him for what he is, and not what they wish he could be. The film ends on a light note, though, as Lydia calls from a Boston hospital after rushing there for a family emergency. Dom joins her there and proposes, finally feeling good about his life—every pound of it.

Omelet with Bread
Rating: G

2 *eggs*
1 *slice Muenster cheese*
3 *slices tomato*
2 *slices Italian bread*
  Butter
  Jelly
  Hot pepper

Cook eggs as for omelet until done, but surface is still runny. Just before folding over egg, place cheese in center. Slide omelet onto plate. Garnish with tomato and bread slices. Spread butter and jelly on bread. Sprinkle omelet with hot pepper. Serves 1.

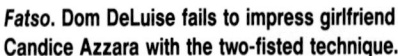

Fatso. Dom DeLuise fails to impress girlfriend Candice Azzara with the two-fisted technique.

Food Scene

All of us have known hunger, even if it's just that white-middle-class hunger for a midnight snack. As a teenager, I almost never walked through the kitchen without getting *something* to eat, even when I wasn't hungry. I called it preventive malnutrition. Cookies were my favorite, and even though the one bag that came into house that was supposed to last the week disappeared only a few hours after shopping, somehow I'd manage to find something that would hold me over until my next trip past the kitchen—about ten minutes later.

Dom Di Napoli knows the siren song of the kitchen as well, only he's no teenager with a hyperactive metabolism to feed. He eats to soothe his soul and because it simply tastes good. The fatal allure of the kitchen holds its grip over Dom night and day, good times and bad. At cousin Sal's funeral for example, with Sal's overfed body lying in final repose, Dom frequents the kitchen to fetch water for his grieving relatives and each time is drawn to the large pot of spaghetti sauce simmering on the stove. Stirring the sauce is therapeutic for his grief, he finds, but with each trip, his craving for therapy also includes cutting a small slice of bread, topping it with a spoonful of sauce, sprinkling it with a little freshly grated Parmesan cheese, and savoring yet another mouthwatering bite.

The whys and wherefores of eating aside, a real food lover like Dom feels that it's very important when you *do* eat to know how to "run your plate," just as you should know how to run your business or run your life. You don't just shovel food off your plate and into your mouth without planning and organization.

Take, for example, the breakfast Dom lovingly prepares for his brother Frankie. First he cooks an omelet to perfection, leaving the center a little runny for soaking up with bread and adding a slice of cheese to melt with the uncooked egg. Then he garnishes the entrée with juicy tomato slices and freshly cut slices of bread. When Frankie sits down and begins to eat, though, Dom disapproves of Frankie's orchestration of the meal and quickly sets him straight.

Fatso Bread
Rating: G

(My Italian brother-in-law Cliff created this fancy way to prepare garlic bread—almost a meal in itself. He calls it Panne Vino; I call it fabulous.)

2 T. butter
½ c. olive oil
⅓ c. minced fresh parsley
2 T. minced fresh basil
3 shallots (3 oz.) minced
3 cloves garlic, mashed
½ t. salt
1 t. freshly ground pepper
4 T. red wine
1 large loaf Italian bread 16 oz.), sliced lengthwise in half
Paprika
Freshly grated Parmesan cheese

Combine butter, olive oil, parsley, basil, shallots, garlic, salt, and pepper in a small saucepan. Heat gently until butter melts. Add the wine. Spread mixture evenly over sliced sides of bread. Sprinkle with paprika and Parmesan cheese. Heat in 350° oven for 10 minutes. Broil under high heat for a few seconds to crisp the top, if desired. Makes 2 halves.

Fatso. Anne Bancroft lends an ear to Dom DeLuise's heavy description of another irresistible morsel.

Picking up a bread slice from Frankie's plate, Dom demonstrates the "dipping" technique. He plunges the crust into the juicy, warm omelet center, explaining to Frankie the higher purpose of the runny center. Bread is also meant for butter and jelly, he tells Frankie, as he proceeds to butter and jelly Frankie's bread. And omelets taste better with hot pepper, he says, sprinkling hot pepper on Frankie's omelet. His well-intended seminar backfires, though, and instead of teaching Frankie how to run his plate, Frankie teaches Dom how fast he can leave a room in exasperation.

Obesity loves company, and Dom always wants everyone to eat (especially bread). Undaunted by the breakfast fiasco, Dom later prepares lasagna for Frankie, even though Dom's in the middle of his own diet and faces a plate of kale and skinless chicken breast. He spoons extra sauce and fresh grated Parmesan cheese on Frankie's plate of lasagna and cuts his brother more bread, just as he would do for himself. But Frankie doesn't love bread like Dom does and, to make his point, he throws the bread on the floor.

Frankie may never learn how to run his plate, and maybe it's sacrilege to eat lasagna without bread, but one thing is for sure: *Fatso* serves big portions of reasons for all kinds of eating—from boredom, sadness, celebration, habit, compulsion, frustration, and pleasure—to even hunger.

No matter what your reason, though, you have to live with it, most likely around your waist.

Kale with Chicken Breast
Rating: PG

½ chicken breast, skin and bones removed
½ lb. kale
Lemon slices
Seasoned salt (see Salt and Pepper, p. 236)

Boil chicken breast until tender, about 45 minutes. Steam kale until tender—about 5 minutes. Sprinkle with lemon juice and seasoned salt. Serves 1.

Lasagna with Bread
Rating: G

(To make a less spicy version, use sweet Italian sausage or a combination of hot and sweet.)

Meat sauce:
- 1 lb. lean ground beef
- 1 lb. hot Italian sausage, skins removed
- 4 large cloves garlic, mashed
- 15 fresh parsley sprigs (about ¾ c.), leaves only, minced
- ¼ c. butter
- ¼ c. olive oil
- 8 oz. mushrooms, sliced
- ¾ lb. onions (about 2 medium-sized), peeled and diced
- 1 lb. fresh Italian plum tomatoes, chopped
- 1½ lbs. canned, peeled, and crushed plum tomatoes with added puree
- 2 15 oz. cans tomato sauce
- 1½ t. salt
- 15 large leaves fresh basil, chopped, or 2 T. dried
- 2 t. dried oregano
- 2 large bay leaves
- ½ c. red wine

Topping sauce:
- 4 T. butter
- 4 T. heavy cream
- 1½ c. tomato sauce (see above)
- 2 T. flour

Filling:
- 2 lbs. ricotta cheese
- 1 c. grated Parmesan cheese
- 1 lb. cooked lasagna noodles

Topping:
- 1½ lbs. mozzarella, shredded
- ½ c. grated Parmesan cheese
  Italian bread, sliced (see Fatso Bread p. 106)

Grind beef and sausage together in a meat grinder or food processor. Brown meat mixture in a large frying pan. Set aside. Using a mallet, mash garlic cloves with parsley. Set aside. In a large pot, melt butter with olive oil. Add mushrooms and onions. Sauté until tender.

Add chopped tomatoes and garlic/parsley mixture. Simmer 10 minutes. Add cooked meat mixture with its meat drippings, canned crushed plum tomatoes, tomato sauce, salt, basil, oregano, bay leaves, and wine. Bring to a boil. Reduce heat and simmer, covered, 1 1/2 hours, stirring occasionally. Correct the seasoning.

Now make the topping sauce. Melt butter in a small saucepan. Add cream and tomato sauce. Heat through. Sprinkle and stir in flour. Set aside. Assemble lasagna: Spoon 3 cups meat sauce evenly into bottom of a 12" x 17" rectangular baking pan. Cover with layer of cooked lasagna noodles. Spread 1 pound ricotta cheese over pasta. Sprinkle with 1/2 cup of the Parmesan cheese. Cover with a second layer of lasagna noodles. Spread evenly with 4 cups of meat sauce. Cover with a third layer of lasagna noodles. Spread with remaining 1 pound ricotta and remaining 1/2 cup Parmesan cheese.

Cover with a fourth layer of lasagna noodles. Spread with 3 cups meat sauce. Spread topping sauce over all. Sprinkle with mozzarella and 1/2 cup Parmesan cheese topping. Cover pan with aluminum foil and bake at 350° for 20 minutes. Remove foil and bake an additional 20 minutes, or until bubbly. Serve with sliced Italian bread. Serves 8.

Spaghetti Sauce with Bread
Rating: G

(This is a wonderful meatless, pesto-type spaghetti sauce created by my Italian brother-in-law, Tim. You may use it for dipping bread, but the magic of the sauce comes together best if served over the special pasta.)

- ¼ c. olive oil
- 2 cloves garlic, mashed
  Scant ¼ lb. fresh basil leaves
- 2¼ t. freshly ground black pepper
- 1 28 oz. can crushed tomatoes with added puree
- 4 lbs. fresh Italian plum tomatoes, sliced thin
- 3 T. butter
- 1 T. salt (or to taste)
- ¼ c. freshly grated Parmesan cheese
- 1 T. sugar
  Sliced Italian bread or the following

Special pasta:
- 1½ lb. large pasta (i.e., rigatoni)
  Salt for pasta water
- ¼ c. olive oil
- 4 medium garlic cloves, mashed
- 5 medium-sized fresh basil leaves, minced
- ¼ t. freshly ground black pepper
- ¼ c. freshly grated Parmesan cheese

In a small saucepan, gently heat olive oil and garlic without browning the garlic. Coarsely chop 5 medium-sized basil leaves and add to warmed oil mixture. Add 1/4 teaspoon of the pepper. Swirl, remove from heat, and set aside.

Pour canned, crushed tomatoes with pureé into food processor with mincing blade. Add 1/8 pound basil leaves and rotate blade until basil is well minced with the tomato puree. Pour oil mixture into a large pot and heat. When sizzling, add tomato/basil mixture. Heat to boiling. Add sliced tomatoes and butter. Sprinkle in salt, remaining pepper, cheese, and sugar. Heat to boiling. Reduce heat to a slow boil and cook 10 minutes, stirring frequently. Crush tomatoes against side of pot with flat side of a large spoon to help break up the slices. Coarsely slice 5 more large basil leaves and add to sauce.

Cook sauce for 40 more minutes at a slow boil, stirring frequently. About 10 minutes before cooking time is over, add 5 small whole basil leaves. Serve over bread or special pasta. Makes about 2 quarts of sauce.

To make special pasta: Cook pasta according to package directions. While pasta cooks, heat oil and garlic together in a small saucepan until warmed. Add minced basil to oil mixture. Set aside. Drain pasta. Return pasta to the pot it cooked in while still hot. Add warmed oil mixture, pepper, and cheese. Gently toss to coat evenly. Serve immediately with sauce.

The Four Seaons

Nutshell

"Apple trees, cheese, wine and bread, and laughter and life itself." That is what Alan Alda as writer, director, and actor is going to show us a slice of in his film, *The Four Seasons*, even if it means serving up twelve loaves of bread and thirteen eggplants to do it. He doesn't waste a frame getting started, either. Before the introductory credits finish rolling, we are bombarded with so much chatter about food that we instantly know one thing for sure: *The Four Seasons* is going to put on a good spread.

Lest we think this is merely a film about folks who use each other's company as an excuse for marathon eating, Alda supplies a story structure as organized as a calendar. He takes three couples to different vacation spots over the course of four seasons, wanting us to recognize the changing "seasons" in friendships and life. The friendships are occasionally seasoned with a mite too much spice, but the meals made and consumed are always a mouth-watering treat.

First there's Jack Burroughs (Alan Alda), the lawyer who's made a science of self-control, and his well-organized *Fortune* magazine editor wife, Kate (Carol Burnett). Then there's Danny Zimmer (Jack Weston), a wealthy dentist, and Claudia (Rita Moreno), his Italian artist wife. Nick Raskin (Len Cariou) is a successful insurance man who's intent on finding a replacement for his flaky wife, Anne (Sandy Dennis). Ginny (Bess Armstrong) is the beautiful young successor to Anne who wants only to be accepted by the group that shows disapproval—or rather jealousy—of her giddy happiness with Nick.

Over the seasons, the couples wine and dine while going at life in a cabin retreat in spring, a sailboat yacht in summer, a college campus in fall, and a ski chalet in winter. During each vacation, they explore to exhaustion their individual personalities, their mutual relationships, and their mid-life crises, which they seem to have bought wholesale. As good as they are at feeding on each other, though, they are even better at feeding their well-developed palates.

Food Scene

In the spring, it's a Chinese dinner. Many who have tried cooking a Chinese meal have subsequently either sold their woks at a garage sale or turned them into planters. Perfectly well-adjusted cooks have been reduced to frantic, uncontrollable tremors trying to execute a full-course Chinese meal, not to mention the debilitating effects of sleeplessness due to pre-meal preparation anxiety. If you're good, you can get the chopping down to under three hours, but the additional hours of organizing, mixing, soaking and stir-frying can cause such a nerve battering that the novice cook may collapse into a bone-benumbed sleep halfway through the meal. Any rave reviews handed out the next morning by happy, satisfied diners hardly seem worth the days of preparation and post-meal convalescence. That's why when we think Chinese, we think take-out.

Fun See (Chinese Cellophane Noodles)
Rating: G

(Fun see, sometimes called cellophane, transparent, or glass noodles, have no distinctive flavor, but add texture and visual appeal to any meal, as well as being exciting to cook. They puff up instantly when plunged into hot oil and therefore require your undivided attention for a few seconds. Primarily used as a garnish by the Chinese, they can also be combined with chopped or shredded meat and vegetables.)

2 c. vegetable oil
1 pkg. cellophane noodles (1 oz.) loosened

Preheat oil in a saucepan to 480°, as Danny suggests, if you want your kitchen filled with hot oil smoke. (If so, change the rating to PG.) Otherwise, use 375° for a G rating. Carefully add noodles and fry 20 seconds on each side. Drain on absorbent towels. Serve with your favorite Chinese meal. Serves 2.

The Four Seasons. A floating summer vacation spot is the setting for Clams Casino.

The Four Seasons. Rita Moreno, left, and Carol Burnett, right, gaze at Sandy Dennis's photographs of vegetables while their husbands cook an elaborate Chinese dinner.

The Four Seasons. "Apple trees, cheese, wine and bread, and laughter and life itself," Alan Alda, center, proselytizes to his friends Sandy Dennis, Len Cariou, Carol Burnett, Rita Moreno, and Jack Weston, as they bask in the warm autumn sun.

Be that as it may, there are still plenty of adventurous cooks who willingly tackle the event, especially if they have help, like the guys in *The Four Seasons.* Collectively, they take two weeks to plan and organize the dinner, but they wind up with two pounds of ginger, one pound of garlic, eight little eggplants from Jack, five salami sized eggplants from Danny, a big wok, a little wok, and a cleaver.

The couples have driven off to Jack and Kate's cabin for a relaxing fall vacation and the Big Dinner. The women sit quietly in the living room sipping wine and admiring Anne's photographs of vegetables, while the men whoop it up in the kitchen. As the air begins to fill with the smoke of hot oil, Danny chokes out instructions. When cooking Chinese food, he says, you must heat the oil to 480°. This is a scientific fact, discovered by Sir Isaac Newton, inventor of mushu pork.

After Jack fries the spectacular "fun see," the merry group digs into their sumptuous feast of white rice, Chinese chicken salad, shrimp, fun see, and Chinese beer. Then the oft-asked question arises: Was it worth it? Nick says that after three hours of shopping for it and four hours of chopping it, he's not only going to eat it, he's going to make love to it!

The couples have barely digested their evening's feast the following day when they're lounging in a large dinghy on a small pond, snacking on wine and cheese and filling nature with talk of more food. "How about Indian food next time? We can make our own mango chutney...fry a little chapati." Or Indonesian. Or Italian.

"Get this," muses Danny, "Homemade pasta, Florentine chicken on a bed of spinach, and a hot antipasto of mussels in Marinara sauce!" These people recite menus as if they were poetry.

Danny keeps the conversation moving at dinnertime with a speech about the misunderstood bean. While they shovel bitefuls of this legume into their mouths, he gives away important bean trivia. If you eat them with rice, he tells them, you never have to eat meat because of their complex set of amino acids!

By their summertime vacation, Nick has replaced Anne with his younger, more attractive girlfriend Ginny. On the sailboat yacht they've rented, it's obvious that they should have stuck to their lakeside dinghy.

Beans
Rating: G

- 1½ c. dried beans
- 6 c. water
- ¼ c. chopped onion
- 2 T. firmly packed brown sugar
- 1 T. dry mustard
- 1 t. salt
- 3 T. catsup
- ½ c. beer
- 1 t. vinegar
- ¼ lb. salt pork cut in 1" cubes

In a saucepan, soak beans in the water overnight. Remove any that float. Bring to a slow boil in the soaking water and simmer 1/2 hour or until tender. Drain, reserving the liquid. Combine beans with remaining ingredients and pour into a greased baker. Cover. Bake at 250° for 6-9 hours. Add bean juice if the mixture begins to dry out. Uncover during last hour of cooking. Serves 4.

In no time the yacht runs aground, making it impossible for the group to make even so much as a peanut butter sandwich in the galley, which is listing heavily to one side. But it's not too much for Nick, wonderboy. With his new girlfriend and newfound carefree approach to life, he not only makes his friends green with envy, but manages to whip up a surprise batch of Clams Casino.

The fall and winter vacations for the three couples offer much smaller portions of culinary triumphs, but this is more than amply compensated by second and third helpings of their complex interpersonal relationships.

In the end critic Judith Crist boiled it all down this way, "The conclusion is that relationships are not easy, concessions and effort must be made because, as Woody Allen's *Annie Hall* made clear, we need the 'eggs.'" (Please read about *Annie Hall*.)

Fried Shrimp
Rating: G

(Use bleached white flour for this, or the batter will be an unattractive grayish color.)

- 12 jumbo shrimp (about 1½ lb.)
- ½ t. garlic juice
- ¼ t. salt
- Vegetable oil for deep frying
- Lettuce

Batter:
- 1½ c. white flour
- ½ t. salt
- 1 T. baking powder
- ½ c. vegetable oil
- 1 c. cold water

Remove shrimp from shells, leaving tails intact. Cut shrimp from the underside almost through to the back, without cutting completely through. Remove veins and wash well. Dry with paper towels.

Lay shrimp split side up on a plate. Rub each with a little garlic juice. Sprinkle each with a little salt. Set aside. Mix flour, salt, and baking powder together in a mixing bowl. Add oil gradually, stirring until ingredients form a ball and leave the sides of the bowl. Add water gradually, stirring until dough has the consistency of pancake batter. (The less water you add, the thicker the crust will be.) Heat oil in a deep fryer or wok to 350°–360°.

Holding a shrimp by the tail, dip into the batter. Carefully place into the hot oil, one at a time. Fry a few at a time for at least 1 minute or until golden brown. Remove with a slotted spoon.

Drain on absorbent towels. Serve on a plate of lettuce leaves. (You may keep the shrimp warm in a 180° oven for about a half hour without sacrificing its crispiness.) Serves 4.

Chinese White Rice
Rating: G

- 3 c. Chinese rice
- 3 c. cold water

Wash rice in a pan of water and rinse until clear. Drain. Place rice and water in a saucepan and let stand 30 minutes. Bring to boiling over high heat and let boil 1 minute. Cover, reduce heat, and simmer 20 minutes, being sure not to open lid while cooking. Remove from heat and let stand, covered, for 10 more minutes (without lifting the lid). Serves 6.

Chinese Chicken Salad
Rating: G

- 1½ c. celery, shredded
- 2 c. cooked chicken, shredded
- 1½ cucumbers, shredded
- 1 scallion, minced
- ½ t. mashed ginger
- 4 t. vegetable oil
- 1 t. sugar
- 1 T. wine vinegar
- 1 t. sesame oil
- 3 T. light soy sauce

Blanch shredded celery in boiling water for 1 minute. Rinse with cold water. Mix minced scallion with ginger in a bowl. Add remaining ingredients and stir well. Chill. Serve alone or on lettuce leaves. Serves 4.

Clams Casino
Rating: G

(This is a wonderful contribution from my father who, as another proponent of eyeball cooking, is dubious that this painstakingly measured recipe will work. [We tried it though, and it does.] He'd rather have turned you loose with a suggested list of ingredients—the minimum requirements being clams, bacon, and green pepper.)

- 2 c. minced clams
- 4 slices bacon, cooked and finely crumbled
- ¼ green pepper, finely chopped
- 2 cloves garlic, mashed
- 1 c. seasoned bread crumbs
- 2 T. grated Parmesan cheese
- Paprika

Combine all ingredients (except paprika) in a bowl. Generously fill a dozen empty large clam or quahog shells with the mixture and sprinkle with paprika. Bake at 350° for about 20 minutes, or until done. Serves 4.

Frenzy

Nutshell

When asked why he made *Frenzy*, Alfred Hitchcock said, "I always wanted to make a film about potatoes." *Frenzy* is Hitchcock's potato film. Five years earlier, in 1968 when shooting a scene in *Torn Curtain* in which a man is brutally murdered with garden tools, Hitchcock is reported to have said that he was going to make a film someday in which vegetables were prominently featured. *Frenzy* is not only about vegetables, it's a film filled with all manner of food in both starring and cameo roles.

On one level, *Frenzy* is about the search for a sexual psychopath—the "wrong man" plot that served Hitchcock so well over the years. The story is set in London's bustling wholesale vegetable and produce market, Covent Garden. A politician's public promise to clean up the Thames of industrial waste is interrupted when a nude woman is found floating head-first in said river, a necktie wrapped around her neck. "Another necktie murder!" cries the assembled crowd. And the story is off and running.

Richard Blaney (Jon Finch), the wrong man, is an ill-tempered, down-and-out former R.A.F. squadron leader who's resentful of the fact that his life is going nowhere. He's out on the town in a generally foul mood after losing his bartending job in an argument with his boss, Forsythe (Bernard Cribbins), who's jealous of Blaney's relationship with barmaid Babs (Anna Massey). In his angered, self-pitying state, Blaney refuses help from his friend Robert Rusk (Barry Foster), a good-natured fruit vendor, and spends his last money on a drink rather than a horse Rusk tipped him on, which comes in to win at twenty to one. He then visits his ex-wife Brenda (Barbara Leigh-Hunt) at her successful matrimonial agency and vents his hostility at the world to her and within earshot of her secretary. Later, when Brenda is found as the necktie killer's most recent victim, Blaney emerges as the number-one suspect.

Unlike many murder mysteries, Hitchcock introduces the real killer early on. It's Rusk, Blaney's friendly, local fruit vendor who's losing his ties around the necks of young women. When the sexually deviant Rusk fails to enlist Brenda's help in landing a mate for himself, he rapes and strangles her too. Before leaving the scene, Rusk finishes off his victim's half-eaten apple and picks his teeth clean with a lapel pin.

With Scotland Yard Inspector Oxford (Alec McCowen) hot on his trail, Blaney finds temporary asylum with a former R.A.F. comrade and his unsympathetic wife, but gets turned out when Babs turns up as the necktie killer's next victim. Rusk had disposed of her body in the back of a potato truck, but after discovering that his lapel pin is missing, he climbs back into the truck and engages in a hilariously macabre wrestling match with Bab's corpse as he tries to free the lapel pin from her clenched, stiffened fist. (To conceal the corpse's more private parts, Hitchcock had a bikini made out of potatoes strapped onto the body.)

Cailles Aux Raisins (Quail with Grapes)
Rating: G

- 6 fresh quail, cleaned and dressed
- Salt, pepper
- 6 dozen peeled white grapes
- Butter for rubbing
- 6 preserved (jarred) grape leaves
- Salt pork
- 4 T. butter, melted
- ½ c. dry white wine
- 1 c. rich veal or chicken stock
- Bunch grapes (for garnish)

Rub inside of birds with salt and pepper. Stuff each with 6 grapes. Truss neck opening closed and legs close to the body using a needle and thread. Rub outsides with butter. Sprinkle with salt and pepper. Wrap each bird in a grape leaf. Secure leaves with thin slices of salt pork.

Roast birds, breast side up, in a roasting pan with 4 tablespoons melted butter for 15-20 minutes at 400° or until tender and done. Remove to a heated platter. Discard trussing thread and keep warm. Pour off all fat from roasting pan.

Pour wine into pan and cook over medium heat until reduced to 1/4 cup, scraping the pan thoroughly and often. Add stock and bring to a boil. Add remaining 3 dozen grapes and heat gently without boiling. Correct the seasoning with salt and pepper.

Pour sauce over the quail, arranging the heated grapes around each bird. Garnish with small grape bunches. Serves 6.

Rusk escapes his close call, of course, and Blaney is finally captured, tried, and sentenced for the necktie murders. But Oxford, the acerbic chief inspector who had been piecing together the case while enduring his wife's (Vivien Merchant) experiments in gourmet cuisine, remains unsettled enough about his findings to reopen the investigation. New clues link Rusk to the last murder victim and convince Oxford that they've sent the wrong man to prison. When he learns of Blaney's escape, he immediately heads for Rusk's apartment, where he catches the real murderer tieless and red-handed, preparing to dispose of yet another victim.

Food Scene

The food scenes in *Frenzy* inspired some of the finest comic moments Hitchcock ever committed to film. Two of the best involve Chief Inspector Oxford, who quietly suffers his wife's attempts to become a gourmet cook. Through her efforts, Hitchcock puts the "gore" back in gourmet.

Oxford is nearing acute starvation at home, where his wife's hâute cuisine includes breakfasts of coffee with floating bits of boiling milk and sweet buns half full of air. To compensate, he eagerly rips into fried eggs, sausages, ham, and toast at the office while denouncing his wife's unfortunate enrollment in the Continental School of Gourmet Cooking.

At home, the chirrupy Mrs. Oxford greets him by proudly presenting more hideous continental concoctions. One night he comes home to a table elaborately set with candles, flowers, and formal place settings. As he sits down and launches into a discourse on the necktie murder case, Mrs. Oxford sets before him a bowl of soupe de poissons. She then putters off to the kitchen, encouraging him to continue talking, while he begins his own investigation into the soup. He sniffs and shudders at the sight of a small, black fish head, mouth agape and eyes bulging (not unlike the bobbing eyeball soup served in *Indiana Jones and the Temple of Doom*). His next scoop reveals the unrecognizeable, mangled remains of another piscine creature. What could these mysterious ingredients be, he asks with guarded curiosity, to which she grandly replies—conger eel, smelts, ling, John Dory, pilcher and frog fish.

Despairing of ever finding anything edible at home again, he ventures a few sips of broth. He's encountered autopsies with more relish. He pours the soup back into the tureen just before her arrival with the next course—one that she promises will be less filling—cailles aux raisins. Carefully, she places one miniscule bird and two grapes on his plate and, having been attentive to her husband's running dissertation on the case, says he's wrong about Blaney.

Blaney, of course, is sent to jail in spite of Mrs. Oxford's intuitions, and the inspector is consigned to his fate at her dinner table. Again, he sifts and weighs the facts of the case aloud to his wife in order to avoid the feast set before him. This time it's pied de porc á la mode de Caens (pig's trotter in heavy sauce). She's prepared the feet in the same sauce the French use for tripe, she boasts. They continue to discuss the grisly details of the case (complete with visual puns—she snapping a bread stick as he tells her how the killer broke the fingers on the corpse), and he launches into his equally grisly meal. Putting his full weight behind knife and fork, he manages to separate the slippery foot and find one tiny morsel of meat. He politely tries to chew his prize, but gives up when he hits bone. Just then, the doorbell rings.

At the door is Sergeant Spearman (Michael Bates), who's come with news about the potato dust that will clear Blaney (a delightful Hitchcockian conceit), but he, too, is unable to escape Mrs. Oxford's best intentions. She brings him a novel drink made of tequila, triple sec, and

Soupe de Poissons (Fish Soup)
Rating: G

(You may use a wide assortment of fresh and/or salt water fish for this soup, which is really thick enough to be a stew. Mrs. Oxford used such fascinating Neptunian creatures as John Dory, conger eel, ling, smelts and frog fish, but lacking those, you can substitute just about any other type, from carp and perch to halibut and squid. If your selections require tenderizing or special cleaning, please do so before they enter the broth. The trick is in choosing fish that take about the same amount of time to cook or pre-cooking those that require more time.)

1 lg. onion
2 cloves garlic, mashed
3 T. butter
2 T. chopped celery leaves
1 bay leaf
2 T. minced parsley
1 sprig fresh dill (or ½ t. dried)
  Pinch cinnamon
  Pinch nutmeg
  Salt, freshly ground black pepper
2 c. dry white wine
1 jigger brandy
½ lb. whole button mushrooms
1 dozen small onions, peeled and boiled
  Butter
2 lbs. fish, whole if small, or cut in thick slices

In a saucepan, sauté onion and garlic in the butter. Add celery leaves, bay leaf, parsley, dill, spices, salt and pepper to taste, and wine. Bring to a boil. Light the brandy with a match and add to the broth. Simmer 30 minutes.

Lightly brown the boiled onions and button mushrooms in butter while broth cooks. Set aside. Strain broth and return to cleaned pot. Add fish, onions, and mushrooms. Simmer for 10 minutes or until all fish is cooked through. Serves 4-6.

fresh lemon juice, all served in a rim-salted glass—a margarita (as foreign to the British as the guacamole is to Michael Caine's character in *California Suite*). Spearman no sooner has his obligatory sip than he's off to turn in the evidence, leaving Mrs. Oxford with her own brand of domestic crime and Mr. Oxford the eternal gastronomic victim.

Frenzy. Vivien Merchant introduces margaritas to Scotland Yard's Alec McCowen, center, and Michael Bates.

Margarita
Rating: G

- ¾ c. cracked ice
- 5 jiggers tequila
- ½ jigger triple sec
- 2½ jiggers lemon juice
- Lemon rind
- Coarse salt

Stir ice, tequila, triple sec, and lemon juice in a small pitcher. Moisten rims of 2 shallow wine glasses with lemon rind, then dip rims in salt. Fill glasses and serve. Serves 2.

Pied de Porc á la Mode de Caens
(Pigs Feet in French Tripe Sauce)
Rating: G

- 6 pig's feet
- Baking soda
- Boiling water
- Salt
- ½ c. chopped carrots
- ½ c. chopped celery
- ¼ c. chopped green pepper
- 1 bay leaf
- ½ t. thyme
- ½ t. whole peppercorns
- 6 fresh parsley sprigs
- 1 c. white wine vinegar
- 1 c. dry white wine

Tripe sauce:
- 1½ lbs. fresh tripe, cut in 2" strips
- 1 c. beef broth
- 1 c. dry white wine
- 2 T. capers
- 2 thin slices peeled lemon (seeds removed)
- ½ t. marjoram
- 4 sprigs fresh parsley
- Salt, pepper
- Dash cayenne
- 3 egg yolks
- Dash nutmeg

Scrub pig's feet thoroughly while soaking them in several changes of cold water, adding baking soda to the last change at the rate of 1 teaspoon per gallon. Drain and dry with absorbent towels. Place in a large pot, cover with boiling water, and salt to taste.

Bring to a boil and boil for 4 minutes. Reduce heat and simmer 2 hours, removing scum as it collects on the surface. Add carrots, celery, green pepper, bay leaf, thyme, peppercorns, and parsley. Bring to a boil and cook for 20 minutes, or until reduced to 1/2 of its original volume. Add wine vinegar and white wine. Bring to a boil again. Reduce heat, cover, and simmer gently for 2 hours. (Keep warm in the broth until ready to serve.) Meanwhile, prepare the tripe sauce.

Combine tripe strips, broth, wine, capers, lemon slices, marjoram, and parsley in a stewpot. Cook for 3 hours, or until tripe is tender. Remove tripe and strain liquid. Return liquid to the pot and reduce to 1 generous cup by boiling. Add salt and pepper to taste and a dash of cayenne. Beat yolks with nutmeg and gradually add to boiling liquid, stirring briskly and constantly with a wire whip. Cook until slightly thickened. (The tripe may be served with this sauce or fried and served separately. This recipe makes about 1 cup of sauce. If more is desired, simply double ingredients.) Pour sauce over pig's feet and serve immediately. Serves 4-6.

The Godfather

Nutshell

One of the most fascinating and authentic portrayals of the Italian subculture in America comes to us in Francis Ford Coppola's *The Godfather*. Coppola attains remarkable authenticity in his adaptation of Mario Puzo's novel by paying attention to details—aided, no doubt, by his own Italian-American heritage, which enabled him to show the uniqueness of these people down to the subtleties in the way they talk, kiss, and even eat their food.

To be Italian is to be reverent of good food. This singular characteristic is apparent in the film time and again in such events as the opening wedding scene, where even traditional bridal cookies are passed out to guests. Later, mob leaders meet to discuss family business around a table of grapes and wine, and a mobster rescues a box of cannoli from the back seat of a car in which he's just killed another gang member. Perhaps the most memorable is when Clemenza (Richard Castellano) delivers a soliloqy on how to make spaghetti sauce, in spite of his gang family being in the midst of a mob siege.

The Godfather immerses us in the saga of the Corleones, a New York Mafia family engaged in ongoing territorial disputes with rival families. Murder is SOP—standard operating procedure—and the men conduct family business by both day and night in darkened rooms. The family offers protection to its members in exchange for their unfailing loyalty and obedience, but ultimately it's a thin shield against the incessantly violent world they've created for themselves.

The screen story of the Corleones begins innocently enough with the wedding of aging Cosa Nostra chieftan Don Vito Corleone's (Marlon Brando) daughter Connie (Talia Shire) to Carlo Rizzi (Gianni Ruzzo). But even during the wedding, the Don conducts business by meeting with beseeching guests in his shadowy office and doling out lethal favors as easily as his daughter passes out wedding cookies.

Mafia life, however, is not a bowl of cherries. Following a series of brutal attacks instigated by new underworld operators seeking to undercut the Corleones' power, Don Corleone is critically wounded. His gang holes up in his mansion for a long siege, while his life and mob control hang in the balance. The attack on his father and the ambush murder of his older brother Sonny (James Caan) eventually lures the youngest Corleone, Michael (Al Pacino) off his straight and narrow Ivy League path and into the family inner circle, where he soon assumes control, leading the family in a bloody counterattack on its various enemies and successfully avenging his father and brother.

The Godfather. Another day at the office, as typical business meetings are conducted over fruit and wine.

Food Scene

During the siege at the Don's estate, Clemenza is faced with responsibility for having to cook for a houseful of mobsters. With murder and mayhem swirling about him, Clemenza calmly takes time to instruct young Michael on his own personal secrets for cooking up a real Sicilian spaghetti sauce. Although preoccupied with his father's medical condition, Michael politely listens as Clemenza stands over a hot stove, pours his ingredients into a big pot and explains, "You start with a little bit of oil. Fry some garlic. Throw in some tomatoes. Fry it up. (Make sure it doesn't stick.) Get it all to a boil. Shove in all your sausage and meatballs. Add a little bit of wine and a little bit of sugar. And that's my trick!" If you're Italian, measurements like "a little bit of this, a pinch of that, throw in some of those," and "a handful of these" might mean something to you. Maybe there's some kind of ethnic secret code here, and you can do better at interpreting such directions than those of us cursed with a kitchen full of measuring cups. If you need more specific instructions, however, the sauce recipe that follows is a version that Kay (Diane Keaton), Michael's innocent, blonde-haired WASPy wife from New Hampshire might have made. Since I'm also sort of an innocent, blonde-haired WASP from New Hampshire married to a Sicilian, I'd guess that Kay probably prepares her sauce as I do—with intimidation (after all, we are cooking for Sicilians!) and with measurements.

Kay's Spaghetti Sauce
Rating: G

1 lb. Italian sausages

Meatballs:

2 slices white bread, crusts removed
1 lb. twice ground lean beef
1 c. parsley sprigs, minced
2-3 garlic cloves, minced
¼ t. salt
⅛ t. pepper

Sauce:

¼ c. olive oil
1 medium onion, chopped
¾ c. parsley sprigs, minced
3 cloves garlic, mashed
1 6 oz. can tomato paste
2 28 oz. cans crushed, peeled, Italian tomatoes
1 bay leaf
1½ t. crushed oregano leaves
1½ t. salt
½ c. dry red Italian wine

Brown sausages in frying pan. Drench bread in water. Place wet bread in bowl with ground beef. Using a mallet, mash the 1 cup minced parsley sprigs with the 2-3 cloves of garlic. Add to the beef mixture. Add the salt and pepper. Mix thoroughly (use your hands or a food processor) and shape into meatballs, using an ice cream scoop.

When sausages are done, remove from pan, cover and keep warm. In the same sausage pan, brown meatballs thoroughly (pour off some fat if necessary). While meatballs cook, start the sauce. Heat olive oil in a large pot. Add onion and cook until transparent. Mash the minced 3/4 cup parsley sprigs with the garlic as before. Add to the onions. Heat through for one minute. Add and stir in the remaining ingredients, the sausages, and meatballs. (Add a little meat fat for extra flavor if desired and skim off later before serving.) Bring to a boil, reduce heat, cover, and simmer for 3 hours, stirring occasionally. Add more wine if sauce gets too thick. Correct seasoning. Serve over your favorite pasta. Serves 4-6.

The Godfather. While his adversaries Sterling Hayden, center, and Al Lettieri, right, consider dinner entrées, Al Pacino plans, then executes their fiery final course.

The Loved One

Nutshell

One of Tony Richardson's specialties as a director is using food as sex (as he did in *Tom Jones*), and his food scenes in *The Loved One* are no exception. He even surpasses himself here by reaching new heights in grotesque "orgiastic gourmandism." While critics debated whether or not the film delivered on its tagline, "The motion picture to offend everyone," one point is indisputable: the eating performed by Ayllene Gibbons as Mrs. Joyboy sets a standard for all-out grotesquerie.

Exaggerated eating scenes were hardly the centerpiece of the Evelyn Waugh novel that inspired this movie. *The Loved One* is essentially about burials and moviemaking. During English novelist Waugh's stay in Hollywood to script his book *Brideshead Revisited*, he was inspired to write a short novel about the last shreds of the British Empire in the American film industry, which would include his observations on "tinsel town's" garish cemeteries. To Waugh, these businesses seemed curiously linked in their lavish, grandiose productions. The resulting story, adapted by Hollywood film-makers as a knowing satire on their own world, is a grim-themed farce that's humor ranges wildly from the blackest black to the hilariously slapstick.

To recount, an English ne'er-do-well, renegade poet, Dennis Barlow (Robert Morse), arrives in Hollywood seeking his fortune. He no sooner takes up residency with an uncle who is employed as an artist in the film industry than he is arranging for the uncle's funeral at the local cemetery—a poshly elaborate burial ground named Whispering Glades. Barlow is overwhelmed by the rococo-style profusion of statues and monuments and gauche amenities such as a gift shop, wedding chapel, talking statue, and Xanadu waterfalls.

Mr. Starker (Liberace), an unctuous casket salesman who shows smug disdain to anyone who buys in the "middle price range," successfully convinces Dennis to purchase a higher-priced, soundproof, waterproof, moistureproof, satin- and silk-lined box for his uncle.

His tour of the grounds is led by devoted Whispering Glades cosmetician, Aimee Thanatogenos (Anjanette Comer), whose beauty immediately inspires Dennis to try to win her affections by taking a job at the cemetery's dead pet division known as Happy Hunting Grounds and reading her love poems during breaks. But Aimee is also being pursued by the cemetery's embalmer, Mr. Joyboy (Rod Steiger), who tapes love notes to her on passing corpses.

Eventually, Aimee is disillusioned by these romantic advances, discovering that Dennis is a fraudulent poet and Joyboy is thoroughly repugnant. She also discovers that the cemetery's founding father, the Reverend Wilbur Glenworthy (Jonathan Winters), whom she worships, is nothing more than a sanctimonious lecher, and her disillusionment grows to mortal confusion. When the guru newspaper columnist who's been giving her advice is revealed as a drunken bum who can't counsel

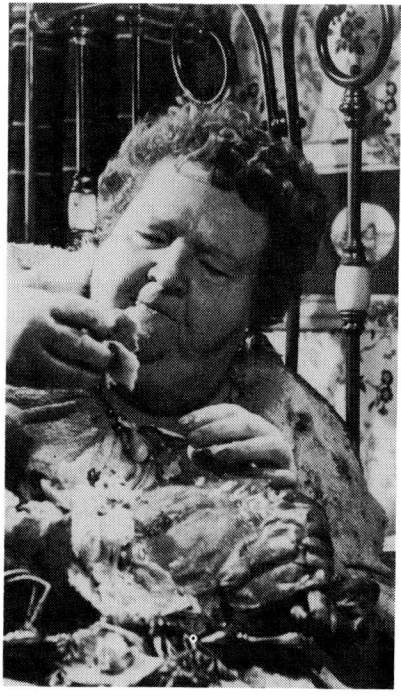

The Loved One. Ayllene Gibbons with a mother of an appetite.

her when she needs it most, Aimee retreats to the everlasting peace she has painted on so many faces by injecting herself with embalming fluid.

Meanwhile, the Blessed Reverend has been scheming to get out of the cemetery business by...ahem...turning the grounds into a senior citizens' city, the advantage being a "brisk turnover" and better use of the limited land. His immediate problem of disinterment is solved when he discovers that a brainy kid and the employees of his Happy Hunting Ground have built a rocket capable of launching bodies into orbit. With the blessings of the Air Force and with great pomp and ceremony, he inaugurates his new plan by propelling the first dead "resident" into space. There, the loved one will float forever in a blissful "orbit of eternal grace."

Food Scene

Aimee is a sweetly naive romantic whose first date with the plump, effeminate Mr. Joyboy is not exactly the stuff of a Harlequin Romance. She'd have been better off staying home to organize her spice rack.

He invites her for a home-cooked dinner with his mother, who turns out to be an obese bedroom recluse. Joyboy dons an apron and prepares roast suckling pig, serving it in his mother's bed like the true swine he is. Together, the Joyboys savagely maul the suckling's body, lustfully grabbing at legs and body parts and reveling in the grease that smears their hands and face, while the demure Ms. Thanatogenos stares in wide-eyed horror at the spectacle.

Aimee's disillusionment over the Joyboys' eating habits, however, is just the beginning of her nightmare. She also discovers that Dennis has been reading fraudulent love poems to her—a sham she finds worse than Joyboy's bad (or in this case bed) table manners. She flees Dennis's embrace and races to Joyboy for consolation, but when she arrives at his house again, she is greeted instead by the ever-eating Mrs. Joyboy, now engaged in an energetic attempt to finish off the contents of the refrigerator.

Mrs. Joyboy tosses food out of the icebox for Aimee to hold, ignoring the girl's urgent questioning about her son's whereabouts. Panicked by the sound of Dennis's arrival, Aimee drops the food and flees.

Dennis enters the kitchen to find Mrs. Joyboy tugging at a turkey carcass wedged between the refrigerator shelves. Grunting and groaning, she plants her foot on the shelves for better leverage and manages not only to free the bird, but also bring the entire refrigerator down on top of her enormous, gelatinous body. Seeing this woman completely covered with food *and* a major appliance, Dennis rushes to her assistance, but the only help she wants is in finding the cranberry sauce for her drumstick.

Roast Suckling Pig
Rating: G

12-15 lb. suckling pig
2½-3 qts. pork stuffing (optional)
1 garlic clove, cut in half
Softened butter
1 medium red apple
1 can whole cranberries
Watercress or parsley

Clean and dress the pig, removing eyeballs and closing eyelids. Fill with dressing if desired. Sew cavity closed to prevent drying out. Secure legs by skewering front legs in a forward position, hind legs in a crouched position. Insert block of wood in mouth.

Rub entire body with cut garlic and softened butter. Cover ears and tail with aluminum foil to prevent burning. Roast in roasting pan, uncovered, at 450° for 15 minutes. Reduce heat to 325° and continue roasting until tender, allowing 30 minutes to the pound for estimating total cooking time. To prevent drying out, baste every 15-20 minutes with pan drippings.

To serve, remove stuffing, set aside, and keep warm. Unskewer legs and remove foil and wood. Fill eye cavities with as many cranberries as they will hold and insert apple in mouth. Place on a decorative platter in a bed of watercress or parsley. (You may also garnish with baked apples or yams.) Eat bare-handed directly from the platter. Serves 6-8.

My Dinner with André

Nutshell

My Dinner with André is a "tale of two talkers." Two old theater acquaintances meet in a posh French restaurant and engage in one hundred minutes of nonstop dinner conversation about their lives, art, theater, and other mysteries, while dining over a three-course dinner. In theory, this could be a grandiose eating scene, but the kind of nourishment that passes between their lips is strictly food for thought.

Wally (Wallace Shawn) narrates the opening sequences and explains that he's been invited to meet his old friend André (André Gregory), whom he hasn't seen in years. Both have been living on their various levels of achievements (or frustrations) in the theater, and while Wally is looking forward to the reunion, he's also not at all sure why it's taking place. André has developed considerable notoriety for himself as an innovative theater director, but Wally is still a struggling writer/actor.

No sooner do they meet than they're seated and engaged in riveting conversation, taking only seconds out of their dialogue to order dinner. The talkfest centers on André's personal account of his search for himself and the meaning of existence. His self-indulgent quest, he explains, took him halfway around the world—to the forests of Poland, the arid sands of the Sahara, the heaths of Scotland, the mountains of India and Tibet, and finally to a Long Island estate backyard.

As a writer, words are Wally's business, although he hardly gets more than a "golly" or a "wow" in between André's stream of consciousness monologue. Fascinating as it is, they eventually enter into a more balanced dialogue, and we are privy to two very distinct views of life.

Both being thinking men, yet physical and philosophical opposites, their individual contributions to the converstion bear equal merit. Wally, the voice of self-assured wisdom, is apparently content in his orderly life, while André seeks the mystical, the extraordinary, and finds fulfillment in the extremes of his theater art.

As much as they are opposites, though, they both share inconsistencies that complicate any notions they may have in summing up what's what in life. Wally is the "raging beast" in stage performances, but is saddled with an exterior life as a comparatively bland human being whose ultimate contribution as a dilettante will mostly go unnoticed. He worries about money when he would rather be obsessed with art, but finds happiness in the small comforts of life, like his electric blanket and time with his girl friend Debby. André searches for magic in order to survive the harshness and chaos of life, and he plays the "tailored aesthetic" who never has to worry about money. He admits, though, that his escapades have led him to no loftier ideals, and that he, too, finds great comfort in the more familiar confines of his home and family. Although Wally believes that one can find himself at the corner cigar store as easily as on top of Mt. Everest, they both agree on the overriding need for people to reach out to each other.

Peppered Quail
Rating: G

4 medium onions
Red wine
4 plump young quail, dressed
¼ c. (or more) melted bacon fat
Coarsely ground black pepper
Curry powder

In a saucepan, cover onions with water and boil for 1 hour. Drain. Cover with red wine and soak overnight. Stuff each bird with a wine-soaked onion. Dip quail in melted bacon fat. Mix equal parts pepper and curry. Rub birds liberally with mixture. Broil until tender and browned (time will depend on size of bird, anywhere from 12-20 minutes, but turn birds frequently and avoid overcooking). Sprinkle with a little more pepper/curry before serving. Serves 4.

My Dinner with André. Wally Shawn, left, and André Gregory engage in meaty conversation while waiting for a dinner of quail to fill their empty plates.

Food Scene

Under the direction of Louis Malle, *My Dinner with André* was shot in just sixteen days in the ballroom of an old hotel in Richmond, Virginia, that had just closed down. The immense, unheated room, decorated like a posh French restaurant for the film, posed an additional hardship on the actors when their hot cooked gourmet dinner of quail cooled to the temperature of chicken salad and looked mostly like a couple of shriveled Cock Robins. Wally gazes ruefully at his order, probably wishing André's magic could turn the bird into a plate of burger and fries, while André, ever searching, will always prefer the type of soul food you can't put on a plate.

Neighbors

Nutshell

It takes less than twenty-four hours for Earl Keese (John Belushi) to lose it all in John Avildsen's *Neighbors*—his house, car, checkbook, and family—even his dinner and breakfast. But in the end, he loves losing it all.

This is an off-center picture that tells the story of a man who gets taken for a ride, both really and figuratively, never to return. Keese is an upper-middle-class schmoo whose tapioca life revolves around a Manhattan white-collar job by day and evenings in front of the TV with his wife Enid (Kathryn Walker). For her part, Enid is both bored and boring, the sum of her life being measured in two minute recipes for capon clipped from the morning paper and dinners of frozen waffles for Earl.

One night, their tranquil rut is interrupted forever when new neighbors come calling. Enid welcomes the couple as a breath of fresh air, but Earl sees them as lewd con-artists who are out for all they can get. Within minutes of introductions, the fast-talking Vic (Dan Aykroyd) borrows Earl's car, takes his money, and makes passes at his wife, while the vampish Ramona (Cathy Moriarty) alternately propositions Earl and accuses him of rape. Life as Earl once knew it is over.

With mounting suspicion about Vic and Ramona, Earl decides to investigate to see if Vic's car really does have brake problems. He removes a block from under a tire, and the car rolls uncontrollably into a nearby swamp. Ramona tells Earl she'll accept blackmail money from him if he wants her to keep quiet about his trashing of Vic's souped-up car, but, she explains casually, Vic is going to be irritated because Baby was in it. "Baby," Earl learns after a frantic plunge into the swamp, is Vic's model airplane, which Earl just manages to salvage after a life-and-death struggle in quicksand.

Earl's daughter Elaine (Lauren-Marie Taylor) arrives home after being thrown out of school for stealing, and revives the party with a display of edible underwear that comes in flavors of banana, peach, mint and, naturally, cherry. One crazy thing follows another. Vic goes up on his roof dressed in wetsuit and helmet and starts taking potshots at Earl. When they try to reconcile differences in Vic's kitchen over instant coffee, tension erupts over a dirty coffee cup and Vic's insults about Elaine. At daybreak, Ramona's promise to Earl of an intimate breakfast for two proves to be just another tease to hold him over until Vic and the girls show up with Chinese food.

Eventually—unbelievably—everything gets sorted out. Vic's car gets hauled out of the swamp; his remote-control plane crashes and sets fire to the house he and Ramona never really bought; Elaine's name is cleared of the theft charges and she rushes back to school; and Enid splits with a macho Indian for an emergency meeting of her Native American studies.

Neighbors. Dan Aykroyd feigns innocence as he holds up a jar of his Aunt Minota's secret, sacred spaghetti sauce that he's used to make an Italian takeout dinner.

Taken-for Takeout Dinner
Rating: PG

- 1 set gullible neighbors
- 1 lb. spaghetti, cooked
- 1 large jar prepared spaghetti sauce, heated
- 1 loaf garlic bread
- 1 green tossed salad with bottled dressing
- 1 gallon red jug Chianti

Talk neighbors into giving you their car keys and money for a restaurant take-out dinner. Drive their car to your house and assemble above dishes at home from ingredients on hand. Take prepared dinner back to neighbors' house, crack bad jokes, and make them feel grateful for your efforts. Serves 4.

In the light of day, Earl sees Vic and Ramona as just fun-loving folks, with perfectly acceptable explanations for their behavior—so acceptable, in fact, that he decides to join them in their madcap adventures and leave his humdrum life forever. Making the break with old world values is as easy as smashing his TV, which he does, causing *his* house to go up in a blaze too. The merry trio then blasts off on their romp to who knows where.

Food Scene

Vic and Ramona are absolutely gonzo-shysters who immediately take the Keeses' lives by storm. They don't bother with the traditional icebreakers, such as borrowing sugar or meeting for cocktails. Vic's first deed is to extort Earl's car keys and $32 for an Italian takeout dinner for the four of them. Initially Earl actually works up excitement over the food Vic says he'll bring back from the fabulous new Italian restaurant—ravioli, stuffed clams, scampi with plenty of garlic. But minutes later, when Earl discovers Ramona in his bed and Vic pawing through his checkbook, his suspicions are confirmed. His new neighbors are nuts.

Worried about his investment in the meal, Earl spies on Vic when he leaves for the restaurant and sees him merely drive next door to his house. Through a window, he watches Vic heat up a jar of store-bought spaghetti sauce while dancing to the tunes of The Doors. To make matters worse, when he gets home, he catches Enid throwing steaks out the back door to Vic's dog, an act of altruism he finds especially annoying since she's been feeding him frozen waffles for dinner.

Chef Vic arrives back at the Keeses' with Chianti, salad, garlic bread, and the "homemade" spaghetti. "Let's dig into this stuff before the sauce turns into penicillin!" he jokes. Conversation at the dinner table is hardly as stale as Vic's humor, what with Ramona's charging Earl with attempted rape and Vic's lewd, nonstop verbal patter.

Earl tries to get the upper hand by confronting Vic about the truth of their meal. But Vic's slick confession instead makes *Earl* look like the heel for not appreciating Vic's trouble in heating up a jar of his Aunt Minota's secret, sacred spaghetti sauce. After all, Earl learns later, it's the *fun* in getting taken for takeout that counts.

Neighbors (left to right). Daughter Lauren-Marie Taylor, wife Kathryn Walker, and neighbor Cathy Moriarty are amused by Dan Aykroyd's mouth-watering description of Lauren-Marie's edible underpants, while the father of the daughter who wears them, John Belushi, is not.

Neighbors. After a full night of wild practical jokes, breakfast for the suburbanites is a Chinese takeout dinner.

Neighbors. Belushi shows the crowded living conditions in the coffee cup his neighbor's offered him.

The Odd Couple

Nutshell

In the beginning there was dirt and dust and cigar butts and moldy sandwiches and litters of smelly laundry. And then, enveloped in a mist of aerosol room fresheners, Felix came and vacuumed, dusted, ironed, cooked gourmet meals, and said, "It is good."

Walter Matthau wears the pants and Jack Lemmon sports an apron in this comedy of mismatched fratrimony. As two marriage-on-the-rocks bachelor roommates, their domestic habits mix like caustic oil and water, which eventually leads to a burning meat loaf and a flying plate of linguine.

When the slovenly, cigar-chomping sportswriter Oscar Madison (Walter Matthau) takes pity on his suicidal pal, TV newswriter Felix Unger (Jack Lemmon), and invites him to take up residence in his bachelor pad, he quickly learns that the only thing they have in common is separation from their wives. Oscar loves to live like a slob and continues to do so, while Felix follows him like an investigator from *Good Housekeeping*.

Felix's incessant housecleaning soon takes all the fun out of Oscar's carefree messmaking, and the two fall into the squabbles of a typically ill-suited couple. Try as they might to find compatible ground, Felix invariably winds up sounding like a fishwife, while Oscar responds as the harried husband.

Among other things, Felix breaks up Oscar's beloved poker game with his incessant tidying up. He displays more ailments than there are symptoms known to man, and his cooking, crying, moose calls, and little "we are out of corn flakes" notes, together with Oscar's active disregard for the basic rules of sanitation, make it impossible for either one of them to really "clear the air," aerosol or otherwise. They wind up separated once again, but managing to part as friends and a little wiser for the wear.

Food Scene

Never let it be said that the neatness-obsessed Felix is not without his good qualities. The guy really knows his way around the kitchen, but even that somehow manages to get the best of him. It first costs him his marriage, when he shows up his wife's homemaking skills, and then exasperates his best friend into throwing him out too. (Many of us tougher breeds, though, could easily withstand the rigors of full-time domestic help.)

To the total distraction of Oscar's poker group, Felix serves them mixed drinks on coasters, and BLT's on crustless pumpernickel toast—only using the soft part of the lettuce! Instead of killing Felix with his bare hands, Oscar decides instead to try to change this freak of nature by getting him into "something soft"—like upstair tenants Cecily and Gwendolyn Pigeon (Monica Evans and Carole Shelley).

Meat Loaf
Rating: R

- 1 lb. gound beef
- ½ lb. ground veal
- ½ lb. ground pork (lean)
- 1 c. chopped parsley
- ¼ c. minced onion
- ¼ c. sliced green onion
- 1 T. dried basil
- 1½ t. salt
- ½ t. pepper
- 2 eggs
- ½ c. bread crumbs
- Bacon slices to cover

Place all the ingredients (except the bacon) in a large mixing bowl. Using your hands, lightly but thoroughly mix together. Shape into an oval loaf and place in a foil-lined baking dish. Cover with bacon slices. Bake at 350° for hours, until smoking and burned. Intended to serve 4.

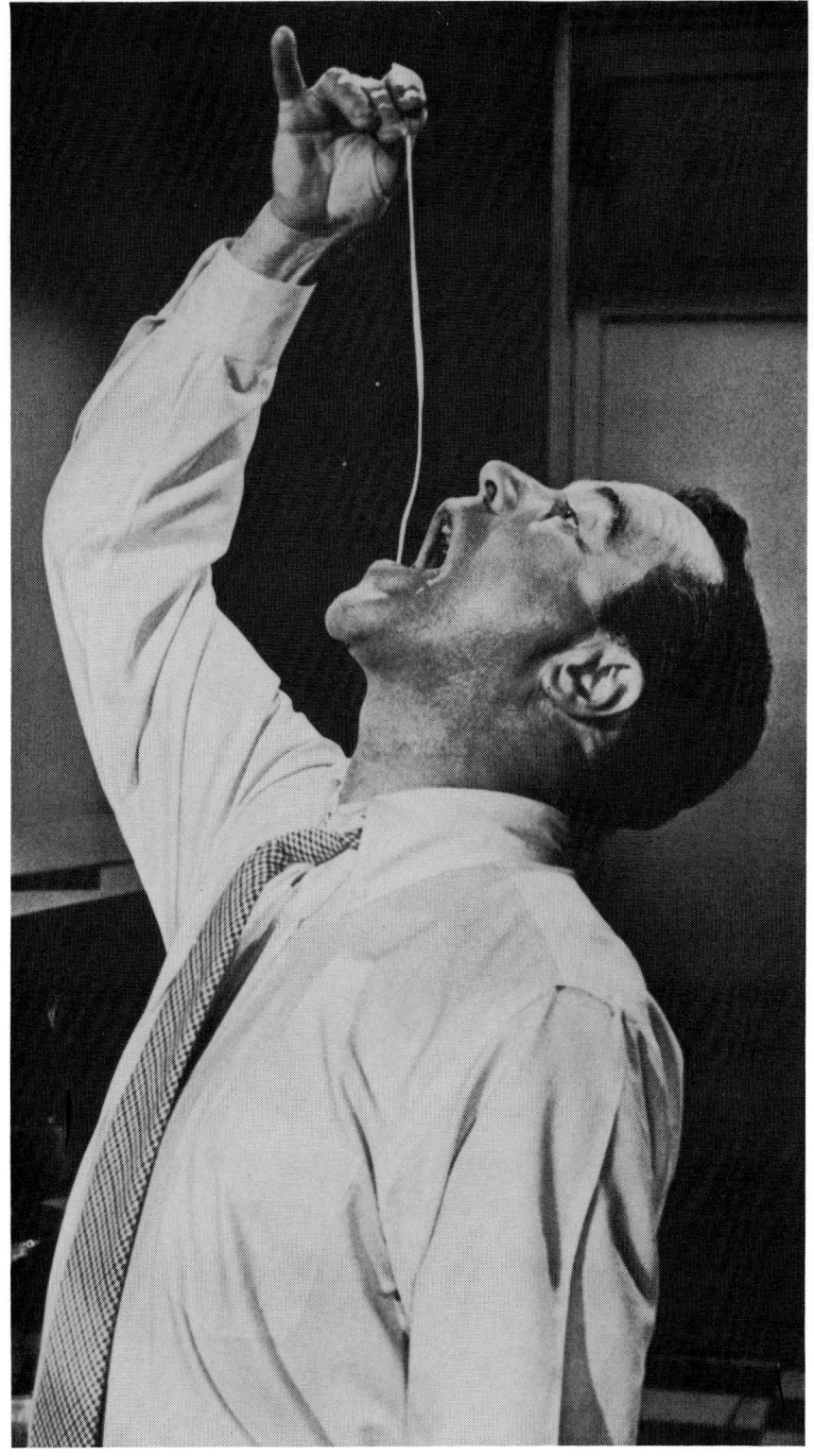

The Odd Couple. Jack Lemmon tests his wet noodle...er..."linguine."

The big date night comes. Felix has been slaving over a hot stove for hours preparing his wife's meat loaf recipe, when Oscar shows up late, only minutes before the girls are due. Waving his soup ladle about the kitchen, Felix chews out Oscar for his irresponsibility and is nothing less than furious about the possibility of his meat loaf drying out. But this tiff is just the appetizer for the disastrous courses that follow. Cocktails barely start when Felix uncontrollably gets himself and the Pigeons

The Odd Couple. Jack Lemmon *is* a wet noodle when he dumps news of his divorce to Wednesday-night poker pals, left to right, Walter Matthau, John Fiedler, Herbert Edelman, David Sheiner, and Larry Haines.

The Odd Couple. Lemmon gets a taste of his own medicine.

in tears over his broken home, and the unattended meat loaf burns to a smoldering cinder. Finally, the grief-stricken househusband is too depressed to continue with all this merrymaking in the girls' apartment when they invite him and Oscar for impromtu potluck that will replace the burned meat loaf dinner. As with many couples in combat, it takes only one big battle to end the war. For Oscar and Felix, the final skirmish takes place over a plate of linguine. Determined to retaliate for his ruined evening and the unbearable weeks of cleanliness, Oscar finally makes himself at home by messing up his apartment. Victory is close when he demands that Felix remove a plate of spaghetti from *his* poker table. Ha! "It's not spaghetti, it's linguine," Felix retorts. Oscar heaves the plate at the kitchen wall and smartly corrects him, "Now it's garbage."

But it's Felix who gets the last laugh in this comedy. After Oscar throws him out, Felix pops back to announce that he has moved in with the Pigeon sisters who, by the way, think he's all that a man should be—warm, wonderful, and sensitive. But are they up to tidy?

Starman

Nutshell

One of the most endearing qualities about *Starman* is that within its story of alien/earthling love on the run, the alien lives on truckstop food, and, incredible as it may seem to us, develops a fondness for our world not in *spite* of our food, but *because* of it. In fact, it's one of the few things he says he'll miss back home on his own planet.

To the critics, *Starman* distinguished itself as one of the few sci-fi movies ever made to emphasize something other than special effects. Lasers, flying saucers, and hi-tech gadgetry are secondary to the human relationships—or, rather, the human and non-human relationships. Director John Carpenter, heretofore known as a master of ghastly horrors (*Halloween* and *The Thing*), wanted *It Happened One Night*, a 1940s style road picture featuring an extra-terrestrial, and got it by weaving a unique twenty-first century love story with an old-fashioned chase.

The premise of *Starman* is the United States' actual launch of the 1970s Voyager space probe, containing greetings in numerous languages and an open invitation to aliens to visit earth. The film begins when another planet intercepts the U.S. probe and sends its own emmissary of good will to earth. The alien visitor's (Jeff Bridges) arrival does not go unnoticed, but instead of rolling out the red carpets and throwing tickertape parades, there are panic bells and whistles in the military's defense system. A government UFO official, Mark Shermin (Charles Martin Smith), is alerted. At the same time, a bluish-glowing ball enters a remote Wisconsin cabin and metamorphoses into the form of a recently widowed woman's husband. The bereaved, thoroughly confused and frightened woman, Jenny Hayden (Karen Allen), at first serves as the alien's unwilling chauffeur in his flight from hostile government agents. But, during their race across the West to meet up with the mother spaceship that will take him home, he and Jenny fall in love.

The road trip takes Jenny and Scott (so named after the man whose image he assumed) across the veritable backlot of the United States, from Wisconsin to Las Vegas, then to Winslow, Arizona's, Meteor Crater and Monument Valley. Scott's jerky, birdlike movements remind us that the alien is not completely at home in his new body. In spite of his idiosyncracies, though, Jenny's distrust and fear turn to awe, understanding, and love when he displays his gentle and kind character and uses magical balls of light for doing such good deeds as reviving a dead deer and saving her life.

Their military pursuers are never far behind them, however, and eventually they corner the couple at a roadside cafe before the Starman can meet the mother ship. Shermin, head of SFETI (Search for Extra-Terrestrial Intelligence), is so angered with the military's plan to capture and dissect the alien that he gives up his chance to learn about the alien by engineering his escape.

Chocolate Malt
Rating: G

Chocolate syrup:
- 8 oz. semi-sweet chocolate
- 1 c. boiling water
- 14 oz. can sweetened condensed milk
- ½ c. sugar

Malt mix:
- 1 c. cold milk
- 3 t. instant malted milk powder
- 1 scoop vanilla ice cream

Melt chocolate in top of a double boiler over hot water. Using a wire whip, slowly stir in the boiling water and condensed milk. Add the sugar and stir until dissolved. Cool. To make the malt, pour cold milk into a tall glass. Add the malted milk powder, 1/4 cup of the chocolate syrup, and stir to combine. Add scoop of ice cream on top. Serve with a spoon and straw. (Store remaining syrup covered tightly in the refrigerator for up to 10 days.) Makes about 3 cups syrup, enough for 12 malts.

Starman. Karen Allen and alien Jeff Bridges stop at a food station for "fuel."

With no time to spare, Jenny and Scott reach the spaceship rendezvous point only moments before a battery of military machinery descends on them. Bullets aimed to kill whiz past the couple as they stumble to the base of the massive meteor crater. Only the arrival of the mother spaceship saves the alien from the hail of bullets and his now failing human health. Snow falls in the eerie light from the ship as Jenny and Scott, knowing that they will never see each other again, search for a way to say good-bye. In a final gesture of kindness before the aliens beam up Scott, he gives Jenny his last ball of light as a gift for the unborn child he has given her—a child who will grow up as a teacher of men and who has inherited knowledge of the ball from his father, the Starman.

Food Scene

During his brief, frenzied stay on earth, the Starman develops a real fondness for Dutch apple pie. This comes as a bit of a surprise when one considers that all he eats in his short visit is road food. We presume that, because of his travels in the universe and his cosmic experiences, he would have acquired more discriminating tastes.

After traveling in the car with Jenny for hours, Scott notices a terrible emptiness in his new body, which Jenny explains is hunger. Scott has learned that cars need fuel from a gas station in order to move, so now he asks Jenny to stop for body fuel at a food station. At a truckstop, they place a mega-calorie order of deviled egg on toast, a superburger, french fries, chocolate malts, and Dutch apple pies with whipped cream. The pie gets rave reviews from the waitress, and Scott wastes no time in digging into the dessert. Jenny is quick to point out, though, that people, while a primitive species, have earned points by developing the custom of eating sandwiches first, dessert last. But Scott is unimpressed with this contribution to higher evolution and happily continues to fuel up on Dutch apple pie *before* his sandwich.

Dutch Apple Pie
Rating: G

Crumble topping:
 1 c. firmly packed brown sugar
 ¾ c. flour
 ½ c. butter, softened
 1½ t. cinnamon
 ¼ t. salt

Filling:
5-6 medium-sized tart apples
 1 unbaked 9" pie shell
   Whipped cream

Combine the crumble topping ingredients in a bowl with a fork until mixture forms into moist clumps. Peel, core, and thinly slice apples. Fill pie shell with apples and top with crumble topping. Bake at 350° for 45 minutes, or until apples are tender. Serve cool with whipped cream (or hot with ice cream—out of this world!!). Serves 6.

Later, as they near their destination, the two enter another roadside cafe, and Scott eagerly asks for his beloved Dutch apple pie. Having none, though, he settles for another dessert with whipped cream, baked specially by the owner's wife. It too is good, Scott notes, as he enjoys one of his final moments of peace on earth, dining on cherry cobbler.

According to property master Larry Bird, it was important to director John Carpenter to capture the real American look in the props, down to the crust on the pies. The Dutch apple pie scene was shot in an abandoned Tennessee restaurant that was completely refurbished for the movie. Temporary grills were set up, and food was supplied by the studio caterer, who was well aquainted with the look of truckstop food. For the cherry cobbler scene, Larry was able to find an old restaurant in Tiptonia, Tennessee, that still makes old-fashioned cherry cobbler in deep tin pans with a crisscross dough on the top. Carpenter was delighted with the find, and apparently it tasted as good as it looked.

Superburger
Rating: G

- ¼ lb. freshly ground beef
- Fresh sesame seed hamburger bun
- 2 slices tomato
- Mustard
- Catsup
- Dilled onions rings (see p. 233)

Form burger into patty and grill to desired doneness. Place on bun and top with tomato slices, condiments, and a generous helping of dilled onion rings. Serves 1.

Deviled Egg on Toast
Rating: G

Filling:
- 2 eggs, hard boiled
- 3 T. mayonnaise
- ¼ t. lemon juice
- 1 T. sweet pickle
- ⅛ t. paprika
- ¼ t. dry mustard
- 2 T. chopped celery
- Salt, freshly ground black pepper
- Chilled lettuce leaves
- 2 slices toast

Remove shells from eggs; chop. Add remaining filling ingredients and stir well. Heap on a slice of toast, top with lettuce leaves and another slice of toast. Makes 1 sandwich.

Road Fries
Rating; G

- Mature baking potatoes
- Oil for deep frying
- Salt
- Catsup

Peel potatoes and slice into long strips, 3/8"-1/2" thick. Soak 15 minutes in 90° water. Drain and dry thoroughly with a towel. Slowly heat oil to 330° in a saucepan or deep fryer. Drop in potatoes, about 1 cup at a time, and fry for 2 minutes.

Remove with slotted spoon and drain on absorbent towels. Continue frying remainder of the potatoes at 330°. Cool at least 5 minutes before final cooking stage. Increase oil heat to 375°. Finish frying the potatoes in batches as before, for about 3 minutes or until golden brown and crisp. Remove with a slotted spoon (or cook in a wire basket if you have one to make removal easier) and drain on absorbent towels. Sprinkle with salt. Serve immediately. Pass the catsup.

Cherry Cobbler
Rating: G

Dough:
- 1 c. cake flour
- 1¼ t. baking powder
- ½ t. salt
- 1½ T. sugar
- 2½ T. butter, softened
- ⅓ c. light cream

Filling:
- 1 c. sugar
- 3 T. quick-cooking tapioca
- ¼ t. salt
- ¾ t. cinnamon
- 2 1lb. cans pitted tart red cherries, packed in water
- ⅓ c. cherry juice
- 1½ t. lemon juice
- ¼ t. almond extract
- 5 drops red food coloring
- 1 T. butter
- Whipped cream

Make the dough first by sifting flour, baking powder, salt, and sugar together. Cut butter in with a pastry blender until the texture resembles cornmeal. Using a fork, lightly stir in the cream. Set aside. Make the filling by combining the sugar, tapioca, salt and cinnamon in a saucepan. Drain the cherries, reserving 1/3 cup of the juice. Add the cherries and reserved juice to the sugar mixture.

Stir in the lemon juice, almond extract, and food coloring. Stir to blend and let sit 15 minutes. Bring to a full boil over high heat. Immediately pour into a buttered 6" x 10" baking pan. Dot with butter. Using your fingers, place long, thin dollops of biscuit dough over the top in a crisscross-type pattern. Bake at 350° for about 1/2 hour, or until dough is lightly browned. Cool. Serve with whipped cream. Serves 4-6.

Tom Jones

Nutshell

John Osborne's movie adaptation of Henry Fielding's eighteenth century novel, *Tom Jones, A Foundling* (1749), together with Tony Richardson's direction, provides one of the greatest cinematic eating scenes of all time. No other film to date can hold a drumstick to its hilariously bawdy sensuality, its attention to every mouth-watering morsel, and its effortless display of the basest pleasures in eating, course after course after course after course after course.

To fully reconstruct the plot here would require a few pages of flowcharts and family trees. Coleridge once said of Fielding's novel, "Upon my word, I think *Tom Jones* is one of the most perfect plots ever planned." Although Osborne's adaptation is somewhat distanced from Fielding's original plot, the gist is maintained with enough cinematic pluses to make up for story losses. Suffice it to say that a Somerset squire named Allworthy (George Devine), takes in a bastard son to raise as his own, banishing the supposed parents, Jenny Jones (Joyce Redman) and Partridge (Jack MacGowran) from his estate. He names the boy Tom Jones (Albert Finney) and treats him as an equal with his legitimate heir, Blifil (David Warner).

Tom grows into a handsome, good-natured, earthy young man, well liked by all except the jealous, pimple-faced Blifil. Tom falls in love with Sophie Western (Susannah York), the beautiful daughter of a neighboring squire, but cannot keep control of his earthy appetite for Molly (Diane Cilento), a local woman of wanton ways. His escapades with Molly bring disgrace to the family, inspiring an arranged marriage between Sophie and Blifil by her busybody aunt (Dame Edith Evans) and the two squires. When Sophie refuses to marry anyone but her true love Tom, he is banished from the estate and forced to seek his own way in life.

On his way to London, Tom meets, dines with, and beds a Mrs. Waters, AKA Jenny Jones, his supposed mother. Later by chance, he also meets and befriends a man named Partridge, his supposed father.

Once Tom reaches his destination, he involves himself in another fling, this time with the sophisticated Lady Bellaston (Joan Greenwood), but is soon joined by Sophie, who wishes to escape matrimony with Blifil. Blifil though, being as nasty as his complexion, won't stand for this mockery and has Tom framed for robbery.

Sentenced to be hanged, Tom is spared when an important note written by his mother at the time of his birth is produced in the nick of time. Although still illegitimate, the note reveals that he is actually the son of Bridget Allworthy, the squire's deceased sister.

Tom is promptly reinstated into the Allworthy family and, amidst cheers of joy, finally given permission to marry Sophie.

Soup
Rating: G

(This is a Scotch broth, as popular to Americans as the British Oxtail soup. It is a hearty "broth" by our standards and may therefore stand alone as a complete meal, but in this case try to save room for the many other courses to follow!)

- 2 lbs. lamb or mutton with bone, cut into 6" pieces
- 2 quarts cold water.
- ½ c. barley
- Salt, freshly ground pepper
- 1 leek (white part only), finely diced
- 2 carrots, finely diced
- 2 ribs celery, finely diced
- 1 medium onion, finely diced
- ½ c. finely diced turnip
- ¼ c. minced fresh parsley

Place the meat in a heavy kettle and add the water. Bring to a boil and skim the top as scum forms. Add the barley, salt, and pepper. Reduce heat, cover, and simmer for 1 hour. Add the remaining ingredients. Bring to a boil. Reduce heat to low; cover and simmer for 2 hours. Transfer the meat to a cutting board and discard the bones, gristle, and fat, reserving the meat. Cut meat into small cubes and return to the soup pot. Skim unwanted fat from the surface. Heat through for a few minutes. Correct the seasoning. Serves 8–12.

Food Scene

While on their way to London, Tom and Mrs. Waters, in a wayside inn, double-handedly awaken every sensory receptor in their bodies by eating a five-course dinner without exchanging one word of conversation. All we see and hear is the sight and sound of food moving from hand to mouth. Only an occasional chuckle breaks the sound of chewing. Richardson didn't need much script detail to direct the eating, either. Given the finger-licking menu, the apparent lack of utensils, and the voracious, carnal appetites of the principal characters, the actors only have to do what comes naturally.

Soup. A nice beginning. Tom heartily slurps the broth in his spoon, holding his head only inches from the bowl, too preoccupied with his hunger to notice the still refined manners of his table companion.

Lobster. Tom pounds the body of his armored crustacean with his fist for a quick demolition. He grabs a leg, wrenches it out of the body, and crunches down on the gam with almost no reward for his efforts. Mrs. Waters, however, has another approach. Eyeing him ever so steadily, she delicately bites down on her morsel, slowly extracting a long, red, limp piece of meat. She smiles triumphantly.

Turkey. Greasy-mouthed, bare-handed, leg-gnawing Tom finally puts his feeding in abeyance and is fully attentive to the artful Mrs. Waters. He grins at her suggestively again and grabs at his meat. She follows his lead and grabs a leg, tears into it with her teeth, then yanks it free. Later she finds a wishbone and offers the free end to Tom.

Oysters. Raw and glistening wet, long-heralded as nature's aphrodisiac. Tom's appetite has reached the point where he can afford to be generous. He offers a choice bivalve to Mrs. Waters. She willingly accepts. Turning her profile to Tom, she tilts her head back, holding the shell to her mouth, and slowly pours the slippery meat to its warm destination. She turns full face, staring into Tom's eyes, then, from out of her mouth comes the oyster! With satisfied, half closed eyes, Mrs. Waters rests the bite on her lips for one last brief moment. Then, quietly, she sucks it down her throat.

Pears. Dripping wet. Now Mrs. Waters takes slow, long, deep bites. Juice drips on the table. Pear pieces hang from her nose. Tom spits out seeds and chuckles.

Wine and candlelight. Their distance narrows as the satiated diners lean into the center of the table, wine glasses poised at their lips. They slowly drink the shimmering nectar, and though completely stuffed, rush off to bed in fast-forward speed.

The movie *Tom Jones* was a terrific box-office hit. Its hell-raising style, its reckless eighteenth-century abandon, and its surprisingly accurate portrayal of King George II's England, made it fresh entertainment of the early 1960s. Since the concept of sequels had not yet taken over Hollywood, the film merely inspired a trail of imitations. In doing so, though, they only force us to recall our fondness for the original, the one and only *Tom Jones*.

Lobster
Rating: G

2 live lobsters, 1½–2½ lbs. each
Sea salt

Fill large cooking pot with cold water to within a few inches of the top. Sprinkle in a teaspoon or so of salt, depending on size of pot. Add the lobsters. Bring to a boil and cook over high heat for 5 minutes. Reduce heat and simmer 15 more minutes. Drain. Serve whole. Serves 2.

Turkey
Rating: G

1 10–20 lb. turkey, cleaned and dressed

Wash bird thoroughly inside and out. Place breast-side down on a rack in roasting pan. Cover tightly with lid or aluminum foil and bake at 350° at the rate of 20 minutes per pound. Remove cover and flip bird breast-side up during last 30 minutes of baking to brown the skin. Let sit 20 minutes before digging in.

Oysters
Rating: G

(The muscles of these mollusks are powerful and should be treated with due caution and respect.)

1 doz. fresh live oysters

Scrub shells well with a stiff brush. Open shells: Hold one oyster in palm of hand, "deep" shell down; insert blade of an oyster knife into hinge area. Turn knife until upper shell lifts, then cut along hinge muscle; cut around edges to lift and open shell. (To protect your hand while cutting, place oyster in a double-wrapped cloth napkin before resting in palm of hand. Lift out meat with knife and rinse in cold water. Rinse shells. Replace meat in shells and serve on the "half shell." Serves 2.

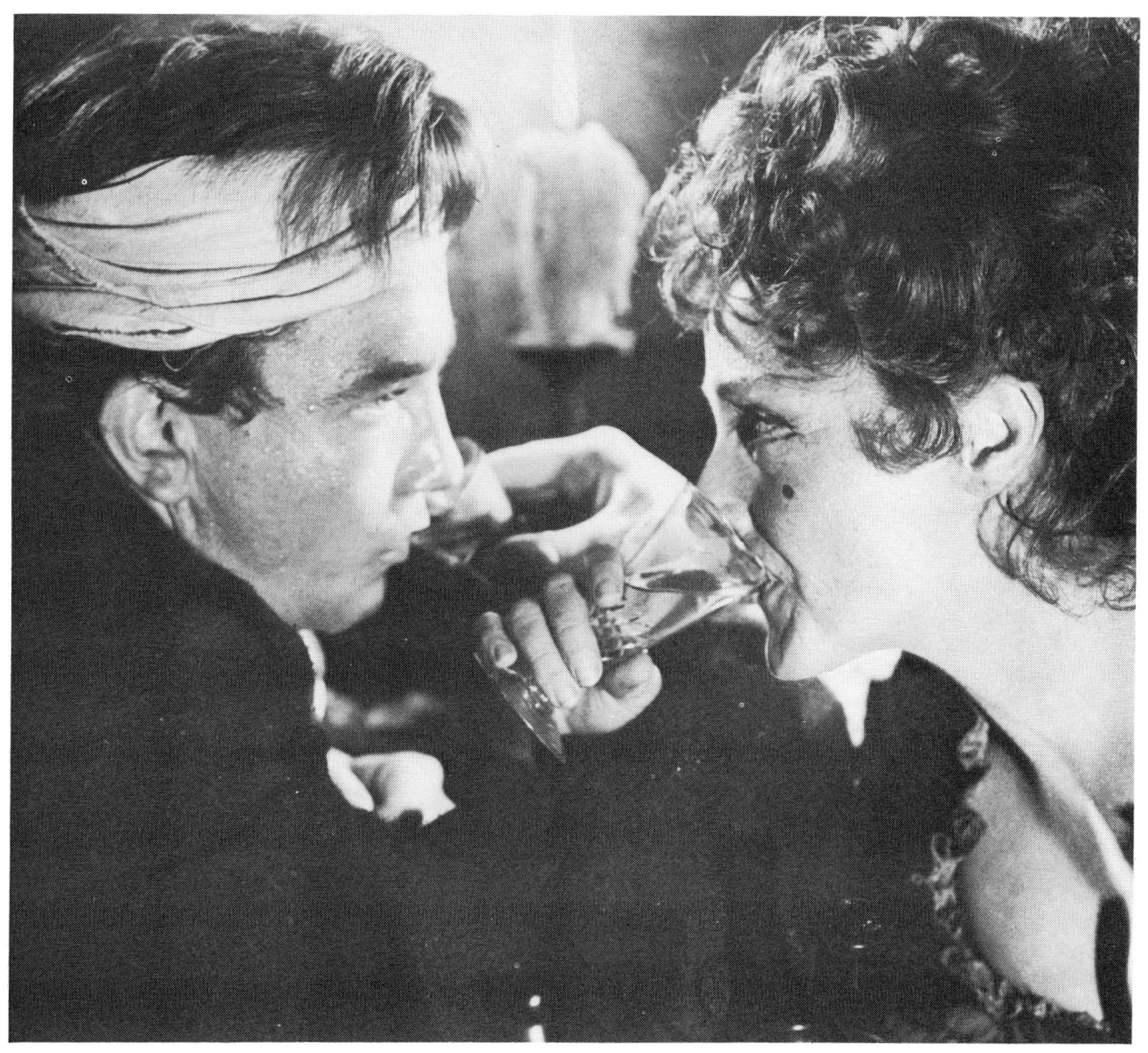

Tom Jones. Albert Finney and Joyce Redman sip after dinner wine.

Victor/Victoria

Nutshell

Plot is to *Victor/Victoria* what twists are to braided bread. For starters, we've got an American remake of a German film taking place in France about a woman pretending to be a man pretending to be a woman. Then Julie Andrews is added as the male impersonator and James Garner as the man romantically drawn to this...this man, and it seems that nothing in life is predictable anymore ever again.

It starts off with a starving would-be cabaret singer Victoria (Julie Andrews) who fails her audition in a hot nightclub. Perhaps it was her choice of the wimpy recital piece "Cherry Ripe" and her Eliza Doolittle togs. In any event, she uses her last shred of ingenuity to bag a fabulous dinner while accidentally meeting the man who will change the course of her life and the gender of her sex.

It's the gay Toddy (Robert Preston) who convinces Victoria that by cropping her hair and lowering her voice, she can go to the top as a female impersonator. The metamorphosis takes place, and Toddy introduces his creation to his theatrical agent, Cassell (John Rhys-Davies), as Count Victor from Poland. Victor/Victoria's career is launched.

Victoria is so good masquerading as a man impersonating a woman, and her performance is so alluring, that she does go right to the top. On the way, she enchants the virile Chicago nightclub owner, King (James Garner). Against all his powers of reason, morality, and manliness, he allows himself to fall for Victor, and, as a consequence, puts his moll Norma (Leslie Ann Warren) in hysterics while risking scandal and ridicule in his show biz world.

Of course, when he goes to consummate his love for Victor, he discovers that his masculinity is still intact, as he learns the true sexual identity of Victor. They go on to live happily ever after as man and woman, while Toddy and King's bodyguard Squash (Alex Karras) end up entwined in true gay love.

Food Scene

It's sheer desperation that gets Victoria her start, beginning with a clever, but overworked scheme for a free meal. Weak and crazed from hunger, she beats a cockroach with a hotel bible and drops it into her purse, intending to use it as payment in full for an all-you-can-eat dinner. In the restaurant, surrounded by bowls of fruit, fresh pies on pedestals, and sumptuous aromas, she orders a bottle of white 1934, two dinners, two salads, and two desserts.

First, with trembling hands, she cuts into a piece of roast pork and brings it to her lips. At long last! Food! And now a little potato, some green beans. When the waiter returns in a few minutes, she is finished and ready to consume her second selection—roast chicken. Preparing it

Double Dinner Salad
Rating: G

- ½ head crisp lettuce, washed and torn in pieces
- 4 radishes, sliced thin
- ½ c. sliced red cabbage
- 2 small tomatoes, each quartered
- 1 cockroach (optional)
- French Dressing (see p. 233)

Toss salad ingredients. Add desired amount of dressing. Serves 1.

"Roast" Pork
Rating: G

- ¼ c. butter
- 1 4 lb. pork roast
- Salt, freshly ground pepper
- 1 medium onion studded with 4 cloves
- 2 cloves garlic, sliced
- 1 t. rosemary leaves
- ½ t. ground sage
- Pinch thyme
- 1 c. dry white wine

Melt butter in a Dutch oven. Brown meat on all sides in the butter. Sprinkle with salt and pepper to taste. Cut onion in quarters and place around meat. Add remaining ingredients around base of meat. Bring to a boil. Reduce heat and simmer, covered, for 2 hours. Strain sauce and skim fat. Serve with the meat. Serves 4–6.

Victor/Victoria. As a down-and-out singer, Julie Andrews yearns for a taste of the good things in life, starting with a square meal.

Victor/Victoria. As a successful nightclub performer, Ms. Andrews yearns for a new kind of nourishment.

could take as long as thirty minutes, she's informed, so she quickly chooses the boeuf bourguignon, then demands that her two salads be served on one plate. "Do you want to order your two desserts," the waiter asks. "Apple Flan to Coupe Jacques is a nice parlay," he adds.

Toddy, who has spied Victoria in her euphoria, joins her at the table. She offers him "the best goddamned dinner you ever had" and explains her payment plan. Victoria quickly flips her opened purse over the huge salad with the aim of dumping the dead roach somewhere between the lettuce and radishes. But the roach, only stunned from his beating with the bible, celebrates his second coming by climbing onto Victoria's thumb. Pandemonium ensues, and she and Toddy use it to make a hasty and unnoticed escape to the even bigger upset that awaits them in the entertainment world.

Coupe Jacques
Rating: G

(The coupe is a dessert of French origin, generally served in a stemmed glass like that used for champagne.)

Vanilla ice cream
Mixed fruits, cut in small cubes

Spoon vertical lengths of ice cream into a serving glass, separating the layers with diced mixed fruit.

Boeuf Bourguignon
Rating: G

(There are many variations of Boeuf Bourguignon, perhaps as many as there are ways to stuff meat in a pot. The common denominator, though, is beef cooked in wine. Anything else is just gravy.)

- 2 T. olive oil
- 2 T. butter
- 3 T. bacon fat
- 2 lbs. chuck, cut into 1½" cubes
- Salt, pepper
- Juice of ½ lemon
- 4 shallots
- 2 medium onions, coarsely chopped
- 2 cloves garlic, mashed
- ½ lb. mushrooms, sliced
- ¼ c. minced fresh parsley
- ½ bottle burgundy
- 1 bay leaf
- ½ t. thyme
- 1 t. salt
- ½ t. freshly ground pepper
- 2 T. flour
- 1½ c. diced carrots

Heat the oil, butter, and fat together in a frying pan. Meanwhile, sprinkle meat with salt and pepper. Brown meat on all sides in the fat. Transfer to a 2-quart stove-top casserole (leaving the fat in the pan) and cover to keep warm.

In the same pan, add the lemon juice to the meat juices and gently sauté the shallots, onions, garlic, mushrooms, and parsley until tender. Transfer to the casserole and mix with the meat. Combine remaining ingredients in a bowl and pour over the meat mixture. Stir. Salt and pepper to taste. Place over high heat until mixture begins to simmer. Reduce heat, cover, and simmer 3 1/2-4 hours. The mixture should barely bubble while cooking. Serve over rice. Serves 4-6.

Apple Flan
Rating: G

Crust:
- 1½ c. sifted flour
- ½ t. salt
- ½ c. shortening
- 3 T. water

Custard:
- 3 eggs, slightly beaten
- ½ c. sugar
- ¼ t. salt
- 1 c. light cream
- 1 c. milk
- 2 t. vanilla
- ¼ t. nutmeg

Topping:
- 2 c. thinly sliced apple, with peel removed
- 1 c. water

Glaze:
- 2 T. water
- ½ c. sugar
- ½ c. fresh or frozen strawberries
- 1 medium-sized apple, peeled and chopped
- 1 T. butter

Sift salt with flour. Cut in the shortening with a pastry blender until the mixture forms into pea-sized lumps. Sprinkle water evenly throughout the dough and mix until the dough forms a ball when pressed together. (Handle as little as possible to prevent toughening.)

Roll out the dough and line a 9" pie plate. Flute the edges. Prick bottom and sides to prevent air pockets from forming. Bake at 425° for 12 to 15 minutes, or until lightly browned. Cool before filling.

Meanwhile, combine the ingredients for the custard in a bowl. Pour into a greased 9" pie plate and bake at 325° for about 30 minutes, or until just firm. Cool. While the custard is baking, place the apples and water in a saucepan and cook until tender. Drain and set apples aside.

Place the glaze ingredients in a small saucepan and boil to the soft jelly stage, or 200° on a candy thermometer. (You will reach the jelly stage when, after about 10 minutes of boiling, the mixture will fall in two heavy drops from the lengthwise edge of a spoon.) Cooking time will depend upon the amount of sugar, the kinds of fruits used, and the amount of juice produced from the fruit. Cool, but do not let it set.

To assemble the flan, carefully run a spatula underneath the cooled custard to loosen. Gently slide into the cooled shell. Top with cooked apple slices and brush with the fruit glaze. Serve at room temperature within 3 hours of baking or refrigerate to prevent spoiling. Serves 6.

What's Up Tiger Lily?

Nutshell

It is written that Woody Allen is crazy about Hershey bars and girls who are "pretty, funny, bright and neurotic." It is also written that "he who has the best egg salad recipe rules over heaven and earth," or so says Allen's Far Eastern James-Bondian spy spoof, *What's Up Tiger Lily?*

In the mid 1960s, Woody Allen was approached by Hank Saperstein and asked to rearrange a "Made-in-Japan" junk spy film by dubbing in a new sound track. The result is an irreverently shredded and altogether new spy yarn featuring a cast of unknown Japanese actors speaking with the heavily New York accented voices of Woody Allen and friends. The film is a crazy amalgam of all-for-fun, fun-for-all verbal slapstick, puns, wisecracks, and inane plot twists. In a particularly heated moment, for example, the hero calls out for dynamite to save the endangered life of one oriental lovely. She adds to the order by calling out for a regular coffee and a toasted corn muffin!

Typical of Allen's idiosyncratic approach to film making, he opens the film with himself in a mock interview, explaining how he has come to supervise this "definitive" spy story: "Because, if you know me, you know that death is my bread, danger my butter. No, death is my butter, danger my bread." Finally, abandoning all hope for terse brevity, "Death and danger are my various breads and butters."

The story that follows concerns an international hunt for the perfect egg salad recipe. Phil Moscowitz (Tatsuya Mihashi), a "lovable rogue," is first seduced, then abducted by two sisters, Suki Yaki (Akiko Wakayabayashi) and Terri Yaki (Mie Hana), who lead him to an anonymous Asian potentate who alerts Phil of a developing crisis: The secret recipe for the best egg salad ever has been stolen by gangster egg salad addict Shepherd Wong (Tadao Nakamaru). Since everybody knows that possession of the recipe means supreme rule over heaven and earth, all free countries are in danger until the recipe is recovered.

Phil and Teri begin their search on the wrong foot—or wing—by getting on the bad side of another bad-guy organization headed by the ruthless Wing Fat (Susumu Kurobe), who is in search of the recipe for his own financial gain. Suki, who has infiltrated Shepherd Wong's gambling/bordello ship, blows her cover and ends up bound in the bilges. Wing Fat and Phil temporarily join forces and, after an assortment of adventures, finally locate the recipe in Wong's ship's safe.

True to his bad-guy nature, though, Wing Fat steals the recipe again and leaves Phil and the sisters tied up under the watchful eye of a deadly cobra. Justice prevails in the end, however. Wing Fat kills Shepherd Wong, whose last dying request is that he be stuffed with crabmeat. Wing Fat is turned in to the authorities by Phil, and Phil thinks he has turned himself into a Pan Am jet. Just your everyday recipe thriller.

Decoded Egg Salad
Rating: G

2 *hard boiled eggs, chopped*
2 *T. mayonnaise*
  Pinch of salt
2 *T. finely chopped celery*
1 *T. finely chopped green onion*
1 *T. finely chopped green olives*
2 *t. minced fresh parsley*
½ *t. white wine vinegar with tarragon herb*
  Freshly ground pepper
  Paprika for garnish

Combine all ingredients (except the paprika) in a bowl and stir well. Serve in a sandwich, on crackers, or sprinkled with paprika on a bed of lettuce. Serves 1–2.

What's Up Tiger Lily? Woody Allen casts a furtive glance as he bites into an apple served by an Asian temptress.

Food Scene

The long-awaited moment is at hand when Phil and Wing Fat locate the stolen recipe. But drat! It's all in code! Fortunately, Phil's 007 sleuthing skills allow him to decipher the message so that we can all find out, once and for all, how much mayo to use to make the world's greatest egg salad. Unfortunately, his voice trails off. . . .

> Take two chopped hard boiled eggs,
> 2 T. of mayonnaise
> Add a pinch of salt...

and we never get the whole picture.

Who's Killing the Great Chefs of Europe?

Nutshell

Finding bouillon cubes in the bouillabaisse is probably the worst crime conceivable in a four-star restaurant, unless the restaurant is one of those in *Who's Killing the Great Chefs of Europe*. In this film, renowned European restaurants not only serve the most exquisite hâute cuisine ever to grace a fork, but also provide the most sumptuous settings for murder. It's a lighthearted, epicurean epic, wherein a diabolical killer systematically murders his way through a fabulous dinner menu, dispatching three of the world's greatest chefs in styles related to their most famous recipes.

With murder as the backdrop, the story takes dead aim at a squabbling divorced couple who are personally and professionally at opposite ends of the table. Natasha (Jacqueline Bisset) is a premiere American pastry chef, who spends hours lacing fabulous desserts with Devonshire cream and worships at the altar of delicate meringues. Robby (George Segal), her ex-husband, is a fast-paced, fast-food franchiser who figures that any meal worth its salt should cost about $1.30 and take only half that time to prepare.

Thickening the plot is the massive Max Vanderveere (Robert Morley), gourmet extraordinaire and publisher of *Epicurus* magazine. (Mr. Morley is the real-life restaurant critic for *Punch* magazine.) We no sooner learn of his serious medical condition due to overweight and hear his doctor's warning that he diet or *else*, than he's off to the Royal Grill restaurant, where German chef Louis Kohner (Jean-Pierre Cassel) will prepare him an early lunch of a dozen poached oysters in bechamel sauce, baked with Parmesan cheese, roast woodcock with an orange, ginger and port sauce, endive and beet salad, cheese, and vanilla meringue glacé with chantilly cream and shaved bitter chocolate. (In deference to the diet, he omits the cheese.)

Coincidentally, the divorcees are staying in the same London hotel—Natasha to prepare the dessert course for a royal banquet Max has planned for the queen; Robby to set up a fast food omelet chain. Natasha manages to fend off Robby's advances and get to the palace in time to prepare her fabulous Le Bombe Richelieu.

The royal kitchen is a mass of activity. Between steps in assembling the dessert, Natasha assists Louis Kohner with his pigeon en croûte (wild game bird sealed in spiced pastry), trimming crusts, arranging chopped aspic, and garnishes of watercress. One by one, courses are carted into the royal dining room, comprising a menu fit for a queen: Consommé au Porto, Pigeon en Croûte, Gigot de Veau, Pommes Dauphine, Carrots Vichy, Salade, Fromages, and Le Bombe Richelieu.

Shortly before dessert is presented, Natasha adorns her masterpiece with the final touches. She drenches the bombe with chocolate sauce, surrounds it with whipped cream and fresh raspberries, splashes it with framboise liqueur, and ignites it into a fiery blaze for a spectacular entrance.

Who's Killing the Great Chefs of Europe? Robert Morley needs more than Alka-Seltzer to pull himself out of this jam. Suicide by overdosing on food is just desserts?

Who's Killing the Great Chefs of Europe? Left to right: George Segal, Robert Morley, and Jacqueline Bisset pose with the loaded Bombe Richelieu.

Later, Natasha shares Louis' bed, and while they eagerly maul a late-night plate of cold pigeon and red wine, Louis tells Natasha his "big secret." Do the shopping yourself, he says. You cannot make the best if you don't start with the best. Fully contented, he promises to prepare a fabulous breakfast for Natasha in the morning. For Natasha, it's the beginning of her nightmare.

Louis is found cooking the next morning, but in his own oven! He's been gruesomely baked to a crisp for no apparent reason. Soon, one by one, chefs all over Europe are found murdered in equally diabolical fashions. The incomparable Italian chef Fausto Zoppi, who was about to divulge the recipe for his inspired aragosto à la garciofo (lobster with artichokes), is found floating in his lobster tank. The legendary French chef Moulineau, creator of an impressive pressed duck, is found with his head crushed in his duck press. Chefs all over Europe fear for their lives as they realize only the best chefs are being murdered. But, they wonder, is it worse to be murdered or passed over?

Piecing clues together, Natasha deduces that the murderer must be someone who hates Max, for the killer is systematically knocking off the chefs who prepare the courses in Max's favorite dinner—a menu he once printed in his magazine as the perfect meal: Louis' pigeon en croûte, Zoppi's lobster, Jean-Claude's pressed duck, and finally, Natasha's bombe. Natasha would be next!

Luckily, Robby, who would love to get Natasha to join him in the leftovers of their marriage, never lets her far from his sight and is able to save her from being blown to smithereens during a TV cooking demonstration.

Max is found in the velvet-drenched Café Royal near Piccadilly Circus, painfully ill from having feasted single-handedly on a banquet that could have fed the Russian army. Glassy-eyed, he stares at the debris of his gluttony: six lobsters, twenty-four stuffed artichokes, thirty-six oysters, a side of beef Wellington, a hog's head stuffed with chestnuts and apples, iced prawns, salvers of poached salmon, an entire baby lamb trussed with paper frills, plates of pastrami, platters of pâtés, shimmering sauces, mounds of potatoes, noodles, tarts, pastries, custards, wheels of cheese, crepes, and gleaming sidecars overflowing with apricot puddings, strudels, fruits, and floating islands en flambé.

Nothing spells relief for a man in this condition, for Max has intentionally committed gastronomic hara-kiri. Before he passes on, his last few blubbering words lead everyone to believe that he's the murderer, but it's Beecham (Madge Ryan), his secretary, who comes forward as the guilty party. She's murdered the chefs to keep Max on his diet. Max couldn't go on living knowing he was the cause of the demise of so much culinary genius, and Beecham couldn't go on without Max. In his final act as the true gourmet, Max slumps to his death, head first into the strawberries Romanoff.

Food Scene

Who's Killing the Great Chefs of Europe? could well be considered the Grand Prix of food films. There isn't scene in it in which food isn't being discussed, prepared, or eaten.

Woven into its whodunit plot is a "cook's tour" of Europe's finest kitchens and eateries. Filmed in London, Munich, Venice, and Paris, elaborate sets include the interiors of the Lido nightclub on the Champs-Elysees (used as a substitute for the kitchen of Buckingham Palace), the famous Maxim's and Tour d' Argent restaurants in Paris, with La Perouse, Lucas-Carton, Faugeron, and the fish markets of Venice as backdrops.

Gigot de Veau (Roast Leg of Veal)
Rating: G

(For convenience, have your butcher lard the veal by wrapping it with fat and tying securely.)

1 4 lb. boneless leg of veal, larded
   Salt, freshly ground black pepper
½ lb. salt pork, cut in thin strips
1 large onion, quartered
2 carrots, coarsely chopped
2 cloves garlic, sliced
1 bay leaf, broken in half
1 t. rosemary
½ c. butter, melted
1 c. dry white wine

Rub larded leg with salt and pepper. Cover with strips of salt pork. Place in roasting pan with meat thermometer inserted into thickest part of the meat. Surround with onion, carrots, garlic, bay leaf, and rosemary.

Roast (uncovered) at 300° for about 2 hours or until thermometer reaches 170°. While roasting, baste frequently with a mixture of the melted butter and wine. Strain juices and skim fat. Serve sauce with meat. Serves 6.

Strawberries Romanoff
Rating: G

½ c. heavy cream, beaten stiff
1 c. softened vanilla ice cream, slightly whipped
   Juice of 1/2 lemon
4 T. Cointreau
   Sugar
1 quart hulled, whole strawberries, chilled
   Strawberries for garnish

Fold whipped cream into softened ice cream. Stir in lemon juice and Cointreau. Sprinkle a little sugar over the strawberries. Pour cream mixture over strawberries and blend quickly. Serve in decorative dessert bowls. Garnish with additional strawberries. Serves 4.

Its culinary creations, budgeted at more than $180,000 (with one scene of fish alone eating up $3,000) and personally supervised by master chef Paul Bocuse (holder of France's most coveted culinary award, the Meilleur Ouvrier de France Cuisinier), were authentic masterpieces, down to the last raspberry. Says Bocuse, "I had to make sure that the food was well prepared, that it looked right, and that it tasted as good as it looked." It was a performance that endeared him to cast and crew alike. Director Ted Kotcheff, himself a gourmet from a family of restauranteurs, heartily supported Bocuse's persnickety approach and called in award-winning cinematographer John Alcott to make sure that the food was filmed in the most ideal light.

Writer Peter Stone, who adapted Nan and Ivan Lyons' novel to the screen, points out that food is a subject rarely touched on in American movies. As a society, we are more and more interested in good food, but are actually eating more and more junk food. France on the other hand, where food is sacrosanct, produced a major statement four years prior to "Chefs" in its 1974 release of Marco Ferreri's *La Grande Bouffe* (The Big Feast), the highly controversial satire on gluttony in which four men commit suicide by eating themselves to death.

The actors in "Chefs" could have met a similar fate. At one point, Jacqueline Bisset reports having to eat seventeen pigeons. Paul Bocuse had individually prepared all thirty-one pigeon en croûtes, the recipe comprising two full pages of text and requiring two days of preparation. Every time the actors broke into the crust, the dish had to be replaced with a new one, and after the last take and the seventeenth pigeon, Ms. Bisset had had enough.

Not only did Miss Bisset's eating scenes put her acting skills to the test, but her cooking scenes weren't any piece of cake either. A self-confessed flop at making piecrust, she was required to act her way through the construction of a raspberry bombe for the film and make it look effortless in the process. As Natasha, she had to talk with a distinct air of authority about the simple sugar syrup needed for the custard filling: "After the eggs (yolks) are fully beaten, we'll add the sugar syrup. The reason we use syrup is that granulated sugar added to raw eggs would not dissolve properly, causing a grainy mix that would be unappetizing as well as difficult to freeze."

Property master Horst Grandt recalls that four or five prop bombes were made by a four star German chef, with Paul Bocuse acting as technical advisor. Each took approximately four days to make, requiring twenty-four hours between layers for proper freezing. Unless you're serving eighteen as Natasha did for the royal banquet, you'll find the recipe given here considerably more manageable, suitable for serving twelve, and requiring little more than a freezer, proper tools, and a modicum of skill to assemble.

Many of the gourmet recipes that follow were contributed by our own resident French chef, Claude Farina of Le Normandie restaurant in Thousand Oaks, California. To some of the more basic gourmet French dishes, Claude has added his personal touch, while others are wholly innovative. (Those contributed by Claude are so indicated at the end of the recipe.) My deep appreciation goes to Claude for sharing his techniques and special combinations of ingredients.

Fillet of Sea Bass
Rating: G

2 T. dry white wine
2 sea bass fillets, about 1 lb.
2 T. minced shallots
1 t. minced chives
   Salt, freshly ground pepper
   Softened butter
   Lemon wedges

Pour 1 tablespoon wine over top surface of fillets (1/2 tablespoon for each). Sprinkle tops evenly with half of the seasoning ingredients: 1 tablespoon shallots, 1/2 teaspoon chives, salt and pepper to taste. Dot each with butter. Broil for 5 minutes. Turn fillets over and top as before with remaining ingredients (wine, shallots, chives, salt, pepper, and butter). Broil 5 more minutes. Serve with lemon wedges. Serves 2.

Le Bombe Richelieu
Rating: G

(The plus side of this spectacular dessert is that most of it can [and should] be prepared ahead of time. Freezing times will vary depending on the temperature of your freezer and the type of ice cream used, but if you prepare and freeze one layer each night, the layering process will be worry-free. When baking the bombe, the sides as well as the top of the meringue coating must be evenly browned to support the weight of the chocolate sauce, so choose a baking platter or dish that will not obstruct proper heat flow in your oven.)

Chocolate sauce:

6 oz. semi-sweet chocolate
2 eggs, well beaten
2 c. sugar
1½ c. evaporated milk
1 T. vanilla

Chocolate ice cream layer:
- 1 quart chocolate ice cream, softened
- 1 t. grated orange peel
- 1 t. orange extract
- ¼ c. coarsely chopped, toasted almonds

Vanilla ice cream layer:
- 1 quart vanilla ice cream, softened

Raspberry sherbet layer:
- 1 pint raspberry sherbet

Custard filling:
- ⅔ c. granulated sugar
- ⅓ c. water
- 8 egg yolks, beaten
- ½ c. heavy cream
- 1 t. vanilla

Orange pound cake (see Bread and Chocolate, p.216)

Meringue:
- 8 egg whites at room temperature
- ⅓ c. sugar
- Whipped cream
- Fresh raspberries
- ½ c. framboise liqueur (raspberry)

First, prepare the chocolate sauce: Melt chocolate in top of double boiler over hot (not boiling) water. Combine the eggs, sugar, and evaporated milk in a small bowl. Stir into the melted chocolate. Cook for 20 minutes, stirring occasionally with a wire whip. Remove from heat and beat for one minute with an electric mixer. Cool slightly and stir in vanilla. This makes about 4 cups, and will store well in the refrigerator for days if tightly sealed. Warm sauce before using.

Chill each: 1- 2- and 3-quart metal mixing bowls and beaters.

Thoroughly stir grated orange peel and orange extract into softened chocolate ice cream. Spoon into bottom of the chilled 3-quart mixing bowl. Line outside of the chilled 2-quart mixing bowl as smoothly as possible with plastic wrap. Push wrapped bowl into chocolate ice cream, pushing ice cream evenly up the sides to within 1/2" of top of 3-quart bowl.

Place a weight (I used clean rocks) in bottom of 2-quart bowl (enough to prevent ice cream from sliding back down the sides) and freeze until firm. Remove 2-quart bowl and peel away plastic wrap. Smooth ice cream with back of a spoon and refreeze if necessary to firm up, about 15-30 minutes.

Stir almonds into softened vanilla ice cream and spoon into chocolate ice cream shell, pushing up the sides as before, this time using a plastic-wrapped 1-quart bowl. Repeat as before, freezing until firm, removing bowl and wrap when ready for the next layer. Break up raspberry sherbet and spoon into ice cream-lined mixing bowl.

Using the back of a large spoon, evenly line the third layer, this time with sherbet. Cover surfaces with plastic wrap and freeze until firm.

Make a simple syrup by combining the 2/3 cup sugar and water in a small saucepan, cooking over low heat until sugar dissolves.

Place beaten egg yolks in a larger saucepan. With a wire whip, gradually stir in cream and syrup, stirring constantly over low heat until mixture begins to boil and thicken. (Don't overcook, or custard will become lumpy!) Cool slightly and stir in vanilla. Cool completely. (Makes about 1 cup.) Remove plastic wrap and spoon custard into center of ice cream lined bowl. Cover surface again with plastic wrap and freeze for a few hours. (The bowl should now be evenly lined to within 1/2" of the top.)

Remove bowl from freezer and arrange 1/2" slices of orange pound cake on top, cutting pieces to fit snugly (this will act as extra insulation while baking).

Unmold by dipping bowl into room-temperature water for about 1 minute, being careful not to get water near the rim. Remove from water and dry sides of bowl. Place ovenproof platter over top of bowl and invert, gently removing mixing bowl. Clean any drips on the platter with absorbent towels. Place in freezer uncovered to harden outer surface while egg whites are prepared.

Beat egg whites with an electric mixer until soft peaks form. Gradually add sugar while continuing to beat until stiff and glossy. Remove bombe from freezer. Cover mound completely and smoothly with beaten egg whites. Bake at 450° for about 4-5, minutes or until browned on all surfaces. (Freeze again if serving later.) Carefully pour chocolate sauce over all. Pipe whipped cream through a pastry bag to make decorative garnishes. Dot with fresh raspberries. At the serving table, gently heat framboise in a chafing dish and ignite with a match. Pour over bombe. Serve immediately. Serves 12.

Carrots Vichy
Rating: G

- 2 dozen tiny whole carrots
- 2 c. water (salted)
- 3 oz. butter
- Dash white pepper
- Fresh minced parsley

Cook carrots in 2 cups salted water until tender. Drain. Season with butter, white pepper, and a generous sprinkling of minced parsley. Serves 2-3.
(By Claude Farina)

Pommes Dauphine
Rating: G

(The pommes Dauphine recipe is a combination of two other recipes: pommes Duchess and pâte à choux.)

Pommes Duchess:
- 2 lbs. potatoes, (about 6 medium) peeled
- 2 whole eggs
- 2 egg yolks
- 2 T. butter
- 1 t. salt
- Pepper
- Pinch nutmeg

Pâte à choux:
- 1 c. milk or water
- 2 T. butter
- ½ t. salt
- 1 c. flour
- 4 eggs

  Oil for frying (peanut, corn, etc. Not solid shortening)
  Salt to taste

First, prepare the pommes Duchess. Cut potatoes into quarters. Bring a large pot of cold, salted water to boiling. Add potatoes (there should be enough water to cover), cover, and cook until tender but not mushy. Drain. Immediately return potatoes to the hot pot and dry thoroughly by shaking pan over a heated burner until all moisture evaporates. Put potatoes through a ricer or fine sieve. Work mixture with a wooden spoon until smooth.

Combine whole eggs with egg yolks and beat slightly with a fork. Add eggs, butter, salt, pepper, and nutmeg to potatoes and beat with an electric mixer until light and fluffy. Keep warm. (These "mashed potatoes" can be made in advance and kept for later use by brushing top with melted butter to prevent a crust from forming. Reheat over low heat if necessary, stirring constantly.)

Next, prepare the pâte à choux. Combine in a saucepan 1 cup milk or water, 2 tablespoons butter, and 1/2 teaspoon salt. Bring to a boil and add the flour all at once, stirring well until the mixture forms a ball and leaves the sides of the pan. Remove from heat. Add the eggs one at a time, stirring well after each addition. Combine 2 cups of the warm pommes Duchess with 2 cups of the pâte à choux. Spoon into a pastry bag. Squeeze out 1" or 2" strips directly into hot (380°) deep fat (use a knife to cut off desired lengths) and fry until puffed and brown. Remove with a slotted spoon and drain on absorbent towels. Salt to taste. Serve hot. Serves 6.
(By Claude Farina)

Truffle Soup
Rating: G

(Truffles, not to be confused with chocolate bonbons of the same name, are fungi found only in the root system of certain trees. Truffle-loving pigs or dogs are used to locate the little treasures, and each nodule must then be rooted out by hand. This, and the fact that they defy controlled farming, accounts for their high cost of about $120 per pound. Even the broken shreddings are sold with a high price tag. If using only a portion of a can of dry truffle shreddings, cover remainder with sherry and refrigerate. It will keep fresh for about four weeks. Or freeze in its own juice, add a little Madeira if juice is lacking, and freeze. The distinctive taste is released by gently heating, and may be used in other dishes, such as eggs, hors d'oeuvres, and pâtés.)

- 1½ quarts beef consommé (stock)
- 7 oz. breaking truffle (truffle shreddings)
- 1 oz. cognac

Bring consommé to a boil. Reduce heat and gradually sprinkle in the breaking truffle. Simmer 5-6 minutes. When ready to serve, add cognac. Serves 4.
(By Claude Farina)

Consommé au Port
Rating: G

- 2 carrots
- 2 celery hearts
- 2 leeks
- 1 white turnip
- 1 parsnip
- 2 quarts beef stock
- 4 c. port wine

Cut carrots, celery hearts, white part of the leeks, turnip, and parsnip in fine julienne, or strips the thickness of kitchen matches, about 1" long. Cook in the beef stock according to their cooking time. Drain well (reserving beef stock), cover vegetables, and set aside. Reduce the beef stock to 1/2 its original volume by slowly boiling over low heat. Add port and vegetables to the reduced stock. Cover and bring to a boil. Reduce heat and simmer just until vegetables are heated though. Serve in heated bowls. Serves 4.
(By Claude Farina)

Oyster Stew
Rating: G

(Oyster liquor is the natural liquid found in unopened oysters. When opening oysters [see Tom Jones oyster recipe for instructions on opening] save the juice and strain it through a fine mesh or metal strainer to remove any sand.)

- 5 T. butter
- ⅛ t. paprika
- ⅛ t. celery salt
- ¼ t. Worcestershire sauce
- 14 freshly opened oysters
- 1 c. oyster liquor (see above)
- 2 c. milk
- 1 c. cream (optional)
- Paprika for garnish

In a deep saucepan, heat 4 tablespoons of the butter with the paprika, celery salt, and Worcestershire sauce. When the butter bubbles, add freshly opened oysters and oyster liquor. Simmer until oyster edges curl. Add the 2 cups milk, or 1 cup each of milk and cream. Bring to boiling point. Pour stew into 4 soup bowls. Top each with a little paprika and equal portions of the remaining 1 tablespoon butter. Serves 4.
(By Claude Farina)

Pigeon en Croûte
Rating: G

Filling:
- 6 *young pigeons (10 oz. each), dressed, cleaned, and trussed*
- *Salt pork fat*
- 3 *c. boiling water*
- ¼ *t. green peppercorns (canned)*
- 1 *small onion, sliced*
- 1 *small carrot, sliced*
- 2 *sprigs fresh parsley*
- 2 *stalks celery, chopped*
- 3 *T. flour*
- 3 *T. melted shortening*

Pastry:
- 2 *c. sifted flour*
- ¾ *t. salt*
- ⅔ *c. shortening*
- 4-6 *T. cold water*
- 1 *egg, beaten*

To prepare filling, sauté pigeons in salt pork fat until well browned. Place browned pigeons in a kettle. Add 3 cups boiling water, peppercorns, onion, carrot, parsley, and celery. Simmer until tender, 2-3 hours. While filling is cooking, prepare the pastry. Sift flour and salt together. Cut in shortening with 2 knives or pastry blender until it reaches the consistency of coarse meal. Add water, a little at a time, just until the mixture holds together. Divide dough into 2 parts. Roll out one part to desired size, large enough to cover the top of a 9" pie plate or shallow casserole with at least 1" excess all around. (You may freeze the other half and use at a later time.) Remove pigeons from kettle. Cover and set aside. Strain and reserve broth in kettle. Blend flour and melted shortening together into a paste consistency. Add to broth, cooking and stirring until thickened. Reheat pigeons in thickened broth. Place in 9" pie plate or shallow casserole and top with pastry crust. Crimp edges, cut air slits in crust, and brush with beaten egg. Bake at 375° for about 10 minutes, or until crust is golden. Serves 6.
(By Claude Farina)

Pressed Duck
Rating: G

(To execute this recipe, the ducklings must be killed by strangulation to conserve the blood—the essential ingredient in pressed duck. You'll also need a good duck press.)

- 1 *5 lb. duckling*
- 3 *young ducklings, 1½-2 lbs., plucked and dressed*
- 3 *raw duckling livers*
- 6 *oz. sweet butter (approximately)*
- 6 *oz. Madeira*
- 6 *oz. port*
- *Juice of 1 large lemon*
- ¼ *c. brandy*
- *Salt, pepper*

Roast the 5-pound duckling in a roasting pan at 350° until done, at the rate of 20 minutes per pound. Skim fat from the pan juices, reserving 1/2 cup greaseless stock. Set stock aside. Roast smaller ducklings at 450° for 15 minutes, turning every few minutes to brown evenly. Carve carcass meat into thin slices. Cover slices and set aside. Remove legs. (These may be broiled and served on the side.)

Crush carcass bones in a duck press. Reserve resultant juices and set aside. (Discard carcass or use in soup stock.) Rinse duck press well by pouring the 1/2 cup greaseless duck stock through. Mash raw livers with an equal amount of sweet butter in a skillet or chafing dish over low heat.

Add Madeira, port, and pressed carcass juices, stirring constantly for about 8-10 minutes, until thickened. Add sliced duck meat and lemon juice to the liver sauce, stirring constantly. Pour brandy over and set aflame. (Color should be dark brown like chocolate and thickened.) Salt and pepper to taste. Serve hot. (Broiled legs may be served on the side.) Serves 4.
(By Claude Farina.)

Pâté de Fois Gras
Rating: G

½ c. goose liver
2 T. goose fat
3 hard cooked eggs
   Salt, pepper

Sauté goose liver in goose fat until tender. Mash (or use food processor) into a paste with the eggs. Salt and pepper to taste. (If too stiff, add additional goose fat.) Serves 2-3.
(By Claude Farina)

Aragosto à la Garciofo (Lobster with Artichokes)
Rating: G

2 artichokes, stems removed and steamed
3 T. butter
3 T. olive oil
2 shallots, minced
3 garlic cloves, mashed
3 T. flour
2 c. milk
¼ c. Parmesan cheese
1 c. cooked lobster
   Salt, freshly ground pepper
1 lb. cooked pasta

Scrape inside of artichoke leaves, removing pulp. Remove fuzzy core and cut up artichoke center base. Set pulp and chopped center aside. Melt butter and olive oil together in large skillet or saucepan. Add shallots and garlic. Sauté 5 minutes without browning. Add flour and stir with a wire whip for 2 minutes. Gradually add milk, stirring with whip until thickened. Stir in Parmesan cheese, lobster, and artichoke pulp. Salt and pepper to taste. Heat through. Serve over hot pasta. Serves 4-6.

Veal Massenet
Rating: G

8 2 oz. thin slices veal scallops (1 lb.)
   Flour for dusting
   Salt, pepper
2 T. butter
1 T. olive oil
1 large bay leaf (broken in bits)
¼ t. dried sage
2 T. unsalted butter
2 T. minced fresh parsley
¼ t. meat glaze (see below)
¼ c. white wine
2 t. heavy cream

Pound veal with side of cleaver or meat mallet. Dust lightly with flour (shake off excess). Season with salt and pepper. Melt butter and olive oil together in a large skillet or frying pan. Add meat. Sprinkle meat evenly with bay leaf and sage. Quickly brown 2-3 minutes on each side. Remove meat to a heated platter. Cover and keep warm. Cream butter and parsley together. Set aside.

Pour off all but 1/4 teaspoon meat juices from the frying pan. (This is the meat glaze). Add wine and cook over high heat a minute or so until slightly reduced and thickened. Remove from heat. Add parsley butter and stir to melt. Stir in cream. Pour sauce over veal and serve immediately. Serves 2.
(By Claude Farina)

TAGS AND TRAILERS

> *If I have to lie, steal, cheat or kill, as God is my witness, I'll never go hungry again.*

Vivien Leigh's oath to the heavens in David O. Selznick's *Gone With the Wind*.

Comfort and Joy

Nutshell

Comfort and Joy is an unexpected comedy treat. It dishes up humor as light as meringue and trouble as heavy as whipping cream. And for connoisseurs of food in film, it even features a mouth-watering confection as the central element in its plot resolution.

Scottish writer/director Bill Forsyth got the idea for this marvelous little story while directing his earlier film, *Gregory's Girl*. Shooting of that film was constantly interrupted by the jingle of a passing ice cream truck. The interruptions were a nuisance, but served to plant the kernel of an idea that would eventually develop into *Comfort and Joy*.

The story, as described by Forsyth, is "a serious comedy about a man who has one of those weeks where everything goes wrong." It begins in Glasgow, a week before Christmas, when the attractive, kleptomaniacal, live-in girlfriend of good-natured radio DJ Alan "Dickie" Bird (Bill Paterson) walks out on him. The parting has come without any prior warning and leaves Dickie with an apartment nearly bereft of furnishings. His sporty red BMW convertible with black velour upholstery is seemingly the only love he has left.

Alan's married friend Colin (Patrick Malahide) encourages him to take advantage of his new freedom and set a fresh direction for his life. But at this point the sum total of Dickie's life consists of recording silly voice-overs for snack commercials and making banal "happy-talk" on his early morning radio show.

When Alan catches the eye of a pretty girl selling ice cream from a Mr. Bunny truck, however, he decides to follow her on her route, and his life takes a decided turn for the more interesting. On a remote neighborhood hilltop outside the city, he becomes the only witness to a brutal assault on the Mr. Bunny van by a gang in ski masks. Before splitting the scene, one of the gang members recognizes "Dickie" Bird and asks him for an autograph, while advising to keep mum about the attack. In the confusion, Alan's recently purchased scoop of ice cream falls onto the hood of his beloved BMW, signaling the beginning of the end of his prized possession.

Alan is exhilarated by this recent brush with the reality of life outside his broadcasting booth and asks his boss Hilary (Rikki Fulton) for permission to do a special documentary on the underbelly of the city. No sooner has he been granted grudging consent to pursue his big story than he finds his upholstery dotted with ice cream cones and himself in the middle of an ice cream war. Mr. Bunny's rival, the Italian ice cream mogul Mr. McCool (Roberto Bernardi), enlists Alan's help as a go-between in trying to settle a territorial dispute between the two companies. Alan, sensing an opportunity to do something worthwhile with his life, dives right into the fray, delivering cryptic messages to the warring sides via his radio broadcasts, and consequently raising doubts in his boss's mind about the DJ's sanity. Alan tries to explain to Hilary the turn of events

Fried Ice Cream
Rating: G

(This particular rendition of fried ice cream is used by a local Mexican restaurant. It's so simple, it's a can't-fail.)

1 c. cereal flakes (i.e., Team), crushed fairly fine
½ t. cinnamon
1 t. sugar
1 scoop vanilla ice cream
1 egg, well beaten
Vegetable oil for deep frying
Crushed fresh strawberries sweetened to taste or
Hot fudge (see California Split, p. 218)

Combine crushed cereal, cinnamon, and sugar in a small bowl. Roll ice cream ball in cereal mixture, pressing crushed flakes into the ice cream as you roll. Use about half the cereal in this step. Roll flake-coated ice cream ball in beaten egg. Roll ball in remaining cereal mixture, again pressing in the flakes as you would pack a snow ball.

Freeze ball at least 30 minutes to firm up. When ready to fry, preheat oil to 375°. Fry ball in hot oil for 30 seconds. Remove with slotted spoon. Drain briefly on absorbent towels. Serve immediately, straight up or with your choice of sauce. Serves 1.

Comfort and Joy. An escalation in cold warfare, as Bill Paterson is attacked by an unknown ice cream assailant after he witnesses the destruction of a defenseless Mr. Bunny truck.

in his life, telling him that until now he's been the wrong flavor—the wrong ice cream. He was raspberry ice cream when he should have been vanilla. A shrink, recommended by Hilary, hears a more elaborate version. Alan was apple cake, he says, when he should be kunsel cake. But his relationship with Maddy, well...that was pure chocolate mousse.

Meanwhile, the war between the ice cream companies escalates even further when Mr. McCool's gang vandalizes Mr. Bunny's warehouse. During the fracas, Alan becomes peeved to learn that the two sides are actually related, and that he's stuck in the middle of a family dispute. Trevor (Alex Norton), the owner of Mr. Bunny and nephew to Mr. McCool, gave up his fish and chips business to ally himself with Mr. McCool's daughter Charlotte (C.P. Grogan).

Just when he's feeling helpless at ever resolving the family feud, Alan hears a radio cookery broadcast that gives him a brainstorm. He gathers the two warring ice cream vendors together and suggests a compromise product to be made that will yield profit for both sides: ice cream fritters. The families go wild with enthusiasm over the lucrative solution, even to the point of letting Alan keep a hefty percentage of the profits in exchange for the secret recipe.

A week after Maddy's departure, Alan finds himself alone in the radio studio on Christmas day, broadcasting yuletide cheer to his listening audience, eating Christmas pudding, and looking forward to his new life in fried ice cream.

Food Scene

It is said that the Chinese are the masters of the difficult ice cream fritter, or fried ice cream. Not surprisingly, I experienced my first ice cream fritter in a tiny Chinese restaurant in San Francisco. It was as fascinating to see on the plate as it was to eat. Crunchy-fried hot on the outside, smooth and creamy cold on the inside. No wonder it was the perfect solution to a family of fried fish merchants and ice cream vendors at war with one another.

In introducing the revolutionary new product, Alan gathers the families in the empty kitchen of an ice cream shop conveniently located next door to a fish and chips eatery. With an apron securely tied around his suit and the group huddled around the counter, he commences cooking. He opens a packet and dumps secret powdery contents onto a plate.

Comfort and Joy. As Bill Paterson opens a package containing the secret ingredient in making fried ice cream, hostile factions of the ice cream war (left to right) Alex Norton, Billy McElhaney, C.P. Grogan, and Roberto Bernardi, watch intently.

Then he rolls two scoops of ice cream in the secret powder, dips the scoops quickly into the batter, and fries them quickly in hot oil. We learn that the contents of the powdery packet is the secret adhesive that prevents the ice cream from turning into a sticky gooey mess.

With the precision of an alchemist, Alan pulls the fritters out of the hot fat and cuts them up for sampling. After only one bite, the entire family is convinced that it's a money-maker, and they can't wait to exploit it with marketing strategies, new flavors, and syrups. Alan quickly reminds them of the essential secret ingredient, earning himself a hefty cut of the business and a new outlook on life as kunsel cake.

The Heartbreak Kid

Nutshell

To be abandoned on your honeymoon with nothing more than a pecan pie to show for your heartache is a cruel fate indeed, no matter how good the pie is. Such is the plight of the unforgettably klutzy Lila Kolodny (director Elaine May's real-life daughter, Jeannie Berlin), in *The Heartbreak Kid*.

This film, inspired by a four-page Bruce J. Friedman short story called "A Change of Plan," was Elaine May's second directoral effort. She successfully paced the usual laugh-a-minute style of writer Neil Simon to allow a story to unfold with painfully funny results.

Following a brief, pristine courtship, Lila and Len (Charles Grodin) marry and head south for a Florida honeymoon. Len is an ambitious, insincere sporting goods salesman who is distressed to suddenly find unsettling quirks in his bride's personality, such as her habit of eating candy bars in bed after lovemaking, her slobbish table manners, and her nonstop, off-key singing of commercial jingles.

Almost immediately upon their arrival in Miami, Lila's penchant for excess gets her a whopping sunburn, forcing her to remain in their hotel room covered with ointment, while Len's roving eye falls on a beautiful, nubile silky-blonde coed, Kelly Corcoran (Cybill Shepherd), who is vacationing with her parents. Her cool, sophisticated manner—in every way the opposite of Lila—prompts Len into declaring his marriage a disaster, and frantically setting out in hot pursuit of his new golden dream girl.

Kelly is bemused by Len's persistent advances, but she especially enjoys watching her father (Eddie Albert) become unhinged at Len's attentions. Len has fabricated a series of outrageous stories to explain his long absences to the despondent Lila back at the hotel room, but in the security of a crowded restaurant, he finally breaks the news that he's decided to end the marriage.

With his marriage out of the way, Len takes off to pursue Kelly full-time in her snowy Minnesota habitat. He first succeeds in ingeniously prying the ice-maiden away from her Herculean boyfriend. Then, after winning enough of Kelly's interest to secure a dinner invitation to her family's house, he tries to win approval from her father with unctuous compliments about the food. He finds honesty in the corn, he says. There's no deceit in the cauliflower, he says. Is he for real? That's what Kelly's dad asks when he offers Len a $25,000 bribe to leave Kelly alone. When Len refuses, his fate is sealed.

At the wedding reception, Len sits alone on the sofa looking like a guy whose fun ends when the chase is over. An inaccessible goal has become just another acquisition. His blank stare underscores his salesman's essential smarminess and vacuity, and leaves one wondering, but not much caring, what's next for the Heartbreak Kid?

Pecan Pie
Rating: G

1 c. firmly packed brown sugar
¼ c. butter, softened
3 eggs
½ c. light corn syrup
1½ c. coarsely chopped pecans
2 t. rum extract
½ t. salt
Single piecrust

Cream the sugar and butter together. Add the eggs, one at a time, beating after each addition. Stir in the corn syrup, pecans, rum, and salt. Pour into the piecrust shell and bake at 450° for 40 minutes, or until a knife when inserted in filling comes out clean. Serves 6.

The Heartbreak Kid. The last course.

The Heartbreak Kid. Jeannie Berlin enjoys herself in a Miami seafood restaurant, unaware of the bomb husband Charles Grodin, center, is about to set off when the pecan pie is served.

Food Scene

For Len and Lila, it's their last supper. For us, it's a glimpse of one of those rare cinematic moments when roaringly funny performances smack head-on with tragedy, producing a rich and powerful climax not easily forgotten.

After Len has determined to marry Kelly, he decides the only way to make the divorce news more palatable to Lila is by treating her to a good dinner. With Lila's sunburn sufficiently under control, Len feigns excitement over the recovery as an excuse to take her to a seafood restaurant for lobster—her favorite.

After Lila gorges herself on the main course, Len orders her favorite dessert—pecan pie. For Len, affairs of the heart are like closing a sale—timing is everything, so he tries to slip in the news about his intentions like the small print in a contract. As the words gradually clear his mouth, Lila's disbelief turns to gagging nausea. But as she begins to panic and shriek, he puts a tight hold on her to prevent her from fleeing to the ladies' room. To the astonishment of onlooking diners, he holds her to her seat and tries to talk her out of her torment by listing all the benefits of their breakup. Like a beached whale taking its last deep and desperate breaths, Lila resigns to the news in the arms of the Heartbreak Kid, but decides to pass on the pecan pie.

Housecalls

Nutshell

One way to get a decent piece of cheesecake is to live in New York City. Another is to import it from New York City. The middle-aged doctor in director Howard Zieff's *Housecalls*, however, does neither. Instead he tries to marry someone whose profession is cheesecakes.

Newly widowed Dr. Nichols (Walter Matthau) returns to Kensington General Hospital after three months of R & R in Hawaii, ready and rarin' to make up for lost "playing the field" time. For a doctor who's been out of circulation since 1945, that means dating starry-eyed nurses and evaluating the charts of choice female patients for potential vital signs.

It's in the midst of this pursuit that he encounters attractive divorcee Ann Atkinson (Glenda Jackson), whose broken jaw has been shut tight in a helmet by senile Dr. Willoughby (Art Carney), a specialist in useless and antiquated medical treatments. Out of the bigness of his heart Nichols rewires Ms. Atkinson's jaw and gets himself into trouble with Willoughby, who he then must placate by agreeing to reappoint and support Willoughby for another term as chief of staff.

Dr. Nichols' interest in the jaw case is heightened when he has a chance meeting with the fully recovered Ms. Atkinson on a TV talk show. There he learns that she's an outspoken proponent of consumer rights and has an opinionated, independent streak that he finds irresistible. What's more, she makes cheesecakes for a living!

The relationship between the two quickly grows into romance. Ann, however, has been put off relationships by a philandering ex-husband and insists that the reluctant doctor commit to her a two-week trial period of exclusive dating rights.

The plot thickens when Willoughby forces Nichols to spend an evening with a not-so-dumb-blonde named Ellen Grady (Candice Azzara), in hopes that she'll drop her ten million dollar lawsuit against the hospital for the operating room death of her rich husband. Although Nichols is technically innocent of any wrongdoing with Ms. Grady, Ann will not be mollified when she believes that he's sampled another kind of "pastry." She hides his clothes in the freezer and storms out of the relationship.

Dressed in nothing but a lovely feather-trimmed dressing gown and matching slippers from Ann's wardrobe, Dr. Nichols marches off to the hospital a changed man. Heroically, he retracts his nomination to reinstate Willoughby for another term, and gallantly chases after Ann to bargain for more of her time—and cheesecake.

Cheesecake
Rating: G

(This is one of the best and absolutely creamiest cheese cakes I've ever tasted—adapted from a recipe by my Italian mother-in-law, who doesn't even live in New York.)

Crust:
- 1/3 c. butter, melted
- 2 c. crushed graham crackers

Cake:
- 3 8 oz. pkgs. cream cheese, softened
- 1 c. sugar
- 2 t. vanilla
- 2 eggs

Topping:
- 1 pt. sour cream
- 3 T. sugar
- 1/2 t. vanilla
- 2 pts. fresh strawberries, crushed and sweetened to taste

Toss the butter and crushed graham crackers in a bowl until crumbs are well coated. Pack into a buttered 13"x 9" pan. Refrigerate. Combine the cake ingredients in a bowl and beat with an electric mixer until smooth. Pour into the prepared pan and bake at 350° for 20 minutes. (It will be slightly loose, but lightly browned around the edges.) Cool 5 minutes. Beat the sour cream, sugar, and vanilla together in a bowl with an electric mixer for 5 minutes. Pour over cake and bake at 450° for 5 minutes. Cool completely. Serve with crushed strawberries or fresh fruit of your choice. Serves 10–12.

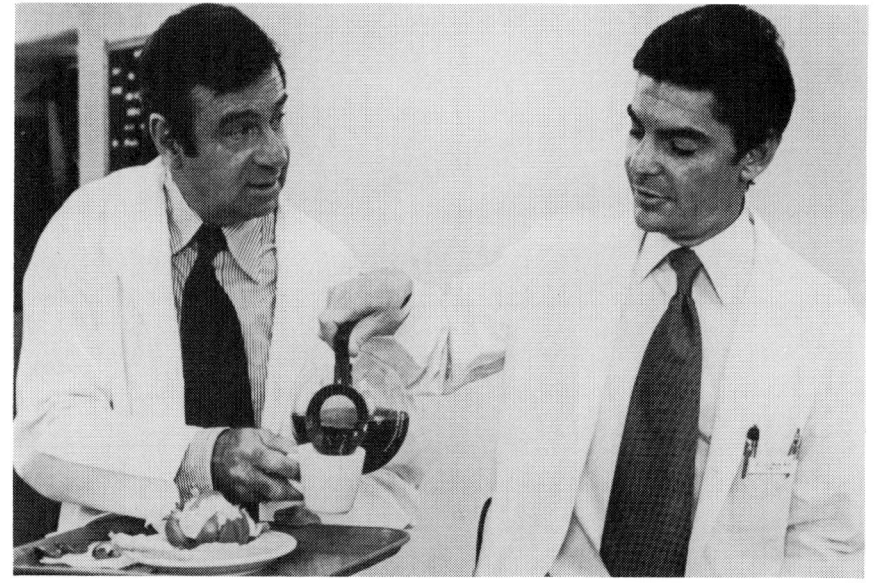

House Calls. Richard Benjamin, right, tops off Walter Matthau's cafeteria "Tuna Surprise" with cafeteria mud.

House Calls. "This is absolutely superb!" Walter Matthau tells Glenda Jackson of her freshly baked cheesecake.

Food Scene

Ann is a sharp-tongued, stubborn woman, who's also charged with enough sensibility, maturity, and intelligence to make a man who's starved for mental stimulation want to give up the ongoing pleasures of the dating game just for her. In addition, of course, she makes a great cheesecake.

Before their courtship actually begins, Dr. Nichols calls on Ann by surprise one night. He's been stranded with car trouble after wining and dining a "foxy lawyer from the racket club." Ann's been busy that night baking her living in the kitchen. While Nichols uses Ann's phone to call the auto club for help, she graciously brings him a complimentary slice of her fresh-baked cheesecake. For a moment, he forgets his inconvenience as he's thoroughly swept away by the moist, creamy-smooth dish. "This is absolutely superb!" he declares after his first bite. It's better than anything he's had that night—and a lot cheaper!

He's impressed enough to ask Ann for their first date—Chinese takeout the following day. One thing leads to another, but before she can whip up some eggs for him for breakfast, he's heading out the door with a promise to fit her into his dating schedule.

Little could Dr. Nichols have known that his first bite would not be his last. Once he got a taste of quality "cheesecake" made by a quality woman, he was hooked and ready to swear off all other "pastries" for good. Especially "tarts."

Mocha Cheesecake
Rating: G

1 12 oz. pkg. chocolate chips
½ c. very strong coffee
1½ lbs. cream cheese, softened (at room temperature)
1 c. sugar
4 eggs
4 T. flour
1 c. heavy cream

Melt chocolate chips with coffee in top of double boiler. Set aside. Put cream cheese in mixing bowl and gradually beat in sugar with an electric mixer. Beat in eggs, one at a time. Then, sprinkling in flour gradually, blend just until mixed. Blend in cream. Stir in chocolate mixture, blending well. Pour into greased 10" spring-form pan. Bake at 350° for 1 hour. Turn off oven, open door, and allow cheesecake to cool completely before removing. Serves 16.

Mildred Pierce

Nutshell

James M. Cain's blockbuster novel turns film murder mystery in this classic "woman's pix" of the 1940s. Movies released during this time were typically soap-operatic, tearjerker types, aimed at women's interests in social status, romance, and motherhood. *Mildred Pierce* was every bit of this formula, but Ms. Crawford's milestone performance as the infamous pie-maker Mildred Pierce, together with the film's exceptional scope, took it beyond the soap. It quickly became one of the most talked about films of the decade.

As an impassioned, honest, hard-working, single mother-on-the-rise, Joan Crawford is the "total woman" in her role as Mildred Pierce. The film begins with the murder of a man, and events quickly move to a police station, where Ms. Pierce, taken in on suspicion of the murder, tells the story of her unhappy life in a series of flashbacks that take us to 1931—the heart of the Depression. Ms. Pierce, a newly separated mother of two (having thrown her philandering husband out of the house), is penniless and with no real job skills to sell except for her obvious culinary talents. Her part-time work baking pies and cakes at home for profit has been bringing in a little extra money, but she determines to find a "good job" to give her girls the best money can buy.

After a discouraging search for a prestigious job, she gratefully takes a position as a lunchroom waitress, but tries to keep her employment a secret from her children to spare them the embarrassment of having a mother who works in a uniform as hired help. Her desire to be the best and provide for her family, though, quickly earns Mildred notoriety as an outstanding waitress. In just a few months, the additional money she earns from baking pies and cakes for the restaurant enables Mildred to open her own chain of classy drive-in restaurants in California.

Over the years, as she makes a steady rise to financial success, Mildred's best intentions are repeatedly turned against her by people she loves or trusts. Instead of the money bringing happiness and security, she is constantly burdened with grief. Her real estate partner double-crosses her; her younger daughter dies; and the men in her life prove unfaithful. But none of these heartaches compares to what she suffers from the unbounded greed of her older daughter, Veda (Ann Blythe).

From childhood, Veda is filled with pretentious airs about fashion, society, and the arts. She grows more obnoxious and demanding as a teen, eventually suckering a suave socialite into a secret marriage that is soon exposed and annulled, but not until she succeeds in blackmailing the groom's family with a fake pregnancy. Disgusted with her mother's lowly line of work with "chickens and pies," Veda storms out of Mildred's life and indulges in a seamier life as a singer at a dockside bar. When she does come back to Mom, it's only to secretly resume her affair with her mother's second husband—the unscrupulous playboy and eventual murder victim, Monte Beragon (Zachary Scott).

Pumpkin Pie
Rating: G

Filling:

- 1½ c. canned or fresh pumpkin puree
- ½ c. half and half
- 1 c. sour cream
- 1½ t. vanilla
- 1 c. firmly packed brown sugar
- 1 T. flour
- 1 t. ground cinnamon
- ½ t. ground nutmeg
- ½ t. ground allspice
- ½ t. ground ginger
- ¼ t. ground cloves
- ½ t. salt
- 3 eggs, beaten
- 1 unbaked 9" single crust pie shell
- Whipped cream

Combine filling ingredients in a bowl and mix well with a wire whip. Pour into pie shell. Bake at 400° for 20 minutes. Reduce heat to 350° and continue baking 40 more minutes. Cool. Serve with whipped cream. Serves 6.

Mildred's years as a doting, self-sacrificing parent are partly to blame for her daughter's ways, but Veda never makes an effort to check her own greed. Eventually Veda becomes too evil even for her own good, and when she needs her mother most, Mildred finally says no.

Food Scene

There are few who would dispute Mildred Pierce as the rightful heir to Mable Normand's title as *First Lady of Pies*. Not since Normand's airborne custard pie has there been a cinematic character so closely allied to this pastry.

Mildred's character in the book varies from the movie in one notable sense. She is much more critical about her first place of employment and vows to change it. About her new job as a waitress, Cain the novelist writes:

> She held aloof from the restaurant itself, and the people connected with it. This wasn't entirely due to her ideas of social superiority. In her own mind, she was highly critical of the kitchen, and was afraid to get drawn into talk, for fear she would say what she thought and lose her job. Her special grievance was the pies. They were bought from the Handy Baking Company...uninviting in appearance with sticky, tasteless filling and hard, indigestible crusts.

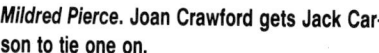

Mildred Pierce. Joan Crawford gets Jack Carson to tie one on.

Lemon Meringue Pie
Rating: G

Lemon filling:
1 c. sugar
6 T. cornstarch
¼ t. salt
1 c. milk
1 c. water
4 egg yolks, beaten
3 T. butter
⅓ c. lemon juice
4 t. grated lemon rind
1 baked single pie shell

Meringue:
4 egg whites
½ t. cream of tartar
4 T. powdered sugar

Combine the sugar, cornstarch, and salt in the top of a double boiler over hot (not boiling) water. Gradually add the milk and water, stirring while adding, and cook about 10 minutes until thickened, stirring constantly. Cover and cook an additional 10 minutes, stirring occasionally. Remove top of double boiler from heat. Measure out about 1/4 cup of the cooked sugar mixture and beat it into the egg yolks. Pour egg mixture into cooked sugar mixture in double boiler. Return to heat and stir for 5 minutes, cooking over boiler water. Remove top of double boiler from heat and stir in the butter, lemon juice, and rind. Cool, stirring gently to release steam. Pour into cooled single piecrust. Whip the egg whites with a beater just until frothy. Add the cream of tartar and beat until stiff, but not dry. Gradually sprinkle in the sugar while continuing to beat, being careful not to overbeat. Spoon meringue over the lemon filling and bake pie at 350° for about 10–15 minutes, until lightly browned. Serves 6.

Mildred resolves to end the problem by taking over the pie contract and does so by smuggling in three of her own pies (pumpkin, apple, and lemon meringue), which sell out in an hour and win her the coveted contract—three dozen a week at 35¢ a piece. Waiting on tables by day and baking by night, she parlays her savings into the fortune that keeps her daughter in lavender and lace.

The movie version gives a more sketchy portrayal of her early involvement at the restaurant, and in quick montage sequences depicts Mildred as a hard-working waitress who gets to be among the best, eagerly learning the business and earning extra money by baking pies on the side for the restaurant, too.

Butterfly McQueen as Mildred's "maid," and Eve Arden as Ida the business friend add comic relief to this otherwise heavy-duty wrap of love gone awry and ingratitude in baker's dozens. The love and gratitude Mildred so desperately wants to see from her daughter comes instead from the delighted customers who appreciate her real gift—flaky-light crusts and fresh tasting pie fillings.

Apple Pie
Rating: G

- 6 medium-sized tart apples (about 2 lbs.)
- 1/3 c. butter
- 1/4 c. white sugar
- 1/4 c. firmly packed brown sugar
- 1 t. ground cinnamon
- 1/2 t. ground nutmeg
- 1 T. lemon juice
- 1/4 c. Applejack
- 1/2 t. grated lemon rind
- 2 T. cornstarch
  Pastry for two-crust 9" pie, unbaked
- 1 T. milk
  Granulated sugar for sprinkling

Peel, core, and quarter the apples. Cut each quarter into 3 or 4 slices. Set aside. Melt the butter in a large frying pan. Mix the sugars with the cinnamon and nutmeg and add to the butter. Cook until sugars melt, stirring constantly. Add apple slices and stir gently to coat with the sugar mixture. Cook over medium heat, until apples begin to soften but are still fairly crisp, about 5 minutes (this will vary with the type of apple and thickness). Remove from heat. Add the lemon juice to the Applejack and pour over the apples. Spoon by layers into a 9" pie shell lined with unbaked crust, sprinkling layers with the lemon rind and cornstarch. Pour any remaining juices from the frying pan over the top. Top with piecrust, crimping and trimming the edges. Cut slits in top to allow steam to escape while baking. Brush crust with milk, and sprinkle lightly with granulated sugar. Bake at 350° for about 45 minutes, or until crust is browned and apples are tender. Serves 6.

On Golden Pond

Nutshell

On Golden Pond is the popular, award-winning 1981 film that brought together for the first time on the camera three of the screen's great actors. Two of those actors, of course, were father and daughter Henry and Jane Fonda, and the third was the incomparable Katharine Hepburn who, though a contemporary of Henry Fonda's with a simultaneously long career, had never met him until the casting of this film.

Ms. Fonda called the experience of working with these two giants "the highlight of her career," and said her acceptance of the role as Fonda's daughter in the film was intended as a "present" for her father. Ironically, it is her *character*'s arrival at her father's birthday celebration that provides initial spark for the story.

A quaint, waterfront cottage in the Winnepausaukee lakes region of New Hampshire is the familiar setting for Norman (Henry Fonda) and Ethel Thayer's (Katharine Hepburn) forty-eighth summer visit to Golden Pond. The cottage is filled with memorabilia from their many happy years together and mementos of Norman's pre-retirement years as a university professor.

Ethel is jubilant over the sight of little wildflowers and the welcoming sounds of the loon, but Norman's frustration with his failing senses and general preoccupation with his own mortality have turned him into a crotchety old "poop," whose morbidly caustic humor pleases no one. To get Norm's mind off his age, Ethel sends him out to pick wild strawberries in the nearby woods, with the promise of strawberry shortcake for lunch, but even that backfires when he suffers a momentary loss of memory and loses his bearings in the woods.

To make matters worse as far as Norman's disposition is concerned, Ethel has secretly invited daughter Chelsea (Jane Fonda) in from Los Angeles to help celebrate his eightieth birthday. Norman and Chelsea have never really seen eye to eye, and the reunion is strained at best, made even more so because Chelsea's brought along her latest boyfriend, dentist Bill Ray (Dabney Coleman) and his thirteen-year-old son Billy Ray (Doug McKeon).

Chelsea and Bill have made plans for a month-long European vacation and call upon Ethel and Norman to act as surrogate grandparents for Billy Ray while they're away. With Billy displaying standard adolescent impatience and disrespect for elders, Ethel and Norman are not in for an easy time of it. But through plenty of swimming, boating, and fishing—and one particularly harrowing experience out on the pond—plus a fair amount of jabbing at each other's individual abrasivenesses, Norman and Billy Ray soon develop healthier outlooks on life and each other.

On Golden Pond. The birthday board, ablaze with eighty candles, is successfully extinguished by the combined efforts of Dabney Coleman, Jane Fonda, Katharine Hepburn, Henry Fonda, and Doug McKeon.

When Chelsea and Bill return, now as husband and wife, Norm seems pleased and happy about his daughter for the first time. A tentative, unspoken truce is declared, and when Chelsea heads back to L.A. with her new family, she leaves feeling positive about Norman as both a father and a friend.

Food Scene

When you reach the age of eighty and celebrate the occasion with a party and cake, as Norman Thayer does, you may face the distinct possibility of having too many candles for too little cake.

At Norman's birthday party, Ethel brings in the cake ablaze with eighty lighted candles. While the candles burn, Norman makes a short speech, thanking the group for attending this historic event, then quickly asks for help in blowing out the candles, whose dripping wax is threatening to float the cake away.

Fortunately, the problem of dripping wax and too many candles for too little cake was brilliantly solved by Katharine Hepburn herself, reports property master Emily Ferry. Ms. Hepburn suggested the use of a "birthday board," which a friend of hers in New England had been using for years.

The birthday board is a round pine board with a raised center platform, large enough to hold an average sized round cake. Holes to support the candles are then drilled around the outside of the platform area on the rim. In this way, the candles are placed *around* the cake, not on, allowing salutations such as "HAPPY BIRTHDAY NORMAN" to be clearly visible and free from wax drippings.

When asked what kind of cake should appear in the scene, Ms. Hepburn stated that every man she ever knew wanted angel-food cake with chocolate frosting. It was an agreeable-enough suggestion, but lighting requirements necessitated the use of a lighter colored frosting. The scene was to be shot in a cozy candlelight setting and chocolate frosting would have appeared to disappear into the night air. Instead, Norman was served angel-food cake with a mocha frosting, a compromise with their lighting problems, but not the taste.

Angel Food Cake with Mocha Frosting
Rating: G

(It's best to make this cake a day before serving, as it "ripens" to improved flavor and texture.)

Cake:
1½ c. egg whites (10-12) at room temperature
¼ t. salt
1¼ t. cream of tartar
1 t. almond extract
1 t. vanilla
1¼ c. superfine granulated sugar
1 c. sifted cake flour

Frosting:
2 T. instant coffee
¼ c. boiling water
1 lb. confectioners' sugar
⅓ c. butter, softened
¼ t. salt
½ oz. (1/2 square) unsweetened chocolate, melted
1-2 t. cream

Beat egg whites with a beater until foamy. Add salt and cream of tartar and beat until whites stand up in soft peaks. Add the almond and vanilla extracts. Sift together the sugar and flour four times. Using a spatula, carefully fold the sugar-flour mixture into the beaten whites, 2 tablespoons at a time. Continue folding over and over until no flour shows and mixture is evenly blended. Spoon into ungreased 10" tube pan and bake at 325° for about 1 hour. Invert on a wire rack and let cool in pan at least 1 hour.

To prepare frosting, dissolve coffee in the boiling water. When mixture has cooled to room temperature, combine all ingredients in a bowl (except cream) and beat with an electric mixer until smooth. If frosting is too thick, stir in cream to increase spreadability. When cake has completely cooled, frost all surfaces. Serves 8.

Once Upon a Time in America

Nutshell

A familiar theme in American films, like *Angels with Dirty Faces* and *Bonnie and Clyde*, has been the impact of hard economic times in creating criminal behavior. Such is the case with famed director Sergio Leone's critically acclaimed masterpiece, *Once Upon a Time in America*.

After a ten-year absence, the master-chef of "Spaghetti Westerns" rides into town delivering not another cowboy hero, but a wholly new cast of characters in his saga of the rise and fall of a group of American gangsters. While food-related hunger in this film is certainly a factor in establishing early motives for crime, the hunger soon turns to a thirst for the material wealth and power promised in the American dream.

Deftly spanning five decades from the 1920s to the 1960s, the film portrays a gang of young ghetto-born Jews growing up with a fiercely twisted sense of loyalties. Leone abandons the more literal styles of cinematic story-telling and chooses, instead, to film in quasi dreamlike settings of flashbacks and fast forwards while swinging from unpredictable hard story realities to mystical story fantasies. What emerges is truly a unique and artful piece of filmmaking.

He begins the story in the middle, where Noodles (Robert De Niro) as a full-grown gang leader is high on hash over the death of gang co-leader Max (James Wood) and other gang friends killed during their involvement in a government heist. He too is hunted, but escapes to find that the suitcase of loot earned by the gang over the years has mysteriously disappeared.

A fast forward to Noodles thiry-five years later brings him back to gang member Fat Moe's bar in the old neighborhood, from which he had fled so many years ago. Who sent for him, he wants to know. He learns that the bodies of his dead friends have been moved to a fancy tomb.

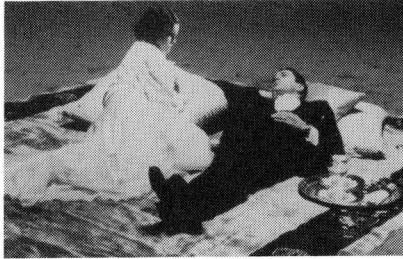

Once Upon a Time in America. Robert DeNiro woos Elizabeth McGovern with a lavish dinner and a romantic interlude by the ocean, but fails to win her heart.

Once Upon a Time in America. James Wood celebrates the end of Prohibition with cake and champagne.

His gaze on a photograph of Moe's sister Deborah (Elizabeth McGovern) cuts to...Deborah as a child dancing....

The story moves on from here to the "beginning" revealing the early romantic involvements of Noodles and Deborah, the formation of the gang, and the boys' progression from heists and muscle jobs to big-time rum-running, speakeasy operations, and prostitution. The young lovers' momentum is derailed early on, however, when Noodles is sent to prison for killing a gun-toting bully who murdered a younger gang member. Upon his release, Noodles is taken to the gang's prosperous speakeasy, where he is reacquainted with Deborah and his partners in crime. There they plan and eventually pull off a diamond heist that puts them in the big-time, including acting as the muscle in labor racketeering.

But it's short-lived glory for the group. Noodles tries to rebuild his long-distanced romance with Deborah in a lavish private dinner for two, but winds up raping her after she tells him her plans for going to Hollywood to start an acting career. The gang's illegal booze business hits bottom with the repeal of the Volstead Act and the subsequent end of Prohibition.

The need for new business tempts Max into planning a hit on the Federal Reserve Bank; however, the high-risk insanity of Max's plan prompts Noodles to set up him and the others to save their lives. Noodles' plan backfires, though, and his friends are shot during the heist—or so it seems.

A cut to thirty-five years later shows the final outcome of the gang, and a bitter-sweet truth behind the American dream.

Food Scene

As a teenager, Noodles is a sensitive romantic who retreats to the public bathroom in his apartment building to read in peace, away from fighting parents and crying babies. One day, when his reading is interrupted by a teenage girl needing the bathroom for purposes other than a library, their natural curiosities collide. The sensuous but calculating girl quickly seizes the opportunity to get what she wants by offering her body in exchange for a Charlotte Russe—and with whipped cream and a cherry on top, she'll do anything!

Word spreads, and soon afterward an obliging gang member stands at the restaurant dessert section laying down his five cents for a Charlotte Russe. When he reaches the girl's apartment, her unsuspecting mother asks him to wait outside the door while the girl finishes bathing.

As he waits, the boy decides to sneak a little taste of the Russe for himself, knowing his sample will never be missed. Then maybe just wiping off the whipped cream from the paper wrapper would be OK too. But as soon as the cherry disappears into his mouth, his fate is doomed—no turning back—and he completely surrenders to the whipped ecstasy before him.

When the girl finally emerges from her apartment, the boy's empty-handed embarrassment sends him scampering down the stairs into the street, less a "man," but also less hungry.

Charlotte Russe
Rating: G

(This dessert classic was served "individual" style in the movie, but the more traditional presentation appears as a large 1- or 2-quart, straight-sided mold lined with ladyfingers. Either way, it has the same divine taste. As this is generally a vanilla custard dessert, you may substitute There's Always Vanilla (see p. *240*) for this coffee-flavored variation.)

½ c. sugar
4 egg yolks
1 c. milk
1 envelope unflavored gelatin
2 T. cold water
¼ c. strong coffee
1 t. vanilla
1 c. heavy cream, whipped
  Ladyfingers
  Chocolate sauce (optional)

Using a wooden spoon, stir the sugar and yolks together in the top of an unheated double boiler until smooth. Bring the milk to the boiling point and gradually add to the yolk mixture, stirring constantly with a wire whip.

Place over boiling water and cook until thickened. Soften the gelatin in the cold water and quickly add to the custard. Stir until the gelatin dissolves. Remove from heat and stir in the coffee and vanilla. Cool without letting the custard set. Fold the whipped cream into the custard. Line a 1-quart, cylindrical charlotte mold as follows: Place a small round of ladyfinger in the center of the bottom. Arrange whole ladyfingers daisy-petal fashion, radiating from the center piece. Fill in spaces with triangular pieces. Line the sides by standing ladyfingers upright, side-by-side close together. Pour the custard mixture into the mold and refrigerate until set, about 2 hours. Unmold onto serving dish dressed with a doily. Serve with chocolate sauce if desired. Serves 4.

Prizzi's Honor

Nutshell

After *The Godfather*, few would have thought that Mafia life would be the stuff of which comedies are made, yet director John Huston employed the typical elements of mob drama—vengeance, murder, and family honor—to turn in a truly devilish comedy in *Prizzi's Honor*. The focus of the film is on the unlikely romance of two mob hit men—or, in this case, hit people, Charley Partanna (Jack Nicholson) and Irene Walker (Kathleen Turner).

Like *The Godfather*, *Prizzi's Honor* begins with a big wedding. It's at this festive occasion that Charley, the chief hitperson for the Prizzi family, experiences love at first sight when he sees the mysterious and beautiful woman in lavender—Irene. He no sooner engages the svelte blonde on the dance floor than their whirlwind romance is off and running. Matters are complicated, however, when Charley learns that she's the wife of a low level crook he's supposed to "ice" for stealing some $700,000 of the Prizzi's money.

Unaware of Irene's occupation, and not wanting to believe she had anything to do with the stolen money, Charley prepares a spaghetti dinner for his "Pop" (John Randolf) to announce his intention of marrying her. When Charley shows Pop the picture of his fiance, however, he learns from the wise old mafioso that Irene was the "pieceman" for the family's most recent contract murder. His girl is a free-lance killer, and now he's faced with an unusual dilemma. Could it be that Irene is double-dealing? Is it possible she may have helped swindle the Prizzi family money? With Hamlet-like perplexity, Charlie wonders, "Do I ice her, or marry her?" To answer the question, he seeks the advice of his former girlfriend, Maerose (Angelica Huston), who tells him to go ahead and marry the girl.

Charley and Irene set up housekeeping just like any ordinary, happy young couple, although Charley is not pleased about his wife's continuing to work. Reluctantly, Charley collaborates with her on a difficult and important murder-kidnaping. Although they conclude the day's work with a peck on the cheek and Irene's wifey promise to "see you at dinner," Irene has really botched the job by accidentally murdering an innocent bystander—the police chief's wife. Havoc breaks out when police crack down on the New York mob families, demanding that they turn in the killer.

Festering beneath these familiar cops and robbers machinations is the delicious subplot of Maerose's revenge. Quietly suffering over an earlier breakup with Charley, and bitter over being banished from the family by her slow-witted, hot-tempered father Dominic (Lee Richardson), Maerose sets the wheels in motion for a delectably diabolical denouement. First she enflames her father with a lurid tale about Charley raping her and then presents her grandfather, Don Corrado (William Hickey), the frail and drowsy, but razor-sharp head of the Prizzi family,

Sicilian Sesame Cookies
Rating: G

(This is an authentic Sicilian cookie recipe that's been cut down to a practical size for today's smaller families. The original recipe called for ingredients in pounds and made enough for a family of 15.)

3 eggs
¼ c. milk
2 t. vanilla
4 c. flour
1 c. sugar
1 T. baking powder
¼ c. vegetable shortening
¼ c. butter, softened
2 oz. sesame seeds, toasted

In a small bowl, beat eggs, milk, and vanilla together with a wire whip. Set aside. In a large bowl, sift flour, sugar, and baking powder together. Cut in shortening and butter with a pastry blender. Add egg mixture and stir until throughly combined. (Consistency will resemble heavy pie pastry.) Roll 1 tablespoon of dough in palms of hands briefly. Roll in sesame seeds. Roll again on a smooth surface into a 3/4" × 3" log. Place on ungreased baking sheet. Repeat procedure until all are rolled. Bake at 375° about 15 minutes, or until barely golden. Makes about 4 1/2 dozen.

Prizzi's Honor. Jack Nicholson and Kathleen Turner savor their brewing romance over lunch in LA.

with evidence that Irene actually did rip off the family money. Dominic, forever short of the puzzle pieces, hires that free-lance hit lady, Irene Walker, to do a job on Charley Partanna, never realizing of course, that Charley and Irene are Mr. and Mrs.

Meanwhile, pressure on the Prizzis from the rival families to turn over the "second man" in the murder of the police chief's wife becomes so great that the family is no longer willing to protect Irene, and with her duplicitous activities now fully out in the open, Charley has to decide which family's honor must be protected—Mr. and Mrs. Partanna's or the Prizzi's?

Food Scene

Unlike their French culinary rivals, Italians often flag when it comes to concocting elaborate desserts. Italians, usually so sated from their main feasting, wisely limit dessert to a selection of fresh fruits. They have, however, produced a few popular sweets. Aside from their ice cream called gelato, perhaps the most famous is cannoli, a crisp-fried, thin pastry tube stuffed with flavored ricotta cheese. They also offer a few cookies that are gaining wider popularity now that ethnic food is so very much in vogue. Several of these cookies were obtained by property master Russ Goble from a Brooklyn Italian bakery to be used as props in one of the pivotal scenes in *Prizzi's Honor*.

The "cookie scene" was shot in the interior of what was once a Rockefeller residence in Brooklyn, but is now a series of high-end apartments. We're in the ornately decorated living room of the Don when Maerose comes to call. She's grateful to the Don for bringing her back into the family and tells him so. Touched by the moment, the Don raises the pitch of his gravelly old voice, as though talking to a child, and asks his granddaughter, "Hey, would you like a cookie?" Politely, Maerose takes one from the nearby table, but she's eager to present the gift she's brought for him—evidence of Irene's perfidy toward the family. Without wasting time to eat her cookie, Maerose relays an eyewitness account proving Irene stole the money and even killed the family's bagman in the process. She demands retribution—to protect the family honor she claims—but what she really wants, of course, is personal revenge over "the other woman."

The Don is reluctant to hurt Charley and tells her to "Shut up!" Dutifully she takes another cookie. This time Maerose bites down hard on it, calculating that it may be all she'll get for her "gift."

Willy Wonka and the Chocolate Factory

Nutshell

"Scrumdidilyumptious." That's the mouthful used to describe the prize-winning chocolate bar in this story of a boy, a candymaker, and his wonderful chocolate factory. Undoubtedly, *Willy Wonka and the Chocolate Factory* is the sweetest movie ever made; one in which candy is not only eaten, but flows like a river, doubles for furniture, grows in gardens, is played with, swam in, sat on, ridden on, walked on, and floated on.

Adapted from Roald Dahl's classic children's book, *Charlie and the Chocolate Factory*, the movie begins by introducing a young boy, Charlie Bucket (Peter Ostrum) who, as the breadwinner of his impoverished family, supports his mother and four grandparents on his paper route money, earning just enough for a steady diet of cabbage water. They live in a quiet town built around a mysterious, iron-fenced candy factory, where no one ever goes in and no one ever comes out. Until one day....

Wonka mania breaks out when a clever marketing gimmick is unleashed on the world by the factory's owner, Willy Wonka (Gene Wilder), announcing a contest that offers a tour of the factory and a lifetime supply of candy to the five lucky winners who uncover a gold certificate under the wrapper of a chocolate Wonka Bar. The entire world goes bananas buying up bushels, crates, even factories full of the bars in search of the precious certificates. One by one they are found, all by "bad" children who are afflicted with nasty habits like tantrum-throwing, gluttony, non-stop gum chewing, and too much TV watching—all except for the fifth winner, Charlie, who is kind, considerate, honest, and hardworking, but who is also enough of a fun lover to keep from being a sap.

On the appointed day, into the factory they go, accompanied by parents who feed their children's bad habits as surely as they are exasperated by them. Inside, the group follows Willy Wonka around his Oz-like wonder factory, filled with all manner of sweets—like lickable wallpaper, polkadot cream toadstools, chocolate rivers, giant striped lollipop flowers, candy cane trees, and everlasting gobstoppers (candy you can suck on forever and it'll never wear out!)—all made by busy, singing and dancing midgets called Oompa Loompas. With "so much time, and so little to see," the tour continues through the factory as, one by one, each of the rotten egg kids is eliminated when he or she misbehaves, getting just the dessert they deserve. The fat boy falls in the chocolate river; the gum-chewer turns into an enormous blueberry; the spoiled tantrum thrower gets dumped down the garbage shoot; and the TV watcher gets miniaturized inside a TV tube. Even the fun-loving Charlie and his Grandpa (Jack Albertson) misbehave by sampling the forbidden liquid gas, making it look like all five certificate holders have been disqualified from winning the grand prize Wonka has kept unannounced. Charlie's good deed of returning his everlasting gobstopper hits the jackpot, though, and he and his family inherit the factory as their new home, as well as a lifetime of all-you-can-eat sweets.

Willy Wonka. Albertson and young Ostrum sample giant candy cane trees in the factory.

Willy Wonka. That's the ticket!

Willy Wonka. In the wonderland of edible sweets, Michael Bollner gets more than a chocolate mess on his hands when, as the first victim of his own greed, he falls into the factory's river of chocolate.

Willy Wonka. The hopes and dreams of Jack Albertson, left, and Peter Ostrum rest somewhere between the wrapper and the chocolate of a Wonka Bar.

Food Scene

Willy Wonka and the Chocolate Factory was brought to you by another food factory, Quaker Oats, whose marketing strategists had no trouble imagining the profits from mixing food and film, and wasted no time in selling their own version of the Wonka bar after underwriting the film.

There is such nonstop candy eating action in Willy Wonka that to recount any particular eating scene would mean detailing the entire picture. For Charlie, certainly one of his biggest moments comes when he unselfishly buys a Wonka Bar for his grandfather with his last few bits of change, and after unwrapping the "gift" finds the last of the certificates under the wrapper, making him the fifth big winner in the contest.

Willy Wonka. Sneaking a sample of the forbidden, "fizzy-lifting" drink.

If you've never tried making a candy bar at home, don't despair. You don't have to live in a factory to do it. By shopping at a candy making store, you can buy all the ingredients specially tempered for the process, not to mention dozens of interestingly shaped molds for customizing your bars. It's almost as easy as melting butter, and will surely win you scrumdidilyumptious reviews.

Wonka Bars
Rating: G

(Melting chocolate [or chocolate compound coating] differs significantly from real chocolate in that the cocoa butter has been removed, making it more suitable for candymaking. By using melting chocolate instead of real chocolate, you'll eliminate the need to get involved in a lengthy process of melting and cooling called tempering. It is important, however, to melt the melting chocolate over hot, never boiling water, or the melting chocolate will discolor and lose its gleam.)

- 1 lb. semi-sweet melting chocolate, wafers or pieces
- 1½ T. water
- ½ c. plus 2 T. marshmallow cream
- 14 caramel candies (about ¼ lb.)
- 2 T. water
- ½ c. dry roasted peanuts, chopped

Melt 1/2 pound of the melting chocolate in top of a double boiler over hot water. Stir in water and marshmallow cream, blending well. Transfer to a bowl and cool. Melt caramels in top of double boiler over hot water. Add water and stir to combine. Stir in peanuts. Transfer to a bowl and cool. Melt remaining 1/2 pound chocolate in top of a double boiler over hot water. Line 3" × 1" × 1/2" plastic candy bar molds by either one of the following methods: Fill molds to top with melted melting chocolate and invert on non-stick baking sheet to catch drips; or coat inside molds by "painting" chocolate on bottom and sides with a paintbrush. Trim around the edges and return excess to double boiler. Place in freezer for a few minutes until set. Form a small portion of the choco-mallow mixture with your hands into the bottom half of each shell. Top with caramel-nut mixture, leaving about 1/8" at the top for sealing. Seal by spreading chocolate completely over caramel. Trim excess around edges. Refrigerate a few minutes until set. Pop out of molds and repeat process until ingredients are used. (If you have extra choco-mallow filling left over, it makes great "bonbons" when rolled into small balls and then into chopped nuts or coconut.) Wrap individually, hiding a gold certificate under one of the wrappers. Finder of certificate wins a free tour of your kitchen and a lifetime supply of candy. (Offer and prizes may differ according to age, sex, color, creed, and geographic location.) Makes 18 bars.

ROUGH CUTS

> " *I never drink— wine.* "

Dracula.

The Cocoanuts

Nutshell

The Cocoanuts originally opened as a musical stage comedy starring the Marx Brothers, but when it was adapted to film for them and released in 1929, it became the first Marx Brothers' motion picture. With twenty years of trouping behind them, the film version caught the brothers at the height of their stage careers. Sound tracks were a new technology, and it has therefore come to be known as one of the few records of a 1920s musical comedy. It also remains the best record of the Marx Brothers' vaudeville style, fully capturing the zany range of their humor, from Groucho's rampaging puns and put-downs to Harpo's jitterbugging eyes.

The emergence of the Marx Brothers into film stars was natural for their talents, but didn't arrive without problems. *Cocoanuts* was filmed in the morning among the artificial palms of an Astoria, Long Island, studio, while the brothers gave stage performances of their third Broadway hit, *Animal Crackers*, in the evening. Groucho recalled that they were so tired from this gruelling schedule that they would sometimes mix dialogue from the two stories. With their sound equipment still in the experimental stage, they were faced with constant breakdowns that often required twenty to thirty takes of each scene. There were also the ordinary problem of retakes, usually due to unscripted, spontaneous laughter on the set. Between the breakdowns and the crack-ups, they somehow managed to crank out one very funny musical that could now be played everywhere at the same time instead of having to play one city at a time.

The opening sequences, all done in sappy song and dance, establish what passes for plot in the typically anarchistic world of the Marx Brothers. Bob Adams (Oscar Show), a young architect working as a clerk at a hotel, plans to develop the Coconut Grove area, but not without first marrying Polly Potter (Mary Eaton), daughter of the wealthy snob, Mrs. Potter (Margaret Dumont). Harvey Yates (Cyril Ring) also has designs on Polly and the family money, but once he fails at getting the first, he plans to steal the latter. To do so, he enlists the help of his sleazy friend Penelope (Kay Francis) who shares an adjoining hotel room with Mrs. Potter.

Mr. Hammer (Groucho), the owner of the Coconut Hotel in Florida, is busily conning his staff out of their wages and trying to swindle Mrs. Potter on a crooked real estate deal. Harpo and Chico come on the scene, intent on conning other hotel guests, and Groucho immediately recognizes them as his own kind.

While Penelope and Yates steal a valuable necklace from Mrs. Potter, Groucho works on his own scam to sell auctioned real estate lots. To be sure he gets a good price, he recruits Chico to inflate the bids, but the overzealous Chico outbids everyone else, and Groucho's plan backfires. Mrs. Potter then discovers her necklace missing, Penelope implicates Bob in the robbery, and he's sent to jail while Mrs. Potter announces that she has chosen her daughter Polly's fiancé, Harvey Yates.

Buffet d' Harpo
Rating: X

4 blazer buttons
1 sponge, spread with glue
1 fresh flower
1 telephone
2 c. ink

Use items for snacking. Wash down with ink. Serves 1.

The Cocoanuts. Harpo's lunch is at hand—a penholder, ink, and a telephone. (Copyright © by Paramount Pictures. Courtesy of MCA Publishing Rights, a Division of MCA Inc.)

The craziness gets ironed out in the end, with Bob being set free and the brothers producing enough evidence to put Penelope and Yates away. Bob and Polly are reunited for a happy ending and are featured in the last frames, smiling sweetly on the audience.

Food Scene

As with all Marx Brothers' movies, any structure—like a script—was sure to be obliterated by their rebellious natures. This eventually would give rise to lively, combustible comedy that far surpassed what any writer could hope to spell out for them on paper. They were famous for their improvisational genius, and would throw out scripts in order to go scene after scene on their own steam. This, combined with quick film editing that accelerated their helter-skelter movements, gave them a unique style of comedy that's never been duplicated.

Harpo was the toughest to control. The most any script could say would be, "Enter Harpo...." From there on, he would be on his own. Take, for example, his introduction in this film. He and Chico have ransacked the mail cubbies in the hotel, and Harpo sits down for a lunch break. He plucks a button from a bellhop's uniform jacket and pops it into his mouth. Finding it tasty, he goes for another and savors it like an after dinner mint. Later he goes for the desk sponge and carefully seasons it with glue. Groucho, silently observing from the side, proffers a nice vase of flowers to see what his bizarre little hotel guest will do next. Harpo thoughtfully makes a selection and eats it, then washes it down with a nice vintage blue from a nearby inkwell. Still not completely satisfied, he begins to nibble at the telephone. Finding it a bit indigestible though, he reaches for another swallow of ink.

Director Robert Florey shed some light on the method behind Harpo's madness, pointing out that this bit of business, invented by Harpo, was eventually done with real-food doubles, using the ever-popular chocolate mold and Coca-Cola for the ink.

Over the years, however, Harpo could not resist the telephone, for as late as 1946 he was eating them again in *A Night in Casablanca*.

Cool Hand Luke

Nutshell

The late 1960s were years when films with the theme of people in conflict with society were extremely popular. "Anti-hero" and "anti-establishment" were favorite buzzwords of the time. In *Cool Hand Luke*, the ever-cool Paul Newman paints a picture-perfect 1960s hero, cut squarely against the grain. He plays the quintessential individual, unbowed before established authority and wanting only to be free to go his own way. He wants it badly enough to pay for it with his soul and his stomach.

On a hot summer night in 1948, Luke (Paul Newman) is arrested for beheading parking meters and is sentenced to two years' hard labor on a southern chain-gang—a world of grueling regimentation ruled by sadistic guards. Luke is hardly there long enough to learn the rules before he starts breaking them. Not only does his free spirit fly in the face of the prison authorities, but he also runs up against the order of the prison subculture itself that is ruled by the hulking convict "Dragline" (George Kennedy). It isn't long before Dragline has to reassert his dominance by challenging Luke to a fight. Technically Dragline's superior size and strength makes him the winner of the fight, but Luke's indomitable spirit in the face of defeat impresses Dragline and wins Luke the admiration of all the other inmates.

When Luke learns of his mother's death, he's sent to the dreaded "hot box" to prevent him from trying to run off to her funeral. As soon as the authorities are sure she's in the ground, they let him out of the box, and Luke resolves to escape.

Luke's constant challenges to the prison bosses initially amuse and inspire his fellow inmates. But after a series of attempts to escape lead to his recapture, his followers, who expect perfection from their hero, become confused and disenchanted. Weary of his role as their savior, Luke cries out to them, "Stop feedin' off me! Get out there yourself!"

Nevertheless, he makes another escape attempt, and, though he's fatally shot in the process, his reputation among the prison population as the one man the system could never break grows to mythic proportions.

Food Scene

After Dragline's metamorphosis from Luke's chief antagonist to best buddy and promoter, he boasts one night that Luke is the "champion hog gut of the camp." Luke casually adds to the boast that he can eat fifty eggs in one hour. Always ready for a simple diversion from camp drudgery and eager for a safe bet, the men get a pool going on Luke's chances of successfully eating fifty eggs.

Luke trains for his one-hour eggathon following Dragline's prescribed regimen for expanding his stomach by downing plates of beans and extra helpings of dinner.

Eggathon
Rating: R

50 hard-boiled eggs

Peel eggs. Set timer for one hour and eat eggs until hour is up. Serves 1.

Cool Hand Luke. Inmates ready the eggs and place their bets for Paul Newman's eggathon.

On the appointed day and hour, with boiled eggs at the ready, Luke begins stuffing them into his mouth like popcorn. That is, until long about the fortieth egg or so. Then men start to up the ante, as it looks more and more like Luke is going to lose.

But the eggs continue to go in, one by one, stuffed down Luke's exhausted, exploding gullet by Dragline, his tireless trainer, who massages Luke's jaw, pulls down on his neck, rubs his ripe belly, walks him around the room, and talks it up all the way—all the way up to the last second and the very last egg.

Luke is victorious. Lying stretched out on a table, he strikes a Christ-on-the-cross pose, but still manages the faint but satisfied smile of a guy determined to pick his own spots and make his own miracles. "Nobody can eat fifty eggs!" the men mutter as they file by in disbelief. Nobody but Cool Hand Luke.

Down and Out in Beverly Hills

Nutshell

In a town like Beverly Hills, it's not at all unusual to find people who treat their dogs like people—dressing them in diamonds and furs, treating their neuroses with top psychiatric help, laying them to rest in opulent doggie burial grounds. But it takes a real animal lover to do it right and get down on all fours to dine with the dog as Nick Nolte does in *Down and Out in Beverly Hills*.

The scene is pretty unappetizing, but that's not what earned it the distinction of being the first R-rated picture to come out of Disney Studios (under their Touchstone label). It is a loosely based adaptation of Jean Renoir's 1932 black comedy classic, *Boudu Saved from Drowning*, and gives Producer/Director/Writer Paul Mazursky the opportunity to continue his "love-hate" relationship with the upper class and the institution of marriage. The original version told of a suicidal vagabond who, after having jumped into the Seine, was rescued by a bourgeois bookseller. The bookseller then brings the tramp home where the tramp's real troubles begin.

In Mazursky's version, the vagabond is a homeless burn-out named Jerry Baskin (Nick Nolte) who, after losing his dog to a pretty woman with a bag of pastries in Beverly Hills, decides to end it then and there by jumping into the nearest backyard swimming pool. Jerry is rescued, however, by Dave Whiteman (Richard Dreyfuss), who's immediately taken by the guy and his own nobility in rescuing him, and allows Jerry to stay on in his luxurious home.

Jerry learns much about the Whiteman family and their way of life. Dave has made his millions manufacturing clothes hangers and begins each morning with a swig of Pepto-Bismol. Dave's wife Barbara (Bette Midler), who is less than enamored with the idea of Jerry staying, is constantly in search of fulfillment, changing pop therapies as often as clothes. The kids are plagued with teenage afflictions. Daughter Jenny (Tracy Nelson) is near anorexic, and son Max (Evan Richards) is obsessed with becoming a film director, and *second* Whiteman daughter. Carmen (Elizabeth Pena), the housekeeper, is bored with life and longs for something, *anything* to liven it up. Matisse (Mike), is the family dog with his fair share of hang-ups.

No one in this family knows what life is all about until Jerry comes along. He's enough of a creative liar to tell each of them what they want to hear and, like a chameleon, becomes what they want him to be. To Dave, he's his ticket back to the roots of his humanity. To Barb, he becomes the guru she's long been searching for who helps her reach nirvana via a special relaxation technique that incidently requires her to be unfaithful to Dave. To Jennifer, he's the lover who gives her reason to eat again. To Max, whose only communication with his parents is through his homemade video tapes, he's the inspiration he needs to come

Doggie Delight
Rating: R

$1/3$ can *Mighty Dog*
$1/3$ can *Kal Kan with Liver*
$1/3$ can *Puppy Chow*

Combine ingredients in dog dish. Serve to your favorite pooch. Serves 2.

Down and Out in Beverly Hills. It's a dog's life. Mike, right, is instinctively suspicious of any guy, including Nick Nolte, who eats dog food.

Down and Out in Beverly Hills. Nolte caters to his friend—share and share alike.

out of the closet. To Carmen, he's the activist who raises her class consciousness by providing her with books on political oppression. And to Matisse, he's the one human being who really, really understands what a dog's life is all about.

As Jerry becomes increasingly central to the family's existence, Dave is less and less able to look at life's little difficulties with his customary equanimity. The radio for his Rolls Royce is stolen; his backyard bushes are dying; Carmen, his mistress, is beginning to ignore him. By the time the family's holiday party is in full swing, Dave's temper is ready to erupt, which it does when he discovers Jennifer and Jerry's romantic involvement. Screaming hysterically, he chases Jerry, followed by most of the guests, into the swimming pool from which he saved him only weeks earlier. Dave tries to drown Jerry, but is unsuccessful.

In an early morning confession Jerry admits he's a fraud. He says he simply gave the family what they wanted in exchange for a little room and board. As he hits the road again, followed by Matisse, he makes a stop for breakfast at the backyard garbage cans. But, like Matisse, the family has really grown attached to this mutt of a man and invites him back for a cup of capuccino.

Down and Out in Beverly Hills. A catered Thanksgiving feast at the Whiteman house.

Food Scene

One of the most endearing characters in *Down and Out in Beverly Hills* is the medium-sized, black-and-white Scottish border collie named Matisse (actually played by two trained collies). The dog often runs the household, monitoring Dave's nocturnal meetings with Carmen or sending the neighborhood into a frenzy by setting off the burgler alarm. When Jerry first comes to the house, though, Matisse loses his appetite.

Concerned over the dog's welfare, Barbara calls in a dog psychiatrist who traces the cause to an upset in the household—maybe Jerry's arrival? When Jerry leaves, the shrink says, the dog will eat again. But Jerry hasn't let his life go to the dogs for nothing. He knows better. He tells Barbara that Matisse thinks he's human and only wants to eat what people eat. To prove his point, he mixes equal parts of Mighty Dog, Kal Kan with Liver, and Puppy Chow (for crunchiness) in Matisse's bowl. Then, sure of the dog's attention, Jerry demonstrates his point by getting down on his hands and knees, lowering his nose into the bowl and eating like a regular hound. Within seconds, Matisse scampers over to the bowl, and goes nose to nose with Jerry.

It's reported that during the filming of the scene, the second replacement dog used in the second take, reacted a bit differently than the first dog. Instead of agreeably sharing dinner with Nolte, the second dog neatly removed a mouthful from the bowl and dropped it on the floor. When Nolte greedily eyed the morsel, the dog growled a warning, then proceeded to eat his share of the dinner.

After shooting the several takes required for the scene, it's reported that Nolte's wife, who had been observing from the sidelines, glanced at her watch and remarked, "Well, I guess I don't have to worry about dinner tonight."

The Gold Rush

Nutshell

It was the best of meals; it was the worst of meals. It was Thanksgiving dinner, but what was eaten was as tough as shoe leather.

I'm talking about Charlie Chaplin's Little Tramp sitting down to a feast of parboiled boot in Chaplin's *The Gold Rush*. In 1954, an international film jury in Brussels named this the second greatest film of all time. (Potemkin was named the greatest.) For those of us who are connoisseurs of cinematic eating scenes, there's little wonder why, for it contains one of the most famous and brilliantly played eating scenes ever. There hasn't been an eating scene to match the tragi-comic dimensions of this one, or one that shows a filmmaking genius at his most resourceful.

Lured by the prospect of finding gold, the Little Tramp (Chaplin) tromps off to the Yukon with hundreds of other hopefuls, only to end up with another prospector, Big Jim (Max Swain), marooned in an isolated cabin belonging to the outlaw Black Larson (Tom Murray). In a three-way cut of cards, Black Larson loses and has to venture outside into a blizzard in search of food, while Charlie and Big Jim stay behind to face each other and starvation.

The Tramp defers disaster at first by improvising a dinner with supplies on hand, like his footwear. But Big Jim's persistent hunger drives him to hallucinations featuring the Tramp as a chicken. The two grapple, Jim for his chicken and Charlie for his life. Just in time, however, real food wanders in in the form of a bear, and the Tramp and Big Jim settle down to a real meal.

Later, in a nearby boom town, Charlie meets and falls in love with Georgia (Georgia Hale), a dance-hall girl from the local saloon. But, as always, Chaplin's humble hero has to endure a series of indignities before he emerges from tramp to champ. He is made the constant butt of barroom jokes, gets snow thrown in his face, and is stood up by the love of his life and her friends after meticulously preparing a Christmas dinner for them. But his dignity—and luck—prevails in the end. He strikes gold, wins Georgia's heart, and sails into a happily-ever-after sunset.

Food Scene

It's Thanksgiving Day, and not even starving people should starve on Thanksgiving. The Tramp has graciously contributed his boot to the soup pot and attentively watches over the bubbling broth, stirring occasionally. Then, beaming with pride, he carries the feast to the table and, after a brisk sharpening of the knife, he cuts into the steaming boot.

The Tramp faces this lowliest of dinners with the refined elegance of an aristocrat. He twirls the shoelaces around his fork like spaghetti and nibbles on the cobbler nails as if they were succulent chicken bones. When he finds one of the nails bent into the shape of a wishbone, he hooks it onto his little finger and extends the free end to Big Jim (a gesture repeated in the famous eating scene in *Tom Jones*). With the last

The Gold Rush. Finger lickin' good, Chaplin nibbles on nails like succulent chicken bones.

Boiled Boot
Rating: X

1 leather boot

Fill a large pot with water and bring to boiling. Add boot and simmer until tender, about 6 hours, adding more water if necessary. Serves 2.

The Gold Rush. Chaplin's Little Tramp reluctantly shares a bone with an uninvited dinner companion.

The Gold Rush. Guess who's not coming to dinner?

bite, the Tramp settles back in a satiated repose, exuding immense satisfaction with this humble repast. Only the inedible portion remains on his plate, the nails sticking up from the sole like freshly cleaned fish bones.

Later the Tramp goes out looking for more food, and, finding none, offers to cook up his other boot. Jim recoils with horror. An honest response, no doubt. The real boot consumed by the actors was made of licorice. More than twenty pairs of boots were consumed in just a few days of shooting. Max Swain found the confection a bit rough on his digestive tract and probably would have preferred to eat a store full of shoe leather instead!

Chaplin's utilization of food for developing his character is not limited to shoe leather, but extends to dinner rolls as well, as depicted in the famous "Dance of the Rolls" or "Oceana Rolls" scene.

After preparing a Christmas dinner for Georgia and her friends and waiting in vain for them, he falls asleep and dreams they actually do show up and join him in a joyous holiday celebration. To entertain them, he places two rolls on the ends of two forks. With his head placed over the fork handles like a giant Mr. Potato Head and the forks and rolls serving as skinny "legs" with oversized "shoes," he performs high-stepping Rockette kicks, cancans, and splits. His gigantic face expressively moves with the antics of the happy feet as the girls giggle with delight. (Diehard Chaplin fans rarely bite into a biscuit without thinking of the frolicksome potential of these modest breads.)

While his intended guests never actually show up to enjoy the Tramp's dancing rolls, the table neatly set with newspaper "linen," or the roast chicken he's prepared, his effort will never really go unappreciated. It's preserved on film, and audiences have been heartily enjoying his performance for almost sixty years.

The Gold Rush. "Dance of the Rolls."

Oceana Rolls
Rating: G

2 biscuits
 (see Gone With the Wind *p.63, or* The Killing of Sister George *p.68 for suitable biscuit recipes*)
2 forks

Push fork prongs through top of biscuit. Repeat for second biscuit. Place one fork handle end in fingertips of each hand, and hold forks side-by-side on tabletop, biscuit side down. Lean head over top of hands and lift fork handles (as though hinged at your hands) in a variety of dance steps; i.e., kicks, cancans, fox trot, etc. Entertains 1.

Iceman

Nutshell

So what's all this talk about sex and violence in the movies? For years, film-makers have been using food to achieve the same end—a strong emotional response from the audience. Just as the sex has become a little kinkier and the violence a little more graphic, the food has become more, well, exotic. Now it's not that we haven't seen a bug eaten on the screen before. Steve McQueen's roach stew in *Papillon* stands out as a vivid example, but in *Iceman*, it's a woman who must eat one—and so the escalation continues.

Dr. Diane Brady (Lindsay Crouse) is attached to a mining company that, during expeditionary drilling in the Arctic, makes the anthropological/archaeological discovery of the century—the frozen remains of a forty-thousand-year old Neanderthal man. At first the scientists are eager to thaw out the man's body and cut him up to study cryogenics (low temperatures), but during an attempt to revivify his cells, the ancient body begins to synthesize DNA and comes to life. Recalling an earlier discovery of a well-preserved frozen mammoth who had stuffed himself on buttercups, Dr. Brady speculates that perhaps it was something the man ate that prevented his cells from crystallizing and dying.

Investigating that theory gets sidetracked, however, when anthropologist Shephard (Timothy Hutton) arrives on the scene and convinces the others that the Neanderthal, later named Charlie (John Lone), is worth more to science alive than dead. The others grant Shephard two weeks to conduct his own studies in the vivarium they've built.

Charlie wakes up in this simulated world of plants and rocks and gets right into acting his natural Neanderthal self. From high behind windows, he's observed crushing berries, smiling, grunting, trying to catch a bird, making fire by hitting two rocks together, and killing a boar. When he tries to eat the garden hose sprinkler, however, his curiosity leads him to the hose's wall connection, whereupon he wildly demonstrates the agonizing realization that he is lost.

Later, Shephard goes into the vivarium to meet Charlie. Together they develop a mutual trust and even crude communication. A linguist is called in to interpret, but it doesn't take an expert to see that Charlie is miserable. Shephard learns that all the man really wants to do is complete the walk he was on so many thousands of years earlier—before his lights went out. The scientists conclude that the man had a god, and, like religious men through the ages, was probably on a journey of atonement.

Beetle Mania
Rating: R

Assorted beetles
Cultured cockroaches

Roast beetles over an open fire until crispy, or eat raw. Serve to guests for lunch.

Iceman. Lindsay Crouse braces herself against Timothy Hutton as Iceman John Lone invites her to lunch on beetles.

Eventually Charlie escapes into the laboratories, where he accidentally spears one of the men hunting for him. Fearing for Charlie's safety now, Shephard leads him back to the frozen cave where he was originally discovered. A rescue helicopter appears on the scene and Charlie, believing it to be his god, grabs onto the craft as it ascends into the air. There's a futile attempt to pull the Iceman aboard that ends with him falling hundreds of feet to his final, long-delayed death.

Food Scene

After Shephard has established a rapport with Charlie, he offers Diane an opportunity to learn more about him up close by accompanying him on a visit into the vivarium. Inside, Shephard makes the introductions, and Charlie, being a good host, serves refreshments. He likes his newest guest and prepares Diane "lunch" from his finest stash of beetles. Shephard wisely advises Diane to accept if she knows what's good for her. Shephard asks her how it tastes? "Like a beetle," she replies.

In truth, it probably tasted like a Hershey Bar. As with Steve McQueen's bug eating scene, little chocolate bodies were molded to resemble beetles, making us all believe in the undaunted courage of this scientist.

All this bug eating reminds me of the time I ate a chocolate covered ant on my own with absolutely no encouragement from MGM or Twentieth Century Fox. It actually wasn't so bad. (But, then, what is when it's covered with chocolate?) It looked like a Raisinette with whiskers and tasted like a peanutty chocolate-covered Rice Krispy. Sound tempting? You might want to pour a little melted Hershey's semi-sweet over the recipe here if you're thinking of serving it to guests.

King Rat

Nutshell

Over the years, we've seen all manner of "food" consumed in movies, from the utterly revolting to the positively divine. In *King Rat*, we're shown that under the most extreme conditions, one can easily become the other.

We could go on at some nauseating length about the gross and disgusting tidbits that have been consumed on film for the greater glory of the cinematic art. Cannibalism, of course, has served as a centerpiece of such films as the black comedy *Eating Raoul* and the futuristic, sci-fi thriller *Soylent Green*. (Cannibalism serves a historical purpose, too, as in the tragic, true-life story *Alive*, or the one about early man, *Quest for Fire*.) Lizards were eaten in *Walk About*; maggots eaten in *Greystoke: The Legend of Tarzan*; and—king (or queen) of the grossouts—Divine eating real dog excrement in the cult film, *Pink Flamingo*.

All this makes the menu for *King Rat* look no less appetizing than a can of cold beans, which Dustin Hoffman gladly enjoys as a down-and-outer in *Midnight Cowboy*.

As the title suggests, rodents are no mere walk-ons in *King Rat*. Written by James Clavell and based on his experiences as a POW, the story takes place in the notorious Japanese internment camp on Singapore Island, Changi Prison, during the final days of World War II. Like *Papillon*, the drama examines the kinds of inhuman conditions that men must endure to survive in confinement, where a precious premium is placed on the basics of life—like food. Unlike others of this genre, though, *Stalag 17* or *Bridge on the River Kwai* for a couple of examples, *King Rat* isn't an escape story, but a story about endurance.

Residents of the camp, American and British prisoners, find that the morality of normal society doesn't necessarily apply to the aberrational environment of a prison camp. The inmates starve to death or die of disease, while a lucky, amoral few prosper by stealing rations from other prisoners or trading in the black market.

The most prosperous inmate and underground leader, Corporal King "Rat" (George Segal), keeps himself and those on his payroll in cigarettes and other luxuries through secret dealings with crooked enemy guards, selling off the valuables of fellow inmates at great profit to himself. His scheming Yankee business prowess earns him the respect and subservience of all those who aspire to a piece of his pie, including officers who are supposed to act as moral arbitrators. King's only real enemy is the provost marshall, Lt. Grey (Tom Courtenay), a British military policeman whose job it is to preserve law and order in the camp and whose main ambition, which constantly eludes him, is to trap King in one of his illegal deals and put him away for good.

Early on, King allies himself with British flight lieutenant Peter Marlowe (James Fox). Marlowe is initially put off by King's manipulation of people, but soon falls under his influence thanks to the intoxicating power of a decent cigarette and a fresh fried egg.

Dog Stew
Rating: R

1 10 lb. dog, dressed
4 qts. water
Salt

Cut meat from bone in 1" chunks. Brown quickly on all sides, add water, and simmer until tender. Salt to taste. Serves 6–8.

Ratatouille—Prison Style
Rating: R

1 dozen plump rat hind legs, dressed
Salt

Sprinkle salt in bottom of frying pan. Sauté legs over medium heat until done (total cooking time will depend on size of legs.) Serves 6.

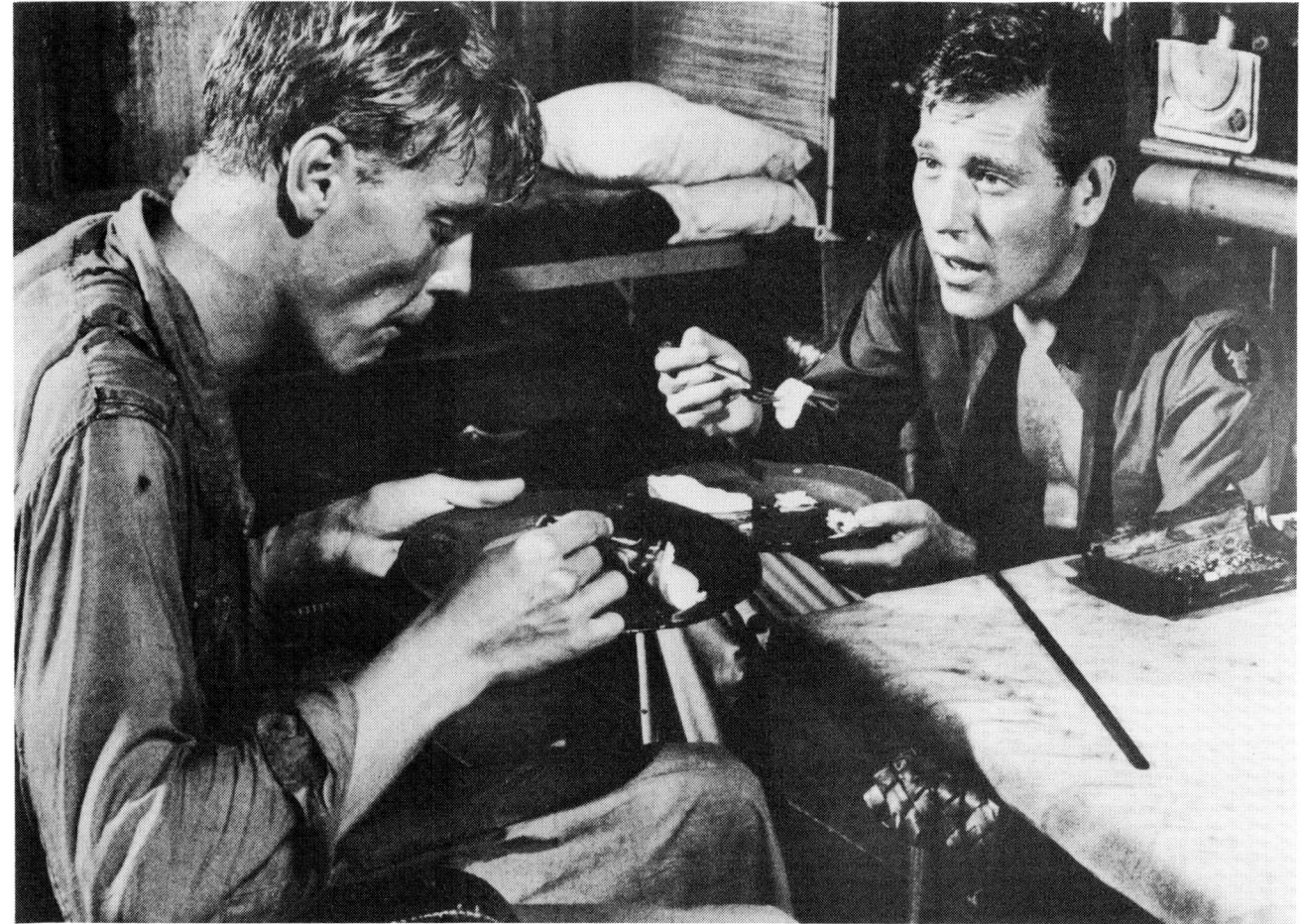

King Rat. Bribery and temptation are SOP for George Segal's business as he attempts to lure James Fox, left, onto his payroll by serving him a rare prison commodity—fresh eggs.

Tension mounts when hut rations are discovered missing, and, under camp justice, the accused is killed by suffocation in a bore hole. Ironically, it's the same bore hole that also breeds thousands of cockroaches, which Marlowe and another inmate collect in pails to use for protein in their diet.

King, Marlowe, and King's gang plan and execute several money-making scams, from hawking cooked rat meat to selling a large diamond to the Japanese. King's plan has been to use the money to buy their way out of prison, but he winds up using some of it on drugs to save Marlowe's life after a near-fatal accident.

Just when it looks like the Japanese will ceremoniously kill an inmate caught with a radio, the end of the war is announced. The allies have won, but as quickly as the news comes through, King loses his position and becomes a nobody from the States again. He cuts off his once-valued friendship with Marlowe and leaves the camp, a king dethroned by the reestablishment of peacetime conventions of civilized behavior.

Food Scene

No one survives Changi Prison without a reason. King and his hired subjects find both a way to survive and a reason for living by exploiting others. No one actually suffers under their exploitation, and our sympathies as an audience are guided to this gang of cunning con-artists rather than the ordinary Joes who follow the rules.

One of the gang's big money-makers is the rat-breeding business. King first conceives of the idea when the gang captures one of these filth-scavaging rodents and, instead of killing it, turns it into a furry little money-maker. He devises a plan whereby they will breed the critters and market the meaty hind legs to officers as a culinary delicacy from a local "miniature jungle deer."

They study rat behavior from an inmate who's a mammal expert and then supply their starter stud with a member of the opposite sex. Before long, their rat farm is booming, and they're cooking up sumptuous dinners for the brass. The officers eagerly devour the legs picnic-style and, never the wiser, describe the dish as "splendid." A bit stringy . . . but splendid.

The men's consciences do not allow them to sell the meat to their friends, but King doesn't think twice about serving his own associates dog meat. Again he turns a bad situation into profit, this time taking advantage of the necessity of killing an inmate's pet dog for its attack on a chicken.

King invites selected friends to a secret location, and when they are greeted by the sight of a meaty bone and a soup pot, they whoop it up in expectation of a pork dinner. King cuts big chunks from the bone, then they all watch the pot boil. King is the first to sample it. It needs a little more salt. Once that situation's been corrected, they all dig in, until King drops the news.

At first the men are appalled. After all, it was Hawkin's pet dog they were eating. But the quick thinking King, unencumbered by fine moral distinctions, explains to them that dogs *and* cats are normal dishes in other countries, and eating one is no worse than boiling live lobsters. As always, the men are gratefully persuaded by King's rationalizations, and they return to their feast with relish.

Marathon Man

Nutshell

Like a jigsaw puzzle, *Marathon Man* starts as a seemingly confused array of unrelated pieces and develops into a rock-solid picture, snapped into place by its own suspenseful momentum. As the story races to its conclusion, the exchange of power that takes place between the two leading characters elevates movie cuisine to new heights of originality, while serving up the roughest cut "carat" known to man.

William Goldman turned his best-selling novel into the screenplay thriller that treated movie audiences to pure, heart-quickening suspense. Played against two of the world's leading cities, New York and Paris, the opening puzzle pieces include the incineration of a New York German in a car crash; the blossoming romance between a Columbia University Ph.D. candidate cum marathon runner and a pretty Swiss woman; a series of mysterious murders in Paris involving bandage boxes, bombs, and chocolates; a mugging in Central Park; a white-haired German living in Uraguay who shaves his head, disguises himself as a peasant woman, and arrives in New York in a business suit; and a family reunion between two brothers.

The puzzle begins to interlock when one of the brothers, Doc (Roy Scheider), is slashed to death by the Uruguayan German, Christian Szell (Laurence Olivier). The murder leads Szell to Doc's brother "Babe" Levy (Dustin Hoffman), whom he relentlessly pursues and tortures because he believes Doc passed valuable information on to Babe before dying.

More of the picture takes shape when we learn about Szell's background. Known as "The White Angel," he is an infamous ex-Nazi dentist who made a fortune digging gold out of the mouths of concentration camp victims and converting it to diamonds. The death of his brother in the opening car crash forced him to come out of hiding to collect the gems in a New York safe deposit box. Doc, a double agent and one of Szell's couriers, has supposedly cleared the way for the White Angel to safely collect the gems without fear of capture. This is the information Szell hopes to extract from Babe by drilling holes in his teeth. "Is it safe yet?" he asks over and over again. But Babe doesn't have the slightest idea what he's talking about. He answers every way possible just to avoid the torture, but the sadist drills on until he's convinced himself of Babe's ignorance.

The tension eases up a bit when Szell gives Babe oil of clove to ease the pain. Babe is soon rescued by Janeway (William DeVane), another double agent who claims to be a friend of Doc's. But Janeway, as well as Babe's girlfriend Elsa (Marthe Keller), are both part of the plot to claim the diamonds and are about as "safe" for Babe as Szell's drill. Marathon chases and a shoot-out lead to the propulsive final scenes in New York's Forty-seventh Street diamond center, where Szell narrowly avoids recognition while collecting his fortune.

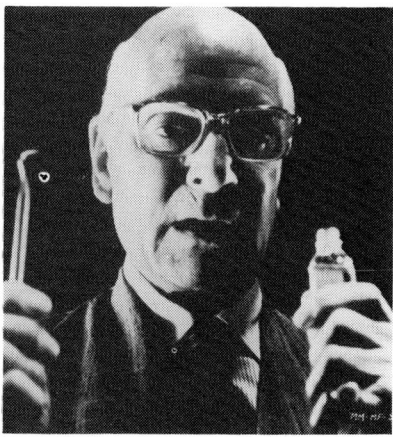

Marathon Man. After torturing Dustin Hoffman by drilling his teeth full of holes, Laurence Olivier offers him oil of clove to ease the pain.

Diamond Delight
Rating: X

(Carats can be found in jewelry stores and are available in all seasons. Refined, or cut diamonds, are more pleasing to the eye than raw, unrefined gems. However, the taste is identical. Choose only those with the most brilliant sparkle.)

One 2-carat cut diamond or YAG

Eat plain, or serve in lemon-butter for variety.

Marathon Man. "Essen!" Hoffman yells as he begins to throw diamonds at Olivier.

In the climactic closing moments, Babe catches up with Szell and forces him at gunpoint into the nearest building—Central Park's Reservoir tank. Inside, Babe and Szell confront each other, while hundreds of tons of water thunder around a wrought-iron bridge. The last puzzle piece falls into place when Babe throws the diamonds down the stairs, and Szell goes tumbling after.

Food Scene

In an exact replica of the New York Reservoir tank, Laurence Olivier, as Szell, is called upon to do some of the most unorthodox eating of his long, distinguished career. Babe nervously assures Szell at gunpoint that he's not going to kill him. In fact, he can have as many diamonds as he can eat. "Essen," Babe demands, throwing handfuls of gems at the Nazi. Most fall through the grid flooring into the swirling water below. Szell slowly takes a large diamond from the palm of his hand and reluctantly places it in his mouth, opening his lips wide enough to show the stone perfectly clamped between his front teeth. He swallows, but finding the humiliation too great, he decides to take his chances in a fight with Babe that sends him to a deadly reunion with his precious stones.

Of course, Olivier didn't put a real diamond in his mouth for that shot—that would be a bit much, even with a multi-million dollar film budget. Property master Billy MacSems reports that the stone was a simulated paste diamond known in the industry at that time as a "YAG" (short for yttrium aluminum garnet). MacSems was able to find the hundreds of YAGs needed for the film—a suitcase full, in fact—in various specialty shops around the New York area. After approximately one week of shooting the reservoir scene, Olivier became adept at creating the illusion of swallowing while never really letting the phony stone pass beyond his cheeks. It was, in short, another gem of a performance by Sir Larry.

Never Cry Wolf

Nutshell

It's been a season of sea change at the Disney Studios in recent years. A naked woman in *Splash* and R-rated language in *Down and Out in Beverly Hills*. But meeska, mooska, Mouseketeers, who ever thought we'd see the day when the studio that Mickey built would sanction mouse-eating right up there on the silver screen? Such is the case in the Disney financed adventure film *Never Cry Wolf*.

Tyler (Charles Martin Smith), a young biologist, has been selected by the government to go to the Arctic for a year to prove that wolves are responsible for endangering the population of caribou herds. As he lands at his destination, however, Tyler not only realizes the insanity of his one-man mission, but the fact that he's stuck with it and there's no turning back.

At the final outpost of civilization, he meets Rosie (Brian Dennehy), a bush pilot, gambler, and real estate tycoon, who's going to fly Tyler to his remote destination, but not without first showing him how to make Moose Juice, a favorite local drink consisting of equal parts Moose Brand beer and ethyl alcohol.

As a consequence of his introduction to Moose Juice, whatever money Tyler had goes to buying cases of Moose Head beer. And that's what he's left with when Rosie drops him off in the middle of a vast expanse of snow and ice—Moose Head and the survival kit supplied him by his government sponsors, consisting of canned asparagus spears, light bulbs, and requisition forms in triplicate. Fortunately for Tyler, he remembered to bring along his bassoon.

Through a series of near miracles, Tyler manages to survive a bevy of near misses (such as falling through the thawing ice of a lake) and is able, at last, to begin his study and enjoy his asparagus tips.

After closely observing the behavior of a family of wolves, Tyler makes an important discovery. Wolves occasionally kill caribou, but only the sick and weak ones. The primary staple of their diet is mice. Hundreds of thousands of little rodents scamper about the countryside, providing more than enough food for the wolves. And enough for Tyler, too, as it turns out.

In order to avoid the inevitable skepticism of the scientific community, Tyler realizes that he'll have to prove his findings in a controlled study. With no one around for thousands of miles, he has but one choice of volunteer—himself. And he sets out to prove that humans as well as wolves can live on mice.

In the process, he also learns that the real enemy of the caribou herds are two-legged, rifle-armed hunters, not the wolves—and that not even the wolves are safe from the hunters.

After developing an understanding and respect for the natural balance of life in the Arctic and making two valuable Innuit friends there, Tyler decides to stay and try to protect the land.

Never Cry Wolf. "Tell-tail" remnants dangle from the mouth of scientist Charles Martin Smith.

Food Scene

Tyler displays real adroitness with a Bunsen burner when preparing meals for his study. In a grossly comical montage, we see Tyler actually delight in his culinary triumphs—mice tempura, mice shishkabob, mice 'n' blankets, and best of all, souris à la crème.

For his first "experiment," Tyler neatly sets his table with a spoon, knife, fork, and of course, scissors. Without even so much as a blink, he digs into his creamed mice stew. The tiny mouse bones are a mild inconvenience, but Tyler's in quest of scientific truth and there's no stopping this snowbound Darwin once he gets started, not even the dozens of Mickey's relatives who scamper around Tyler's tent in a panic over the masticating massacre taking place before their disbelieving little eyes.

I am told however, that Charles Martin Smith did not share Tyler's enthusiasm for proving the nutritional value of field mice. Instead he managed to work out an agreeable arrangement with property masters Wayne McLaughlin and Grant Swain and enjoyed some rather terrific steak and chicken.

Dozens of little rodents were carved out of cooked meat, all in an attempt to simulate a realistic likeness. Linguine and rawhide made great wiggling tails, but often slid out the "end" of the meat causing many a retake. Mr. Smith was eager to make suggestions about how he was going to eat all these mice, and even recommended using real mice (or lemmings and voles) in the cracker sandwich scene, tails and legs hanging out to the cameras. Little did we know that chicken was waiting for him on the other side of the sandwich.

Inspiration for these and other scenes in the film came from Farley Mowat's real-life studies in the Arctic and his autobiographical book, *Never Cry Wolf*. Farley really did study wolves in the freezing cold and tells us he really ate mice. He writes: "Eating these small mammals presented something of a problem at first because of the numerous minute bones; however, I found that the bones could be chewed and swallowed without much difficulty. The taste of the mice—purely a subjective factor and not the least relevant to the experiment—was pleasing, if rather bland. As the experiment progressed, this blandness led to a degree of boredom and consequent loss of appetite and I was forced to seek variety in my methods of preparation." Thus evolved his most ambitious achievement and his favorite recipe—souris à la crème.

It should be noted that before you launch into this dish, or duplicate his meals, that Mr. Mowat lived quite comfortably for one week on this diet, but soon developed a craving for fats. He realized that his experiment, up to this point, was partially invalid due to an oversight. The wolves ate the whole mouse, but he had been meticulously discarding the gut. His dissections of mice revealed that they store most of their fat in their abdominal cavity, "adhering to the intestinal mesenteries, rather than subcutaneously or in the muscular tissue." After this insight, he no longer discriminated against body parts, but cooked and ate the whole thing ("without the skin of course").

The following is Farley Mowat's recipe for Souris à la Crème, taken directly from his book, *Never Cry Wolf*.

Souris à la Crème
Rating: R

("Sowbelly is normally only available in the Arctic, but salt pork can be substituted.")

1 doz. fat mice
1 c. white flour
1 piece sowbelly
  Salt, pepper
  Cloves
  Ethyl alcohol

"Skin and gut the mice, but do not remove the heads; wash, then place in a pot with enough alcohol to cover the carcasses. Allow to marinate for about two hours. Cut sowbelly into small cubes and fry slowly until most of the fat has been rendered. Now remove the carcasses from the alcohol and roll them in a mixture of salt, pepper, and flour; then place in frying pan and sauté for about 5 minutes (being careful not to allow the pan to get too hot, or the delicate meat will dry out and become too tough and stringy). Now add a cup of alcohol and six or eight cloves. Cover the pan and allow to simmer slowly for about 15 minutes. The cream sauce can be made according to any standard recipe. When the sauce is ready, drench the carcasses with it, cover and allow to rest in a warm place for ten minutes before serving."
Serves 1.

Papillon

Nutshell

Intermittent degradation, brutality, and despair for an intense one-hundred fifty minutes could be tough going on any movie-goer. But if the picture is based on the first-person story of a man named Papillon, then at least we know there's a glimmer of hope in it, for the man lives to tell his story. Papillon's determination to survive the inhumanities he suffers in various French prisons forces him, among other things, to adopt unorthodox eating habits that keep him alive through a total of seven years in solitary confinement.

Steve McQueen plays the role of Henri Charriere, otherwise known as Papillon, the real-life French safecracker framed for murdering a pimp, who is sentenced to the prisons of French Guiana. While aboard the ship bound for the prison, the muscular Papillon meets heavily bespectacled Louis Dega (Dustin Hoffman), a brainy, but frail counterfeiter. Although opposites in most every way, they arrange a mutually beneficial "business partnership" whereby Papillon agrees to be Dega's bodyguard in exchange for Dega underwriting Papillon's escape.

Once at the prison, an unsuccessful attempt to buy their way out of the more difficult work camps backfires, landing them both in the most wretched one of all—the swamps. The cruel rigors and violence of penal life there nearly do them in, but Dega's money allows them to buy an escape plan. A senseless beating of Dega by a particularly vicious guard, however, prompts Papillon to defend his friend on impulse, thereby forcing him to flee earlier than planned. Bounty hunters make easy sport of him, earning Papillon a lengthy sentence in solitary confinement.

A cell five paces wide is his home for the next two years, six months of which are spent in total darkenss with half-rations. He survives the incarceration only because he submits to eating anything to stay alive, even if it crawls. In the end of his confinement he emerges alive, but as an emaciated, stammering shell of his former self, unable to utter an single coherent thought without superhuman effort.

While regaining his strength in the prison infirmary, Dega and other inmates plan another escape that succeeds in getting them as far as Honduras, but in the end they're arrested again. For this second escape attempt, Papillon is given five years' solitary confinement.

Miraculously he survives once more, and, having paid his debt to France, is sent to Devil's Island in the Caribbean to live out his years. Although once called the Salvation Island by missionaries who fled there from an epidemic of malaria centuries before, Papillon still considers this island exile as a prison and resolves again to escape. Coincidentally, he finds Dega already settled on the island, but Dega cannot be persuaded to join Papillon in another attempt at freedom. The plan requires Papillon to jump from the island's high cliffs into treacherous waves and float on a sack of coconuts. Incredibly, he succeeds this time, and Papillon's determination and luck allow him to live out his days as a free man.

Papillon. In solitary confinement, Steve McQueen adds anything that crawls to his diet of reduced rations.

Survival Soup
Rating: R

1 c. clear reddish broth
1 yellow butterfly or moth
2 large cockroaches
1 huge centipede, pinchers removed

Place broth in tin pot. Break off bite-size portion of butterfly wing and stir into broth. Toss in roaches and centipede. Chop centipede with spoon. Stir. Serves 1.

Papillon. During one of his escapes, Steve McQueen shares a feast with a native girl in one of the film's few moments of contentment.

Papillon. Fresh eggs.

Food Scene

Papillon is a story of human survival in extremes—of both the fierce loyalty of men toward one another and their ferocious brutality. It's about how low some men will go to rob others of their humanity and how far others will go to save their humanity.

When, in his first two years of solitary, Papillon's already meager rations are cut in half for his refusal to expose Dega as the man who smuggled him a few coconuts, he determines to survive whatever harshness the officials inflict on him. Instinctively he knows that in order to do this he must be resourceful.

In the one small speck of light that eeks its way through a crack in his cell's darkness, Papillon prepares his survival soup. His tin meal pot holds a one-cup ration of broth, to which he adds one part broken butterfly wing, two large cockroaches, and one huge centipede cut up with his spoon. Then, in the depths of human existence, he slurps down his meal without hesitation.

Property master Dennis Parrish went beyond the call of duty for the filming of *Papillon.* First he faced the problem of finding large cockroaches and bugs for the eating scenes, which, because they were on location in Jamaica, was not major. He simply enlisted the help of a local Rastifarian who knew where the hairiest, king-sized insects could be found. The problem of building up Steve McQueen's nerve to deal with the scampering cockroaches and pretend to eat them was another matter. To help, Parrish allowed live bugs to crawl over his body (not unlike Kate Capshaw's memorable "body bug" scene in *Indiana Jones and the Temple of Doom*). Within a short time, McQueen got the idea, and the star was not only able to touch the creepy crawlies, but handle them for his eating scenes as well. The actual eating of the bugs was a problem Parrish handled by having molded impressions made from real roaches, from which authentic looking chocolate cockroaches were made (Mrs. See, is this the shape of things to come?) Eventually, however, molded rubber bugs were substituted, because after a week of shooting, the steady diet of chocolate roaches was wearing thin. Rubber bugs were a welcome change of pace.

Papillon. On a ship bound for the prison island, obedient prisoners like Dustin Hoffman enjoy the luxury of "silver service" (aluminum bucket) rations.

Splash. In a posh New York City restaurant, Daryl Hannah negotiates a lobster, mermaid style.

Splash

Nutshell

As most movie-goers know, there are often scenes in films that require the use of stand-ins or doubles. Usually scenes involving some degree of risk to the star will use a stunt double, and stand-ins are used for even broader applications. These are the necessary tricks of the filmmaker so critical to the creation of the grand illusion that is the cinema. Whoever heard of a stunt lobster? But then, who ever heard of a mermaid loose with a credit card at Bloomingdales...until *Splash* came along.

Splash is the modern story of a mythical character whose popularity rivals that of the unicorn—the mermaid. Director Ron Howard and his team were able to successfully overcome some of the obvious difficulties associated with mermaids, like underwater filming and sufficiently covering the top of the maid's body for the newly liberated, yet still conservative, Disney Studios, not to mention maneuvering a thirty-pound plexiglass-and-latex tail stuck on the legs of the leading lady.

It opens with a hazy black-and-white flashback sequence in which a young tourist, Allen Bauer (later played by Tom Hanks as an adult), leaps from a Cape Cod cruise ship into the deep blue sea. Under normal circumstances, this might very well be the end of the boy, but Allen's unusually lucky. A little girl mermaid just happens to be swimming in the area. Underwater with her, Allen's safe from drowning (a switch from the old folklore about mermaids drowning admiring sailors) and within seconds, a lasting bond is struck between them. The mermaid is saddened when he is quickly rescued and taken back on board ship.

A fast forward in time shows Allen and his brother Freddie (John Candy) as young men, running, or trying to run the family's fresh produce business in New York City. The hassles of managing slimy cherries, the playboy escapades of Freddie, and a break-up with his female friend all convince Allen that he needs an escape to Cape Cod, the place he's held dearest ever since his childhood. Unfortunately for Allen, Cape Cod does not return the affection, and he finds himself abandoned in an outboard dinghy off her shores, dunked again in her waters, looted of his wallet by her drifting currents, and nearly drowned again amidst her fishes and seaweed.

Once again, though, he's rescued and pulled ashore to safety by the mermaid (Daryl Hannah) of his childhood, now fully grown. He wakens from his unconscious state to see this beautiful naked woman on the beach. She cannot speak to him, but kisses him passionately before running back into the water. "Oh, why didn't I learn how to swim!" yells Allen.

The story develops into a frothy mix of improbable romance and comic intrigue. The finned sea Ms. makes her way into Gotham, sprouts land-legs, and finds Allen. They fall madly in love, wine and dine for six fun-filled days, and vow to marry, although Madison (as the mermaid names herself) never quite gets around to telling Allen that the woman he's fallen in love with is really a fish.

Stunt Lobster
Rating: R

> 1 large boiled potato, cooked in its jacket
> Salt, pepper
> 1 can hearts of palm, drained
> 1½–2½ lb. lobster, boiled (see Tom Jones p. 132)
> Butter and lemon (optional)

Peel and dice potato into 1" cubes. Salt and pepper to taste (add butter and lemon if desired). Cut hearts of palm into irregular-sized pieces, allowing some to shred like lobster meat. Combine with potatoes. Split lobster down the center on the underside and carefully remove insides. Fill carcass with the potato-palm mixture and close up body around the filling. Serve on a platter with drawn butter and lemon (optional). Serves 1 vegetarian.

Matters are complicated when an obsessed marine scientist dumps water on Allen's bride to be, causing her legs to metamorphose into one big orange fin and revealing her aquatic heritage to the world. The temporarily disillusioned Allen comes to his senses, though, and rescues Madison from the hooks of the incompetent military. Together they escape their military pursuers, rushing to freedom with a plunge into the New York City harbor. In Neptune's kingdom, they are finally joined in true love.

Food Scene

Madison is a charming mermaid, but turns into a delightfully funny person on land when she uses some of her aquatic customs in unexpected places, like when she and Allen dine at a swank New York restaurant. The couple is heavily into the six-day love affair by this time, and Allen only has a vague understanding from Madison's Lorelei quirks that she's from out of town. When their order of lobster arrives at the table, the famished mermaid grabs the entire body and gnaws right into the top of this easy catch, crust and all. Happily she munches through the shell as juicy white meat falls out of the carcass. As surprised diners gaze on the spectacle in disbelief, Allen wonders if maybe his out-of-town guest is out-of-her-mind as well.

As it turns out, the person eating the lobster, actress Daryl Hannah, is a vegetarian. "I get real hysterical at the thought of eating dead things," she is reported as saying, and loves fish so much that she doesn't eat them at all. This posed only a minor problem for property master Dennis Parrish, who ingeniously stuffed an empty lobster shell with a mixture of boiled potatoes and hearts of palm that created another cinematic first—the world's first stunt lobster.

Whatever Happened to Baby Jane?

Nutshell

During the early 1960s, one of the best thrillers to hit the movie scene since Hitchcock's *Psycho* was Robert Aldrich's *Whatever Happened to Baby Jane?* By ignoring traditional rules of movie making, it brought together two of Hollywood's biggest names for the first time and doubled its box-office appeal. Bette Davis plays the lead as a drunken, mentally deranged has-been child actress who plans on making a comeback by starving to death her invalid sister, played by Joan Crawford.

We're given the background for the story in the opening minutes when child star Baby Jane Hudson is shown doing her vaudeville song and dance routine on stage, while her plain-Jane sister Blanche watches from the wings. Baby Jane is adored by her public, but offstage she is a spoiled monster who bullies Blanche and her preening parents.

Years pass, and both of the sisters are making movies, but now it's Blanche who's blossomed and is making it as Hollywood's top star. Jane, unable to develop beyond her childhood talents, only gets work because Blanche has the clout to force studios into giving her parts. A disastrous car accident, however, leaves Blanche a cripple and ends her career. Jane, now totally dependent upon her sister for money, is forced into taking care of Blanche as her bitterness grows unabated.

The sisters live in semi-isolation in their Hollywood home. Jane has become a deranged lush, almost completely reverting to her successful days by singing her old hit songs and sporting corkscrew curls, flouncy dresses, and garish baby-doll makeup, while Blanche lives a more dignified, albeit wheelchair-bound existence, alone in her second-floor bedroom. Only an occasional visit from the cleaning woman, Elvira (Maidie Norman), breaks the monotony of TV and needlepoint for Blanche, until Jane decides to try to make a comeback.

Dwindling finances have forced Blanche into putting her house on the market. Jane accidentally learns about it and, fearing that she might be put in a home, determines to get rid of her burdensome sister once and for all and take vaudeville by storm.

She initiates her scheme by serving Blanche a highly questionable bill of fare, cleverly intimidating Blanche into starving herself. Once Blanche's demise is well underway, Jane hires the first musician who responds to her ad and begins rehearsals. The accompanist, Edwin Flagg (Victor Buono), is a huge, scheming lout who strings Jane along with false compliments to get the money he needs to leave his domineering mother.

Jane binds and gags Blanche after Blanche attempts to contact their neighbor for help. When Elvira manages to overcome Jane's barriers in order to rescue Blanche, Jane kills the maid with a hammer. Edwin, who's grown increasingly suspicious about Jane, snoops around the house and discovers Blanche near death and immediately calls the authorities.

Parboiled Parakeet
Rating: X

1 parakeet
Tomato slices

Plunge bird into boiling water and boil for 20 minutes, or until done. (Total cooking time will depend on size of the bird.) Arrange tomato slices decoratively around rim of serving plate and place bird in the center. Serves 1.

Whatever Happened to Baby Jane? Corkscrew curls and corkscrew bottles.

Whatever Happened to Baby Jane? Joan Crawford faces a lunch of roasted pet parakeet.

Whatever Happened to Baby Jane? The ice cream cones Bette Davis was bringing as a peace offering to her starving sister never reach Joan Crawford. Ms. Davis becomes distracted by the arrival of police officers and an "audience" of curious beachgoers.

Jane makes a fast getaway by packing Blanche into the car and taking off for the beach. There, under the hot sun, Blanche knows she is dying and tells Jane the truth about the car accident that cost Blanche her career. Once Jane learns this truth, she forgives Blanche and even admits to feeling sorry for all those years she hated her. In this new, fleeting moment of sisterhood, Jane buys them both ice cream cones, but she's so far into her Baby Jane fantasy that she doesn't even notice the police who rush in to save her dying sister.

Food Scene

In order to prevent the sale of the house, Jane decides the best solution is to get rid of the problem—Blanche. For years, Jane has been preparing the meals that keep Blanche alive so she can run their financial affairs, but with the finances running low and her home jeopardized, Jane concludes that Blanche's purpose in life is over. Jane is too clever to blatantly murder her sister, so she hatches a scheme whereby Blanche will kill herself.

On the first day of the plan, Jane serves her sister lunch on a beautiful silver tray. Earlier she had cleaned out the birdcage and prepared Blanche's pet parakeet as the entrée, neatly garnished with a ring of tomato slices. When Blanche unsuspectingly lifts the lid, she is shocked and horrified by the sight of the dead bird. Now she knows the extent of her sister's insanity and fears becoming the victim of her open hatred.

The next day, when she delivers another food tray, Jane drops a casual warning about rats in the basement. Blanche's hunger forces her to overcome her fear, but she wishes it hadn't when she lifts the lid and finds a large, dead rat.

In the end, Blanche becomes a limp, helpless mass of skin and bones. Her every attempt at escape is a failure. By the time Jane hauls her off to the beach, she is resigned to her own death, but at least makes peace with her conscience.

A PIE FOR ALL REASONS

Let's clear the air about pies. For more than half a century, the pie as a prop has occupied the most honored place of all foods in the history of film. Pies add atmosphere and authenticity to eating scenes like the one in *Starman*. Plots can pivot on pies, as in *Mildred Pierce*. But most of all, pies are funny—especially a pie in the face. It's an axiom as old as Hollywood itself—if your film needs a quick and easy laugh, just arm your actors with pies and let 'em fly. Over the years, almost every kind of pie ever assembled has been thrown across the silver screen. But where did this madness begin?

According to legend, there are two instances (not unrelated) credited with being the first pie thrown on film. The first is that during a break in filming at the Keystone Studios, comedienne Mabel Normand grabbed someone's luncheon dessert of custard cream pie and heaved it across the set. A cameraman standing nearby was quick to catch the impromptu scene on film, thus recording it for posterity. Another source agrees that it was indeed Mabel Normand who first launched pie into flight in film, but says it was during the 1913 Keystone Studio silent movie, *A Noise from the Deep*. The target of Mabel's pie was Fatty Arbuckle, another popular star of silent films. In either case, the gesture was such a hit that it was to be repeated many times in years to come, with Mabel, more often than not, on the receiving end of many of Arbuckle's pies. Nonetheless, Mabel Normand secured her status as the greatest comedienne of the silent era by being the first to prove that pies could fly and get laughs.

The Keystone Studios, of which Mabel was a part, was largely responsible for the early evolution of cinematic pie throwing. Studio head Max Sennett recognized pie throwing as a viable form of comedy and quickly incorporated it into his broader plan to create classic American slapstick. The use of airborne pies in Max Sennett's comedies became as much his studio trademark as the roaring lion was for another.

As for Fatty Arbuckle, he rose to new comedic heights as a pie thrower. With a deadly aim and dexterity that belied his ample girth, he elevated the act of pie throwing to an art form by tossing two at once in opposite directions.

And what of the pies themselves? Originally Keystone Studios ordered them from a nearby "pâtisserie" called Greenberg's, which dutifully made the real McCoy on demand. When it was discovered, however, that the genuine article tended to disintegrate in midair, Greenberg invented a heavy-duty "ballistic" version using a double thick pastry and a filling of flour, water, and whipped cream—guaranteed to be sloppy. His pies became such an important ingredient of Max Sennett's Keystone Comedies, that he closed his bakery to the public and dedicated himself to making thousands of pies exclusively for the studio.

Then along came Laurel and Hardy—two more big proponents of pie throwing. Occasionally they would toss a custard cream or meringue around the set until 1927, when the pie was about to make its biggest splatter. Fourteen years after its debut with Mable Normand, Hal Roach wrote, produced, and directed (with Clyde A. Bruckman) a Laurel and Hardy two-reeler called *The Battle of the Century*. We know from what remains of the film (only the second half of the film is extant), that it contains nearly three thousand pies, the largest number of pies ever thrown in a film sequence. It is the *Apocolypse Now* of pie fights.

Not to be deceived by the title, there are two big "battles" in *The Battle of the Century*. Originally titled *The Big Fight*, the main fighting event is a boxing match between Thunder-Clap Callahan (Noah Young) and Canvasback Clump (Stan), who is managed by Ollie. After the ringside spectacle, a banana peel becomes the catalyst for the *really* big fight.

Ollie has taken out a $5 insurance policy on Stan so that, in the event of an injury, Ollie will collect. When Stan slips on the banana peel in front of a store and bumps his head, Ollie is elated over his potential windfall "I'll get one thousand dollars for that pineapple!" he boasts, gazing upon Stan's lump. But with the banana peel still on the ground, an unsuspecting pie vendor (Charlie Hall) then slips. A squabble between Stan and Ollie begins and ends with one of the vendor's pies in Ollie's face. More and more passersby enter the enveloping battle with pies flying in every direction.

An innocent victim sitting in a dentist's chair gets a mouth full; another victim takes a direct hit and falls into a garbage can; a dowager poised in her limousine takes one in the puss; and on and on it goes to heightened hilarity. When a cop spies Stan and Ollie chortling at the spectacle, he asks if *they* were the ones who started it. "What pie fight?" Ollie asks innocently, as the battle grows to a frenzied pitch. Finally the cop gets a face full himself

The Battle of the Century, with Laurel and Hardy, features one of the classic pie throwing free-for-alls of all time.

Group shot of the Keystone Cops in uniform.

After all those ballpeen hammer blows to the head, pies provide a welcome respite for The Three Stooges in *In Sweet Pie and Pie*.

Ed Brophy, Polly Moran, and Marie Dressler in *Prosperity*.

Not even a blueberry touches hero Tony Curtis as he calmly walks through the melee of pies thrown in the palace kitchen in *The Great Race*.

Then there's the very serious application of pies as *real* ammunition by the all-child cast of *Bugsy Malone*. Made as a spoof on gangsters and gangster movies, warring mobs get their muscle from seltzer bottles and a new weapon called the "splurge gun." The gun "scrambles" the opposition by shooting balls of whipped cream at the intended victim with a direct, fast, clean hit. One gang leader realizes that cream pie artillery is . . . well, just old fashioned, and spends a good part of the story trying to get his hands on one of those newfangled whipped cream guns. Leave it to the movies to bring us humble pie, then raise it to state-of-the-art technology.

More recently, the humorous but biting *Heartburn* offers us, according to Pauline Kael, the first cinematic pie ever thrown in real anger. Written by Nora Ephron and based on her best-selling semi-autobiographical novel, both the book and movie are chock full of great dishes, mostly because the leading character, Rachel (Meryl Streep), is a food columnist. But she's also a wife and mother whose happy marriage is breaking up. As the screen story of her meeting and subsequent unstable marriage to writer Mark (Jack Nicholson), unfolds, so does her culinary wizardry. She dazzles the audience, if not her mate, with a delicious selection, including carbonara, guacamole, lemon chicken, linguine with clam sauce, and pork chop with mustard and cream. There's also rice pudding (her favorite) and paella, which are presented as gifts for Rachel while she's in the hospital.

After enduring the pain and heartache of her husband's philandering, however, she chooses a friend's dinner party to make a final statement on food and marriage. With the main course of lobster out of the way, Rachel tops the Key Lime pie she's brought for dessert with an abundance of whipped cream and plants it directly in Mark's face with the icy detatchment of a paid assassin. In Ephron's book, Rachel only wished that she'd made a blueberry pie so that it would stain Mark's new blazer. Also in the book, Ms. Ephron thoughtfully supplies recipes for some of the dishes mentioned, Key Lime pie being one of them. It's a quick and easy version that makes a nice parting shot if needed.

Whether it's custard or cream, tossed or eaten, the pie has played a significant role in movie humor (and madness) ever since the silent days. Assembled here are just a few unforgettable moments of the Hollywood pie in action over the years.

Group shot of the Keystone Cops in uniform.

After all those ballpeen hammer blows to the head, pies provide a welcome respite for The Three Stooges in *In Sweet Pie and Pie*.

Ed Brophy, Polly Moran, and Marie Dressler in *Prosperity*.

and sets off in pursuit of Stan and Ollie to end *the* biggest pie fight of all time.

Hardly enough can be said about the routine use of pies by The Three Stooges, Moe Howard, Larry Fine, and Curly Howard. We'd be splitting hairs to try to name them all, but there are a few that stand out in the crowd. The 1947 short, *Half-Wit's Holiday*, contained so much pie throwing footage that much of it was reused in many of their other films, like *Pies and Guys, Stop! Look! and Laugh!, The Pest Man Wins*, and *Scheming Schemers. Half-Wit's Holiday* is also remembered for its "invisible" food in which, as part of a bet, the Stooges are being trained to eat (and behave) like gentlemen. They cut into invisible food, swallow invisible peas, and drink invisible liquids, but we still hear the sound effects these actions normally make. The attempted transformation of the Stooges from bumbling bums to gentle gents ends with their starting a pie-throwing meleé that finishes off the fashionable dinner party and ends the bet.

A similar transformation was attempted earlier in 1941 when *In Sweet Pie and Pie*, three sisters follow the advice of their attorney and marry the Stooges in order to collect a $7,000,000 inheritance with the stipulation that they must be married in order to collect. Since the Stooges are convicts facing public hanging, the sisters will be able to collect the full amount immediately following their execution. But the real killer confesses and the sisters are stuck with the Stooges. To the chagrin of their wives, they try to become gentlemen, but instead are once again responsible for ending the social dig of the year with a messy pie fight.

Actor Larry Fine said the most grueling scenes were always those involving pies. Often they would run out of pies, so the prop man would scoop "used" pie goop off the floor, complete with tacks, splinters, and nails, and reassemble into a pie tin for recycling. Then there's the problem of pretending to be surprised when you know a pie is coming your way. Director Jules White solved the problem by telling Larry that Moe would smack him on the count of three, but Jules would tell Moe to heave it on the count of two.

The pie fight continues to make periodic comebacks in Hollywood films. In *The Great Race*, a turn-of-the-century spoof about a madcap 'round-the-world auto race, released in 1965, the Great Leslie (Tony Curtis) and his gleaming white, brass-trimmed, red-leather-seated phaeton goes up against villainous Professor Fate's (Jack Lemmon) sinister square black monster, the Hannibal Eight. Along for the ride and the fun is staunch feminist Maggie DuBois (Natalie Wood). The race takes its contestants from New York City through the blistering West, up to blizzardly cold Alaska, then by iceberg over the Bering Straits and into Russia, where the race is interrupted for one of the great pie fights in modern films before heading off to the finish line in Paris.

In the mythical kingdom of Potzdorf, Carpania, the Leslie and Fate group of racers becomes unwittingly involved in a plot to overthrow the reigning prince, who's an exact look-alike of Professor Fate. The professor, up to his handlebar moustache in royal fakery, falls off the stairs in the royal bakery into a 1,500 pound, three-tiered cake and kicks off the mayhem. Pies of every description are soon being hurled about the kitchen by the bakers, revolutionaries, counter-revolutionaries and folks just passing by on their way to Paris.

The prince, a well-known boozer, gets hit with a brandy cream that prompts him to ask for more. When he gets it with rum instead, he drunkenly declares, "I never mix my pies!" In a terrific sight gag, the Great Leslie, all decked out in his customary white, glides through the whizzing cream carnage, untouched by even so much as a blueberry until Ms. DuBois, completely covered in cream herself and unable to see, whirls around and nails our pristine hero dead on. Not since the early days of Sennett, Chaplin, or Laurel and Hardy has the screen seen such a colorful fusillade of custard, fruit, and cream pies.

The agony and ecstasy. Alice Faye in *Hollywood Cavalcade*.

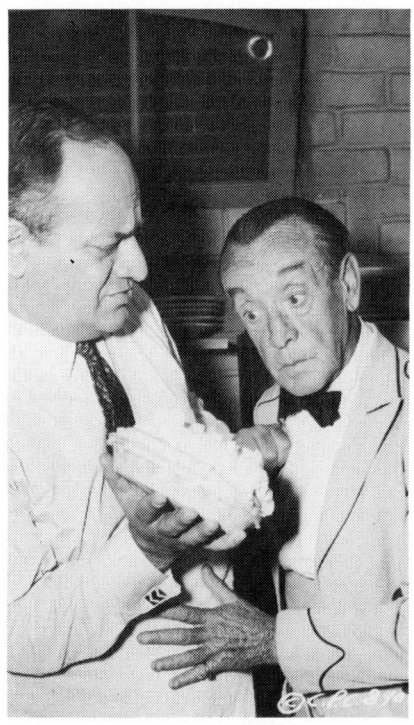

Famed silent screen comedian Snub Pollard, right, who was first hit with pies in 1915 by Buster Keaton and Harold Lloyd, is about to be smacked with the five-thousandth pie of his forty-two-year-old film career by actor Hank Henry for a scene in *Pal Joey*.

Hoodlums are armed and dangerous in *Bugsy Malone*.

The creamy ammunition shot from "splurge gun" in *Bugsy Malone* does its dirty work.

Mabel Normand, right, the First Lady of Pies, is caught red-handed after smacking Marie Dressler in *A Misplaced Foot*.

Not even a blueberry touches hero Tony Curtis as he calmly walks through the melee of pies thrown in the palace kitchen in *The Great Race*.

Then there's the very serious application of pies as *real* ammunition by the all-child cast of *Bugsy Malone*. Made as a spoof on gangsters and gangster movies, warring mobs get their muscle from seltzer bottles and a new weapon called the "splurge gun." The gun "scrambles" the opposition by shooting balls of whipped cream at the intended victim with a direct, fast, clean hit. One gang leader realizes that cream pie artillery is ... well, just old fashioned, and spends a good part of the story trying to get his hands on one of those newfangled whipped cream guns. Leave it to the movies to bring us humble pie, then raise it to state-of-the-art technology.

More recently, the humorous but biting *Heartburn* offers us, according to Pauline Kael, the first cinematic pie ever thrown in real anger. Written by Nora Ephron and based on her best-selling semi-autobiographical novel, both the book and movie are chock full of great dishes, mostly because the leading character, Rachel (Meryl Streep), is a food columnist. But she's also a wife and mother whose happy marriage is breaking up. As the screen story of her meeting and subsequent unstable marriage to writer Mark (Jack Nicholson), unfolds, so does her culinary wizardry. She dazzles the audience, if not her mate, with a delicious selection, including carbonara, guacamole, lemon chicken, linguine with clam sauce, and pork chop with mustard and cream. There's also rice pudding (her favorite) and paella, which are presented as gifts for Rachel while she's in the hospital.

After enduring the pain and heartache of her husband's philandering, however, she chooses a friend's dinner party to make a final statement on food and marriage. With the main course of lobster out of the way, Rachel tops the Key Lime pie she's brought for dessert with an abundance of whipped cream and plants it directly in Mark's face with the icy detachment of a paid assassin. In Ephron's book, Rachel only wished that she'd made a blueberry pie so that it would stain Mark's new blazer. Also in the book, Ms. Ephron thoughtfully supplies recipes for some of the dishes mentioned, Key Lime pie being one of them. It's a quick and easy version that makes a nice parting shot if needed.

Whether it's custard or cream, tossed or eaten, the pie has played a significant role in movie humor (and madness) ever since the silent days. Assembled here are just a few unforgettable moments of the Hollywood pie in action over the years.

Mabel's Cream Pie
Rating: R

- ¼ c. flour
- ½ c. water
- 2 c. whipping cream
  Double thick 9" pie shell, baked and removed from pan

Make a paste of the flour and water, mixing together until smooth. Add flour mixture to cream and whip until thick and cream stands in soft peaks. Spoon into pie shell. For ballistic purposes only. Makes 1 pie.

Key Lime Pie
Rating: G

(This is the list of ingredients Nora Ephron calls for in her novel version of Key lime pie. If you prefer, you can use a regular pie pastry for the crust and meringue for the topping.)

- 6 egg yolks, well beaten
- 1 c. lime juice (fresh or bottled)
- 2 14 oz. cans sweetened condensed milk
- 1 T. grated lime rind
  9" pie plate lined with a graham cracker crust
  Whipped cream

Combine the yolks, lime juice, condensed milk and grated rind. Pour into pie shell and freeze. Just before serving, remove from freezer and spread with whipped cream. Let sit five minutes before serving. Serves 6.

Custard Cream Pie
Rating: G

(This cooking method allows the crust to remain crisp and dry.)

- 4 eggs
- ⅔ c. sugar
- ½ t. nutmeg
- ½ t. salt
- 3 c. milk, scalded and slightly cooled
- 1 t. vanilla extract
  9" pie shell, baked
  Nutmeg for garnish
  Whipped cream

Beat eggs with a beater until well blended. Stir in the sugar, 1/2 teaspoon nutmeg, salt, milk, and vanilla. Pour into 9" buttered glass (or other smooth-sided) pie pan. Set pan into a larger pan and pour water into outer pan to a depth of 1/2". Bake at 375° about 45 minutes or until firm. Cool on wire rack. About 1/2 hour before serving, loosen edge of custard filling with a thin, sharp knife. Gently shake pan to loosen bottom. Holding custard plate over the baked pie shell, gradually tilt the custard, easing filling gently into the shell. Sprinkle with nutmeg and serve with whipped cream. Serves 6.

The face that launched a thousand Spaghetti Westerns: Clint Eastwood.

SPAGHETTI WESTERNS

Spaghetti western is not pasta served with barbecue sauce. Loosely translated, the term "Spaghetti Western" refers to the numerous films made about the early days of the American West that are made just about anywhere in the world—except America. They're the result of foreign filmmakers trying to fill the void created when Hollywood abandoned the genre that was the staple of its economy for so many years—the grade B Western.

Spaghetti became the culinary appellation of this hybrid genre because the godfather of these films was Italian director Sergio Leone, who gave the world *A Fistful of Dollars, For A Few Dollars More,* and *The Good, The Bad and The Ugly.* These films weren't entirely Producto di Italia, however. Their flavor was international. They were generally filmed in Spain and featured American actors, such as Lee Van Cleef, Dan Duryea, Joseph Cotten, Henry Silva, Eli Wallach, Charles Bronson, Ernest Borgnine, Henry Fonda, and, most notably, Clint Eastwood, who rose from the ashes of a cancelled TV show to international stardom through the Leone oaters.

Typically, the Hollywood-made Westerns and those created abroad to mimic them were morally wholesome and clean—especially those that featured the disinfectant powers of Gene Autry, Dale Evans, and Roy Rogers. Under Leone's influence, however, the foreign Western veered off into the blackened abyss of amoral sex and violence. Rape, torture, and gunfights were the usual bill of fare. Audiences lapped it up and came back wanting more.

The Italian Western heroes and villains fashioned by Leone were also part of the overhaul. The hero was no longer easily identifiable, and was not necessarily the "good" guy. Oh he'd do the job all right, but he'd do it as an unshaven, super-efficient, money-grubbing killing machine motivated only by power, greed, revenge, and lechery. Villains, equally unshaven, were only slightly less super-efficient, money-grubbing killing machines motivated by power, greed, revenge, and lechery. The only significant way to tell them apart was by their voices. Heroes were silent types given to lengthy, meaningful stares; villains were noisy, easily identifiable by loud bursts of sinister, throaty laughter, especially if they were Mexican.

Popular themes involved land disputes, power struggles, bank robberies, and no-good-double-crossing sidewinders, etc., between cowboys and Indians, Mexicans and revolutionaries, cavalries and Indians, or Yanks and Johnny Rebs. At any given time, action would generally find the pursuer and pursued in an exhausting chase, covering probably thousands of miles in just ninety minutes of "running" time, from dusty plains and dry deserts to mountains peppered with boulders, never too far from the Mexican border and almost always set against the Civil War or Mexican Revolution. Only once in a while did they need to rest and explain why they were chasing each other, in such dialogue waystations as saloons, whorehouses, forts, teepees, and homesteads. Such is the stuff of which Spaghetti Westerns are made.

Given Leone's lead and foreigners' undying fascination with the Old American West, a whole spate of foreign filmmakers emerged to turn out American Westerns from a variety of foreign locales. It was like going to a restaurant for your favorite Steak au Poivre, then discovering you can make it at home for less whenever you want it and however you want it. American film critics and journalists dubbed these often laughable efforts with culinary nicknames to denote their lands of origination. Thus the phenomenon produced not only "Spaghetti Westerns," but "Curry Westerns," "Sauerkraut Westerns," "Chop Suey Westerns," "Camembert Westerns," and even "Borscht Westerns" from Russia. Basically, all foreign movie stories about the West were being served "Italian style"—inspired by countries whose roots were as foreign to the frontier as garlic is to apple pie.

Hardly a pork chop was eaten in any of them. In fact, other than a bottle of whiskey or the soft end of a cigar, no one put much of anything in their mouths in these films. What little *was* shown were mostly demonstrations of gross eating habits. Instead, they were dedicated to the filling of bodies with lead. The *Movie Lover's Cookbook* pays tribute to these cult classics nonetheless, because anything with a name like "Chop Suey Western" cries out for exploration—in this case a culinary interpretation. What follows are some Americanized versions of international dishes, all altered in some way by a distinct "Western" influence. Just as foreign filmmakers altered the American Western, these recipes are altered foreign dishes, unauthentic versions, full of simmering action but streamlined for convenience and speed in the tradition of American Western cuisine.

Spaghetti Western

- 2 T. olive oil
- 1 large onion, chopped
- 2 cloves garlic, sliced thin
- 3 T. minced fresh parsley
- 1 lb. lean ground beef
- 2 15 oz. cans tomato sauce
- 1 t. oregano
- 1 bay leaf
- 1½ t. sweet basil leaves
- Salt, pepper
- 1 15½ oz. can kidney beans, drained
- Cooked spaghetti for serving

In a 2-quart saucepan, sauté onion in olive oil until tender and transparent. With a wooden mallet, mash garlic thoroughly with the parsley and stir into cooked onion. Add ground beef and cook over medium heat until browned. Stir in sauce and seasonings. Bring to a boil, reduce heat, cover, and simmer 2 hours, stirring occasionally. Add kidney beans and cook 30 minutes more. Skim fat. Serve over cooked spaghetti noodles. Makes about 1 1/2 quarts.

Paella Western

(This is a colorful, festive Spanish dish that we serve every Christmas day. The dish contains so many main dish meats or fish that it pleases everyone.)

- 2 lbs. chicken, cut into serving pieces
- 6 T. olive oil
- 2 t. vinegar
- 1 t. oregano
- 2 cloves garlic, mashed
- 3 peppercorns
- 1½ t. salt
- 2 lbs. hot Spanish sausage (chorizo), in links
- ½ lb. ham steak, cut in strips
- 2 medium-sized onions, peeled and chopped
- 1 green pepper, seeded and chopped
- 2 t. capers
- ¼ c. tomato sauce
- 3 c. rice
- 1 lb. medium shrimp, shells and veins removed
- 1 t. saffron
- Boiling water to cover
- 1 pkg. frozen peas
- Salt
- 1 lb. mussels, scrubbed
- 1 dozen small clams, scrubbed
- 2 cooked lobster tails
- 1 small jar pimientos, drained
- Parsley for garnish

Wash, drain, and dry the chicken. Set aside. Mash oregano, garlic, peppercorns, and salt with 2 tablespoons of the olive oil and the vinegar in a small bowl with a wooden mallet. Brush chicken parts with oil mixture. Brown chicken in the remaining olive oil over medium heat in a large kettle. Meanwhile, cook sausage in a skillet until done. Set aside. When chicken is cooked, stir in cooked sausage, ham, onions, green pepper, and capers. Cook 10 minutes over low heat. Add tomato sauce and rice and cook 5 minutes more. Add shrimp, saffron, and boiling water to cover. Stir to combine and cook until water is absorbed, about 20-30 minutes, stirring occasionally. Add peas midway through cooking. Salt to taste. Steam mussels and clams in a large pot with as little water as possible, until opened. Transfer rice mixture to a large serving platter. Garnish with mussels, clams, lobster tails, pimientos, and parsley. Serves 8-10.

Chop Suey Western

- 2 lbs. chicken breast
- 1 large bunch celery, stems only, sliced thin on bias
- 2 large Bermuda or white onions, peeled and sliced thin
- 1 c. chicken stock
- 2 8 oz. cans bamboo shoots, drained
- 2 16 oz. cans bean sprouts, undrained
- 4 T. all purpose soy sauce
- 4-5 T. cornstarch
- Chow mein noodles or cooked white rice
- Soy sauce to taste

Place chicken breasts in a 2-quart saucepan. Cover with water. Bring to a slow boil and cook until tender and done, about 30 minutes. Remove pan from heat and set aside. Place celery, onions, and chicken stock (use stock in the chicken saucepan) in a large pot. Stir to combine. Bring to a boil. Reduce heat and simmer, covered, until tender, about 25-30 minutes, stirring occasionally. Debone cooked chicken and cut into bite-sized pieces. Add chicken, bamboo shoots, and bean sprouts (including canned liquid) to vegetables and stir. Combine soy sauce and cornstarch and stir until smooth. Add to vegetable mixture and stir to combine. Bring to a slow boil. Reduce heat, cover, and cook until thickened, about 15 minutes. Add more cornstarch if additional thickening is required. Add soy sauce to taste. Serve over chow mein noodles or rice. Serve with soy sauce. Serves 6.

Borscht Western

(This is best when prepared a day in advance.)

1 *quart beef soup stock with meat chunks*
1 *qt. water*
1 *16 oz. can tomatoes, drained and cut into chunks*
¼ *c. finely chopped green pepper*
¼ *c. finely chopped celery*
2 *large cloves garlic, mashed*
2 *T. minced fresh parsley*
½ *t. freshly ground black pepper*
2 *medium potatoes, peeled and diced*
2 *T. butter*
2 *T. wine vinegar*
¼ *head cabbage, sliced thin*
1 *c. julienne carrots*
1 *c. canned julienne beets and juice*
  Salt
  Sour cream for serving

Put soup stock and water in a large pot with the tomatoes, green pepper, celery, garlic, parsley, and pepper. Bring to a boil, reduce heat to a slow boil, and cook for 1/2 hour. Add potatoes and cook another 1/2 hour. Add butter, vinegar, and cabbage. Cook 15 minutes more. Add carrots, beets and beet juice. Cook 15 minutes more. Salt to taste. Serve hot with a dollop of sour cream in each bowl. Serves 6.

Curry Western

(West-coast Westerners are fond of crab, as the Dungeness variety is native to the shore, delicious, and readily available at good prices.)

½ *c. mayonnaise*
1 *t. curry powder*
2 *T. fresh lemon juice*
2 *c. fresh or canned Dungeness crab meat (well drained), chilled*
½ *c. chopped celery*
½ *c. sliced ripe olives*
3 *c. cooked rice, chilled*
3 *T. French dressing (see French Dressing, p.233)*
2 *T. minced fresh parsley*
  Paprika
  Parsley sprigs for garnish

Combine mayonnaise, curry, and lemon juice in a bowl. Add the crab, celery, and 1/3 cup of the ripe olives. Toss gently to combine. Toss the rice, dressing, and minced parsley together. Spread on a serving platter. Top with crab mixture. Sprinkle with paprika and garnish with remaining ripe olives slices and parsley sprigs. Serves 4-6.

Sauerkraut Western

(News for no one: Westerners often use canned foods to shortcut cooking time. Making sauerkraut from scratch requires at least one month of fermenting and de-scumming cabbage brine in stone crocks, at temperatures much cooler than we like to keep our kitchens. Canned sauerkraut is equally good, especially when doctored up with extras, and it takes a fraction of the time.)

2 *T. bacon fat*
1 *medium-sized onion, thinly sliced*
2 *16 oz. cans sauerkraut, undrained*
2 *c. boiling chicken stock*
4 *T. firmly packed brown sugar*

Heat bacon fat in a skillet with a tight-fitting cover. Add onion and sauté until tender and transparent. Add sauerkraut and boiling chicken stock to cover. Bring to a slow boil and cook over medium-low heat, uncovered, for 30 minutes. Reduce heat, cover, and simmer an additional 30 minutes. Add brown sugar and stir until sugar dissolves. Serve with corned beef, pork, ribs, or hot dogs. Makes 1 quart.

MOVIE MENUS

Movie titles can sometimes be misleading. The connoisseur of food in films can often be lured to the local movie house in mouth-watering anticipation of an eating extravaganza by titles like *The Three Musketeers* or *Herbie Goes Bananas*, only to find that food doesn't even make a cameo appearance. No matter how artistic such films may be, they're a disappointment for those who believe the real auteur of great film is the commissary cook. How many have drowned their sorrows in a malted after hearing not word one about fruit in *The Strawberry Statement*, or seeing so much as a glass of wine in *The Grapes of Wrath*? Nonetheless, food movie titles, whether they're misleading or literally descriptive of the content of the film, have other uses. They make excellent menus.

When organized into classically structured menus, movie titles make a meal. Start with an appetizer like *Operation Caviar*, for instance, and move on to an entree of *Lady Caroline Lamb*, with *Le Soufflé Au Cour*, *Forty Carats*, and a salad of *Attack of the Killer Tomatoes* with *The Green Goddess* dressing. Finish up with *Bread and Chocolate*, with beverages of *Café Society* and *Champagne for Caesar*.

There are countless titles to choose from and almost endless combinations. Grouping is ultimately based on individual preferences, but movie menus make better sense if built around a theme. A Southern-style dinner for example, might consist of *King Creole*, *Cornbread, Earl and Me*, with *Watermelon Man* and *Jamaica Rum* for dessert. A theme provides a focal point on which to organize the wide variety of titles available.

Here's just a sample of what can be put together to create original and interesting groups of tantalizing dishes, complete with recipes. If you wish to plan your own menus and recipes, imagination is all you need to produce real show-stopper meals—because, unlike the movies, you have the final cut.

Breakfast

Entree:	A Clockwork Orange
	The Egg and I
	The Toast of New Orleans
Beverage:	Coffee, Tea or Me?
Entree:	Wild Oranges
	A Bout de Soufflé
	The Pumpkin Eater
Beverage:	Tea for Two *with* Diamonds for Breakfast
Entree:	Bananas
	Serial
Beverage:	Expresso Bongo
Entree:	Strawberry, Lemon and Mint
	The Day the Fish Came Out
	The Toast of New York
Beverage:	Café Metropole
Entree:	A Raisin in the Sun
	A Day in the Death of Joe Egg
Beverage:	Tea and Sympathy
Entree:	Smile Orange
	Sunny Side Up
	The Bread Peddler
Beverage:	Coffy
Entree:	How to Frame a Figg
	Egghead on Hill
	Toast of the Legion
Beverage:	Java Head
Entree:	Honeycomb
	The Serpent's Egg
Beverage:	The Luck of Ginger Coffey

Lunch

Entree:	Skippy
	Goodbye Mr. Chips *with* Grease
Dessert:	Lorna Doone *and* Top Banana
Beverage:	Peppermint Soda
Entree:	The Count of Monte Cristo *with* The Strawberry Statement
Dessert:	The Chocolate Soldier
Beverage:	The Seven Ups
Appetizer:	King of Hearts
Entree:	The Ghost and Mr. Chicken
	Bread, Love and Jealousy
Dessert:	The Strawberry Blonde
Beverage:	Punch and Jody
Appetizer:	Tortilla Flat
Entree:	Cantata of Chile *with* Crackers
Dessert:	California Split
Beverage:	The Brave Bulls
Entree:	Summer Stock
	Get Rollin'
Dessert:	Marshmallow Moon
Beverage:	Ring of Bright Water
Appetizer:	There's a Girl in My Soup
Entree:	Prisoner of Shark Island
	The Corn Is Green *with* Salt of the Earth
Dessert:	Rhubarb
Beverage:	Monterey Pop
Appetizer:	Wild Fruit
Entree:	Tuna Clipper
Dessert:	Here Comes Cookie
Beverage:	Lemonade Joe
Appetizer:	Hey, Pineapple!
Entree:	Lady From Chungking
	Ginger in the Morning
Dessert:	The Fortune Cookie
Beverage:	The Bitter Tea of General Yen
Entree:	The Pizza Triangle
Dessert:	The Lemon Drop Kid
Beverage:	Captain Milkshake
Appetizer:	Our Vines Have Tender Grapes
Entree:	Attack of the Crab Monsters
	Blondie in the Dough
Dessert:	The Forbidden Fruit
Beverage:	Under Milk Wood

Dinner

Appetizer:	Operation Caviar
Entree:	Lady Caroline Lamb
	Le Soufflé au Cour
	Forty Carats
	Attack of the Killer Tomatoes *with* The Green Goddess
	Roll, Freddie, Roll
	Salt and Pepper
Dessert:	Sweet Charity
Beverage:	Champagne for Caesar
	Café Society
	Port of New York
Appetizer:	The Amorous Prawn
Entree:	Pork Chop Hill *with* The Gravy Train
	Onionhead *with* French Dressing
Dessert:	Bread and Chocolate
Beverage:	Port of Seven Seas
	Dark Waters
Appetizer:	Octopussy
Entree:	Cold Turkey *with* Pillar of Salt
	One Potato, Two Potato
	The Nutty Professor
Dessert:	A Taste of Honey
Beverage:	Champagne Charlie
	Black Water Gold
Appetizer:	Limelight
Entree:	Clambake
	Adam's Rib
	Freebie and the Bean
	The Biscuit Eater
Dessert:	The Cocoanuts
Beverage:	Knickerbocker Holiday
Appetizer:	Frogs
Entree:	Cisco Pike
	Mrs. Wiggs of the Cabbage Patch
	The Story of Seabiscuit
Dessert:	The Honey Pot
Beverage:	Teahouse of the August Moon
Appetizer:	Wild Strawberries
Entree:	Million Dollar Duck
	The Food of the Gods
	The Doughgirls
Dessert:	The Grasshopper
Beverage:	A Girl in Every Port
Entree:	Chicken Every Sunday
	Bread, Love and Dreams *with* Butterfield 8
Dessert:	Apple Game
Beverage:	Manhattan
	Esther Waters
Appetizer:	Broth of a Boy
Entree:	King Creole
	Cornbread, Earl and Me
Dessert:	Watermelon Man
Beverage:	Jamaica Rum
Appetizer:	Eve Knew Her Apples
Entree:	Michael Strogoff
	Sorrell and Son *with* The Onionfield
Dessert:	There's Always Vanilla
Beverage:	La Marie Du Port
Appetizer:	Attack of the Mushroom People
Entree:	The Kentucky Fried Movie
	Jack and the Beanstalk
	Hot Potato
Dessert:	The Apple Dumpling Gang
Beverage:	Cigarettes, Whiskey and Wild Women
Appetizer:	Duck Soup
Entree:	The Fish That Saved Pittsburgh
	Where the Red Fern Grows
	The Young Girls of Rochefort
Dessert:	The Adventures of Huckleberry Finn
Beverage:	Champagne Waltz
	Brandy Ashore

Movie Snacks

Popcorn
Candy:
   The Milky Way
   The Three Musketeers
   The Babe Ruth Story
   Payday
   Sweethearts

All titles and snacks available at your local movie theater.

Adam's Rib
(Baked "Barbecued" Spare Ribs)

3-4 lbs. country or farmer-style ribs
1 medium onion, sliced and separated
1 lemon, sliced and seeds removed
1 c. catsup
⅓ c. Worcestershire sauce
1 t. chili powder
1 t. salt
2 dashes Tobasco
2 c. water
Cooked rice

Place ribs in a glass baking dish. Arrange onion and lemon slices on top. Bake at 450° for 1/2 hour.

Meanwhile, prepare the sauce by combining the remaining ingredients in a saucepan. Bring to a boil. Reduce heat and simmer for 15 minutes, or until ribs are done. Pour sauce over the meat. Reduce heat to 325° and cook for an additional 1 1/2 hours, basting every 15 minutes or so. Serves 2-4.

The Adventures of Huckleberry Finn
(Huckleberry Tart)

(Huckleberries are practically the twin sister of blueberries, the only real difference being in their size and number of seeds. Huckleberries are generally found growing on mountainsides [like the blueberry], abandoned fields, or pine forests. Feel free to use one in place of the other, or even to mix them. The proper thickening of these berries is guesswork at best, as their juiciness varies like other types of fresh or frozen fruit. You may use more or less tapioca for thickening, but experience will be your best guide.)

Crust:
1 c. flour
½ c. softened butter
1 egg yolk
2 T. grated lemon rind
1 t. vanilla

Filling:
1½ qts. fresh or frozen huckleberries (or blueberries)
½ c. sugar
2 T. firmly packed brown sugar
½ t. cinnamon
1 T. lemon juice
⅓ c. quick cooking tapioca
2 T. butter

Mix the flour, butter, yolk, lemon rind, and vanilla together. Form into a ball and chill one hour. Roll the dough out onto a lightly floured board until slightly larger than a 9" pie plate. Place in the pie plate; flute and trim the edges. Set aside.

Combine the berries, sugars, cinnamon, lemon juice, and tapioca in a bowl. Let sit 15 minutes. Pour berry mixture into the prepared piecrust and dot with butter. Bake at 350° for 45 minutes to 1 hour, until thickened and lightly browned. Serve with ice cream or whipped cream. Serves 6.

The Amorous Prawn
(Broiled Prawn and Artichokes)

1 lb. medium-sized prawn or shrimp
1 9 oz. pkg. frozen artichoke hearts
1 medium-sized onion, minced
3 cloves garlic, mashed
¼ c. olive oil
¼ c. vegetable oil
¼ c. minced fresh parsley
1 T. Worcestershire sauce
Juice of 1 lemon
1 t. dried basil leaves
1 t. salt
1 t. dried mustard

Clean the prawn or shrimp by removing the shell, deveining, and washing under cold water. Drain well. Cook the artichoke hearts according to package directions. Drain and cool. Combine the remaining ingredients in a bowl. Add the prawns and artichokes and marinate at room temperature for 1 1/2 hours.

Place in a single layer on a baking sheet, marinade and all, and broil 6" from medium-high heat for 1 1/2 minutes on each side. (Be sure not to overcook!) Top each prawn with an artichoke chunk and skewer with a toothpick. (You may have to halve some of the artichokes to have enough.) Serve hot. Serves 6.

The Apple Dumpling Gang
(Apple Dumplings with Custard Sauce)

Dumpling:
6 large apples
Juice and grated rind of 1 lemon
¾ c. chopped dates
¼ c. chopped pecans
4 T. firmly packed brown sugar
2 t. ground cinnamon
¼ t. ground nutmeg
Pastry for 3 single piecrusts

Custard:
⅓ c. sugar
3 T. cornstarch
3 large egg yolks
1 c. milk
1 c. light cream
2 t. vanilla

Peel and generously core the apples, leaving about 1/4" of the core at the base. Cut a flat edge at the bottoms to keep the apples upright and level. Brush the inside and outside of each with lemon juice.

In a small bowl, mix the lemon rind, dates, pecans, brown sugar, cinnamon, and nutmeg together. Fill the core of each apple with the date mixture. Divide the pastry into 6 equal portions and roll each out into a 7" square, about 1/4" thick. Place a prepared apple into the center of each square, bringing the four corners of the pastry up to the center. Moisten with milk and pinch top and edges to seal.

Place on a buttered baking sheet and chill in the freezer for 5 minutes. Brush with milk and bake at 375° for 45 minutes, or until golden brown. Meanwhile, prepare the custard sauce.

Preheat water in the bottom of a double boiler until simmering. Combine the sugar and cornstarch in the top of an unheated doubled boiler. Using a wire whisk, beat in the egg yolks and whip until smooth. Heat the milk and cream in a separate saucepan to the boiling point. Add half the milk mixture to the egg mixture, stirring constantly. Stir in the remaining milk.

Now place the top of the double boiler over the simmering water (being sure it does not touch the water) and cook, stirring constantly, until the mixture is thickened and smooth, about 5–10 minutes. Remove from heat and spoon into a serving bowl. Serve immediately with the baked dumplings, or cover surface with plastic wrap to prevent a skin from forming until ready for use. Makes 6 dumplings and 2 cups custard sauce.

Apple Game
(Apple-Surprise Tart with Pecans Glaze)

(Find the surprise apple filling in this all-in-one taste extravaganza!)

Pecans glaze:

- 1 c. perfect pecan halves
- ¾ c. water
- ¼ c. honey
- 3 T. sugar
- ¾ c. vegetable oil

Piecrust:

- 1¾ c. flour
- ¼ t. salt
- 10 T. chilled butter (1¼ sticks) cut in 1" cubes
- 3 T. solid vegetable shortening
- ¼ c. finely chopped pecans
- ½ c. ice water
- 1 egg, beaten

Apple surprise filling:

- 1 medium-sized tart apple
- 1 T. butter, softened
- Scant ⅛ t. salt
- ¼ c. firmly packed brown sugar
- ½ c. coarsely chopped pecans

Pumpkin disguise filling:

- ½ c. evaporated milk
- ½ t. cinnamon
- ¼ t. ground ginger
- ¼ t. salt
- ⅛ t. nutmeg
- ⅛ t. ground cloves
- ½ c. pumpkin puree, canned or fresh
- ¼ c. firmly packed light brown sugar
- 1 egg, slightly beaten
- 2 T. dark rum

Rum cream:

- ½ c. heavy cream
- 1 T. powdered sugar
- 1 t. dark rum

Prepare the pecans glaze by combining the pecan halves with the water and honey in a 1-quart saucepan. Bring to a boil over medium-high heat and boil for 5 minutes. Drain in a colander and return to the hot empty pan over medium heat. Sprinkle with sugar, remove from heat, and gently toss pecans to coat evenly. Arrange pecans in a single layer on a baking sheet lined with wax paper. Let dry 5 minutes.

Meanwhile, wash and dry the saucepan. Add the oil, and heat to 375° over medium-high heat. Deep fry the pecans, stirring gently until the nuts turn light brown and the sugar begins to caramelize, about 2 mintues. Remove the fried nuts with a slotted spoon and drain on a wire mesh (not paper or linen, as they will stick), being sure the pecans do not touch each other as they dry. Cool until crispy. Refrigerate in an airtight container until ready for use. (These make a great snack or holiday food gift.)

Prepare the dough by sifting or blending the flour and salt together in a food processor, using the mincing blade. Cut in the butter, shortening, and pecans by turning the motor on and off until dough resembles coarse meal (or use a pastry cutter or wire whip).

Add the water all at once. Machine or spoon mix just until the ingredients come together without forming into a ball. Remove from the processor and gather into a ball. Cut dough in half. Dust each half lightly with flour, form each into a ball, and seal each tightly in plastic wrap. Refrigerate at least 2 hours before using. (This recipe makes enough dough for 2 single piecrusts, so the leftover dough can be stored in the refrigerator in the plastic wrap for up to 1 week, or frozen for 1 month.)

Butter a 9"×1" fluted tart pan that has a removable bottom. Set aside. Place one chilled dough ball on a lightly floured board and roll out to a thickness of 1/8", forming an 11" circle. Fold in half, place in the prepared pan, unfold and fit to size (there should be little or no excess). Generously prick sides and bottom with a fork at 1/2" intervals. Chill 20 minutes.

Butter a sheet of aluminum foil and place buttered side down over the dough. Fill with rice, beans, or pastry weights. Bake at 425° until set, about 15 minutes. Holding pan by the sides, remove tart pan from oven and uncover crust. Brush with beaten egg and bake at 425° until golden, about 5 minutes. Cool for 10 mintues. Remove outer ring from pan and cool completely on a rack. Return ring to pan before filling.

To prepare the apple filling, peel, core, and thinly slice the apple. Place in a skillet with the butter and cook, covered, over medium heat for 5 minutes, stirring occasionally. Remove from heat. Mix the salt with the brown sugar and add to the apples. Add the pecans. Toss to coat evenly. Spread in the bottom of the cooled crust.

For the pumpkin filling, blend the evaporated milk, cinnamon, ginger, salt, nutmeg, and cloves in a large bowl with a wire whip. Stir in the pumpkin, brown sugar, egg, and rum. Beat until smooth. Carefully spoon pumpkin mixture over apple mixture in the piecrust. Place on a baking sheet and bake at 450° for 10 minutes. Reduce to 350° and continue baking until set, about 35-45 minutes.

Cool on the baking sheet for 15 minutes, then transfer to a wire rack and cool completely. Remove the outer ring and place on serving dish. To finish, whip the cream with the sugar and rum. Spoon into a pastry bag with desired tip and pipe decorative border design on top of pie. Garnish with pecans glaze. Serves 6.

Attack of the Crab Monsters
(Crabs In a Stew)

- 4 T. butter
- 1 T. olive oil
- 1 lb. mushrooms, quartered
- 2 shallots, minced
- 2 green onions, sliced fine
- 3 cloves garlic, mashed
- ¼ c. minced fresh parsley
- 1 10 oz. pkg. frozen petite peas, cooked
- 1 4 oz. jar sliced pimientos, drained
- 1 c. light cream
- 2 T. cornstarch
- 2 T. whiskey
- 1 lb. cooked crabmeat
- 3 c. cooked rice
- Salt, freshly ground pepper

Melt the butter and oil together in a large skillet. Sauté the mushrooms, shallots, green onions, and garlic until tender. Add the parsley, cooked peas, pimientos, and cream. Stir gently and heat through.

Take 1/2 cup of the heated cream from the skillet and dissolve the cornstarch in it. Return cream to the mushroom mixture and heat until the sauce thickens. Gently stir in the crab and whiskey. Heat through and season to taste. Serve over rice. Serves 6.

Attack of the Killer Tomatoes *with* The Green Goddess
(Tomato Wedges with Avocado Dressing)

Dressing:
- 1 ripe avocado
- 1 c. mayonnaise
- ½ t. garlic powder
- 1 T. dried parsley flakes
- 4 T. tarragon-flavored white wine vinegar
- ½ t. salt
- Freshly ground black pepper
- Dash cayenne

- Boston lettuce
- Large vine-ripe tomatoes
- Parsley sprigs

Beat avocado with an electric mixer until smooth and creamy. Add remaining dressing ingredients and beat at low speed until well blended. Chill.

When ready to serve, arrange crisp lettuce leaves on a serving plate. Cut tomatoes (allowing one per person) through stem end into wedges, being careful not to cut entirely through tomato. (This will allow tomato to open, but still remain attached at the center.) Place tomato on lettuce leaves and spoon dressing into the center. Makes about 1 1/2 cups dressing.

Attack of the Mushroom People
(Mushroom Paté)

- ¼ c. minced onion
- 1 lb. mushrooms, chopped
- 2 cloves garlic, mashed
- 3 T. butter
- 2 T. flour
- ¼ c. cream
- Salt, pepper
- 4 hard boiled egg yolks
- 2 T. minced fresh parsley
- 2 T. sherry
- Petite pastry shells or toast points
- Parsley sprigs

Sauté the onion, mushroom, and garlic in the butter until tender. Mix the flour with the cream until smooth and stir into the mushroom mixture. Salt and pepper to taste. Mash 3 of the egg yolks and add to the mixture along with the parsley. Stir in the sherry and heat through. Serve in pastry shells or on toast points garnished with bits of the remaining egg yolk (mashed), and parsley sprigs. Makes about 2 cups.

Bananas
(Broiled Banana)

- 1 banana, peeled and sliced lengthwise
- Pitted dates, sliced lengthwise
- Pineapple slices, coarsely chopped
- 3 slices bacon

Run the end of a spoon lengthwise down the center of each banana half, creating a shallow hollow. Fill one banana half with a thin layer of dates and pineapple slices. Top with remaining banana half, sandwich style. Wrap with bacon slices, slightly overlapping them in a spiral around the outside.

Broil under medium heat, turning as necessary to brown and crisp bacon evenly on all sides. Serves 1.

Biscuit Eater
(Bacon Biscuits)

- 1 pkg. dry yeast
- ½ c. warm water
- 1 c. sour cream
- 3 eggs, beaten with 1/4 c. milk
- ¼ rounded t. salt
- 4 c. flour
- ½ lb. bacon, cooked crisp and crumbled
- Flour for sprinkling
- 1 egg, beaten

Dissolve the yeast in the warm water. Set aside. Mix the sour cream, egg mixture, and salt together with a wire whip until well combined. Add the yeast mixture and stir well. Add the flour a little at a time, stirring after each addition. (The dough will be fairly sticky.) Cover with a clean cloth and let rise in a warm place until doubled. Lightly flour a board and sprinkle with the bacon crumbs. Punch dough down and roll out on the "bacon" board with a floured rolling pin. Sprinkle dough with enough flour to prevent sticking. Fold into quarters and let rise again, covered, in a warm place. Punch down, roll out on a lightly floured board, fold into quarters and let rise as before. Repeat this procedure 1 more time.

On the last roll-out, roll to a thickness of 1/2", cut the dough into 2 1/2" round biscuits, and place on buttered baking sheets. Brush with beaten egg and let rise until doubled a final time. Bake at 350° for 25-30 minutes, or until lightly browned. Makes about 25-30 biscuits.

The Bitter Tea of General Yen
(Herb Tea)

4 T. fresh lemon verbena
2 c. boiled water

Steep leaves in boiled water 3-10 minutes. Serves 2.

Black Water Gold
(Honey Fruited Tea)

1¼ qts. boiling water
2 teabags
10 cloves
1/3 c. honey
1¼ c. orange juice
1 qt. limeade
2 T. lemon juice
    Orange slices
    Mint leaves

Pour boiling water over teabags and cloves. Cover and steep for 5 minutes. Strain. Stir in the honey and cool. Add the orange juice, limeade, and lemon juice. Pour over cracked ice and garnish with orange slices and mint leaves. Serves 12.

Blondie in the Dough
(Million Dollar Spiral Bread)

(This is a spiral herb bread, the herbs being added to the dough jelly-roll fashion before rising.)

Bread dough:
3 c. warm water
3 pkg. yeast
¼ c. honey
1 T. plus 1 t. salt
9 c. flour, approximately
5 T. safflower oil

Herb filling:
1 c. butter, softened
¾ c. minced fresh parsley
½ c. minced green onions (about 3-4)
3 cloves garlic, mashed

Combine the water, yeast, and honey in a large bowl. Stir until yeast dissolves. Add the salt and half the flour, beating until smooth. Add the remaining flour and combine, kneading with your hands if necessary. Pour the oil over the dough and knead 5 minutes in the bowl until smooth and elastic. Cover the bowl with a clean cloth and let rise in a warm place until doubled.

Meanwhile, prepare the herb filling by mashing the filling ingredients together with a mallet. Set aside. When the dough has doubled, punch down and divide into 3 equal parts. Knead slightly on a lightly floured board, then roll each out to a thickness of 1/4" to 1/2". Divide the herb filling into 3 equal parts, and spread each over the rolled dough, bringing the filling to within 1/4" of the edges. Firmly roll up each, jelly-roll fashion, and place in buttered loaf pans, seam side down. Cover with the cloth and let rise again until doubled. Bake at 375° for 30-35 minutes, or until done. Makes 3 loaves.

A Bout de Soufflé
(A Breakfast Egg Soufflé)

Butter
Parmesan cheese
1 lg. onion, chopped fine
1 c. milk
   Salt, pepper
4 T. butter
4 T. flour
5 eggs, separated

Generously butter a 1-quart soufflé mold and dust with Parmesan cheese. Chill.

Combine the onion, milk, and salt and pepper to taste in a small saucepan. Cook over medium heat until onion is tender. Melt the 4 tablespoons butter in a 1-quart saucepan. Using a wire whip, blend in the flour and cook several minutes until thickened and smooth. Gradually add the milk mixture, beating constantly until thick. Cool slightly.

Beat the 5 egg yolks into the thickened milk mixture, one at a time. Beat the egg whites in a bowl until stiff (but not dry). Whip 1/3 of the beaten egg whites into the yolk/milk mixture with a wire whip. Fold in the remainder of the egg whites. Pour into the prepared soufflé mold and bake at 375° for 30-35 minutes, or until well risen and lightly browned. Serve immediately. Serves 4.

Brandy Ashore
(Mulled Brandy)

¼ 32 oz. bottle brandy
¼ 32. oz. bottle port
2 bottles (24 oz. each) red wine
1 T. brown sugar
2 sticks cinnamon
8 whole cloves
½ t. grated nutmeg
   Peel of 1 orange
   Peel of 1 lemon

Combine the ingredients in a saucepan and almost bring to a boil, stirring with a wooden spoon. Simmer 5 minutes. Serve warm in mugs. Serves 8-12.

The Brave Bulls
(Brave Bull Cocktail)

⅝ oz. tequila
⅝ oz. kahlua

Pour over ice. Stir. Serve in old-fashioned glass. Serves 1.

Bread and Chocolate
(Orange Pound Cake with Chocolate Hazelnut Sauce)

(Pound cakes are best when made a day in advance. To make an exceptional cake, all ingredients should be at room temperature and you should use an electric mixer.)

Butter for greasing pan
Flour for dusting
1 c. butter, softened
1 c. sugar
½ t. grated orange rind
2 t. orange extract
1 t. vanilla
5 eggs
2 c. sifted cake flour
½ t. salt

Chocolate hazelnut sauce:
Hot fudge (see California Split p. 218)
1 c. finely chopped hazelnuts

Butter and lightly dust a loaf pan with flour. Set aside. Beat the butter, sugar, and rind together with an electric mixer at medium speed for 3 minutes. Beat in the extracts and eggs one at a time for 1 additional minute. Stir in flour and salt. Beat for 2 more minutes. Pour into prepared loaf pan and bake at 300° for 1 1/2 hours. Cool 10 minutes in the pan. Turn out onto a wire rack and cool completely. Prepare hot fudge and stir in hazelnuts. Cool.

When ready to serve, cut into serving slices and frost one side of each slice with chocolate hazelnut spread. Makes 1 loaf.

Bread, Love and Dreams
(Parmesan "Cloud" Bread)

3 c. boiling water
1⅓ c. butter
¼ c. sugar
2 t. salt
1¼ c. grated Parmesan cheese
2 pkg. dry yeast
⅓ c. lukewarm water
3 eggs, beaten slightly
9-10 c. flour, approximately
½ c. skim-milk powder
2 large cloves garlic, mashed

Combine the boiling water, 1/3 cup of the butter, the sugar, salt, and cheese in a large bowl. Stir until the butter melts. Set aside to cool. Dissolve the yeast in the lukewarm water. Add yeast mixture and the beaten eggs to the cheese mixture when it has cooled to lukewarm. Stir to blend thoroughly.

Sift 7 cups of the flour with the skim-milk powder and stir into the batter, mixing until smooth. Add and knead in up to 3 more cups of flour to make a medium-stiff dough. Knead for 5 minutes on a lightly floured board. Place in a buttered bowl, cover with a clean cloth, and let rise in a warm place until doubled. Punch down, divide into 3 equal pieces, and divide each piece into 12 pieces. Roll the 36 pieces into balls and let rest 10 minutes. Meanwhile, melt the remaining 1 cup butter with the garlic in a small saucepan. Butter 3 loaf pans. Roll balls in the garlic butter and place 12 in each loaf pan, making 2 layers of 6 balls in each. Let rise again until doubled. Bake at 375° for 35-40 minutes or until browned and done. Makes 3 loaves.

Bread, Love and Jealousy
(Bread with Spices, Onion, and Garlic)

5 T. butter
2 T. sugar or honey
1 T. salt
4 cloves garlic, mashed
1¾ c. scalded milk
2 c. minced onion
2 pkgs. dry yeast
½ c. warm water
½ t. rubbed sage
½ t. celery salt
7 c. flour, sifted (approximately)

Put 2 tablespoons of the butter, the sugar (or honey), salt, and garlic in a large bowl. Pour the milk over and stir until the butter is melted. Sauté the minced onion in the remaining 3 tablespoons butter until tender and lightly browned. Cool to warm. Dissolve the yeast in the warm water and add to the cooled milk mixture. Sift the sage and celery salt with 2 cups of the flour and stir into the milk mixture. Mix with a beater until smooth. Stir in the onion. Gradually add the remaining flour, stirring well after each addition. (You may knead the last few cups in for ease in combining.)

Turn out on a lightly floured board and knead for 5 minutes, until smooth and elastic. Add flour as necessary to keep the dough from sticking.

Place in a buttered bowl, cover with a clean cloth, and let rise in a warm area until doubled. (I like to use an unheated oven with a large pan of hot water on the rack below the bread bowl.) Punch down and let rise again for 35 minutes.

Cut the dough into 2 equal parts and shape into 2 loaves on a lightly floured board. Place in buttered loaf pans, cover with a cloth, and let rise in a warm area until doubled. Preheat oven to 400°. Place bread in oven, reduce heat to 350°, and bake 40 minutes or until nicely browned. Makes 2 loaves.

The Bread Peddler
(Lemon-Custard French Toast)

- 6 1½" slices day-old French bread
- 2 eggs, beaten
- 1 c. light cream
- 1 c. milk
- 1 t. vanilla
- 1 T. grated lemon peel
- 2 T. sugar
- ¼ t. salt
- ¼ t. nutmeg
- 2 T. butter
- 2 T. vegetable oil
- Powdered sugar for garnish
- Maple syrup

Arrange bread slices one layer deep in a large glass pie plate or baking dish. Using a wire whip, beat the eggs, cream, milk, vanilla, lemon peel, sugar, salt, and nutmeg together in a bowl. Pour over bread and let soak 5 minutes. Turn slices over. Cover with plastic wrap and refrigerate several hours or overnight.

Heat 1 tablespoon of the butter with 1 tablespoon of the oil on a griddle or large frying pan over medium heat. Cook slices until golden brown, about 5 minutes on each surface (top, bottom, and sides) adding more butter and oil as necessary. (Be sure to cook completely or insides will not be set.) Transfer to a heated platter and sprinkle with powdered sugar. Serve with maple syrup. Serves 4–6.

Broth of a Boy
(Black-Eyed Soup)

(This is one of those magical soups that can handle more water if it gets too thick without sacrificing too much of the flavor. As with most soups, it's even better as a leftover the next day.)

- 2 c. dried black-eyed peas
- 7 c. boiling water
- 1 medium ham hock
- 2 celery ribs with leaves, coarsely chopped
- 2 carrots, coarsely chopped
- 1 medium onion, peeled, halved, and studded with 4 cloves
- 1 bay leaf
- 2 T. minced fresh parsley
- 1 T. butter
- Salt, pepper
- Lemon juice
- 4 thin slices lemon
- Paprika
- Chervil leaves for garnish

Cover the peas with cold water and let soak overnight. Drain and place in a large pot. Cover with the boiling water. Add the ham hock, celery, carrots, onion, bay leaf, parsley, butter, salt, and pepper. Bring to boiling. Reduce heat and simmer until the peas are tender, about 2 1/2–3 hours. (Skim the top as necessary while cooking to remove the scum.) Discard the ham hock and bay leaf.

Puree the soup in a food processor, blender, or sieve. Return to the pot to low heat and season to taste with salt and pepper. Adjust the consistency to your liking by adding water if necessary. Spoon into soup bowls. Sprinkle surface with lemon juice. Garnish tops with a lemon slice sprinkled with paprika and several whole chervil leaves. Serves 4.

Butterfield 8
(Basil-Butter Bread Spread)

(If you plan to use Butterfield 8 for a type of bread other than Parmesan "Cloud" Bread, add a mashed clove of garlic and Parmesan cheese to the spread if desired.)

- 1 c. softened butter
- Juice of 1 small lemon
- ½ t. Worcestershire sauce
- ½ t. dried oregano
- 1 t. dried sweet basil or
- 2 T. minced fresh basil

Mash ingredients together and use as a spread for breads. Makes about 1 cup.

Café Metropole
(Italian Spiced Coffee)

- ½ c. ground coffee
- 1 T. grated orange rind
- 1 T. grated lemon rind
- 1½ t. anise seed
- 3 c. water
- Cream

Combine coffee, grated rinds, and anise seed in the basket of an automatic coffeemaker. Pour water through and let drip. Serve with cream. Serves 2.

Cafe Society
(Spiced Brandy Coffee en Flambé)

- ½ stick cinnamon
- 6 whole cloves
- 1 curl orange peel
- 1 curl lemon peel
- 6 t. sugar
- 2 oz. rum
- 4 oz. brandy
- 3 c. strong coffee

Mix all the ingredients (except the coffee) in a chafing dish. Heat and set afire with a lighted match. Stirring with a ladle, slowly stir in the coffee. Ladle into demitasse cups. Serves 6.

California Split
(Ice Cream Split with Hot Fudge)

Hot fudge:
- ¼ c. butter
- 4 oz. unsweetened chocolate, shaved
- ¼ c. cocoa
- ¾-1 c. sugar
- ½ c. cream
- 2 t. vanilla
- Pinch salt

    Assorted ice creams
    Bananas, peeled and cut in half lengthwise
    Chopped dates
    Whipped cream
    Chopped walnuts
    Shaved coconut

Melt butter in top of double boiler. Add chocolate and stir until smooth. Add remaining hot fudge ingredients and heat to dissolve sugar, stirring frequently. Arrange ice creams, banana halves, and dates in a serving dish. Top with hot fudge, whipped cream, nuts, and coconut. (The sauce can be stored in the refrigerator and reheated as needed.) Makes about 1 1/2-2 cups hot fudge.

Cantata of Chile *with* Crackers
(Chili with Crackers)

- 3 slices bacon
- 1 large onion, diced
- 3 cloves garlic, mashed
- 1 lb. ground beef
- 1 28 oz. can whole peeled tomatoes
- 1 16 oz. can whole peeled tomatoes
- 6 oz. can tomato paste
- ½ green pepper, seeds and membrane removed
- ½ t. celery seed
- ⅛ t. cayenne
- 3 t. ground cumin
- 1 bay leaf
- 2 T. chili powder
- ¼ t. basil
- Salt and pepper to taste
- 1 16 oz. can kidney beans (optional)
- Crackers (saltines, etc.)

Cook bacon in a large saucepan until crisp. Remove bacon and set aside. Add onion and garlic and sauté until onion is tender. Add beef, stirring and cooking until browned. Coarsely chop the canned tomatoes and add juice and all to the meat mixture. Stir in the paste. Crumble cooked bacon and add to the mixture.

Dice the green pepper and add along with the remaining ingredients (except the beans and crackers). Bring to a boil. Reduce heat and simmer, covered, for 2 hours. Before serving, add kidney beans if desired and heat through. Serve with crackers. Serves 4.

Captain Milkshake
(Banana Brown Cow Milkshake)

- 1 ripe banana
- 1 c. cold milk
- 2 T. chocolate syrup
- ¼ t. vanilla
- Whipped cream
- Ground cinnamon

Beat the banana with an electric mixer until smooth. Add the milk, chocolate syrup, and vanilla. Blend well. Pour into serving glass. Top with whipped cream dusted with cinnamon. Serves 1.

Champagne Charlie
(Dressed Champagne)

    Chilled champagne
    Lillet (a fine French aperitif)
    Twist of orange rind

Put an ice cube into a large champagne glass. Add champagne and Lillet to taste. Garnish with twist of orange rind. Serves 1.

Champagne for Caesar
(Champagne Punch)

- 2 bottles champagne, well-chilled
- ¾ bottle sauterne, well-chilled
- 2 lemons, sliced
- 2 oranges, sliced
- 2 fresh mint leaves
- ¼ c. sugar
- 10 sticks pineapple
- ¾ qt. fresh strawberries
- ¾ c. brandy

Pour one bottle of champagne and the sauterne into a large bowl. Add the lemon and orange slices, mint, sugar, and pineapple. Stir until the sugar dissolves. Place a large ice chunk in the bowl and add the strawberries and brandy. Just before serving, add the remaining bottle of champagne. Serve in chilled champagne glasses or punch cups. Serves about 10.

Champagne Waltz
(Wine Champagne)

- 1½ c. chilled sauterne
- ½ c. lemon-flavored sparkling mineral water
- 2 lemon twists

Combine the wine and water and pour over ice into 2 wine glasses. Garnish with lemon twists. Serves 2.

Chicken Every Sunday
(Parmesan-Herb Roast Chicken)

- 1 6 lb. roasting chicken
- 3-4 T. butter, softened
- 1 t. crushed basil leaves
- ½ t. tarragon
- ¼ t. garlic powder
- Salt, pepper
- ½ c. grated Parmesan cheese
- 2 medium-sized onions, sliced
- 6 medium-sized potatoes, quartered
- 1 lemon cut in ½" slices
- 1 pkg. frozen peas, cooked
- Flour for gravy

Wash the chicken and let drain. Rub the top, sides, and bottom with butter. Sprinkle top with basil, tarragon, garlic powder, salt, pepper, and 1/4 cup of the Parmesan cheese. Place breast side down in a deep roasting pan or Dutch oven so that the meat will cook in its own seasoned juices. Tuck the sliced onions and potatoes around the bird. Squeeze the lemon slices over all and place rinds on top.

Cover and roast at 350°, allowing about 20-25 minutes per pound. Total roasting time will depend on how deep the roasting pan is and how closely it is surrounded by vegetables.

At the last half hour of roasting, add the cooked peas (mixing with the juices) and sprinkle with the remaining 1/4 cup Parmesan cheese. Continue roasting, uncovered, until done. Discard the lemon slices.

Transfer the roast chicken and vegetables to a large bowl and cover to keep warm. Prepare gravy by thickening the pan juices with 1/4-1/2 cup flour (made into a paste with the juices) and adding water if necessary. Salt and pepper to taste. Skim fat. Serves 4-6.

The Chocolate Soldier
(Chocolate Cookie Men)

- 1/2 c. margarine
- 1 c. sugar
- 1 egg
- 2 t. vanilla
- 2 oz. unsweetened chocolate, melted
- 1½ c. flour
- 1/2 t. salt
- 1½ t. baking powder
- 1 c. miniature chocolate bits
- Powered sugar (optional)

Cream margarine and sugar together. Beat in the egg, vanilla, and chocolate. Sift flour, salt, and baking powder together and stir into the dough. Stir in the chocolate bits.

With a floured rolling pin, roll dough out on a floured board to 1/4" thickness. Cut "soldiers" with 5" gingerbread man cookie cutter. Transfer to unbuttered baking sheets with a spatula. Bake at 325° for 10 minutes. Remove from oven and sprinkle with sifted powdered sugar, or let cool and decorate with colored frostings. Makes about 18 men.

Cigarettes, Whiskey and Wild Woman
(Hot Toddy)

- 1 jigger bourbon
- 1 t. sugar
- 1 jigger apple juice
- 1 stick cinnamon
- ½ c. very hot water
- 1 twist of lemon peel
- Sprinkle of ground cloves

Put the bourbon, sugar, apple juice, and cinnamon in a mug with a spoon in it. (The spoon will help prevent the mug from cracking when the hot water is added.) Pour in very hot water. Garnish with lemon twist and light sprinkle of clove. Serves 1.

Cisco Pike
(Wine-Eyed Pike)

(Pike is one of the better-tasting fresh water fishes. It is juicy and flavorful, without being "fishy," and therefore needs little adornment.)

- 3 lbs. fresh walleyed pike
- 1 egg, beaten
- Flour for dredging
- Salt, pepper
- 1/4 c. butter
- 1/4 c. oil
- 2 T. lemon juice
- 1/4 c. white wine
- 1 T. minced fresh parsley

Cut fillets from fish and divide into serving pieces. (If more than 1" thick, cut in half.) Dip each fillet into beaten egg and dredge with flour that has been seasoned with salt and pepper. Melt butter in a large skillet. Add the oil and heat together.

Brown fillets lightly on both sides, sprinkling with lemon juice and wine as they cook. When still moist, but flaky when tested with a fork, remove from heat, sprinkle with parsley, and serve. Serves 2-3.

Clambake
(New England Clambake)

(If you live in an area where these fixings are scarce, your local variety of shellfish will no doubt taste just as good.)

- 3 dozen steamer clams
- 3 dozen cherrystone clams
- 2 dozen mussels
- 3 1½-2 lb. live Maine lobsters
- 1 lb. washed seaweed or cornhusks
- 1 qt. water
- 6 ears corn, husked
- 1 lb. butter
- Juice of one lemon

Thoroughly scrub the clams and mussels with a stiff brush and rinse under cold water to remove sand. Rinse the lobsters. Rinse the seaweed. (If you are using cornhusks, soak them in water first.) Cover the bottom of a large clambake kettle with seaweed (or cornhusks) 4" deep. Pour in 1 quart water and bring to a boil. Put the lobsters in the pot and cover with a layer of seaweed (or cornhusks). Cover and steam 20 minutes. Add the corn, cover, and cook an additional 10 minutes. Add the clams and mussels. Cover with a layer of seaweed (or cornhusks). Cover and steam until the shells open—about 15 minutes.

Meanwhile, melt the butter in a small saucepan. Add the lemon juice and keep warm until the shellfish are done. Serve, beginning with the top layer and working down to the lobster. Pass the lemon-butter and the kettle juices. Serves 4-6.

A Clockwork Orange
(Honey-spiced Citrus Cups)

- 1 large grapefruit
- 1 medium orange
- 1 T. lemon juice
- 1 T. honey
- ⅛ t. cinnamon
- Cherries

Slice grapefruit crosswise in half. Using a grapefruit knife, remove pulp in one piece without tearing the outer rind. Set empty "cups" aside. Cut a 1/4" slice of grapefruit from the widest end of each pulp half. Set aside. Peel orange and cut pulp into bite-sized pieces. Combine lemon juice, honey, and cinnamon. Toss with the orange pieces. Spoon equal amounts of the orange mixture into the grapefruit cups, topping each with the grapefruit slice. Cut cherries into 1/8" × 1/2" strips. Arrange strips around outer edge of top slice to resemble hour marks on a clock. Serves 2.

The Cocoanuts
(Coconut-Chocolate Brownies)

- 1 c. firmly packed brown sugar
- ¼ c. melted butter
- ¾ c. flour
- ½ t. salt
- 1 t. baking powder
- 1 c. flaked coconut
- 1 egg
- 1 t. vanilla
- 1 6 oz. bag semi-sweet chocolate chips

Cream brown sugar and butter together in a mixing bowl. Combine flour, salt, baking powder, and coconut in a separate mixing bowl by lightly stirring with a fork. Add egg and vanilla to the butter-sugar mixture and beat well with a spoon. Add the dry ingredients and mix thoroughly. Stir in the chips. Spread in a greased 8" square pan and bake at 350° for 30 minutes. Cool 15 minutes and cut into squares. Makes about 16.

Coffee, Tea or Me?
(Spiced Coffee and Mulled Tea)

Spiced coffee

- 2 sticks cinnamon
- 15 whole cloves
- ¾ c. ground coffee
- 4½ c. water
- Whipped cream
- Ground cinnamon
- Sugar (optional)

Combine the cinnamon sticks, cloves and coffee in the drip basket of a coffeemaker. Pour water into coffeemaker and brew. Pour into mugs and top with a dollop of whipped cream. Sprinkle with cinnamon. Sugar to taste. Makes about 6 servings.

Mulled tea

- 1 qt. water
- 4 teabags
- 20 whole cloves
- 2 sticks cinnamon
- 2 c. apple juice or cider
- 2 T. firmly packed brown sugar

Bring water to a boil in a saucepan. Remove from heat.

Add the teabags, cloves, and cinnamon. Cover and steep for 8 minutes.

Remove the teabags and spices. Stir in the juice and sugar. Serve hot with cinnamon stick garnish if desired. Makes about 1 1/2 quarts.

Coffy
(Instant Fancy Coffee)

(This instant mix stores well for future use if refrigerated in an airtight container.)

- ¼ c. cocoa (or instant cocoa)
- ¼ c. sugar
- 1 t. grated lemon rind
- 1 drop aromatic bitters
- Hot freshly brewed coffee
- Cream or milk

Combine the cocoa, sugar, lemon rind, and bitters. For each cup to be served, place 1 1/2 t. of the cocoa mixture in the bottom of a mug. Pour in 6-8 oz. fresh coffee. Stir to combine. Add cream or milk to taste. Makes about 24 cups.

Cold Turkey
(Turkey Aspic)

- ¾ c. water
- 1 envelope (1 T.) gelatine
- ¾ c. mayonnaise
- 1 c. cooked turkey, cut in small pieces
- ¼ c. chopped green pepper
- ½ c. chopped celery
- 2 T. chopped pimiento
- 2 T. sliced green olives
- Salt and pepper
- Lettuce leaves

Heat water in a small saucepan. Sprinkle on gelatin and stir over low heat until gelatin completely dissolves. Cool. Pour into mayonnaise and stir well. Add remaining ingredients (a scant amount of salt and pepper), except lettuce, and mix well. Mold and chill. Unmold on lettuce leaves and serve. Serves 4.

The Corn Is Green with Salt of the Earth
(Husk-steamed Corn with Sea Salt)

(Cooking vegetables or meat in husks is a natural flavor enhancer. This dish calls for cooking fresh corn in individual husk "pouches.")

- 4 ears unhusked corn
- 2 c. water or chicken stock
- Sea salt

Husk corn, taking care to keep the husks whole. Remove silk. Plunge husks into a large pot of boiling water. Remove from heat, cover, and let husks sit in the water 5 minutes. Drain. Using a sharp knife, remove corn from the cob by running the blade lengthwise down the sides.

To form the cooking pouch, select 3 husks and lay them side by side on a flat surface, overlapping the sides about 1 1/2". Place about 1/4 cup corn in the center husk. Fold the 2 outer husks into the center, then fold the opposite ends into the center, overlapping as much as possible. Secure by tying a 12" length of string around the outside. Repeat process until all corn is wrapped. Boil the water or chicken stock. Add the pouches. Cover and cook over medium heat for 12 minutes. Serve corn in pouches. Pass the sea salt. Makes about 10 pouches, serves 4-6.

Cornbread, Earl and Me
(Southern Buttermilk Cornbread)

1/3 c. softened butter
1/2 c. boiling water
1 c. yellow cornmeal
3 T. sugar
1 t. salt
2 eggs, beaten
1 c. buttermilk
1 c. flour
1 t. baking soda
2 t. baking powder

Melt the butter in the boiling water. Combine the cornmeal, sugar, and salt in a bowl. Pour in the butter-water and stir to combine. Stir in the eggs and buttermilk. Sift the remaining ingredients together and stir into the batter, mixing just until blended. Pour into a greased 6"×10" baking pan. Bake at 350° for 30-40 minutes, until cooked through. Serves 6-8.

The Count of Monte Cristo *with* The Strawberry Statement
(Monte Cristo Sandwich with Strawberry Preserves)

(To make an equally great "non-sweet" version, add mustard and pickles to the sandwich before frying and eliminate the sugars and preserves.)

Batter:

1 c. flour
1/4 t. salt
1 t. baking powder
2 T. sugar
2 eggs
2/3 c. flat beer

Sandwich:

8 thin ham slices
4 slices Swiss cheese
8 slices white bread, crusts removed (sourdough is especially good)
Oil for deep frying
Confectioners' sugar, sifted
Strawberry preserves

Sift the flour, salt, baking powder, and sugar together. Set aside. In a separate bowl, beat the eggs with a beater until fluffy. Stir in the beer. Add the flour to the egg mixture and stir just until the ingredients are combined.

Construct a ham and cheese sandwich using 2 slices of ham and one slice of cheese for each. Cut diagonally in half. Thoroughly coat each half with the batter. Carefully lower into preheated oil and deep-fry until browned and crispy. Sift a light dust of confectioners' sugar over the tops and serve with strawberry preserves on the side. Makes 4 sandwiches.

Dark Waters
(Tea with Mint Syrup)

3 t. sugar
1 1/2 c. water
3/4 c. clover honey
2 c. fresh mint leaves, bruised
Freshly brewed tea

Combine the sugar and water in a saucepan. Bring to a boil, reduce heat to medium, and cook 10 minutes. Add the honey and stir to dissolve. Place mint leaves in a heat-resistant bowl and pour water mixture over. Let cool. Strain. Store the syrup by refrigerating in an airtight container. When ready to serve, prepare tea and add mint syrup to taste. Makes about 1 3/4 cups mint syrup.

A Day in the Death of Joe Egg
(Poached Egg on Canadian Bacon with Mornay Sauce)

2 T. butter
2 T. flour
1/4 t. dried mustard
1 c. milk
1 small onion studded with 4 whole cloves
1 egg yolk
1/4 c. grated Swiss cheese
1/8 t. salt
Freshly ground black pepper
1 T. white vinegar
4 eggs
4 slices Canadian bacon

Melt butter in a small saucepan (do not let it brown). Beat in flour and mustard with a wire whip until smooth. Slowly add the milk, stirring constantly with the whip until smooth. Cut onion in half and add halves to the milk mixture. Add salt and pepper. Cook, uncovered, for 12 minutes until thickened, stirring occasionally to keep sauce smooth. Cover and remove from heat.

While sauce is thickening, fill a shallow skillet 3/4 full with water. Add vinegar and bring to a boil. Reduce heat to simmer. Break an egg into a cup and slide gently into the simmering water, holding cup as close to the water as possible. Repeat for remaining eggs.

Poach for 3-5 minutes or to desired firmness. Lift eggs out of water with a slotted spoon and drain on absorbent towels. While the eggs are poaching, heat Canadian Bacon on both sides in a separate skillet until hot. Just before serving, fold cheese into the warm sauce with a rubber spatula. Place each poached egg on a Canadian Bacon slice and top with sauce. Serves 4.

The Day the Fish Came Out
(Brook Trout Meuniére-Almandine)

- 4 brook trout
- ¼ c. milk
- ½ c. flour
- ½ t. salt
- Pepper
- Peanut oil
- ½ c. butter
- 2 lemons, cut in slices
- 2 t. minced fresh parsley
- ½ c. slivered almonds, toasted in butter

Wash, scale, and clean trout, leaving heads and tails on, but removing the fins. Dip in milk. Combine flour, salt, and pepper to taste. Dredge fish. Pour peanut oil in a skillet to a depth of 1/4" and heat to frying temperature. Fry fish on both sides over medium heat until done. (This will depend on the size and weight of each fish, but when firm and browned, test for doneness—it should be white and flaky.)

Transfer to a heated platter and keep warm. Pour fat out of skillet and wipe pan with absorbent towels. Melt butter in the same skillet and heat until lightly browned. Pour over trout. Sprinkle with parsley and toasted almonds. Garnish with lemon slices. Serves 4.

Diamonds for Breakfast
(Rock Candy)

(Rock candy is an elegant substitute for sugar in coffee or tea.)

- 5 c. sugar
- 2 c. water

First prepare the pan that will form the candy crystals. Using an 8" square foil pan, punch a total of 14 equally spaced holes a generous 1/4" from the bottom on opposite sides (7 holes on each side). Lace a string through each hole from one side to the other, leaving a few inches of string free at the ends. Place the foil pan in a slightly larger pan to catch syrup drips.

Put the sugar and water in a saucepan, bring to a boil over high heat without stirring and heat to 250°. Pour mixture into the prepared pan, being sure the string runs through the center of the sugar mixture. Cover the candy surface with foil and wait for crystals to form (it can take up to a week). When fully crystallized, cut strings, dislodge the candy, and break into desired serving pieces. Rinse under cold water and dry on rack in a very low-temperature oven (200°). Diamonds are served.

The Doughgirls
(Seedy Dinner Rolls)

- 1 T. salt
- ⅓ c. honey
- ⅓ c. butter
- 1 c. boiling water
- 1 c. lukewarm water
- 2 cakes yeast
- 3 eggs, beaten
- 7 c. flour, approximately
- Seeds—poppy, sesame, caraway, celery
- 1 egg, beaten

Combine the salt, honey, butter, and boiling water together in a large bowl. Melt the butter by stirring, then add the lukewarm water. When the entire mixture is lukewarm, add the yeast and dissolve. Beat in the eggs and 2 cups of the flour with an electric mixer until smooth. Add the remaining flour and stir with a spoon until combined.

Knead on a floured board 3 minutes, adding more flour as necessary to keep from sticking. Place in a buttered bowl, cover with a cloth, and let rise in a warm place until doubled. Punch down and knead lightly on a floured board. Roll out with a rolling pin to a thickness of 1/2"-3/4". Cut into desired shapes with a cutter and place on buttered baking sheets. Let rise in a warm place until doubled.

Brush with beaten egg and sprinkle with desired seeds before baking. Bake at 375° for 20 minutes or until golden brown. Makes about 28 3" rolls.

Duck Soup
(Duck Soup)

- 1 meaty duck carcass
- 1¼ qts. cold water
- 1 c. chopped celery (with leaves)
- 1 c. chopped onion
- 2 shallots, halved
- 2 carrots, quartered
- ¼ c. minced fresh parsley
- ½ t. mixed pickling spice
- 1 bay leaf
- 4 sprigs chervil (or 1 t. dried)
- 1 t. salt
- 1 c. white rice
- ½ c. wild rice
- 1 pkg. frozen artichoke hearts
- 1 c. dry vermouth
- 1¼ qts. chicken stock
- Salt, pepper

Place the carcass in a large pot with the cold water. Add the celery, onion, shallots, carrots, parsley, pickling spice, bay leaf, chervil, and salt. Bring to a boil, reduce heat, cover, and simmer for 1 1/2 hours. Strain the soup and chill the broth. Skim the fat from the broth and place in a pot along with the white and wild rice, artichoke hearts, and 1/3 cup of the vermouth. Add the chicken stock, bring to a boil, reduce heat, cover, and simmer until the rice and artichokes are tender. Pour in the remaining 2/3 cup vermouth and correct the seasoning. Serves 6.

The Egg and I
(Egg-stuffed Idaho Potatoes)

- 2 large Idaho potatoes
- 3-4 T. butter
- 1 T. minced onion
- 4 eggs, beaten
- ½ c. grated jack or cheddar cheese
- 1 T. minced fresh parsley
- Paprika
- Salt, pepper
- Sour cream or plain yogurt

Scrub potatoes and prick several times with a fork. Bake at 350° for one hour or until tender. Cut lengthwise in half and remove insides. Melt 3 tablespoons of the butter in a frying pan. Sauté onion until tender. Add 1 cup of the cooked potato and fry until lightly golden, stirring frequently. Add more butter if necessary to prevent sticking. Add the eggs, cheese, and parsley. Cook scrambled style. Salt and pepper to taste. Fill potato skins with equal amounts of the potato-egg mixture. Top with sour cream or yogurt. Sprinkle with paprika. Serves 4.

Egghead on Hill
(Shirred Eggs with Sausages)

(Shirred eggs, or *oeufs sur le plat* [eggs on the plate], are traditionally cooked and served in small individual baking dishes called "shirrers." Individual soufflé dishes or ramekins will do as well.)

- 6 small pork sausages
- 2 T. butter
- 2 T. flour
- 1 c. tomato juice or cocktail
- 2 t. lemon juice
- Salt, pepper
- 6 eggs
- Grated Parmesan cheese

Cut the sausages into 1/2" pieces and cook in a skillet over medium heat until done, about 10 minutes. Meanwhile, melt the butter in a small saucepan. Using a wire whip, stir in the flour. Slowly add the tomato and lemon juice. Stir with the whip until thickened. Salt and pepper to taste.

When the sausages are done, drain and add the thickened tomato sauce. Spoon equal amounts into 6 egg shirrers. Break 1 egg into each dish. Bake at 400° until almost done to your taste, from 5-10 minutes. A couple of minutes before the eggs are finished cooking, sprinkle tops with Parmesan cheese and broil under high heat until lightly browned and crispy. Serves 6.

Esther Waters
(Iced Honey Coffee)

- 4 c. strong hot coffee
- ¼ c. honey
- 1 t. cinnamon
- 4 c. milk
- Whipped cream
- Cinnamon for dusting

Add the honey and cinnamon to the coffee and stir to dissolve the honey. Add the milk and chill. Serve over cracked ice with a dollop of whipped cream dusted with cinnamon. Makes 8 1-cup servings.

Eve Knew Her Apples
(Apple-Cheese Canapés)

- 4 medium-sized red apples
- ¼ c. lemon juice
- Cheddar cheese
- Pepper ham, sliced thin
- 32 rectangular club crackers

Slice each apple into 8 wedges. Remove core. Dip each wedge in lemon juice. Place a 1/4" thick wedge of cheese on top of each apple wedge.

Cut ham into 1/2" × 4" strips. Wrap each apple-cheese wedge with a strip of ham and place on baking sheet, cheese side up. Bake at 350° until cheese softens, about 3-5 minutes. Remove with spatula and place each on a club cracker. Makes 32.

Expresso Bongo
(Espresso with a Twist)

(To properly prepare this type of strong, heavy bodied coffee, you will need an expresso coffeemaker.)

- Finely ground Italian roasted coffee
- Lemon peel twists
- Orange peel twists

Prepare espresso following manufacturer instructions for your coffeemaker. Serve in demitasse cups with a twist of lemon and orange peel.

The Fish That Saved Pittsburgh
(Holy Mackerel)

- 4 8 oz. mackerel fillets
- 2 cloves garlic, mashed
- Juice of 1 lemon
- 2 T. olive oil
- Pinch thyme
- Salt, pepper
- 4 Italian plum tomatoes, chopped
- 1 medium onion, coarsely chopped

Place the fillets, skin side down, in an oiled baking dish. Rub surface with garlic. Sprinkle with the lemon juice and olive oil. Season with thyme, salt and pepper to taste. Combine the tomatoes and onions. Spoon over and around the fish. Bake at 425° until fish is done, about 10 minutes per inch thickness of fish. Serves 4.

The Food of the Gods
(Mixed Greens with Goddess Dressing)

½ head chicory
½ head escarole
½ head Boston
½ head Buttercrunch
   Croutons (optional)
   Freshly ground black pepper

Dressing:

1 clove garlic, mashed
1 c. mayonnaise
¾ c. thinly sliced scallions
   (about 3)
1 T. chopped fresh chives
2 t. minced shallots
¼ c. finely minced fresh parsley
3 T. tarragon vinegar, or white
   wine vinegar with
   tarragon herb
⅓ c. sour cream

Wash the lettuce heads, tear into bite-sized pieces, and chill. Combine the dressing ingredients in a blender and blend a few seconds until smooth. Chill 1 hour before serving. Serve with freshly grated black pepper. Makes about 1 1/2 cup dressing.

The Forbidden Fruit
(Apple Cake with Hot Rum Sauce)

(This is one of those traditional family favorites that I grew up with and associate with the holidays as much as I do pine trees, snow, and warm family gatherings. Now living in California, I've given up snow and the picturesque New England countryside, but I continue to ring in the New Year with a batch of hot apple-rum cake. It's a memory-maker.)

1 c. sugar
¼ c. butter, softened
1 egg
1 c. flour
1 t. baking soda
1 t. ground cinnamon
½ t. nutmeg
3 medium-sized apples, peeled
   and chopped fine
½ c. chopped walnuts

Rum sauce:

⅓ c. sugar
⅓ c. firmly packed brown sugar
½ c. whipping cream
¼ c. butter
1 T. rum flavoring

Cream the sugar and butter together. Add the egg and stir well to combine. Sift the flour, baking soda, cinnamon, and nutmeg together and stir into the sugar mixture. Stir in the apples and nuts. Spoon into a buttered tube cake pan (as for angel or bundt cake) and bake at 325° for 1 hour.

Meanwhile, prepare the sauce by placing the ingredients in the top of a double boiler over hot water. Stir to combine, melting the butter and dissolving the sugars. Serve hot over the cake. (Reheat sauce as necessary to serve with the cake.) Serves 6–8.

The Fortune Cookie
(Fortune Cookies)

(Many people wonder if fortune cookies are authentically Chinese. No matter which side you take, you're right. In China, messages such as birth announcements were sometimes sent wrapped in a sweet dough, and an ancient Chinese game involved writing wise and witty quips on paper that were inserted into cakes. In America, the invention of the fortune cookie as we know it is credited to George Jung, founder of the Hong Kong Noodle Company in 1916. His motive, it is said, was entertainment and religion. Today, many of the cookie slogans ranging from funny to grotesque, are written by professional writers. They can be, and have been, used for much more than entertainment, such as their starring role in an advertising campaign for the Matthau-Lemmon comedy, *The Fortune Cookie*. Perhaps the biggest challenge in making these cookies at home is making them worth reading, much less eating.

This recipe was adapted by my twin sister Lorraine, who found a way to form the cookie while still warm and then complete the baking to desired crispness.)

½ c. cake flour
1 egg white
3 T. sugar
½ t. vanilla
3 T. water

Write fortunes on 1/2"×2" strips of white paper. (You will need about 10 for one batch.) Combine flour, egg white, sugar, and vanilla. Mix well. Add water, 1 tablespoon at a time, mixing well.

Spoon 1 tablespoon of batter on a lightly greased skillet, making a 3" circle. (An electric skillet works best for this.) Heat 5-6 minutes. Flip over and heat an additional 4 minutes. Working quickly, remove cookie and place fortune on upper half of cookie. Fold in half, up over the fortune, then place the folded edge crosswise on rim of a bowl and bend corners down to form the classic fortune cookie shape. Place in muffin tin. Continue procedure until all cookies are formed. Bake at 350° for 10-15 minutes until lightly browned and crisp. Makes 8-10.

Forty Carats
(Lemon-Glazed Carrots)

40 tiny young carrots
   Salt
2 T. butter
2 T. sugar
4 thin slices lemon

Scrub the carrots and place in boiling salted water. Cover and simmer until done, but still slightly crisp. Drain and keep warm. Melt the butter in a saucepan, add the sugar, and stir until dissolved. Add the lemon slices and carrots, tossing gently until carrots are well coated with the glaze. Serves 6.

Freebie and the Bean
(Easy Boston Baked Beans)

- 1   28 oz. can Boston baked beans
- 2   T. firmly packed brown sugar
- 2   T. minced onion
- 1   T. Dijon mustard
- ¼   c. dry sherry
- 1   t. instant coffee

Combine the ingredients in a casserole dish. Bake at 350° for about 30 minutes or until bubbly. Serves 4-6.

Frogs
(Garlic-Butter Frog Legs)

- 8   large frog legs, cleaned and skinned
-     Salt, pepper
- 5   T. butter
-     Lemon juice
-     Minced fresh parsley
- 2   cloves garlic, mashed

Soak the legs in cold water for 2 hours. Dry the legs thoroughly and sprinkle with salt and pepper. In a saucepan, sauté the legs in 2 tablespoons of the butter until golden brown. Remove to a heated serving platter and sprinkle with lemon juice and minced parsley. Keep warm. Melt the remaining 3 tablespoons butter in the saucepan and add the garlic when the butter is nut-brown. Heat the garlic for a few seconds and quickly pour over the legs. Serve immediately while the butter is still foaming. Serves 4.

Get Rollin'
(Refrigerator Rolls)

(These rolls are exceptionally convenient, because the dough can be prepared ahead of time and will stay fresh in the refrigerator for up to one week. They can also be turned into just about any shape you'd like—twists, Parker House, braids, cloverleaf, spirals, etc.)

- 1   c. sugar
- 1   T. salt
- 1   c. butter, softened
- 2   c. mashed potatoes (about 4 medium)
- 2   c. hot potato water
- 2   pkgs. yeast
- 1   c. warm water
- 3   large eggs, slightly beaten
- 12-13   c. flour
-     Butter for greasing pans
-     Beaten egg for glaze
-     Sesame, poppy, or caraway seeds (optional)

Beat together the sugar, salt, butter, mashed potatoes, and hot potato water with an electric mixer. Dissolve yeast in the warm water. When the potato mixture has cooled to lukewarm, beat in the eggs and yeast mixture on low speed until throughly blended.

Stir in flour, adding more as necessary to make a non-sticky, fairly stiff dough. Turn out on a floured board and knead 5 minutes. Place in a buttered bowl. Cover tightly with plastic wrap and refrigerate. If dough rises, punch down as often as necessary until it reaches refrigerator temperature and stops rising (to keep it from turning sour).

When ready to make rolls, remove any desired amount from refrigerator. Turn into chosen shapes on a floured board. Place on buttered baking sheets and let rise until doubled. Brush with beaten egg and sprinkle with seeds, if desired. Bake at 375° for about 30 minutes, or until browned. Makes about 4 dozen.

The Ghost and Mr. Chicken
(Parmesan Chicken with Mashed Potatoes)

- 6   chicken breast halves
- 6   T. butter
- ½   lb. fresh mushrooms, sliced
- ½   c. chopped onion
- 3   c. milk
- ½   c. flour
- 1   c. grated Parmesan cheese
- ½   t. salt
-     Pepper
- 6   c. hot mashed potato

Wash chicken breasts and place in a large pot. Cover with water and bring to a boil. Reduce heat and simmer, covered, for 45 minutes, or until tender. Reserve the broth. Debone chicken and cut into bite-sized pieces, covering to prevent drying out. Set aside. Melt butter in a large saucepan. Add mushroom and onions. Cook over medium heat until tender.

Add the milk, 1 1/2 cups of the reserved chicken broth, and 1/2 cup of the Parmesan cheese. Stir and heat through. Take 1 cup of the milk-cheese mixture and add to the flour, mixing thoroughly to the consistency of smooth liquid paste. Slowly add the flour mixture to the milk-cheese mixture, stirring constantly with a wire whip. Add the chicken. Add salt and pepper to taste. Cover and simmer 1 hour, stirring occasionally.

When ready to serve, arrange equal amounts of potato in the bottom of 6 individual casserole dishes. Spoon chicken mixture over and sprinkle with remaining Parmesan cheese. Broil under high heat for a few minutes until cheese lightly browns. Serves 6.

Ginger in the Morning
(Gingered String Beans)

1 lb. fresh Chinese (or French) string beans
½ oz. dried shrimp, soaked
Oil for deep frying
2 green onions, chopped
½ t. dried ginger
2 t. sugar
1 t. salt
2 T. chicken stock
2 T. wine vinegar
½ t. sesame seed oil

Wash beans and trim ends. Cut into 4" lengths. Finely chop shrimp. Set aside. Heat oil in a wok and deep-fry beans 1 1/2 minutes. Drain on absorbent towels. Pour out all oil except for 1 tablespoon. Stir-fry chopped shrimp in the oil for 1 minute. Combine remaining ingredients. Add beans and green onion mixture to wok and stir-fry 1–2 minutes. Serve immediately. Serves 4.

A Girl in Every Port
(White Port Cocktail)

1½ oz. dry white port
1 oz. sweet vermouth
Few drops lemon juice

Shake with ice. Strain into a cocktail glass. Serves 1.

Good-bye Mr. Chips
(Fried Vegetable Chips)

Aged Idaho potatoes, carrots, or sweet potatoes
Peanut oil
Corn oil
Safflower oil
Sea salt or seasoned salt (see p. 236)

Wash vegetables and slice thin. (My daughter discovered that a metal cheese slicer works great for this.) Soak slices in cold water (use ice if necessary) for 2 hours, changing the water after 1 hour. Drain in a colander and dry well with absorbent towels. Pour equal amounts of the oils into a deep-fat fryer. Heat oils to 380°. Fry slices in a frying basket, shaking it frequently while cooking to prevent sticking. (If you are making several types of chips, fry each type separately as cooking time will vary.) Fry until lightly browned. Drain on absorbent towels and sprinkle with salt. Repeat process until all are cooked.

The Grasshopper
(Grasshopper Pie)

21 chocolate layer cookies
¼ c. butter, melted
½ c. milk
10 marshmallows
1 c. whipping cream
1 oz. creme de menthe
1 oz. creme de cacao

Crush 20 of the cookies into crumbs and combine with melted butter. Pat into a 9" pie shell and chill. In a saucepan, melt marshmallows in milk over medium heat, stirring constantly. Set aside to cool. Whip cream just until it begins to thicken, then continue to whip while slowly drizzling in the liqueurs. Whip until stiff.

Add the cooled marshmallow mixture and stir to combine. Spoon into the refrigerated pie shell. Crush remaining cookie into crumbs and sprinkle on top for garnish. Chill at least 2 hours before serving. Serves 6.

Here Comes Cookie
(Applesauce-Spice Cookies)

2 c. flour
1 t. salt
1 t. baking soda
1 t. ground nutmeg
1 t. ground cinnamon
½ t. ground cloves
½ c. butter, softened
½ c. white sugar
½ c. firmly packed light brown sugar
1 egg
2 t. vanilla
1 c. applesauce
1 c. currants
1 c. chopped walnuts

Sift the flour, salt, soda, and spices together. Set aside. Cream the butter and sugars together in a separate bowl. Beat in the egg, vanilla, and applesauce. Add the flour mixture and stir well. Add the currants and nuts, mixing thoroughly. Drop by tablespoons onto baking sheets and bake at 400° for 8–10 minutes or until lightly browned. Makes about 5 dozen cookies.

Hey, Pineapple!
(Batter-Fried Pineapple)

Batter:
¾ c. flour
1 t. sugar
Pinch salt
1 egg, separated
⅓ c. warm beer
2 T. butter, melted
About 5 T. water

½ fresh pineapple
Oil for deep frying
Sweet and sour sauce for dipping

Combine the flour, sugar, and salt in a bowl. Stir in the egg yolk. Add the beer in 3 intervals, stirring briefly after each addition. Do not beat the batter, and stir only until ingredients are combined. Stir in the melted butter. With a wire whip, stir in only enough water to bring the batter to the consistency of very heavy cream. (The batter will have lumps like pancake batter.) Cover loosely with plastic wrap or a plate and let sit one hour at room temperature.

Meanwhile, quarter the pineapple and remove core and rind. Cut into 1/2" thick slices. When the batter is ready, beat the egg white until stiff and fold gently into the batter. Heat the oil. Coat several pineapple pieces with batter and carefully lower into the hot oil. (Do not try to fry too many at the same time.) When browned on both sides, remove with a slotted spoon and drain on absorbent towels. Serve with sweet and sour sauce. Serves 4.

The Honey Pot
(Baked Honey Custard)

  4 eggs
  ¼ c. honey
  ¼ t. salt
  1 t. vanilla
2½ c. scalded milk
    Nutmeg
    Toasted coconut

Beat the eggs with a fork until well combined. Add the honey, salt, and vanilla. Gradually add the scalded milk, stirring constantly. Pour equal amounts into individual custard cups or 6-ounce ramekins. Sprinkle tops with nutmeg.

Place cups in a glass baking dish. Fill baking dish with water so that the water level almost reaches the tops of the custard cups. Carefully place in oven and bake at 325° for about 50 minutes, or until a knife inserted into the center comes out clean. Remove cups from the water. Serve hot or cold with toasted coconut sprinkled on top and with more honey if desired. (This dessert may also be baked in a 1-quart casserole or mold. Place in pan of water as above and bake until done.) Serves 6.

Honeycomb
(Buttermilk Waffles with Honey-Orange Sauce)

Waffles:

  2 c. sifted flour
  ¼ t. baking soda
  2 t. baking powder
  1 t. salt
1½ T. sugar
  2 eggs, separated
1¾ c. buttermilk
  6 T. melted butter

Sauce:

1 c. honey
¼ c. finely chopped orange rind
⅛ t. salt

Sift the flour, baking soda, baking powder, salt, and sugar together into a large mixing bowl. Set aside. In a smaller bowl, beat the yolks with a fork. Stir in the buttermilk and butter. Pour the yolk-milk mixture into the flour mixture and stir just until the dry ingredients are moistened. Beat egg whites until stiff but not dry. Fold into the batter.

Thoroughly grease a preheated waffle iron. Spoon batter onto cooking surface. Close lid and cook about 4–5 minutes, or until golden brown. Continue until all the batter is used. Make sauce while waffles are cooking: Combine ingredients in a small saucepan. Heat through for 5 minutes without boiling. Serve waffles with the hot honey sauce. Makes about 10 waffles and 1 cup sauce.

Hot Potato
(Baked Potato Skins)

4 large Russet potatoes
2 T. oil
2 T. bacon fat
1 4 oz. can diced mild green chilies
¼ c. diced green onions
½ c. grated longhorn cheddar cheese
½ c. grated monterey jack cheese
    Sour cream or plain yogurt
    Bacon bits

Scrub potatoes and prick several times with a fork. Bake at 350° for one hour or until tender. Cut into quarters and scoop out the insides, leaving 1/4" of the potato on the skin. Heat oil and bacon fat in a frying pan until hot. Fry skins for 1 minute on each side. Drain on absorbent towels. Place on a baking sheet and sprinkle with equal amounts of chilies, green onions, and cheeses. Bake at 400° for 15 minutes, or until cheese melts. Top with bacon bits. Serve hot with sour cream or plain yogurt. Serves 4.

How to Frame a Fig
(Stewed Ginger Figs)

1 lb. dried figs
   cold water to cover
2 T. lemon juice
1 T. coarsely grated lemon rind
2 t. dried ground ginger
   Sugar
   Cornstarch
   Vanilla

Place figs in a saucepan and add cold water to cover. Add lemon juice, lemon rind, and ginger. Bring to a boil. Reduce heat and simmer, covered, until tender—about 20–30 minutes. Drain, reserving the liquid. Measure the liquid and return to the saucepan. For each 1 cup of liquid, add 1/4 cup sugar. Bring to boiling, reduce heat to medium.

For each 1 cup of liquid originally measured, add 3 teaspoons cornstarch by mixing it first with a small amount of the hot syrup, then stirring it into the saucepan. Cook until thickened, stirring frequently. Add 1/2 teaspoon vanilla for each 1 cup of liquid originally measured. Add figs and serve warm. Serves 6.

Jack and the Beanstalk
(Hasty Bean Salad)

½ c. canned kidney beans
½ c. canned chick peas
1 c. canned green beans
1 c. canned waxed green beans
¼ c. minced onion
½ diced green pepper, seeds and membrane removed
½ diced red pepper, seeds and membrane removed
   French Dressing (see p. 233)

Combine all ingredients in a bowl (be sure all the beans are well drained) and pour desired amount of dressing over. Chill for 1 hour before serving. Serves 4.

Jamaica Rum
(Jamaican Rum Cocktail)

2 oz. Jamaican rum
1 t. bar sugar
Juice of ½ lime

Combine in a shaker with ice cubes. Shake. Strain and serve in a chilled cocktail glass. Serves 1.

Java Head
(Cocoa-Java)

4 oz. semi-sweet chocolate
2 c. strong, hot, mocha-java coffee
2 c. hot milk
Whipped cream
Ground cinnamon or cocoa

Melt chocolate over low heat in a 1-quart saucepan. Gradually stir in the coffee with a wire whip. Increase heat to medium high. Gradually add the milk, beating until the mixture reaches the boiling point and foams. Serve in mugs with whipped cream dusted with cinnamon or cocoa. Makes 4 cups.

The Kentucky Fried Movie
(Kentucky Fried Chicken)

1 c. bread crumbs
½ c. flour
3 t. dried parsley
¼ t. rubbed sage
1 t. dried basil
½ t. dried oregano
1½ t. garlic powder
2 t. onion powder
1 t. paprika
½ t. dried thyme
½ t. dried marjoram
1 t. salt
1½ t. black pepper
1 2½-3 lb. frying chicken, washed and cut into serving pieces
2-3 eggs, beaten in a bowl
Shortening for frying

Combine the bread crumbs, flour, and 11 different herbs and spices in a paper bag. Coat the chicken with the beaten egg. Place pieces, a few at a time, in the bag and shake to coat with the breadcrumb mixture. Repeat egg-dipping and shaking. Skillet-fry the chicken in 1" of preheated oil until tender and golden brown, about 30-40 minutes. Serves 4-6.

King Creole
(Shrimp Creole)

(This is a slightly spicy-hot Cajun dish. If you want a milder or hotter version, simply adjust the amount of cayenne to your taste.)

3 T. bacon fat
2 c. coarsely chopped onion
3 cloves garlic, mashed
1 green pepper, diced
3 ribs celery, coarsely chopped
3 medium tomatoes, coarsely chopped
½ t. dried thyme
1 bay leaf
¼ t. cayenne
Salt
2 lbs. raw shrimp, shelled and deveined
2 t. Worcestershire sauce
Cooked rice for serving

Heat the bacon fat in a large saucepan. Add the onion, garlic, green pepper, and celery. Cook over medium-low heat until tender, but not browned. Add the tomatoes, thyme, bay leaf, cayenne, and salt. Simmer, uncovered, for 10 minutes, stirring occasionally. Add the shrimp and simmer, covered, for 10 minutes. Season with Worcestershire sauce and serve over cooked rice. Serves 4-6.

King of Hearts
(Heart of Artichoke, Palm and Celery Salad with Tarragon Dressing)

1 14 oz. can artichoke hearts, drained and quartered
1 c. hearts of palm chunks
1 c. sliced celery hearts

Dressing:

2 T. freshly squeezed lemon juice
1 medium clove garlic, mashed
1½ t. Dijon mustard
¼ t. dried tarragon leaves
½ t. sugar
1 egg yolk
¼ c. olive oil
¼ c. vegetable oil
Salt and freshly ground pepper
½ c. diced sweet red bell pepper
1 t. capers
½-1 head romaine lettuce, washed and dried
½ c. croutons

Combine the artichokes, hearts of palm, and celery hearts in a colander to drain thoroughly. Set aside. Combine the lemon juice, garlic, mustard, tarragon, sugar, and yolk in a bowl with a wire whip. Gradually add the oils while beating constantly with the whip. Salt and pepper to taste.

When ready to serve, combine "hearts" with red pepper and capers in a bowl. Pour in desired amount of dressing and toss gently. Spoon over lettuce leaves and top with croutons. Makes 3/4 cup dressing. Serves 4-6.

Knickerbocker Holiday
(Knickerbocker Cocktail)

1 t. orange juice
1 t. lemon juice
1 t. raspberry syrup
2 oz. light Puerto Rican rum
½ t. curacao
pineapple slice

Combine ingredients in a shaker with ice cubes. Shake well. Strain into chilled cocktail glass and garnish with pineapple slice. Serves 1.

La Marie Du Port
(Savoy Sangaree)

(This is an anglicization of the Spanish *sangria*.)

- 8 oz. port
- 1 t. powdered sugar
- 1 slice orange
- 1 twist lemon peel
- Nutmeg

Combine the port and sugar in a glass. Stir well to dissolve the sugar. Pour into an old fashioned glass over ice. Garnish with the orange slice and lemon peel. Dust with nutmeg. Serves 1.

Lady Caroline Lamb
(Lamb in White Wine with Mushrooms)

- 1 lb. lean lamb, cut into 1½" cubes
- 2 cloves garlic, mashed
- Salt, pepper
- 3 T. butter
- 1 c. chopped onion
- ½ lb. button mushrooms
- 1 T. minced fresh parsley
- 1½ T. flour
- 1 c. dry white wine
- Mint leaves
- Mint jelly

Rub the lamb cubes with the mashed garlic, being sure each piece is "peppered" with garlic bits. Sprinkle with salt and pepper. Melt 1 tablespoon of the butter in a frying pan. Add the prepared lamb and brown on all sides. Transfer to a covered casserole and keep warm. Melt the remaining butter in the same pan and sauté the onion, mushrooms, and parsley until tender. Stir in the flour, blending well. Gradually add the wine, stirring constantly until thickened and bubbling. Pour over lamb cubes. Cover and bake 45 minutes to 1 hour, or until tender. Garnish with mint leaves and serve with mint jelly. Serves 4.

Lady from Chungking
(Chunking Vinegar Chicken)

(This is a "cooled down" version of a very spicy dish, coming to us from Szechwan's largest city, Chunking. If you wish to abide by the more authentic fire of Szechwan cooking, add 3 or 4 finely chopped dried red chilies [that have been soaked in water] to the wok at cooking time.)

- ½ lb. boneless white chicken breast
- 1 egg white, slightly beaten with a fork
- 2 T. sherry
- 1 t. salt
- 1 T. cornstarch
- 1 c. sliced bamboo shoots
- 3 T. vegetable oil
- ¼ t. sesame seed oil

Vinegar sauce:

- 1 T. sugar
- 1 T. cornstarch
- ¼ t. dried ginger
- 1 green onion, finely chopped
- 1 large clove garlic, minced
- 1 T. soy sauce
- 1 T. wine vinegar
- 3 T. chicken stock

Skin the breasts and crisscross-score the tops in 1/2" sections. Cut into chunks, using the score as a cutting guide. Combine the egg white, sherry, salt, and cornstarch in a bowl. Add the chicken and marinate. Combine the ingredients for the sauce in a bowl. Set aside.

Heat the oils in a wok and stir-fry the chicken with its marinade for about 2 minutes. Add the bamboo shoots and cook, stirring constantly, 10 seconds. Add the vinegar sauce, blend well, and cook until thickened. Serve immediately. Serves 4.

Le Soufflé au Cour
(Potato Soufflé)

- Butter
- 6 T. grated Parmesan cheese
- 2 c. thick mashed potatoes (about 4 medium)
- ½ c. cream
- ⅛ t. nutmeg
- 1 t. salt
- 4 egg yolks, beaten
- 4 egg whites

Generously butter a 2-quart soufflé mold and dust with 3 tablespoons of the Parmesan cheese. Chill. Combine mashed potatoes, cream, nutmeg, and salt in a saucepan. Cook over low heat, stirring frequently until mixture is very hot, but not scorching. Remove from heat and add remaining Parmesan cheese.

Slowly add egg yolks while beating potato mixture with an electric mixer at high speed for 1 minute. Wash and dry beaters. Beat egg whites until stiff but not dry. Fold in. Pour into prepared mold (it will be about 3/4 full) and bake at 375° for 30–35 minutes or until lightly browned and well puffed. Serve immediately. Serves 6.

The Lemon Drop Kid
(Lemon Bars)

(This recipe is from my mother's kitchen, a great cook in her own right. I've taken the liberty of cutting back on the sugar and adding lemon rind for a more lemony taste, but feel free to add up to another 1/2 cup sugar for the filling if so desired.)

Crust:
- 2 c. flour
- ½ c. powdered sugar
- 1 c. chilled butter

Topping:
- 1½ c. sugar
- ¼ c. flour
- ½ t. baking powder
- 4 eggs, slightly beaten
- ⅓ c. fresh lemon juice
- 1 t. grated lemon rind
- Sifted confectioners' sugar

Work the flour, powdered sugar, and butter together in a bowl with your hands until well combined. Form into a large ball. Using the palms of your hands, spread the dough into a 9"×12" baking pan. Bake at 350° for 20 minutes. Stir the sugar, flour, and baking powder together in a bowl. Stir in the eggs, lemon juice, and lemon rind. Pour lemon topping over cooked crust. Rebake 25 minutes at 350°. Cool. Sprinkle with powdered sugar and cut into bars. Makes 12-24 bars.

Lemonade Joe
(Old-fashioned Homemade Lemonade)

(My oldest daughter is our resident lemonade expert, as she has been squeezing out gallons of it for years now from the year-round supply of lemons that grow in our backyard. We all agree that this "concentrate" method gives the most flavorful and freshest tasting lemonade ever.)

- 2 c. freshly squeezed lemon juice with pulp
- 5 t. grated lemon rind
- 1½ c. sugar

Combine the ingredients in a glass jar and shake to dissolve the sugar. Cover and chill. To serve, measure 1/4 cup of the lemon mixture into a drinking glass. Fill with ice and 3/4 cup fresh water. Makes about 12 glasses, or 2 2/3 cups lemon concentrate.

Limelight
(Lime-Chicken Kabobs)

(The trick with this barbecue dish, as with any other, is in keeping the food moist while cooking. With an attentive eye and almost constant basting and turning the meat on the grill, this more unusual chicken treatment is a great change of pace.)

- 3 chicken breasts, halved and deboned
- ½ c. lime juice
- ½ c. vegetable oil
- ½ t. salt
- 1 t. dried tarragon
- 1 t. dried rosemary
- 1 T. chopped fresh chives
- 2 T. minced fresh parsley
- 2 shallots, minced
- ¼ t. Tabasco sauce

Wash the chicken and cut into 1" cubes. Impale on 6" bamboo skewers. Combine the remaining ingredients in a 6"×10" glass baking dish. Marinate the skewered chicken in the sauce for 1/2 hour at room temperature. Barbecue over a slow fire, basting with the sauce and turning frequently until done, about 20-30 minutes. Makes about 8 kabobs.

Lorna Doone
(Lemony Shortbread Cookies)

(This is a slightly lemony variation of the traditional store variety called Lorna Doone.)

- 1 c. butter, softened
- ⅔ c. sugar
- 1 egg
- 2 t. vanilla extract
- 2 t. grated lemon rind
- 2½ c. sifted flour
- ½ t. salt
- Powdered sugar

Cream the butter and sugar together. Beat in the egg, vanilla, and lemon rind. Sift the flour and salt together. Stir into the butter mixture. Chill 3 hours. Roll out dough on a floured board to a thickness of 1/4". Cut into 2" squares, or any other desired shape. Place on ungreased baking sheets and bake at 375° for 8-10 minutes or until lightly browned around the edges. Dust with powdered sugar if desired. Makes about 4 dozen 2" square cookies.

The Luck of Ginger Coffey
(Ginger Coffee)

- 2 T. sugar
- ¼ c. honey
- 1 qt. strong, hot coffee
- ½ t. dried ground ginger
- ½ c. whipping cream
- 2 egg whites

Dissolve sugar and honey in the coffee. Chill. Add the remaining ingredients and beat thoroughly with an electric mixer. Fill glasses with cracked ice and pour over. Serves 4-6.

Manhattan
(Manhattan Cocktail)

- 2 jiggers dry vermouth
- 6 jiggers bourbon
- 2 dashes Angostura bitters
- 2 maraschino cherries or lemon peel twists

Combine the vermouth and bourbon. For each drink, put a dash of Angostura bitters in a Manhattan glass. Add ice cubes and equal amounts of the bourbon mixture. Garnish with a cherry or lemon twist. Serves 2.

Marshmallow Moon
(Marshmallow-Mocha Cream Torte)

(I am not a big marshmallow fan, but this mocha cream mixture is one exception. It can easily be used whenever you need a good, strong, coffee-flavored whipped cream.)

½ lb. large marshmallows
1 c. very strong, hot coffee
1 c. whipping cream
1 t. vanilla
28 3" ladyfingers
¼ c. chocolate syrup
    Shaved semi-sweet chocolate
        curls
2 oz. toasted sliced almonds

Put the marshmallows and coffee in a saucepan and cook over low heat, stirring constantly until the marshmallows melt. Refrigerate until slightly thickened. Beat the whipping cream with the vanilla until stiff and fold into the slightly thickened marshmallow mixture. Arrange 14 of the ladyfingers in a single layer on the bottom of a 10"×6"×2" baking dish. Spoon on 1/2 of the mocha-cream mixture. Drizzle the chocolate syrup over the cream in a "marbled" pattern. Repeat with another layer of 14 ladyfingers and the remaining mocha-cream. Refrigerate until set firm. When ready to serve, garnish top with chocolate curls (easily made with a vegetable parer on a square of chocolate) and sliced almonds. Serves 8.

Michael Strogoff
(Beef Stroganoff)

1½ lb. tender beef fillet in a ½"
        slab
    Salt, freshly ground pepper
3 T. butter
2 T. finely chopped onion
1 lb. sliced mushrooms
⅓ c. white wine
1 c. warmed sour cream
2 t. Dijon mustard
2-3 T. flour
8 oz. wide egg noodles, cooked,
        drained, and hot

Pound the meat and cut into 2 1/2" × 1" strips, removing all fat and gristle. Sprinkle with salt and pepper. Set aside. Melt 1 tablespoon of the butter in a large frying pan. Sauté the onion until tender. Add the beef and sauté quickly for about 5 minutes, browning evenly on all sides. Remove beef from the pan, cover and keep warm.

Melt the remaining 2 tablespoons butter in the frying pan. Add the mushrooms, stir to coat well with the juices, and sauté until tender. Return beef to the pan. Reduce heat to low. Add the wine, sour cream, and mustard. Stir to heat through without boiling. If the sauce is too runny, thicken by combining the flour with 1/2 cup of the juices and stirring into the beef. Continue to heat through until thickened. Serve over cooked noodles. Serves 4.

Million Dollar Duck
(Roast Duck à la Beverly Hills with Citrus Sauce Bigarade)

1 5-6 lb. duckling with giblets
2 medium onions, sliced
3 carrots, sliced
1 bouquet garni (preferably
        fresh herbs)
4 parsley sprigs (or 1 t. dried)
4 chervil sprigs (or 1 t. dried)
2 thyme sprigs (or ¼ t. dried)
½ bay leaf
    Salt, pepper
1¾ c. water
2 slices bacon, diced (about
        2 oz.)
2 celery stalks, sliced
2 T. butter, softened

Citrus sauce:
    Rind and juice of 1 Seville
        orange
    Rind of ½ lemon
1¼ c. water
1 c. dry white wine
1 t. lemon juice
6 T. flour
    Salt, pepper

    Flour for dusting
    Smile Orange (p. 237) for
        garnish

Prepare a stock by placing the giblets, 1 sliced onion, 1 sliced carrot, bouquet garni (tie herbs in a bunch together) or dried herbs, salt, pepper, and 1 3/4 cups water in a saucepan. Bring to a boil, reduce heat, cover and simmer 1 hour. Place the bacon, celery, remaining onion, and carrot in the bottom of a casserole-type roasting pan (with lid). Rub the duckling with the butter and place on top of vegetables in the roasting pan. Cover pan tightly with aluminum foil, then cover with the lid and bake at 350° for 20 minutes. (Allow 20 minutes to the pound when estimating total cooking time.) Strain the giblet stock and add 1 cup to the duck pan. Cover as before and continue roasting until done.

When duckling has 40 minutes left to cook, remove from oven and pour the pan juices and vegetables into a bowl. Reserve. Dust bird lightly with flour and return to the oven, uncovered. Continue baking until done and skin is browned and crisp.

About 30 minutes before the end of cooking time, prepare citrus sauce. Pare orange and lemon rind (avoiding the white pith) and slice into very thin strips. Bring 1 1/4 cups water to boiling in a small saucepan. Add rinds and blanch for 5 minutes. Remove from heat and set aside. Reduce wine by 1/2 by boiling in a small saucepan. Remove from heat and set aside.

To complete the sauce, strain pan juices (stock) from the vegetables, reserving the duck stock. Skim fat from the stock, reserving 4 tablespoons of fat. Place the 4 tablespoons fat, 3/4 cup skimmed duck stock, orange juice, reduced white wine, lemon juice, and blanched rinds and rind water into a saucepan. To another 1/2 cup of the skimmed duck stock, add the flour and blend well into a watery paste. Stir into the orange/stock mixture.

Bring to a boil. Reduce heat and simmer, stirring occasionally, until slightly thickened. Correct the seasoning with salt and pepper to taste. Garnish with Smile Orange (broiled orange slices) and serve with the citrus sauce. Serves 4.

Monterey Pop
(Wine Cooler)

- 2 c. fresh orange juice
- 3 c. lemon juice
- 2 c. rock candy syrup
- 1 gallon white jug wine
- 2 qts. club soda
- Orange slices

Combine the juices, syrup, and wine. Chill. When ready to serve, pour into a punch bowl and add the soda. Add an ice block and orange slices for garnish. Makes about thirty 8 oz. drinks.

Mrs. Wiggs of the Cabbage Patch
(Cabbage Salad)

Mrs. Wiggs' dressing:

- 2 T. flour
- 1½ t. sugar
- 1 t. dry mustard
- ½ t. salt
- Few grains cayenne
- 2 egg yolks, slightly beaten
- 2 T. butter
- ¼ c. garlic-flavored wine vinegar
- ¾ c. milk

  Cabbage, shredded for cole slaw
  Minced onion
  Shredded carrots
  Chopped celery
  Green pepper, diced
  Celery seed

Combine the flour, sugar, dry mustard, salt, and cayenne in the top of a double boiler. Combine the yolks, butter, vinegar, and milk in a bowl. Using a wire whip, stir into the dry ingredients, cooking and stirring over boiling water until slightly thickened. Cool. Pour dressing over prepared vegetables at the rate of 1/2 cup dressing for each 2 cups of salad. Makes about 1 cup dressing.

The Nutty Professor
(Berry-Nutty Bread)

- 1 c. sugar
- 2 c. flour
- ½ t. salt
- 1½ t. baking powder
- ½ t. baking soda
- 2 T. butter, melted
- 1 egg, beaten
- ½ c. fresh squeezed orange juice
- 2 T. hot water
- 2 t. grated orange rind
- 2 c. fresh cranberries, cut in half
- ¾ c. coarsely broken walnuts

Sift the sugar, flour, salt, baking powder, and baking soda together in a large bowl. Set aside. Add the butter to the egg. Stir in the juice, hot water, and grated rind. Pour the juice mixture into the flour mixture and stir well. Add the remaining ingredients, stir well, and pour into a greased loaf pan. Bake at 350° for 45 minutes to 1 hour or until done. Cool. Makes 1 loaf.

Octopussy
(Stewed Octopus in Red Wine)

(While octopus is a lean and mild-flavored mollusk, it is also the toughest of all meats. Fortunately, it can be tenderized to enjoy its superb taste and nutritional value. It helps to select smaller octopi at the start, as they are more tender than the larger varieties.)

- 1 lb. octopus, dressed, tenderized*, and cut into 2" pieces
- ¼ c. olive oil
- ¾ c. chopped onion
- 2 cloves garlic, mashed
- ¼ c. chopped celery
- 2 T. minced parsley
- 1 c. dry red wine
- 1 bay leaf
- Salt, freshly ground black pepper

*If the octopus has not been tenderized at the store, you may do it at home with the following method: Pound the meat with a mallet or rolling pin for at least 5 minutes. Wash well and place in a pan with boiling salted water to cover. Add 1/4-1/2 cup vinegar and simmer for 5 minutes. Drain. Peel off the tough skin, cut into 2" pieces if necessary. Set aside.

Heat oil in a saucepan. Add the onion, garlic, celery, and parsley. Sauté until tender. Add the octopus, wine, bay leaf, and salt and pepper to taste. Cover and simmer, stirring occasionally, until tender and the sauce is thickened, about 1 1/2 to 2 hours. Correct the seasoning and serve hot. Serves 2.

One Potato, Two Potato
(Four Potato Salad)

- 4 medium-sized red-skinned potatoes
- ¼ c. vegetable oil
- ¼ c. olive oil
- ¼ c. wine vinegar
- 1 T. dry white wine
- 2 t. minced fresh parsley
- 2 t. chopped fresh chives
- ½ t. salt
- ¼ t. freshly ground black pepper
- 1 t. dried tarragon leaves
- 2 hard boiled eggs, chopped

Scrub potatoes and boil in their jackets until tender, being careful not to let the skin split (this means they're probably overdone). Drain. Set aside. Combine the oils, vinegar, wine, and seasonings in a jar. Cover tightly and shake vigorously. Dice potatoes when they are cool enough to handle. Place in a bowl and pour dressing over. Add eggs and toss gently. Adjust the seasoning. Cool to room temperature. Cover and chill. Serves 4.

Onionhead with French Dressing
(Marinated Dill Onions with French Dressing)

(The marinated onions discovered by my mother make an excellent condiment for hamburgers, hot dogs, or cold cut sandwiches. They will last for months in the refrigerator.)

Marinated onions:
- 1 large Bermuda onion, peeled and cut into ¼" slices
- ¼ c. sugar
- 4 t. salt
- 2 t. dried dill weed
- Cloves garlic, cut in ⅛" slices
- 1 c. white vinegar

Dressing:
- 1 c. vegetable oil
- ½ c. olive oil
- ½ c. wine vinegar
- ¾ t. salt
- ¼ t. ground white pepper
- 1 t. dry mustard

Separate onion slices and place in a glass jar. Combine remaining marinade ingredients in a saucepan and bring to a boil. Pour over onions and cover tightly. Cool to room temperature, shaking jar occasionally. Refrigerate and let marinate 24 hours before serving. Prepare dressing by combining the ingredients in a bottle. Cover tightly and shake. To serve, place marinated onions in a serving bowl, or on a bed of lettuce and pour on desired amount of dressing. Makes about 1 pint marinated onions, 2 cups dressing.

Operation Caviar
(Caviar-stuffed Celery)

- 2 bunches celery, washed
- 8 oz. cream cheese, softened
- 1 T. minced onion
- 1 T. minced scallion
- ⅓ c. minced fresh parsley
- Freshly ground black pepper
- ¼ c. red caviar
- ¼ c. black caviar

Select only the choice, inner stalks of the celery bunches, with leaves intact. Combine the cream cheese, onion, scallion, parsley and pepper to taste. Stuff celery stalks with the cheese mixture. Cut into 1 1/2" serving pieces, leaving the leaves for garnish. Decorate tops of each celery piece with a small dollop of red and black caviar. Serves 6.

Our Vines Have Tender Grapes
(Stuffed Grape Leaves)

- 6 T. olive oil
- 1½ c. finely chopped onion
- ½ c. uncooked long-grain white rice
- 1½ c. water
- ¾ t. salt
- Freshly ground black pepper
- ⅓ c. coarsely chopped pine nuts (pignolia)
- ½ c. dried currants
- 2 qts. water
- 40 preserved (jarred) grape leaves
- 4 T. water
- Juice of 1 lemon

Heat 2 tablespoons of the olive oil in a skillet over medium heat until it smokes slightly. Add onion and cook until tender, about 5 minutes, stirring frequently. Add rice and cook 3 minutes, stirring constantly without letting it brown. Pour in the 1 1/2 cups water. Stir in the salt and pepper to taste. Bring to boiling. Reduce heat, cover and simmer 20 minutes, or until rice is tender and all the water is absorbed. In a small skillet, lightly brown the pine nuts in 1 tablespoon of the oil. Add to the rice. Stir in the currants. Set aside. Bring the 2 quarts water to boiling in a large pot.

Drain leaves and drop into the boiling water. Remove from heat and let stand 1 minute. Drain in a colander and rinse under cold water.

Carefully separate leaves and spread on absorbent towels. Place 10 of the leaves in the bottom of a 2-3 quart pot with a tight fitting lid, thoroughly covering the bottom. Stuff the remaining 30 leaves as follows: Place about 1 tablespoon of the rice mixture in the center of each leaf, dull side up. Fold the stem end up to the center over the rice, then fold in each of the sides to the center, and close by rolling the stem end to the leaf point, making a snug cylinder.

Layer stuffed leaves in the pot, seam side down. Sprinkle with the remaining 3 tablespoons oil and 4 tablespoons cold water over all. Place over low heat, cover tightly, and simmer 50 minutes. Remove cover and cool. Sprinkle lemon juice over all and serve at room temperature, or refrigerate and serve chilled. Makes 30.

Peppermint Soda
(Mint Soda)

- 8 oz. 7-Up
- 2 t. corn syrup
- Scant ⅛ t. peppermint extract
- 1 drop green food coloring
- Mint leaves

Combine the 7-Up, syrup, extract, and food coloring in a glass. Stir. Add crushed ice and garnish with mint leaves. Serves 1.

Pillar of Salt
(Herb Salt)

- 4 T. salt
- 1 T. paprika
- 1 t. celery salt
- 1 t. garlic powder
- 1 t. onion powder
- 1 t. dry mustard

Combine seasonings and store in a dry container. Use in place of regular table salt. Makes about 6 tablespoons.

The Pizza Triangle
(Pesto-Shrimp Pizza)

Dough:
- 2 pkgs. yeast
- 1 c. warm water
- 2 T. firmly packed brown sugar
- 1½ t. salt
- ¼ c. olive oil
- 2 eggs, beaten
- 4 c. or more flour

Pesto:
- 1½ c. fresh basil leaves (about ⅛ lb.)
- 2 or 3 cloves garlic, mashed
- ¼ c. pignoli
- ¾ c. grated Parmesan cheese
- ¾ c. olive oil
- Salt, pepper
- 1 t. dried oregano
- ¼ t. thyme
- Dash of Tabasco

Topping:
- 1 t. dried oregano
- 2 t. paprika
- Up to 1 red onion, sliced thin
- 8 oz. fresh mushrooms, sliced
- 1 lb. cleaned raw medium shrimp
- 12 oz. mozzarella cheese, grated
- ¼ c. grated Parmesan cheese

To make the dough, dissolve the yeast in the warm water. Stir in the sugar, salt, oil, and egg. Gradually mix in the flour. Knead on a floured board for 5 minutes, adding more flour as necessary to prevent sticking. Place in a buttered bowl, cover with a clean cloth, and let rise in a warm area until doubled.

Meanwhile, prepare the pesto by placing the ingredients in a food processor and mincing together. Punch the dough down and divide in half. Roll out each portion on a lightly floured board to a rectangle shape about the size of a baking sheet. Place each on a baking sheet.

Divide the pesto in half (will be about 3/4 cup for each pizza) and spread equal amounts over the dough with a rubber scraper. Arrange or sprinkle toppings evenly over the pesto in the order listed, dividing ingredients in half as before and using equal amounts on each pizza. Bake at 350° for 30 minutes or until dough is cooked through. Makes 2 pizzas.

Pork Chop Hill *with* The Gravy Train
(Baked Stuffed Pork Chops with Lemon Gravy)

- 8 ½" thick pork chops
- Garlic powder
- Pepper
- 1 T. bacon fat

Stuffing:
- ¼ c. butter
- ½ c. chopped onion
- ½ c. chopped celery
- 3 c. ¼" hard bread cubes
- 1 t. sage
- Salt, pepper
- ½ c. water

Gravy:
- 1 T. bacon fat
- 1 T. butter
- 2 T. flour
- 1 c. chicken stock
- 1 T. lemon juice
- Salt, pepper
- Beef coloring sauce (optional)

Pound chops with meat tenderizer mallet to 1/4" thick. Sprinkle with garlic powder. Lightly sprinkle with pepper. Heat bacon fat in a large skillet and brown chops in the fat. Remove to baking dish, cover with foil, and keep warm. Melt butter in the chop skillet and sauté the onion and celery until tender. Stir in bread cubes. Sprinkle with sage, salt, and pepper. Pour in the water. Cook and stir until the bread cubes are softened.

Divide stuffing mixture into 4 equal parts. Place 1 portion on top of one pork chop and top with another chop. Secure the "sandwich" by tying with string. Repeat for remaining stuffing and chops. Place side by side in the baking dish. Cover with foil and bake at 350° for 1 hour, inverting the chops after 1/2 hour.

Meanwhile, prepare the gravy by heating the bacon fat and butter in a saucepan. Stir in the flour with a wire whip until a paste forms. Gradually stir in chicken stock, stirring constantly until thickened.

Stir in the lemon juice. Add beef coloring sauce to darken gravy, if desired. Salt and pepper to taste. Remove string from the baked chops before serving. Pass the gravy. Serves 4. Makes about 1 cup gravy.

Port of New York
(A Port Aperitif)

- 1 oz. port
- 1½ oz. brandy
- ½ t. Cointreau
- Dash of Angostura bitters

Combine in a shaker with ice cubes. Shake. Pour in an old fashioned-type glass over ice cubes. Serves 1.

Port of Seven Seas
(Seven Seas Port Cocktail)

- 2 t. port
- 2 oz. brandy
- 2 t. dry vermouth

Combine and stir in a cocktail glass. Serve with an ice cube. Serves 1.

Prisoner of Shark Island
(Shark Teriyaki)

(Those who enjoyed eating shark meals before the gruesome "eating" scene in *Jaws* was released, probably remain undeterred in their habit. In fact, there are probably more people eating shark than ever before—after all, turnabout is fair play. As unlikely as it seems though, shark meat, or "grayfish" as it is often advertised to unsuspecting buyers, is similar to swordfish in texture [while not as tender] but is infinitely less expensive and more readily available. It varies in color from off-white to salmony red, and can vary in flavor with the species. Any disagreeable taste can be eliminated by marinating or soaking in slightly salted cold milk or water-diluted lemon juice. This particular recipe is a delicious marinade for any type of shark, and is especially good if barbecued.)

Marinade:
- ⅔ c. soy sauce
- ¼ c. vegetable oil
- ¼ t. dried ground ginger
- 2 cloves garlic, mashed
- 1 t. Dijon mustard
- ¼ c. sugar
- 3 T. brandy
- 4 shark (grayfish) fillets or steaks

Combine the marinade ingredients in a glass baking dish. Soak the shark fillets in the mixture for about 1 hour. Broil or barbecue until done (about 10 minutes total for a 1" thick fillet), turning once halfway through cooking. Serves 4.

The Pumpkin Eater
(Pumpkin Bread)

- 3⅓ c. sifted flour
- 2 t. baking soda
- 1½ t. salt
- 2 t. nutmeg
- 2 t. cinnamon
- 3 c. sugar
- 1 c. vegetable oil
- 4 eggs, slightly beaten
- 1 T. vanilla
- ⅔ c. water
- 2 c. pumpkin puree
- 1½ c. raisins
- 1½ c. chopped pecans

Sift together the flour, soda, salt, nutmeg, cinnamon, and sugar into a large bowl. Make a well in the center and add the remaining ingredients. Beat to blend well. Pour equal amounts into 3 greased loaf pans or muffin tins. Bake at 350° for 1 hour if using loaf pans, or 25–30 minutes for muffins. Freeze for later use if so desired. Makes 3 loaves.

Punch and Jody
(Tea Punch)

- 1 qt. hot water
- 4 Constant Comment teabags
- 1 c. sugar
- 2 c. orange juice
- 1 c. lemon juice
- 2 qts. ginger ale
- Fruit garnish

In a saucepan, bring the water to a boil. Add the tea, cover and steep for 5 minutes. Remove teabags, stir in the sugar to dissolve, and let cool. Chill. Add the juices and ginger ale at serving time. Serve in a punch bowl over an ice block with fruit garnish. Serves 12.

A Raisin in the Sun
(Raisin 'n' Sunflower Muffins)

(This healthy raisin muffin recipe is adapted from a friend of my mother's, Jo Bernier, who needed a good milk-free breakfast bread for allergy-stricken members of her family. It is my favorite morning muffin for its all-around exceptional taste, nutritional value, and "stay-with-you" qualities. For variety, you may substitute 2 cups buttermilk for the bananas.)

- ¾ c. honey
- ½ c. molasses
- ½ c. vegetable oil
- 2 eggs, beaten
- 2 c. mashed ripe bananas (about 4 bananas)
- 3 c. warm water
- 1¾ c. bran or bran flakes
- 1 c. wheat germ
- 2¾ c. whole wheat flour
- 2½ t. baking soda
- ½ t. salt
- 2½ c. raisins
- 2 T. grated orange rind
- 1 c. sunflower seeds

Stir together the honey, molasses, oil, eggs, bananas, and water in a large bowl. In a separate bowl, stir together the bran, wheat germ, flour, soda, and salt. Gradually pour the dry ingredients into the wet and stir thoroughly.

Add the raisins, orange rind, and sunflower seeds and mix well. Spoon into greased or paper-lined muffin tins, filling them to the top. Bake at 350° for 30–35 minutes, or until done. Makes about 2 1/2 dozen muffins.

Rhubarb
(Rhubarb Cake)

- 3 T. butter
- ½ c. firmly packed brown sugar
- 3 c. diced rhubarb (about ¾ lb.)
- 4 drops red food coloring
- ¼ c. dry sherry
- 3 egg yolks
- 1 t. lemon juice
- 1 c. sugar
- ¼ c. hot water
- 1 c. sifted flour
- 1½ t. baking powder
- ¼ t. salt
- 3 egg whites
- Whipped cream

Melt butter in a 9"×12" glass baking dish. Remove from heat. Stir in the brown sugar. Spread evenly on the bottom of the dish. Arrange rhubarb evenly over the sugar mixture. (If you are using frozen rhubarb, be sure to defrost it thoroughly and drain all the excess water before adding it to the baking dish.)

Add the food coloring to the sherry and drizzle over the rhubarb. Set aside. In a large bowl, beat the yolks and lemon with an electric mixer at high speed for 1 minute. Continue beating while gradually adding the sugar, beating until light. Turn beater to low speed and beat in hot water. Set aside.

Sift together flour, baking powder, and salt. Add to yolk mixture and stir just until ingredients are combined. Beat egg whites until stiff but not dry. Fold into the batter. Spoon batter evenly over rhubarb. Bake at 325° for 35-40 minutes or until the cake tests done. Let cool 15 minutes. Cut pieces and invert on serving dishes, rhubarb side up. Serve with a dollop of whipped cream. Serves 12.

Ring of Bright Water
(Egg 'n' Beer)

- 1 egg
- 12 oz. beer

Lower egg into a pan of boiling water. Remove from heat and let egg soak for 5 minutes. (This process "cooks" the egg long enough to destroy harmful disease-causing organisms, yet keeps it looking and tasting raw. It also helps to maintain and enhance the delicate balance of vitamins, enzymes, and amino acids in eggs.) Remove egg from water and cool. Break into a cold glass of beer. Serves 1.

Roll, Freddie, Roll
(Dinner Rolls)

- ⅓ c. butter
- 1 c. boiling water
- 1 T. salt
- ⅓ c. sugar
- 1 c. lukewarm water
- 2 cakes yeast
- 3 eggs, beaten
- 6-7 c. flour
- 1 egg, beaten
- Sesame or poppy seeds

Combine the butter, boiling water, salt, and sugar in a large mixing bowl. Stir to melt the butter and dissolve the salt and sugar. Cool by adding the lukewarm water. Dissolve the yeast in the water mixture. Beat in eggs and half the flour. Mix well. Add remaining flour (up to 7 cups in all), stirring until the dough forms a ball and leaves the sides of the bowl. Turn out on a floured board and knead for 3 minutes. Place dough in a greased bowl. Cover with a cloth and let rise in a warm place until doubled, about 1 hour. Punch down and knead lightly on a floured board for 1 minute.

Using a floured rolling pin, roll dough out to a thickness of 3/4". Cut into roll shapes (use the open end of a 3" drinking glass if you do not have a cutter). Place on buttered baking sheets and let rise again, uncovered, until doubled. Brush with beaten egg and sprinkle with desired seeds. Bake at 400° for 20 minutes or until golden brown. Serve hot. Makes about 2 dozen.

Salt and Pepper
(Salt and Pepper Seasoning Mix)

- 2 T. salt
- ¼ t. black pepper
- ½ t. paprika
- ½ t. garlic powder
- ½ t. onion powder
- 1 t. finely crushed dried parsley

Combine seasonings in a shaker and shake to mix well. Sprinkle on meat, vegetables, or salads for added flavor. Makes about 3 tablespoons.

Serial
(Granola)

- 6 c. oatmeal
- 2 c. toasted wheat germ
- 1 c. firmly packed brown sugar
- 1 t. salt
- 2 t. cinnamon
- ½ c. corn syrup
- ½ c. vegetable oil
- 1 t. vanilla
- 1 c. chopped dried dates
- 1 c. raisins
- 1 c. hulled sunflower seeds
- ½ c. chopped peanuts or toasted almonds
- ½ c. chopped walnuts

Mix the oats, wheat germ, brown sugar, salt, and cinnamon. In a separate bowl, combine the syrup, oil, and vanilla. Pour syrup mixture over oat mixture and stir until oats are well coated. Spread on ungreased baking sheets and bake at 200° for 1 hour or until crispy. Stir every 15 minutes or so while baking to prevent burning. Cool. Mix in the remaining ingredients. Store in a tightly covered container in the refrigerator. Makes about 4 quarts.

The Serpent's Egg
(Egg-Stuffed Baked Tomato)

2 large tomatoes
4 T. grated Parmesan cheese
1 T. butter
1 T. olive oil
2 T. finely chopped onion
2 eggs, beaten
2 slices prosciutto, diced
   Salt, pepper
1 t. minced parsley

Slice off tops of tomatoes just below stem area. Scoop out insides, leaving about 1/4" pulp to form a sturdy "cup." Sprinkle insides evenly with 2 tablespoons of the Parmesan cheese. Place on a buttered glass baking dish and bake at 350° for 20 minutes or until tender.

About 10 minutes before the tomatoes are done, melt the butter with the olive oil in a small skillet. Add the onion and sauté until tender and lightly browned. Stir in eggs and prosciutto. Cook scrambled style, stirring frequently until desired doneness. Remove from heat and stir in the remaining 2 tablespoons Parmesan cheese. Salt and pepper to taste. Spoon equal amounts of egg mixture into the baked tomato cups. Sprinkle tops with parsley. Serves 2.

The Seven Ups
(Sparkling Punch)

1 6 oz. can frozen grape juice
      concentrate
1 6 oz. can frozen tangerine juice
      concentrate
1 6 oz. can frozen lemonade
      juice concentrate
4 c. water
1 qt. Seven-Up
   Assorted fruit slices

Combine juice concentrates and the water. Chill several hours. At serving time, slowly add the Seven-Up. Serve with ice and fruit slices. Makes 2 1/2 quarts.

Skippy
(Homemade Peanut Butter Sandwich)

(Peanut butter will keep fresh if stored in an airtight container and refrigerated. If it separates, remix by stirring.)

Peanut butter:
2 c. shelled peanuts
2 T. peanut, vegetable, or
      safflower oil
½ t. salt (optional)

Sandwich:
2 slices whole grain bread
2 T. homemade peanut butter
1 T. crumbled crisp bacon
1 T. chopped raisins
¼ t. toasted sesame seeds
2 T. grated carrots

To make the peanut butter, pour peanuts into a blender. Cover and blend at high speed for five seconds. Add oil and salt. Blend at high speed for 10 seconds. Turn motor to low and continue blending for 50 seconds. (If mixture sticks to container, turn motor off, scrape sides with a rubber spatula, and push peanut butter into the blade. Continue beating until smooth.) For the Skippy sandwich, spread 2 tablespoons of the peanut butter on a slice of bread. Sprinkle with remaining ingredients and top with bread slice. Makes 2 cups peanut butter. Makes 1 sandwich.

Smile Orange
(Broiled Orange "Smile Sections")

(These oranges have a crisp candy crust and make an excellent garnish for a duck dinner.)

2 navel oranges
  Softened butter
  Sifted brown sugar

Peel and section oranges. Place flat side down on a baking sheet. Spread tops with butter and sprinkle evenly with brown sugar. Broil for a few seconds until the sugar melts. Cool slightly. Serves 2-4.

Sorrell and Son *with* The Onion Field
(Sorrel Salad with Onion Dressing)

(Sorrel [sour grass] is a pleasantly unusual variation to the everyday salad. The cloverlike leaves tend to have a slightly acid or lemon-sour taste, and are best when harvested young and combined with other greens.)

4 slices cooked crisp bacon,
      crumbled
   Small, young sorrel leaves
1 head lettuce—Boston, Bibb,
      romaine, or spinach leaves
1 c. croutons
1 hard boiled egg, diced

Dressing:
¼ c. olive oil
¼ c. vegetable oil
¼ c. wine vinegar
2 T. minced onion
1 T. firmly packed brown sugar
½ t. dried mustard
¼ t. salt
   Freshly ground pepper

Wash and dry the salad greens. Tear into pieces and chill. Combine the dressing ingredients in a jar. Cover tightly and shake thoroughly. When ready to serve, add the bacon bits, croutons, and egg to the greens. Toss with desired amount of dressing. Makes about 1 cup dressing. Salad serves 2-4.

The Story of Seabiscuit
(Sea Salt Biscuits)

(Since sea salt has no appreciable taste difference from regular table salt, you may use table salt as a substitute.)

- 3 c. flour
- 1½ t. baking powder
- ¾ t. baking soda
- 1 t. granulated sea salt
- 3 eggs
- 1½ c. sour cream
- Sea salt for sprinkling

Sift the flour, baking powder, baking soda, and sea salt together. Stir in 2 of the eggs and sour cream. Knead gently and briefly on a lightly floured board and roll out to a thickness of 1/2". Punch out biscuit rounds with a 2 1/2" biscuit cutter and place on buttered baking sheets. Beat the remaining egg and brush tops of biscuits. Sprinkle lightly with sea salt. Bake at 425° for 15–20 minutes or until lightly browned. Makes about 16.

The Strawberry Blonde
(Cointreau Strawberries with Crème Blonde)

- Fresh strawberries
- Orange juice
- Cointreau

Creme blonde:
- 1 c. heavy cream
- 2 T. sugar
- ½ t. vanilla
- Few drops yellow food coloring

To fresh berries, add orange juice and Cointreau to taste. Combine crème blonde ingredients in a bowl and whip until mixture stands in soft peaks. Top each serving with a head of crème blonde.

Strawberry, Lemon, and Mint
(Fresh Strawberries with Lemon Sauce and Mint)

Lemon sauce:
- ⅓ c. sugar
- 2 T. cornstarch
- 1 c. water
- 3 T. butter
- 2 T. fresh lemon juice
- ½ t. grated lemon rind
- 3 T. orange juice
- ⅛ t. salt

- Fresh strawberries, sliced
- Mint leaves

Combine sugar, cornstarch, and water in top of a double boiler. Cook over boiling water, stirring occasionally until thickened. Remove from heat and stir in remaining sauce ingredients. Cool. Serve over sliced strawberries. Garnish with mint leaves. Makes about 1 cup sauce.

The Strawberry Statement
(Last-Word Strawberry Preserves)

(The word "perfect" here means berries that are juicy, red-ripe, but solid. Do not use berries with hollow cores.)

- 1 qt. perfect strawberries, stems removed, washed and dried
- 4½–5 c. sugar
- ½ c. fresh squeezed lemon juice

Combine berries and sugar in a saucepan. Let stand 3 hours. Place over heat and bring to boiling, stirring occasionally, until sugar dissolves. Cook over medium heat until thickened, about 20 minutes. Add lemon juice and cook an additional 10 minutes. While boiling hot, pour into sterilized jars. Seal immediately with airtight lids. (If sealing with paraffin, cool completely before pouring into sterile, hot, but dry jars.) Makes about 4 half-pints (cups).

Summer Stock
(Vegetable Soup)

(This soup recipe comes to us from my Sicilian mother-in-law, whose father was something of a soup king back in the old country. He invented soups by the bucket everyday—soups with no name—to feed his family of fourteen and the many neighborhood soup fans who would stop by. Later the grandchildren and great-grandchildren gathered around his fabled soup pot.

Lucky for us he passed on some of his legendary recipes, this one being a hearty sampling of a summer harvest and my personal favorite all-around soup.)

- 1 large onion, diced
- 1 c. diced celery with leaves
- ½ c. olive oil
- ¼ lb. kale, sliced into 1" pieces
- 2 medium zucchini, diced
- 2 medium yellow squash, diced
- 3 medium summer squash, diced
- 3 medium potatoes, diced
- 1 T. dried crushed sweet basil leaves or 8 leaves fresh basil, chopped
- 2 t. dried oregano leaves
- 1 t. dried dill weed
- ⅓ c. minced fresh parsley
- 2 bay leaves
- Salt, pepper

- 1 medium onion, diced
- 2 T. olive oil
- 1 28 oz. can tomatoes, coarsely chopped
- 1 c. fresh peas
- 1½ qts. hot water
- Grated Parmesan cheese

In a large kettle, sauté the diced large onion and celery in the oil until tender. Add remaining ingredients and sauté for 1/2 hour, stirring frequently. Meanwhile, in a separate skillet, sauté the diced medium onion in the 2 tablespoons oil until tender. Add tomatoes with their canned juice and simmer 15 minutes. Pour into the sautéed vegetables. Add peas and hot water. Cover and simmer at least 2 hours (the longer the better). Serve with grated Parmesan cheese. Serves 14.

Sunny Side Up
(Herbed Fried Egg)

- 1-2 T. butter or vegetable oil
- 2 eggs
- 1 t. minced fresh parsley
- Seasoned salt (see p. 236)

Heat butter or oil in a frying pan. When the fat begins to smoke slightly, break eggs into frying pan, being careful not to break the yolks. Reduce heat to low. Baste yolks with the fat until whites become firm and yolks form a light film. Sprinkle with parsley and baste once more. Remove with a spatula to a warm plate and sprinkle with seasoned salt. Serves 1.

Sweet Charity
(Peach Brandy Crêpes Flambé with Meringue)

(You may prepare most of this elegant flaming dessert ahead of time.)

- 16 crêpes (see Swedish pancakes, p. 57)
- 2 lbs. fresh peaches (about 6 medium)
- 1 medium fresh peach (for garnish)
- 2 T. butter
- ¼ c. sugar (or sugar to taste)
- ⅓ c. peach flavored brandy
- 1-2 T. cornstarch
- 2 T. heated apricot preserves, strained

Meringue:

- 2 egg whites, at room temperature
- 2 T. sugar
- ¼ t. cream of tartar
- ½ c. peach flavored brandy

Prepare crêpes. (These can be made ahead of time and stored in the refrigerator until you are ready to assemble them.) Blanch peaches, including the one for garnish, by plunging them into a pot of boiling water and letting sit for 1 minute. Drain. Set the garnish peach aside. Peel and pit peaches (except the one for garnish). Dice.

Melt butter in a saucepan. Add diced peaches and toss to coat. Cover and cook over low heat until tender, stirring occasionally, about 15 minutes. Stir in sugar to taste and brandy.

Mix 1 or 2 tablespoons of cornstarch (depending on amount of juice) with a few tablespoons of the peach juice. Add to the cooked peaches and stir in. Cook, uncovered, for 5 minutes or until thickened and not too runny. (The consistency should be thick enough so that it doesn't drip down the sides of the crêpes, but still easy to spread.)

Place one crêpe on a lightly buttered ovenproof serving dish or glass pie plate. Spread 3 tablespoons of the peach mixture on the crêpe, being sure to reach the edges. Place a second crêpe over the first, and spread with 3 tablespoons of the peach mixture. Repeat procedure until all crêpes are used. (You may prepare the dessert up to this point several hours before serving. Do not refrigerate.)

Shortly before serving, peel the last peach, remove pit, and cut into 16 pieces. Arrange slices in a flower-petal ring on top of the crêpe stack. Brush apricot preserves over peach garnish and top crêpe. Prepare meringue by beating egg whites with an electric mixer until foamy. Add sugar and cream of tartar. Beat until stiff but not dry. Spread meringue around sides of the crêpe stack. Bake at 400° for 6-8 minutes or until lightly browned. At the table, barely warm the brandy in a small chafing dish. Ignite and pour over top of the stack. Serve immediately. Serves 8.

A Taste of Honey
(Honey Pears)

- 4 pears
- ¼ c. pineapple juice
- ¼ c. firmly packed brown sugar
- 1 t. vanilla
- 1 t. lemon juice
- ½ c. chopped pecans
- ¼ c. honey

Parboil the pears 1 minute in boiling water. Drain and plunge into cold water. Peel the skin. Cut in half lengthwise and scoop out core. Fit snugly, flat side down, in a glass baking dish. Pour pineapple juice over. Combine sugar, vanilla, lemon juice, and nuts. Sprinkle over pears. Drizzle honey over pears. Bake at 350° for 30 minutes, or until tender. Serves 4.

Tea and Sympathy
(Hot Minted Tea)

- 4 t. loose black or green tea leaves
- 4 c. water
- 4 fresh mint leaves

Preheat a teapot by partially filling with boiling water and letting stand for 2 minutes. Meanwhile, bring the 4 cups water to a full boil in a saucepan. Drain and dry the teapot. Put loose tea in preheated pot and pour boiling water over tea. Add mint leaves, cover, and let steep for 3-5 minutes, depending on desired strength. Serve immediately. Makes about 4 cups.

Tea for Two
(Basic Brewed Tea)

2 t. tea leaves
1½ c. water, boiled
Sugar
Lemon wedges

Preheat a teapot by partially filling it with boiling water and letting stand for 2 minutes. Meanwhile, bring the 1 1/2 cups water to a full boil in a small saucepan. Drain and dry the teapot. Put loose tea in preheated pot and pour boiling water over tea. Cover and let steep for no less than 3, but no more than 5 minutes, depending on desired strength. Serve immediately. Pass the sugar and lemon. Serves 2.

Teahouse of the August Moon
(Teahouse Tea)

¼ c. black China tea (Oolong or Orange Pekoe)
¼ c. dried jasmine
¼ c. dried rose petals
¼ c. dried violets

Mix thoroughly in a bowl. Store in an airtight tin. When ready to make tea, use 2 heaping tablespoons per pot, and serve without milk or cream. Sweeten to taste if desired. Makes 1 cup dried tea preparation.

There's a Girl in My Soup
(Cream of Artichoke-Mushroom Soup)

1 9 oz. pkg. frozen artichoke hearts
1 chicken bouillon cube
3 T. butter
½ lb. fresh mushrooms, sliced thin
4 T. finely chopped onion
3 T. flour
2 c. milk
1 c. chicken stock
Salt, pepper

Cook artichoke hearts according to package directions. Drain, reserving liquid. Dissolve bouillon cube in the hot artichoke liquid. Set aside. Dice artichoke hearts. Set aside. Melt butter in a large saucepan. Add mushrooms and onion and sauté until onion is tender. Stir in flour. Remove from heat and stir in the artichoke-bouillon liquid. Return to heat and gradually add milk and chicken stock, stirring constantly. Add diced artichoke hearts and cook over medium heat until mixture thickens. Salt and pepper to taste. Serves 4.

There's Always Vanilla
(Vanilla Bavarian Cream)

1 envelope unflavored gelatin
⅓ c. cold water
5 egg yolks
⅔ c. sugar
¼ t. salt
1¼ c. milk
2 t. vanilla extract
1¼ c. heavy cream, whipped stiff
Fruits for garnish (strawberries, bananas, kiwi, raspberries, etc.)

Soften the gelatin in the cold water. Set aside. Combine the yolks, sugar, and salt in the top of a double boiler over hot (not boiling water) and beat with a wooden spoon 1 minute. Scald the milk and gradually add it to the egg mixture, stirring constantly. Continue to cook and stir until smooth and thickened. Stir in the softened gelatin and vanilla. Cool slightly, then chill, stirring occasionally to prevent a skin from forming. Fold in the whipped cream and pour into a decorative 1 quart mold that has been rinsed in cold water. Chill until firm. When ready to serve, unmold (as you would for Jell-O) onto a serving platter and garnish with fresh or frozen, whole or mashed fruit. Serves 6–8.

Toast of the Legion
(Whipped Honey-Butter Toast)

¼ c. butter, softened
2 T. heavy cream
¼ c. honey
½ t. cinnamon
Bread slices, crusts removed
Butter for spreading

Beat butter and cream together with an electric mixer at medium speed, until light. Very slowly drizzle honey into butter mixture while continuing to beat. Add cinnamon and beat until smooth and creamy. Spread 2–3 tablespoons of the honey butter on a slice of bread. Cover with another slice of bread. Lightly butter outer sides of "sandwich." Cut into quarters and toast both sides under a broiler until golden brown. Makes about 1/2 cup honey butter.

The Toast of New Orleans
(Pecan-Cinnamon Toast Roll)

8 slices white bread, crusts removed
Butter
2 T. brown sugar
1 T. white sugar
¼ t. cinnamon
¼ c. finely chopped pecans

Butter bread slices on one side. Combine remaining ingredients. Sprinkle 1 tablespoon of the mixture evenly on butter side of each bread slice. Starting at the corner, roll each slice tightly to the opposite corner, buttering the loose corner to fasten closed. Melt butter in a skillet and pan-toast rolls evenly on all sides. Makes 8 rolls.

The Toast of New York
(Bagels)

1 medium potato, scrubbed
3 c. flour
1 t. salt
4 T. sugar
1 pkg. yeast (1 cake)
3 T. vegetable oil
2 eggs
4 quarts boiling water
1 egg, beaten
  Sesame seeds
  Poppy seeds

Cut potato into 1" cubes. Place in small saucepan, cover with water, and boil until tender. Reserve 2/3 cup of the potato water. (You may use the potato for some other recipe.) Sift flour, salt, and 2 tablespoons of the sugar into a bowl. Dissolve yeast in 1/3 cup of the warm potato water. Add to flour mixture. Add oil to the remaining 1/3 cup potato water and stir into flour mixture. Add eggs and stir until dough forms a ball. Knead on a floured board at least 5 minutes. Place dough in a buttered bowl, cover, and let rise until doubled. Punch down, cover, and let rise again until doubled. Punch down a second time. Knead on a floured board until smooth and elastic. Divide dough into 12 equal portions and shape into 6"×3/4" strips.

Pinch ends of strips together to form doughnut shapes. Add remaining 2 tablespoons sugar to the 4 quarts boiling water. Drop bagels, one at a time, into the boiling water. Cook about 5 at once (depending on size of the pot) for 5 to 6 minutes from the time they rise to the surface of the water. Remove with a long-handled fork and place on a lightly greased cookie sheet. Let cool 5 minutes. Brush tops with beaten egg and sprinkle with seeds if desired. Bake at 375° for 25–30 minutes or until golden brown. Makes 12.

Top Banana
(Banana Popsicles)

2 bananas
  Chocolate sauce
  Finely chopped nuts

Peel bananas. Insert popsicle stick lengthwise in each banana. Wrap individually in plastic wrap and freeze. Brush with chocolate sauce and roll in nuts. Serves 2.

Tortilla Flat
(Corn Tortillas)

(A 6" tortilla press [found in most Mexican and Chinese specialty markets] is useful for making this Mexican "bread." However, failing that, the palms of your hands will do just fine. Tortillas are almost an indispensable part of any Mexican meal and can be used in literally hundreds of recipes.)

½–¾ lb. prepared masa or
2 c. Quaker masa harina and
1⅓ c. water

If using prepared masa, no water is necessary. If using the masa harina, put the 2 cups in a mixing bowl and add the water all at once (to prevent lumps from forming), stirring quickly just until combined. Let rest 20 minutes. Meanwhile, preheat a griddle (two will speed up the cooking) so the tortilla faintly sizzles when placed on the surface.

Before charging on, make a "test" tortilla to adjust the consistency of the dough and temperature of the griddle. Form a 1 1/2" ball of dough and pat it out to a 5" round flat cake. If using a tortilla press, cover the lower part of the press with a plastic bag and place the dough ball on the bag, slightly more toward the hinge.

Place the second bag on top of the ball and close the press. Push the handle down firmly, then open the press carefully and peel off the top bag. Lift the lower bag out and invert, tortilla side down, on your upturned hand, more toward your fingers than your palm, and carefully peel the bag away from the dough. If the bag is difficult to peel away, there is too much moisture in the dough. Add a little more masa to the dough, mix well, and repeat process.

Gently place one tortilla cake on the preheated griddle (if dropped onto the surface, it will form air bubbles and not cook properly). If the cake looks thick, with an uneven, grainy edge, the dough is too dry. Add a small amount of water to the masa in the bowl, mix well, and try again. When the dough reaches the correct consistency without being thick and grainy, cook the tortilla just until it begins to dry out around the edges. Flip over and cook the other side slightly longer, until it begins to color. Flip over again and finish cooking, about 2 minutes total. If the tortilla puffs up when flipped back to the first side, the dough has the correct consistency and is being cooked at the correct heat.

Finish cooking the remainder of the tortillas, adding more water if the dough begins to dry out. Keep tortillas warm and pliable by stacking together and wrapping in a towel as they cook. Makes about 16 tortillas.

Tuna Clipper
(Tuna-Olive Casserole)

- 4 T. butter
- 4 T. flour
- 2 c. milk
- 1 c. shredded cheddar cheese
- 6 oz. elbow macaroni
- 1 13 oz. can white tuna, packed in water
- ½ c. finely chopped green olives
- 3 T. minced fresh parsley
- Salt, freshly ground pepper
- ¼ c. breadcrumbs, tossed with 2 T. melted butter

Melt the butter in a saucepan. Using a wire whip, stir in the flour and cook over low heat for 1 minute, stirring constantly. Slowly add the milk, stirring constantly and cook for 5 minutes until thickened. Add the cheese and stir until melted. Remove from heat and set aside. Cook the macaroni al dente and drain. Add the tuna, olives, and parsley to the cheese mixture. Salt and pepper to taste. Gently toss the tuna mixture with the macaroni and pour into a buttered casserole dish. Top with breadcrumbs and bake at 350° for 20-30 minutes or until bubbly and lightly browned. Serves 4.

Under Milk Wood
(Coffee-Nog Cooler)

- 5 t. instant coffee
- 2½ T. sugar
- 1 egg
- Pinch salt
- 2 c. milk
- ½ t. vanilla

Combine the coffee, sugar, egg, and salt in a bowl. Beat with an electric mixer until the coffee and sugar dissolve. Add the milk and vanilla. Beat well. Chill and serve over cracked ice. Serves 2.

Watermelon Man
(Watermelon Cake)

- 1 c. butter, softened
- 1¾ c. sugar
- 5 eggs
- 2 t. vanilla
- 3 c. flour
- 1½ t. baking powder
- ½ t. salt
- ⅔ c. sherry
- 1¾ c. minced pickled watermelon rind (about three 10 oz. jars)
- 1 c. white raisins
- 1 c. chopped pecans
- 1 c. slivered almonds, toasted in 1 T. butter
- 1 T. butter

Cream the butter with the sugar. Add the eggs, one at a time, beating after each addition. Stir in the vanilla. In a separate bowl, sift the flour, baking powder, and salt together. Stir into the butter mixture alternately with the sherry. Add the watermelon rind, raisins, pecans, and almonds and stir well. Pour equal amounts into 2 well-greased loaf pans. Bake at 325° for 1 hour. Cool. Makes 2 cakes.

Where the Red Fern Grows
(Steamed Fiddleheads)

(These rare, springtime forest edibles are one of the most delectable plants known, and are well worth the effort in locating them. Their taste is somewhere between spinach and artichokes, but their location is much harder to pinpoint. A fiddlehead hunt through a densely wooded area in the spring might produce results. Barring that, some grocers carry them in season or stock them in the frozen section. Basically you are looking for the uppermost curled portion of new fern shoots. If you can find them fresh [or have them given to you by a kindly neighbor as I did] wash them well, drain, and peel off the woolly skin before cooking. If frozen, partially defrost.)

Fresh or frozen young fiddleheads (fern shoots)
Butter
Lemon slices
Salt, pepper

Wash and prepare as indicated and steam as for asparagus—covered for about 12 minutes or until tender. Serve with butter, lemon slices, and salt and pepper.

Wild Fruit
(Broiled Fresh-Fruit Kabobs)

- 2 bananas, peeled and cut in 1" slices
- 2 c. fresh pineapple chunks
- 2 c. whole fresh strawberries
- ½ c. French Dressing (see p. 233)
- ¼ c. clover honey

Alternate fruit on 6" bamboo skewers. Place in a glass baking dish. Combine dressing and honey. Pour over fruit kabobs. Marinate 1/2 hour. Broil 3"-4" from heat, basting and turning until fruit is lightly browned on all sides. Makes 12 skewers.

Wild Oranges
(Spiced Oranges in Juice)

- 2 large oranges, peeled and thinly sliced
- ¼ c. chopped dates
- ½ c. fresh orange juice
- Scant ⅛ t. ground clove
- 2 pieces stick cinnamon
- ¼ c. chopped toasted almonds

Combine all ingredients, except almonds, in a saucepan. Cover and bring to a boil. Remove from heat and cool to warm, keeping covered but stirring occasionally. Remove cinnamon sticks. Spoon into serving dishes and sprinkle with almonds. Serves 4.

Wild Strawberries
(Chilled Strawberry Soup)

2½ c. fresh wild strawberries, tops removed
¼-½ c. sugar
⅔ c. sour cream
2 c. ice water
½ c. red wine
Mint leaves

Puree the berries in a food processor, blender, or food mill. Add sugar to taste and sour cream. Stir well. Add ice water and wine. Correct the sweetness if necessary. Chill. Serve in chilled bowls with mint leaf garnish. Serves 4.

The Young Girls of Rochefort
(Salad with Roquefort Dressing)

½ c. French Dressing (see Onionhead, p. 233)
¼ c. Roquefort cheese, crumbled

Tossed green salad

Prepare French Dressing and combine with Roquefort cheese. Chill. Pour over tossed salad of your choice. Makes about 3/4 cup dressing.

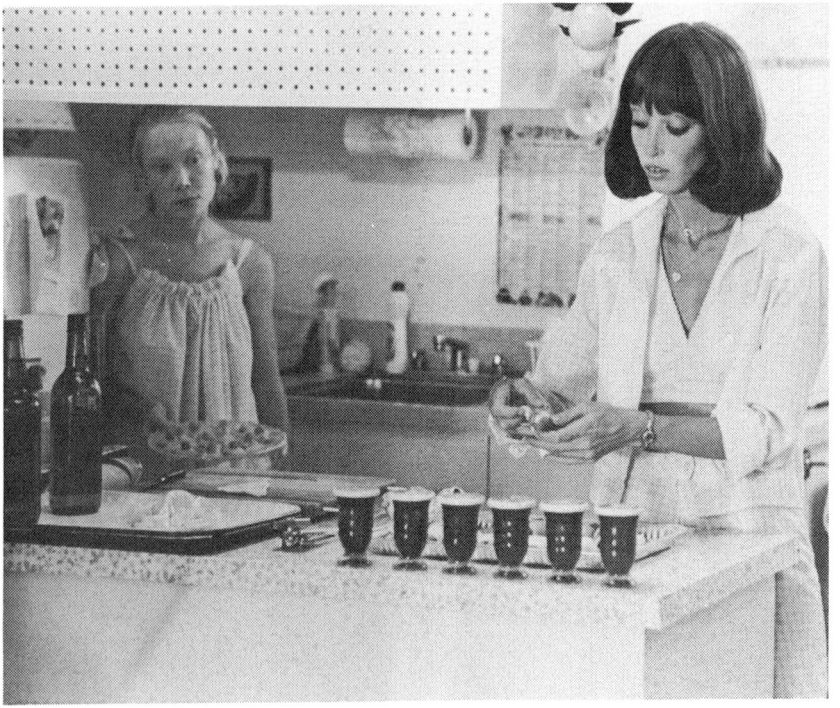

The Private Life of Henry VIII. In what is considered his best role, Charles Laughton plays Henry VIII, the porcine king given to wine, wives, and feasting.

Three Women. In Robert Altman's psychological suspense thriller, Sissy Spacek watches the pseudo-swinging Shelley Duvall, right, ready their date's dinner party fixin's of processed shrimp cocktail cups, hot dogs baked in processed refrigerator rolls, processed pudding cups, and cheap screw-top wine.

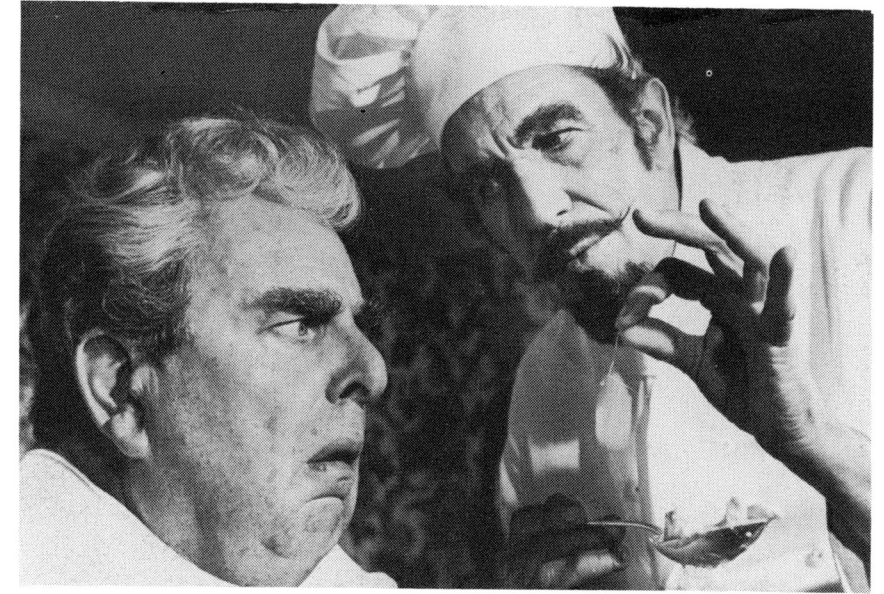

Theater of Blood. Outraged British thespian Edward Lionheart (Vincent Price) systematically murders unsympathetic critics in a manner related to Shakespearian plays. Lionheart, disguised as a French chef, shows theater critic Meredith Merridew (Robert Morley) a hair belonging to one of Merridew's pet poodles, a key ingredient in the "ragout of poodle" that Lionheart and devoted daughter Diana Rigg force-feed the doomed critic as in *Titus Andronicus*.

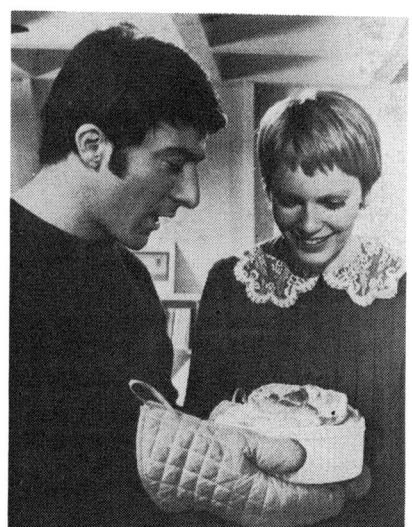

John and Mary. The simple, introspective weekend love story involves two love-wary strangers (Dustin Hoffman and Mia Farrow), who meet, share a bed, and some laughs, cook some meals, and finally work up the courage to introduce themselves.

FEATURED TITLES INDEX AND RECIPES

Animal House, 78
    Food Fight Shopping List, 80
Annie Hall, 81
    Mashed Yeast 'n' Sprouts, 81
    Shiksa Sandwich, 82
Arsenic and Old Lace, 30
    Aunt Martha's Elderberry Wine, 31
Bedtime for Bonzo, 56
    Swedish Pancakes (plättar), 57
Blazing Saddles, 83
    Campfire Beans, 83
    Schnitzengrüben with Sauerkraut, 83
Breakfast at Tiffany's, 59
    Crullers, 60
The Breakfast Club, 85
    Breakfast Club Lunch, 85
California Suite, 10
    Guacamole, 10
Close Encounters of the Third Kind, 87
    Mashed Spudniks, 87
The Cocoanuts, 170
    Buffet d' Harpo, 170
Comfort and Joy, 148
    Fried Ice Cream, 148
Continental Divide, 89
    Grandmother's Goulash, 89
Cool-Hand Luke, 172
    Eggathon, 172
Danton, 91
    Convention Sauce, 95
    Fruit à la Royal Runaway, 95
    Refugee Quail with Wine Onions, 92
    Stuffed Cucumber, 91
    Turbot à la Flunkey, 94
    Vol au Vent, 93

Days of Wine and Roses, 33
    Brandy Alexander, 33
Diary of a Mad Housewife, 96
    Caesar Salad, 96
    Omelet Beaumont, 97
    Orange-Plant Salad, 97
    Oyster-Chestnut Stuffing, 98
Diner, 99
    French Fries and Gravy, 100
    Heated Roast Beef Sandwich, 99
Diva, 61
    Satori Bread, 62
Down and Out in Beverly Hills, 174
    Doggie Delight, 174
Dr. Jekyll and Mr. Hyde, 35
    Zombie, 35
Dr. Strangelove, or:
  How I Learned to Stop Worrying and
  Love the Bomb, 37
    American Vodka, 38
E.T., the Extra-Terrestrial, 101
    Space-iality of the House, 101
The Falcon and the Snowman, 39
    Shredded Margarita, 39
Fatso, 104
    Fatso Bread, 106
    Kale with Chicken Breast, 107
    Lasagna with Bread, 108
    Omelet with Bread, 105
    Spaghetti Sauce with Bread, 108
The Four Seasons, 109
    Beans, 111
    Chinese Chicken Salad, 112
    Chinese White Rice, 112
    Clams Casino, 112
    Fried Shrimp, 112
    Fun See, 109

Frenzy, 113
    Cailles aux Raisins, 113
    Margarita, 115
    Pied de Porc à la Mode de Caens, 115
    Soupe de Poissons, 114
The Godfather, 116
    Kay's Spaghetti Sauce, 117
The Gold Rush, 177
    Boiled Boot, 177
    Oceana Rolls, 179
Gone With the Wind, 63
    Southern Buttermilk Biscuits, 63
Harper, 42
    Detective Coffee, 43
The Heartbreak Kid, 151
    Pecan Pie, 151
Heaven Can Wait, 44
    Hot Chocolate and Marshmallow, 45
    Liver and Whey Shake, 45
Housecalls, 154
    Cheesecake, 154
    Mocha Cheesecake, 155
I Remember Mama, 12
    Kjøttboller, 14
Iceman, 180
    Beetle Mania, 180
The Killing of Sister George, 66
    Scones, 68
King Rat, 182
    Dog Stew, 182
    Ratatouille—Prison Style, 182
Kramer vs Kramer, 69
    French Toast, 70
    Salisbury Steak with Onion Gravy, 69

The Loved One, 119
    Roast Suckling Pig, 120
Ma and Pa Kettle at the Fair, 15
    Crab Apple-Plum Jam, 16
Marathon Man, 185
    Diamond Delight, 185
The Meaning of Life, 17
    Salmon Mousse with Cucumber Dill Sauce, 19
Mildred Pierce, 156
    Apple Pie, 158
    Lemon Meringue Pie, 157
    Pumpkin Pie, 156
Mr. Roberts, 46
    Johnny Walker Red Label, 46
My Dinner with André, 121
    Peppered Quail, 121
My Man Godfrey, 48
    Pixie Juice, 50
Neighbors, 123
    Taken-for Takeout Dinner, 123
Never Cry Wolf, 187
    Souris à la Crême, 189
The Odd Couple, 125
    Meat Loaf, 125
On Golden Pond, 159
    Angel Food Cake with Mocha Frosting, 161
Once Upon a Time in America, 162
    Charlotte Russe, 163
Papillon, 190
    Survival Soup, 190
Prizzi's Honor, 164
    Sicilian Sesame Cookies, 164

Public Enemy, 20
    Fresh Squeezed Grapefruit, 21
The River, 71
    Blackberry Jam, 73
    Oatmeal Butter Cookies, 73
    Pie Pastry Crust, 73
    Three-Loaf Farm Bread, 71
Rocky, 51
    Raw Rockies, 51
Rosemary's Baby, 53
    Tannis Shake, 53
Splash, 192
    Stunt Lobster, 193
Starman, 128
    Cherry Cobbler, 130
    Chocolate Malt, 128
    Deviled Egg on Toast, 130
    Dutch Apple Pie, 129
    Road Fries, 130
    Superburger, 130
The Tin Drum, 22
    Eels Alfred, 22
Tom Jones, 131
    Soup (Scotch Broth), 131
    Lobster, 132
    Turkey, 132
    Oysters, 132
Two for the Road, 24
    Road Food Picnic, 24
Valley Girl, 27
    Val Sushi, 28
Victor/Victoria, 134
    Apple Flan, 136
    Boeuf Bourguignon, 136
    Coupe Jacques, 135
    Double Dinner Salad, 134
    Roast Pork, 134

Whatever Happened to Baby Jane?, 195
    Parboiled Parakeet, 195
What's Up Tiger Lily?, 137
    Decoded Egg Salad, 137
Who's Killing the Great Chefs of Europe?, 139
    Aragosto à la Garciofo, 146
    Carrots Vichy, 143
    Consommé au Port, 144
    Fillet of Sea Bass, 142
    Gigot de Veau, 141
    Le Bombe Richelieu, 142
    Oyster Stew, 145
    Pâté de Fois Gras, 146
    Pigeon en Croûte, 145
    Pommes Dauphine, 144
    Pressed Duck, 145
    Strawberries Romanoff, 141
    Truffle Soup, 144
    Veal Scallop Massenet, 146
Willy Wonka and the Chocolate Factory, 166
    Wonka Bars, 168
Woman of the Year, 74
    Woman of the Year Waffles, 74

MENU SECTION TITLE INDEX AND RECIPES

Adam's Rib, 212
    Baked "Barbecue" Spare Ribs
Adventures of Huckleberry Finn, The, 212
    Huckleberry Tart
Amorous Prawn, The, 212
    Broiled Prawn and Artichoke
Apple Dumpling Gang, The, 212-13
    Apple Dumplings with Custard Sauce
Apple Game, 213-14
    Apple-Surprise Tart with Pecans Glaze
Attack of the Crab Monsters, 214
    Crabs in a Stew
Attack of the Killer Tomatoes, 214
    Tomato Wedges
Attack of the Mushroom People, 214
    Mushroom Pâté
Bananas, 214
    Broiled Banana
Biscuit Eater, The, 214-15
    Bacon Biscuits
Bitter Tea of General Yen, The, 215
    Herb Tea
Black Water Gold, 215
    Honey Fruited Tea
Blondie in the Dough, 215
    Million Dollar Spiral Bread
Bout de Soufflé, A, 215
    A Breakfast Egg Soufflé
Brandy Ashore, 215
    Mulled Brandy
Brave Bulls, The, 216
    Brave Bull Cocktail
Bread and Chocolate, 216
    Orange Pound Cake with Chocolate Hazelnut Spread
Bread, Love and Dreams, 216
    Parmesan "Cloud" Bread
Bread, Love, and Jealousy, 216
    Bread, with Spices, Onion, and Garlic
Bread Peddler, The, 217
    Lemon-Custard French Toast
Broth of a Boy, 217
    Black-Eyed Soup
Butterfield 8, 217
    Basil-Butter Bread Spread
Café Metropole, 217
    Italian Spiced Coffee
Café Society, 217
    Spiced Brandy Coffee en Flambe
California Split, 218
    Ice Cream Split with Hot Fudge
Cantata of Chili, 218
    Chili with Crackers

Captain Milkshake, 218
    Banana Brown Cow Milkshake
Champagne Charlie, 218
    Dressed Champagne
Champagne for Caesar, 218
    Champagne Punch
Champagne Waltz, 218
    Wine Champagne
Chicken Every Sunday, 218-19
    Parmesan-Herb Roast Chicken
Chocolate Soldier, The, 219
    Chocolate Cookie Men
Cigarettes, Whiskey, and Wild Women, 219
    Hot Toddy
Cisco Pike, 219
    Wine-Eyed Pike
Clambake, 219
    New England Clambake
Clockwork Orange, A, 220
    Honey-Spiced Citrus Cups
Cocoanuts, The, 220
    Coconut-Chocolate Brownies
Coffee, Tea, or Me?, 220
    Spiced Coffee and Mulled Tea
Coffy, 220
    Instant Fancy Coffee
Cold Turkey, 220
    Turkey Aspic
Corn Is Green, The, 220-21
    Husk Steamed Corn with Sea Salt
Cornbread, Earl, and Me, 221
    Southern Buttermilk Cornbread
Count of Monte Cristo, The, 221
    Monte Cristo Sandwich
Dark Waters, 221
    Tea with Mint Syrup
Day in the Death of Joe Egg, A, 221
    Poached Egg on Canadian Bacon with Mornay Sauce
Day the Fish Came Out, The, 222
    Brook Trout Meunière-Amandine
Diamonds for Breakfast, 222
    Rock Candy
Doughgirls, The, 222
    Seedy Dinner Rolls
Duck Soup, 222
    Duck Soup
Egg and I, The, 223
    Egg-stuffed Idaho Potatoes
Egghead on Hill, 223
    Shirred Eggs with Sausages
Esther Waters, 223
    Iced Honey Coffee

Eve Knew Her Apples, 223
    Apple-Cheese Canapes
Expresso Bongo, 223
    Espresso with a Twist
Fish That Saved Pittsburgh, The, 223
    Holy Mackerel
Food of the Gods, The, 224
    Mixed Greens with Goddess Dressing
Forbidden Fruit, The, 224
    Apple Cake with Hot Rum Sauce
Fortune Cookie, The, 224
    Fortune Cookies
Forty Carats, 224
    Lemon-glazed Carrots
Freebie and the Bean, 225
    Easy Boston Baked Beans
French Dressing, 233
    French Dressing
Frogs, 225
    Garlic-Butter Frog Legs
Get Rollin', 225
    Refrigerator Rolls
Ghost and Mr. Chicken, The, 225
    Parmesan Chicken with Mashed Potatoes
Ginger in the Morning, 226
    Gingered String Beans
Girl in Every Port, A, 226
    White Port Cocktail,
Good-bye Mr. Chips, 226
    Fried Vegetable Chips
Grasshopper, The, 226
    Grasshopper Pie
Gravy Train, The, 234
    Lemon Gravy
Green Goddess, The, 214
    Avocado Dressing
Here Comes Cookie, 226
    Applesauce-Spice Cookies
Hey, Pineapple!, 226
    Batter-Fried Pineapple
Honey Pot, The, 227
    Baked Honey Custard
Honeycomb, 227
    Buttermilk Waffles with Honey-Orange Sauce
Hot Potato, 227
    Baked Potato Skins
How to Frame a Figg, 227
    Stewed Ginger Figs
Jack and the Beanstalk, 227
    Hasty Bean Salad
Jamaica Rum, 228
    Jamaican Rum Cocktail

Java Head, 228
  Cocoa-Java
Kentucky Fried Movie, The, 228
  Kentucky Fried Chicken
King Creole, 228
  Shrimp Creole
King of Hearts, 228
  Heart of Artichoke, Palm, and Celery Salad with Tarragon Dressing
Knickerbocker Holiday, 228
  Knickerbocker Cocktail
La Marie du Port, 229
  Savoy Sangaree
Lady Caroline Lamb, 229
  Lamb in White Wine and Mushrooms
Lady from Chungking, 229
  Chunking Vinegar Chicken
Le Soufflé au Cour, 229
  Potato Soufflé
Lemon Drop Kid, The, 230
  Lemon Bars
Lemonade Joe, 230
  Old-fashioned Homemade Lemonade
Limelight, 230
  Lime-Chicken Kebabs
Lorna Doone, 230
  Lemony Shortbread Cookies
Luck of Ginger Coffey, The, 230
  Ginger Coffee
Manhattan, 230
  Manhattan Cocktail
Marshmallow Moon, 230–31
  Marshmallow-Mocha Cream Torte
Michael Strogoff, 231
  Beef Stroganoff
Million Dollar Duck, 231
  Roast Duck à la Beverly Hills with Citrus Sauce Bigarade
Monterey Pop, 232
  Wine Cooler
Mrs. Wiggs of the Cabbage Patch, 232
  Cabbage Salad
Nutty Professor, The, 232
  Berry-Nutty Bread
Octopussy, 232
  Stewed Octopus in Red Wine
One Potato, Two Potato, 232
  Four Potato Salad
Onion Field, The, 237
  Onion Dressing
Onionhead, 233
  Marinated Dill Onions with French Dressing
Operation Caviar, 233
  Caviar Stuffed Celery
Our Vines Have Tender Grapes , 233
  Stuffed Grape Leaves
Peppermint Soda, 233
  Mint Soda
Pillar of Salt, 233
  Herb Salt
The Pizza Triangle, 234
  Pesto-Shrimp Pizza
Pork Chop Hill, 234
  Baked Stuffed Pork Chops with Lemon Gravy
Port of New York, 234
  A Port Aperitif
Port of Seven Seas, 234
  Seven Seas Port Cocktail
Prisoner of Shark Island, 235
  Shark Teriyaki
Pumpkin Eater, The, 235
  Pumpkin Bread
Punch and Jody, 235
  Tea Punch
Raisin in the Sun, A, 235
  Raisin 'n' Sunflower Muffins
Rhubarb, 236
  Rhubarb Cake
Ring of Bright Water, 236
  Egg 'n' Beer
Roll, Freddie, Roll, 236
  Dinner Rolls
Salt and Pepper, 236
  Salt and Pepper Seasoning Mix
Salt of the Earth, 220
  Sea Salt
Serial, 236
  Granola
Serpent's Egg, The, 237
  Egg-stuffed Baked Tomato
Seven Ups, The, 237
  Sparkling Punch
Skippy, 237
  Homemade Peanut Butter
Smile Orange, 237
  Broiled Orange "Smile" Sections
Sorrell and Son, 237
  Sorrel Salad with Onion Dressing
Story of Seabiscuit, The, 238
  Sea Salt Biscuits
Strawberry Blonde, The, 238
  Cointreau Strawberries with Crème Blonde
Strawberry, Lemon and Mint, 238
  Fresh Strawberries with Lemon Sauce and Mint
Strawberry Statement, The, 238
  Last-Word Strawberry Preserves
Summer Stock, 238
  Vegetable Soup
Sunny Side Up, 239
  Herbed Fried Egg
Sweet Charity, 239
  Peach Brandy Crêpes Flambé with Meringue
Taste of Honey, A, 239
  Honey Pears
Tea and Sympathy, 239
  Hot Minted Tea
Tea for Two, 240
  Basic Brewed Tea
Teahouse of the August Moon, 240
  Teahouse Tea
There's a Girl in My Soup, 240
  Cream of Artichoke-Mushroom Soup
There's Always Vanilla, 240
  Vanilla Bavarian Cream
Toast of the Legion, 240
  Whipped Honey-Butter Toast
Toast of New Orleans, The, 240
  Pecan-Cinnamon Toast Roll
Toast of New York, The, 241
  Bagels
Top Banana, 241
  Banana Popsicles
Tortilla Flat, 241
  Corn Tortillas
Tuna Clipper, 242
  Tuna-Olive Casserole
Under Milk Wood, 242
  Coffee-Nog Cooler
Watermelon Man, 242
  Watermelon Cake
Where the Red Fern Grows, 242
  Steamed Fiddleheads
Wild Fruit, 242
  Broiled Fresh-Fruit Kabobs
Wild Oranges, 242
  Spiced Oranges in Juice
Wild Strawberries, 243
  Chilled Strawberry Soup
Young Girls of Rochefort, The, 243
  Salad with Roquefort Dressing

MASTER RECIPE INDEX

Appetizers
 Apple-Cheese Canapés, 223
 Broiled Prawn and Artichoke, 212
 Caviar-Stuffed Celery, 233
 Clams Casino, 112
 Kjøttboller, 14
 Stuffed Cucumber, 91
 Stuffed Grape Leaves, 233
 Val Sushi, 28

Apples
 Apple Cake with Hot Rum Sauce, 224
 Apple-Cheese Canapés, 223
 Apple Dumplings with Custard Sauce, 212-13
 Apple Flan, 136
 Apple Pie, 158, 129
 Applesauce-Spice Cookies, 226
 Apple-surprise Tart with Pecans Glaze, 213-14
 Crab Apple-Plum Jam, 16

Artichokes
 Aragosto à la Garciofo, 146
 Broiled Prawn and Artichoke, 212
 Cream of Artichoke-Mushroom Soup, 240
 Heart of Artichoke, Palm, and Celery Salad with Tarragon Dressing, 228

Avocados
 Green Goddess Dressing, 214
 Guacamole, 10

Banana
 Banana Brown Cow Milkshake, 218
 Banana Popsicles, 241
 Broiled Banana, 214

Bars
 Coconut-Chocolate Brownies, 220
 Lemon Bars, 230

Beans
 Beans (Baked), 111
 Black-Eyed Soup, 217
 Campfire Beans, 83
 Easy Boston Baked Beans, 225
 Gingered String Beans, 226
 Hasty Bean Salad, 227

Beef
 Beef Stroganoff, 231
 Boeuf Bourguignon, 136
 Heated Roast Beef Sandwich, 99
 Kjøttboller, 14
 Meat Loaf, 125
 Salisbury Steak with Onion Gravy, 69
 Superburger, 130

Beverages (also see Coffees and Teas)
 Alcoholic:
  A Port Aperitif, 234
  American Vodka, 38
  Aunt Martha's Elderberry Wine, 30
  Brandy Alexander, 33
  Brave Bull Cocktail, 216
  Champagne Punch, 218
  Dressed Champagne, 218
  Hot Toddy, 219
  Jamaican Rum Cocktail, 228
  Johnny Walker Red Label, 46
  Knickerbocker Cocktail, 228
  Manhattan Cocktail, 230
  Margarita, 115
  Mulled Brandy, 215
  Pixie Juice, 50
  Savoy Sangaree, 229
  Seven Seas Port Cocktail, 234
  Shredded Margarita, 39
  Spiced Brandy Coffee en Flambé, 217
  Wine Champagne, 218
  Wine Cooler, 232
  White Port Cocktail, 226
  Zombie, 35
 Non-Alcoholic:
  Banana Brown Cow Milkshake, 218
  Chocolate Malt, 128
  Hot Chocolate and Marshmallow, 45
  Liver and Whey Shake, 45
  Mint Soda, 233
  Old-fashioned Homemade Lemonade, 230
  Raw Rockies, 51
  Sparkling Punch, 237
  Tannis Shake, 53
  Tea Punch, 235

Birds/Fowl (also see by individual names)
 Parboiled Parakeet, 195
 Pigeon en Croûte, 145

Biscuits
 Bacon Biscuits, 214-15
 Sea Salt Biscuits, 238
 Scones, 68
 Southern Buttermilk Biscuits, 63

Breads (also see Biscuits, Rolls, Muffins, and Pastries)
 Bagels, 241
 Berry-Nutty Bread, 232
 Bread with Spices, Onion, and Garlic, 216
 Buttermilk Waffles, 227
 Fatso Bread, 106
 French Toast, 70
 Lemon-Custard French Toast, 217
 Million Dollar Spiral Bread, 215
 Parmesan "Cloud" Bread, 216
 Pecan-Cinnamon Toast Roll, 240
 Pumpkin Bread, 235
 Satori Bread, 62
 Southern Buttermilk Cornbread, 221
 Three-Loaf Farm Bread, 71
 Whipped Honey-Butter Toast, 240

Bugs
 Beetle Mania, 180
 Survival Soup, 190

Butter
 Basil-Butter Bread Spread, 217
 Whipped Honey-Butter Toast, 240

Cakes
 Angel Food Cake with Mocha Frosting, 161
 Apple Cake with Hot Rum Sauce, 224
 Orange Pound Cake with Chocolate Hazelnut Spread, 216
 Rhubarb Cake, 236
 Watermelon Cake, 242

Canapés (see Appetizers)

Candy
 Rock Candy, 222
 Wonka Bars, 168

Carrots
 Carrots Vichy, 143
 Lemon-Glazed Carrots, 224

Casseroles
 Beef Stroganoff, 231
 Boeuf Bourguignon, 136
 Chili with Crackers, 218
 Chop Suey Western, 208
 Curry Western, 209
 Grandmother's Goulash, 89
 Lasagna with Bread, 108
 Paella Western, 208
 Parmesan Chicken with Mashed Potatoes, 225
 Ratatouille-Prison Style, 182
 Shrimp Creole, 228
 Souris à la Crême, 189
 Spaghetti Western, 208
 Tuna-Olive Casserole, 242

Caviar
 Caviar Stuffed Celery, 233
 Satori Bread, 62

Cereal
 Granola, 236

Cheese
 Apple-Cheese Canapés, 223
 Parmesan Chicken with Mashed Potatoes, 225
 Parmesan "Cloud" Bread, 216
 Parmesan-Herb Roast Chicken, 218-19

Cheesecakes
 Cheesecake, 154
 Mocha Cheesecake, 155

Chicken
 Chinese Chicken Salad, 112
 Chunking Vinegar Chicken, 229
 Kale with Chicken Breast, 107
 Kentucky Fried Chicken, 228
 Lime-Chicken Kabobs, 230
 Parmesan Chicken with Mashed Potatoes, 225
 Parmesan-Herb Roast Chicken, 218-19

Chinese
  Chinese Chicken Salad, 112
  Chinese White Rice, 112
  Chunking Vinegar Chicken, 229
  Chop Suey Western, 208
  Fortune Cookies, 224
  Fried Shrimp, 112
  Fun See, 109
  Gingered String Beans, 226
  Herb Tea, 215
Chocolate
  Banana Brown Cow Milkshake, 218
  Chocolate Cookie Men, 219
  Chocolate Malt, 128
  Chocolate Sauce, 216
  Cocoa-Java, 228
  Coconut-Chocolate Brownies, 220
  Hot Chocolate and Marshmallow, 45
  Hot Fudge, 218
Clams
  Clams Casino, 112
  New England Clambake, 219
Coffees
  Cocoa-Java, 228
  Coffee Nog Cooler, 242
  Detective Coffee, 43
  Espresso with a Twist, 223
  Ginger Coffee, 230
  Iced Honey Coffee, 223
  Instant Fancy Coffee, 220
  Italian Spiced Coffee, 217
  Spiced Brandy Coffee en Flambé, 217
  Spiced Coffee and Mulled Tea, 220
Cookies
  Applesauce-Spice Cookies, 226
  Chocolate Cookie Men, 219
  Fortune Cookies, 224
  Lemony Shortbread Cookies, 230
  Oatmeal Butter Cookies, 73
  Sicilian Sesame Cookies, 164
Corn
  Husk Steamed Corn, 220-21
  Southern Buttermilk Cornbread, 221
Crab
  Crabs in a Stew, 214
Cucumbers
  Stuffed Cucumber, 91
  Cucumber Dill Sauce, 19
Custards
  Apple Flan, 136
  Baked Honey Custard, 227
  Charlotte Russe, 163
  Custard Pie, 205
  Custard Sauce, 212-13
  Lemon-Custard French Toast, 217
Desserts (*also see* Cakes and Pies)
  Apple Dumplings with Custard Sauce, 212-13
  Apple Flan, 136
  Apple-surprise Tart with Pecans Glaze, 213-14
  Baked Honey Custard, 227
  Charlotte Russe, 163
  Cheesecake, 154
  Cherry Cobbler, 130
  Coupe Jacques, 135
  Fresh Strawberries with Lemon Sauce and Mint, 238
  Fried Ice Cream, 148
  Honey Pears, 239
  Huckleberry Tart, 212
  Ice Cream Split with Hot Fudge, 218
  Le Bombe Richelieu, 142
  Marshmallow-Mocha Cream Torte, 230-31
  Mocha Cheesecake, 155
  Peach Brandy Crêpes Flambé with Meringue, 239
  Strawberries Romanoff, 141
  Vanilla Bavarian Cream, 240
Dessert Sauces
  Chocolate Sauce, 142
  Custard Sauce, 212-13
  Hot Fudge, 218
  Hot Rum Sauce, 224
Dips
  Guacamole, 10
Dog Food
  Doggie Delight, 174
Doughnuts
  Crullers, 60
Dressings (*see* Salad Dressings)
Duck
  Duck Soup, 222
  Pressed Duck, 145
  Roast Duck à la Beverly Hills with Citrus Sauce Bigarade, 231
Eggs
  A Breakfast Egg Soufflé, 215
  Decoded Egg Salad, 137
  Deviled Egg on Toast, 130
  Egg-stuffed Baked Tomato, 237
  Egg-stuffed Idaho Potatoes, 223
  Eggathon, 172
  Herb Fried Egg, 239
  Omelet Beaumont, 97
  Omelet with Bread, 105
  Poached Egg on Canadian Bacon with Mornay Sauce, 221
  Raw Rockies, 51
  Shirred Eggs with Sausages, 223
Fish
  Brook Trout Meunière-Almandine, 222
  Eels Alfred, 22
  Fillet of Sea Bass, 142
  Holy Mackerel, 223
  New England Clambake, 219
  Salmon Mousse with Cucumber Dill Sauce, 19
  Shark Teriyaki, 235
  Soupe de Poissons, 114
  Tuna-Olive Casserole, 242
  Turbot à la Flunkey, 94
  Val Sushi, 28
  Wine-Eyed Pike, 219
Fowl (*see by individual names*)
French
  Boeuf Bourguignon, 136
  Cailles aux Raisins, 113
  Carrots Vichy, 143
  Consommé au Port, 144
  French Fries and Gravy, 100
  French Toast, 70
  Gigot de Veau, 141
  Le Bombe Richelieu, 142
  Lemon-Custard French Toast, 217
  Pied de Porc à la Mode de Caens, 115
  Pigeon en Croûte, 145
  Pommes Dauphine, 144
  Turbot à la Flunkey, 94
  Veal Scallop Massenet, 146
  Vol Au Vent, 93
Frogs
  Garlic-Butter Frog Legs, 225
Frostings
  Mocha Frosting, 161
Fruit (*also see by individual* names)
  Batter-fried Pineapple, 226
  Broiled Fresh Fruit Kabobs, 242
  Fresh Squeezed Grapefruit, 21
  Fruit à la Royal Runaway, 95
  Honey Pears, 239
  Honey-Spiced Citrus Cups, 220
  Huckleberry Tart, 212
  Peach Brandy Crêpes Flambé with Meringue, 239
  Stewed Ginger Figs, 227
Ginger
  Ginger Coffee, 230
  Gingered String Beans, 226
  Stewed Ginger Figs, 227
Gravies (*also see* Sauces)
  Basic Gravy, 100
  Lemon Gravy, 234
  Onion Gravy, 69
Honey
  Baked Honey Custard, 227
  Honey-fruited Tea, 215
  Honey-Orange Sauce, 227
  Honey Pears, 239
  Honey Spiced Citrus Cups, 220
  Iced Honey Coffee, 223
  Whipped Honey Butter Toast, 240
Hors d'Oeuvres (*see* Appetizers)
Ice Cream
  Coupe Jacques, 135
  Fried Ice Cream, 148
  Ice Cream Split with Hot Fudge, 218
  Le Bombe Richelieu, 142
Italian
  Aragosto à la Garciofo, 146
  Italian Spiced Coffee, 217
  Kay's Spaghetti's Sauce, 117
  Lasagna with Bread, 108
  Pesto-Shrimp Pizza, 234
  Spaghetti Sauce with Bread, 108
  Spaghetti Western, 208
  Taken-for Takeout-Dinner, 123
Jams/Preserves
  Blackberry Jam, 73
  Crab Apple-Plum Jam, 16
  Last-Word Strawberry Preserves, 238
Kabobs
  Broiled Fresh-Fruit Kabobs, 242
  Lime Chicken Kabobs, 230
Lamb
  Lamb in White Wine with Mushrooms, 229
Lemon
  Lemon Bars, 230
  Lemon-Custard French Toast, 217
  Lemon Gravy, 234
  Lemon Meringue Pie, 157
  Lemon Sauce, 238
  Lemony Shortbread Cookies, 230
  Old-fashioned Homemade Lemonade, 230
Lobster
  Aragosto à la Garciofo, 146
  Lobster, Boiled, 132
  Stunt Lobster, 193
Luncheons/Buffets
  Breakfast Club Lunch, 85
  Buffet d' Harpo, 170
  Space-iality of the House, 101

Marshmallow
   Hot Chocolate and Marshmallow, 45
   Marshmallow-Mocha Cream Torte, 230-31
Meatballs
   Kjøttboller, 14
Meats (*see by individual names*)
Menus, 120-11
Mexican
   Corn Tortillas, 241
   Chili with Crackers, 218
Mice
   Souris à la Crême, 189
Miscellaneous
   Boiled Boot, 179
   Diamond Delight, 185
   Dog Stew, 182
   Food Fight Shopping List, 80
   Road Food Picnic, 24
   Taken-for Takeout Dinner, 123
Mocha
   Marshmallow-Mocha Cream Torte, 230-31
   Mocha Frosting, 161
   Mocha Cheesecake, 155
Mousse
   Salmon Mousse with Cucumber Dill Sauce, 19
Muffins
   Raisin 'n' Sunflower Muffins, 235
Mushroom
   Cream of Artichoke and Mushroom Soup, 240
   Mushroom Pâté, 214
   Lamb in White Wine and Mushrooms, 229
Octopus
   Stewed Octopus in Red Wine, 232
Onions
   Marinated Dill Onions with French Dressing, 233
Oranges
   Broiled Orange "Smile" Sections, 237
   Honey-Orange Sauce, 227
   Orange-Plant Salad, 97
   Orange Pound Cake with Chocolate Hazelnut Spread, 216
   Spiced Oranges in Juice, 242
Oysters
   Oysters, 132raw, 98
   Oyster-Chestnut Stuffing, 145
   Oyster Stew, 57
Pancakes (*also see* **Waffles**)
   Swedish Pancakes (plätter), 57
Pastries (*also see* **Pies**)
   Crullers, 60
   Pie Pastry Crust, 73
   Vol Au Vent, 93-94
Patés
   Mushroom Paté, 214
   Pâté de Fois Gras, 146
Peaches
   Peach Brandy Crêpes Flambé with Meringue, 239
Peanuts
   Homemade Peanut Butter, 237
Pears
   Honey Pears, 239

Pecans
   Pecan Cinnamon Toast Roll, 240
   Pecans Glaze, 213-14
   Pecan Pie, 151
Pesto
   Pesto-Shrimp Pizza, 234
Pies
   Apple Pie, 158
   Cherry Cobbler, 130
   Custard Pie, 205
   Dutch Apple Pie, 129
   Grasshopper Pie, 226
   Key Lime Pie, 205
   Lemon Meringue Pie, 157
   Mabel's Cream Pie, 205
   Pecan Pie, 151
   Pie Pastry Crust, 73
   Pumpkin Pie, 156
Pineapple
   Batter-Fried Pineapple, 226
Pizza
   Pesto-Shrimp Pizza, 234
Plums
   Crab Apple-Plum Jam, 16
Pork
   Baked "Barbecue" Spare Ribs, 212
   Baked Stuffed Pork Chops with Lemon Gravy, 234
   Roast Pork, 134
   Roast Suckling Pig, 120
   Pied de Porc à la Mode de Caens, 115
   Schnitzengrüben with Sauerkraut, 83
   Shirred Eggs with Sausages, 223
Potatoes
   Baked Potato Skins, 227
   Egg-stuffed Idaho Potatoes, 223
   Four Potato Salad, 232
   French Fries and Gravy, 100
   Mashed Spudniks, 87
   Pommes Dauphine, 144
   Potato (Vegetable) Chips, 226
   Potato Soufflé, 229
   Road Fries, 130
Poultry (*see by individual names*)
Pumpkin
   Pumpin Bread, 235
   Pumpkin Pie, 156
Punches
   Champagne Punch, 218
   Sparkling Punch, 237
   Tea Punch, 235
Quail
   Cailles aux Raisins, 113
   Peppered Quail, 121
   Refugee Quail with Wine Onions, 92
Raisin
   Cailles aux Raisins, 113
   Raisin 'n' Sunflower Muffins, 235
Rhubarb
   Rhubarb Cake, 236
Rice
   Chinese White Rice, 112
Rolls
   Oceana Rolls, 179
   Pecan Cinnamon Toast Rolls, 240
   Refrigerator Rolls, 225
   Seedy Dinner Rolls, 222

Salads
   Attack of the Killer Tomatoes, 214
   Cabbage Salad, 232
   Caesar Salad, 96
   Chinese Chicken Salad, 112
   Decoded Egg Salad, 137
   Double Dinner Salad, 134
   Four Potato Salad, 232
   Hasty Bean Salad, 227
   Heart of Artichoke, Palm, and Celery Salad, 228
   Marinated Dill Onions, 233
   Mixed Greens, 224
   Orange-Plant Salad, 97
   Roquefort Salad, 243
   Sorrel Salad, 237
Salad Dressings
   Goddess Dressing, 224
   Green Goddess, 214
   French Dressing, 233
   Onion Dressing, 237
   Roquefort Dressing, 243
   Tarragon Dressing, 228
Salmon
   Salmon Mousse with Cucumber Dill Sauce, 19
Salt
   Herb Salt, 233
   Salt and Pepper Seasoning Mix, 236
Sandwiches
   Deviled Egg on Toast, 130
   Heated Roast Beef Sandwich, 99
   Homemade Peanut Butter Sandwich, 237
   Monte Cristo, 221
   Shiksa Sandwich, 82
Sauces (*also see* **Dessert Sauces and Gravies**)
   Convention Sauce, 95
   Dill Sauce, 19
   Honey-Orange Sauce, 227
   Kay's Spaghetti Sauce, 117
   Mornay Sauce, 221
   Spaghetti Sauce with Bread, 108
Shellfish (*see by individual names*)
Shrimp
   Broiled Prawn and Artichoke, 212
   Fried Shrimp, 112
   Pesto-Shrimp Pizza, 234
   Shrimp Creole, 228
Soufflés
   A Breakfast Soufflé, 215
   Potato Soufflé, 229
Soups
   Black-Eyed Soup, 217
   Borscht Western, 209
   Chilled Strawberry Soup, 243
   Consommé au Port, 144
   Cream of Artichoke-Mushroom Soup, 240
   Duck Soup, 222
   Scotch Broth, 131
   Soupe de Poissons, 114
   Survival Soup, 190
   Truffle Soup, 144
   Vegetable Soup, 238
Spaghetti Sauces
   Kay's Spaghetti Sauce, 117
   Spaghetti Sauce with Bread, 108
   Spaghetti Western, 208
Spreads
   Basil-Butter Bread Spread, 217

Stews
  Boeuf Bourguignon, 136
  Crabs in a Stew, 214
  Oyster Stew, 145

Strawberry
  Chilled Strawberry Soup, 243
  Fresh Strawberries with Lemon Sauce and Mint, 238
  Last-Word Strawberry Preserves, 238
  Strawberries Romanoff, 141

Stuffing
  Oyster-Chestnut Stuffing, 98

Sushi
  Val Sushi, 28
  Flying Fish Eggs, 28
  Uni, 28
  Quail Egg, 28

Tarts
  Apple-surprise Tart with Pecans Glaze, 213–14
  Fruit à la Royal Runaway, 95
  Huckleberry Tart, 212

Teas
  Basic Brewed Tea, 240
  Herb Tea, 215
  Honey Fruited Tea, 215
  Hot Minted Tea, 239
  Spiced Coffee and Mulled Tea, 220
  Tea Punch, 235
  Tea with Mint Syrup, 221
  Teahouse Tea, 240

Tomatoes
  Egg-stuffed Baked Tomato, 237
  Tomato Wedges, 214

Truffle
  Truffle Soup, 144

Turkey
  Turkey Aspic, 220
  Turkey (roast), 132

Vanilla
  Vanilla Bavarian Cream, 240

Veal
  Gigot de Veau, 141
  Veal Scallop Massenet, 146

Vegetables (*also see* by individual names)
  Carrots Vichy, 143
  Caviar Stuffed Celery, 233
  Egg-stuffed Baked Tomato, 237
  Fried Vegetable Chips, 226
  Gingered String Beans, 226
  Husk Steamed Corn, 220–21
  Kale with Chicken Breast, 107
  Lemon-Glazed Carrots, 224
  Steamed Fiddleheads, 242
  Vegetable Soup, 238

Waffles
  Buttermilk Waffles with Honey-Orange Sauce, 227
  Woman of the Year Waffles, 74

Watermelon
  Watermelon Cake, 242

Yeast
  Mashed Yeast 'n' Sprouts, 81

ABOUT THE AUTHOR

Lorna Woodsum Riley is a self-described "ex-everything—including ex-pianist, ex-digital font specialist, ex-elementary school teacher, ex-theater usherette, ex-machinist, ex-sales rep, ex-lifeguard, and ex-marketing director for a company that manufactures elevator brains.

Riley was born in New York and raised in Minnesota, graduated high school and college in Connecticut, started a family in New Hampshire, and found true happiness in California where, she says, she was finally able to put it all together by combining a passion for food and movies and creating something she could share with others: *The Movie Lover's Cookbook: Reel Meals.*